THE VICTORIAN MIND

The
Victorian Mind

AN ANTHOLOGY
EDITED AND SELECTED BY
Gerald B. Kauvar
and Gerald C. Sorensen

G. P. Putnam's Sons
New York

Copyright © 1969 by Educational Resources Corporation

Library of Congress Catalog
Card Number: 68-54928

PRINTED IN THE UNITED STATES OF AMERICA

Contents

Preface

WHEN reading volumes jointly edited it is comfortable to know which editor is responsible for each part. In the case of the present volume, the extent of collaboration nearly precludes neat divisions of editorial labor. The idea informing the entire book is held by us both; the selections in each section were mutually agreed upon; each selection was edited by both of us; the ideas presented in the several introductions were developed in a continuing series of conversations; even the headnotes are the products of joint effort. However, Mr. Sorensen is chiefly responsible for the general introduction and for the introductions to the sections concerning social welfare and religion. Mr. Kauvar bears primary responsibility for the introductions to the sections on education, science, and art.

We wish to acknowledge our indebtedness to many who are not visibly connected with this book. The wise and thorough teachings of Lionel Stevenson and G. Robert Stange are reflected in the thesis developed in the introductions, which determined the materials and arrangement of this volume. For valuable and knowledgeable editorial patience and judgment, we are grateful to Charles Sherover, whose contribution to this book is too pervasive to be acknowledged piecemeal. To Professors Barry and Laila Gross go our thanks for early and continuous encouragement. To our wives, Elaine, and Sonja, this book would be dedicated, were it not as much theirs as ours.

GERALD B. KAUVAR
GERALD C. SORENSEN

Introduction

QUEEN VICTORIA reigned in England from 1837 to 1901, and for most Britons it was an age comparable only to that of Elizabeth I. Victoria wielded less power than Elizabeth had, but she governed a country wealthier and more powerful than Elizabeth could have conceived. Long before the turn of the century the British Empire had become one on which "the sun never set." The territorial expansion had been based in part upon unparalleled industrial growth, and both sorts of expansion were causes of a characteristic Victorian attitude: optimism. As early as 1851 the Great Crystal Palace Exhibition gave evidence of this optimism, as well as of the smugness which was sometimes its companion. The "ordinary" Victorian could hardly help feeling that he lived, if not in the best of all possible worlds, at least in a world which was rapidly becoming better and better.

Progress, for the Victorians, was not only material but moral and political, and all three were closely intertwined. Politically the Victorian period is characterized by the development and the consequent establishment of English constitutional monarchy as we now know it. In these processes all Victorians were crucially interested; all of them could not, at first, vote, but pressure could be brought to bear, as in the founding of the powerful political unions in the manufacturing towns, or in the Chartist movement. The party system, particularly as it emerged after the passage of the first Reform Bill, made government a clearer (though by no means perfect) expression of public opinion. The differences between the two major political leaders of the age, Disraeli and Gladstone, were temperamental as well as philosophical, yet our usual understanding of them—Disraeli as the personally flamboyant and adventurous Conservative, and Gladstone the staid, somewhat dull, yet high-minded Liberal—tends to obscure the degree to which both contributed to the greater growth of the Empire. The fact, too, that the two of them held the post of Prime Minister at

3

one time or another for nearly thirty years indicates the general areas of agreement among all Englishmen, and at the same time their willingness to disagree on the specific means to be used to achieve their goals. All too often, it is the area of agreement—of compromise—that we remember, and the unfortunate effect of our selective memories is that much vital, brilliant, relevant controversy is obscured or ignored.

"The Victorian Compromise" is a phrase which, since Gilbert Chesterton first formulated it, has come to convey to most of us a certain truth about the lives and ideas of the Victorians. That compromise, as it is usually understood, was a widespread acceptance of the standards of the middle class. With it we associate moral rigidity and prudery, the gospel of work, the instinct for reform—even the jingoism of Palmerston and the imperialism of the later Victorian age. But if we understand the term as implying that the Victorian age was one of great stability, that all Victorians were "earnest" in their attempt to establish and work from the standards of the middle class, we commit an oversimplification nearly as gross as those we now associate with Lytton Strachey's assaults on the Victorian personality. As George Kitson Clark has suggested in *The Making of Victorian England* (Cambridge, Mass., 1962), the initial difficulty of defining the middle class in the nineteenth century renders impossible any sort of accurate description. Certainly one cannot refer to the heterogeneous mass which is today described as the middle class—or "middle-income group." Ought we, then, to think of the "rising middle class"—the captains of industry to whom Carlyle's *Past and Present* is addressed? Or perhaps of the whole of the group that gained the franchise in the reforms of 1832?

Furthermore, the difficulty of the term "compromise" ought to be immediately apparent. Does it mean simply an area of middle ground, held to because it resulted in the least bother? Or does it mean a balance of opposing forces, sometimes violent ones, an equilibrium not consciously sought but nonetheless effective? So W. L. Burn describes it in *The Age of Equipoise* (London, 1964). No doubt all the major historians of the Victorian period would agree that a great diversity of forces, while not peculiar alone to the time, is one of its leading characteristics. All would agree, too, that by some process the age avoided the extreme, revolutionary violence which led on the Continent, especially in the first half of the century, to the overthrow of nearly all the existing governments. The salient fact about English history of the time is that, though the threat of violence existed and revolution was widely feared—particularly during the three Chartist "risings" of 1839, 1842, and 1848—the development of English society in the nineteenth century was evolutionary, and was measured by the relatively peaceful process of legislative action.

Whether we find as more characteristic of Victorianism its differences (it is hardly possible to grasp fully the breadth of opinion) or its similarities, we are in equal danger of getting only half the truth. The Victorians themselves were vastly more aware of their differences. and would have been harder put to it than we are to decide on the nature of the "Compromise." They were concerned, assuredly, with the development of a governmental system (or society) which would provide each man the maximum of security and at the same time guarantee him the greatest possible freedom. This would have been true of a Manchester manufacturer as well as of a Chartist leader; of a Tractarian, Evangelical, or agnostic; of artist or machine operator equally.

Much of what has been said so far is a good deal unlike the ordinary stereotypes for "Victorian," which are based on the lives of that anomalous middle class. All young women were tenderhearted and pure, and older women conspired to keep them that way. Modesty was a virtue; priggishness was even better. Dark red plush velvet was the favorite drapery material of the Victorians; their furniture was ornately ugly; and later on in the century they used gaslight and lived in a sort of mindless elegance. Yet the Victorians were anything but thoughtless, and the comparison of the Victorian to the Elizabethan age is a valid one insofar as it suggests the degree to which nineteenth-century England was a time of very considerable intellectual ferment.

The contention of this book is that the importance of controversy to the development of Victorian attitudes has not heretofore been sufficiently emphasized. In order to make clear the relevance of the idea of conflict we have organized the material into five areas: education, social welfare and the industrial revolution, religion, science, and art. Such categories cannot, by their nature, be mutually exclusive —we should have a very partial understanding of Victorian religion if we failed to consider the importance to it of scientific discovery, or of scientific habits of mind. Most anthologies (organized by author or by genre) tend to obscure the particulars of controversy. The disagreement between Huxley and Arnold, for example, is widely known, but the similarities in their rhetorical postures, as well as critical differences in the details of their argument, are too easily glossed over or ignored. Focus on the author, or on the *kind* of literary work he was performing, may also lead us to assume that such controversy was characteristic only of the pamphlet, or lecture, or expository essay. Enough purely "imaginative literature" is included here to illustrate that controversy was a point of reference for *all* the Victorians. It appears evident, furthermore, that controversy was to a great degree self-concious and deliberate. Only part of the time was there direct confrontation like that between Newman and Kingsley. Most of these personal controversies are well known—Huxley's and Arnold's for example—but their disagreement has a quality different from the sometimes strident tones of Kingsley. More often we find the clear assumption that gentlemanly behavior is compounded of good breeding and good sense, both of which preclude attacks on personality and remove the argument to the relatively safer grounds of reason. What one ought to find above all is that controversy was a habit of the Victorian mind, acquired through experience and sharpened by constant exercise.

John D. Cooke and Lionel Stevenson, in their wise volume *English Literature of the Victorian Period* (New York, 1949), characterize Victorian controversy in the following way:

They believed in the wisdom of looking at all sides of a question, and they were not convinced that truth was simple enough to be condensed into a single dogma. Each author, each politician had his own beliefs, to be sure; but they were intensely concerned with one another's views, and their controversies were more in the nature of cooperative experiments than campaigns of mutual extermination. An interminable town meeting or panel discussion went on for half a century, every writer contributing his share. For this reason, no author or group of authors can be fully understood without constant reference to what their contemporaries were saying at the same time.

We have eliminated out of hand some controversial pieces with which the reader is likely to be familiar in some detail. Such essays as Robert Buchanan's attack on "The Fleshly School of Poetry" are often referred to but are available rather widely already. To include them here would not significantly advance one's appreciation of the importance of conflict. Some essays familiar to most of us do indeed appear, but wherever possible we have chosen the documents of controversy, many of them by important men, and presented them in the form and context closest to that in which the Victorian reader might have been likely to see them. For this reason, for example, we have chosen to include a large portion of Kingsley's "What, Then, Does Dr. Newman Mean?" which first appeared as a pamphlet and has not since been readily available. Similarly, the portion of the text of Newman's response included here is not that with which most readers of the *Apologia* are familiar. *The Apologia pro Vita Sua* was first published in seven weekly parts in the spring of 1864. When Newman collected the parts for the second edition, in book form, in 1865, he suppressed most of Parts One and Two "as being for the most part directly controversial." We have preferred, here, the arguments "directly controversial," in order to reveal the conflict on its original basis.

Despite the excellent and indispensable work on the Victorians exemplified by such books as G. M. Young's *Victorian England: Portrait of an Age*, J. H. Buckley's *The Victorian Temper*, and Walter E. Houghton's *The Victorian Frame of Mind*, we remain a considerable distance from seeing conflicts like these as facts immanent in the lives of the Victorians. We incline to impose upon them the terms of our own existence, and do not accurately gauge the real differences created by the last century. A case in point is the controversy over "the two cultures," the opposing views established by Dr. F. R. Leavis and Sir Charles Snow, which touched relatively few during the years it was most lively. That is to say, although the "facts" on which the conflict is based have relevance, ultimately, to every member of our society, a disproportionately small number of people (not even all of those who may be grouped under the dubious heading "intellectual") can say what the controversy is, what have been the stages in its development or what it means in the context of modern life. We intend by this example to suggest two central facts about controversy among the Victorians: first, that it was made possible and stimulated by a kind of audience which no longer exists; second, that the problems on which Victorian controversy arose have particular relevance to the present day. In fact, much of what we now think of as modern either is Victorian in its origins or is clearly foreshadowed in the nineteenth century. This is the sense in which one speaks of the mood of isolation in Arnold's poetry as being modern—to be caught between two worlds, the one dead, the other powerless to be born.

One of the major themes of Victorian literature focuses on the role of art: does it exist for its own sake—does it retreat into its own palace, as we see frequently in the earlier Tennyson—or does it have a more specifically social function, is it required to enunciate moral principles? If the latter, then the artist is a prophet, a role in which he is responsible to society as a whole (John Holloway's *The Victorian Sage*). The dilemma this created was important to every Victorian artist; the tension between these alternative roles of art and the artist is a constant in Victorian literature, but for the most part we may say that the audience expected the artist to be didactic. They derived some sort of comfort from being advised that they were culpable, and that by following the one true way they might gain the whole world as well as salvation. The family that sat reading the most recent part of a Dickens novel wanted to be entertained, of course, but they would have felt cheated without an equivalent amount of moralizing. If they were prepared to weep for Little Nell or Paul Dombey they were just as ready to respond to the cruelty of the workhouse system into which Oliver Twist is thrust.

The conditions that created that audience cannot be our concern here, and have been adequately traced in such books as George H. Ford's *Dickens and His Readers* (Princeton, 1955) and Richard D. Altick's *The English Common Reader* (Chicago, 1957). What is important is that we understand that the audience was willing and even anxious to take the pill of moral or didactic purpose, and just as frequently when it was not sugared with fiction. The high expectations of those readers account in part for the adverse intensity of the response which greeted poets like Swinburne, or the Pre-Raphaelites. Conversely, it explains the public stature of such men as Dickens, and especially Tennyson and Browning. And what is true of poets and novelists is only slightly less true of the writers of expository prose. Not only Macaulay's *Lays of Ancient Rome* but also his *History of England* were among Victorian best sellers, as were Smiles' *Self-Help* and even his *Life of George Stephenson, Railway Engineer*, which is represented here. Then too, the variety of forms of publication available in the nineteenth century contributed to the spread of ideas and therefore of controversy. Pamphlets, the penny press, the issue of works (not only novels) in monthly or weekly parts, vast numbers of new periodicals—all helped to make available to large numbers of concerned readers some of the best that was being thought and said. And, although the rate of literacy in the United States today may be higher than that of Victorian England, the Victorian controversialist was nevertheless likely to find an audience wider than his counterpart

would find today, wider not only proportionately but by the absolute measure of quantity as well.

A popular culture (or subculture) existed in Victorian England as it does today. Less attention has been given it than our own has received, and certainly it has not received the attention it merits. In the distance of time, however, the interest of a large proportion of the Victorians seems to have centered on topics of more considerable importance than we ordinarily associate with mass culture. But the problems of the Victorians are strikingly like those we know today, not because men are the same in all ways now as they were in the last century but because the position of man in an urban, industrialized society is a necessary concern of all of us. In one sense, the history of the last 150 years is of a single piece.

Each of the introductions to the five sections represents an individual way of regarding problems raised by controversy in the Victorian age. It is our hope that this approach provides a critical and historical framework sufficient to allow insight into the Victorian mind. Implicit in each, however, is the assumption that Victorian problems are modern ones, and that we have something yet to learn from the past. Relatively little of the material here should appear quaint to the modern reader. No one would today argue, for example, the specific point of Keble's sermon. But the relations between church and state have not yet been clearly sorted out, and are still liable to revision. Nor would the majority argue the point of apostasy—it is a fact established beyond all doubt. Apostasy does not, however, mean only a lapse from the standards of the church militant (as for the Evangelicals) or the rigid Anglicanism of Keble. It means, too, the consciousness of somehow having been separated from worthwhile purpose, becoming aware of the fact of deep division between the ordinary occupations of our lives and what they ought to signify. This consciousness, amounting to sickness, is a prominent tone among the Victorians, and it is especially clear in the documents of men like Ruskin and Morris. In part it is simply a condition of life under industrialism. The separation of worker from product, and the substitution of money for payment in kind, is the first step in the process leading to the assembly lines and the "fragmentation of modern man." This is a problem at once religious and social—it is touched by science, it affects education, and it has become the content of art. The problems revealed by automation are essentially the same as those to which Ruskin addressed himself.

Just so, the Victorian controversy over education has recently been redone with a modern cast. The long struggle to establish a system of public education, culminating in the passage of Forster's Education Act of 1870, was really subordinate to the greater questions of what should be taught, how, and by whom. In the last decade we have worried the same questions, and have not arrived at answers less equivocal than those the Victorians achieved. The conflict between scientific and humanistic goals for education has not been resolved, although Arnold's prophecy that the humanities, after a brief decline, would regain their rightful place has proved somewhat overly optimistic. Inevitably the influence of science has had a greater effect on our lives than it had even through the publication of *The Origin of Species*. The difference, however, is one of degree only. The laws of evidence which substantiated the higher criticism of the Bible and the discoveries of Lyell and Darwin are a first version of our more thoroughgoing materialism. Adherence to the facts of science and the necessity of belief have equally motivated the most exemplary of modern theologians, Pierre Teilhard de Chardin. At once scientist (a paleontologist) and priest, he was forced to find God immanent in man, not in a church or a religion. The quality of his response to the modern situation is not so different from that of Arnold; humanism remains a workable alternative.

Many more of the problems raised in this book will appear familiar, and might easily be transposed into modern terms. But Victorian controversy is here presented not primarily as a means of gaining perspective on our own culture, but in the hope that it will add to our understanding of the past.

I

Education

DURING the Victorian period two areas of controversy about education were prominent. First, in Parliament social questions were debated: Who shall be taught? How long? At whose expense? Under whose supervision? Second, answers to the pedagogical problem of what to teach were offered in lectures and essays by some of the most eminent Victorians.

Answers to the first set of questions became increasingly liberal. The nonsectarian University of London was established as University College in 1825, and its curricula were far broader than those offered at Oxford and Cambridge. Not until 1871 were religious tests eliminated as degree requirements at England's most prestigious and influential universities. Religion, though steadily less important as a social prerequisite, played a vital role in widening the availability of education and in defining its social function. The Broad Church movement was instrumental in the establishment in 1854 of Workingmen's College, where instruction in at least letters and numbers became available to a large and hitherto neglected class. The appointment of John Henry Newman as rector elect of the Catholic University of Ireland in 1852 occasioned the discourses which became *The Idea of a University*, one of the most potent of all Victorian statements on education.

Throughout the period, education became less of an aristocratic privilege and more of a middle-class and lower-class prerogative. Increasingly, too, the state rather than local voluntary organizations or the church assured the availability and adequacy of public elementary schools. A board of inspectors and a national system of curricular requirements and standards were established. Matthew Arnold is surely the most famous of the school inspectors, and in his essay we see how his practical experiences influenced his concept of education.

Arnold's role as a participant in and a commentator on the educational system provides a convenient transition to the second area of controversy, the one of more interest to the student of intellectual backgrounds. What shall be taught? is another of those questions the Victorians learned to ask and we are still learning to answer: whether the natural sciences or the liberal arts should be stressed, whether the schools are responsible for moral instruction and, if so, what system of morals ought to be taught, whether there are pedagogical methods or systems capable of universal application.

Most of these questions appear in the imaginative literature of the time; probably the novelists' interest in individual psychological development and in social reform are both responsible for this phenomenon. For example, in the selection from Dickens' *Hard Times*, belief, fancy, and taste are all equivalent to or replaced by fact. But after hearing Bitzer's definition of horse, would any of us think we know what a horse is or that we could identify one? And even if we could, isn't it true that Sissy Jupe's understanding of *what a horse is* is more profound and closer to what we would want to know? "Would you use a carpet having a representation of flowers upon it?"

The kind of emphasis on science burlesqued by Dickens is inevitably ludicrous, but another kind is more insidious. In Meredith's novel, Richard Feverel's misfortunes are, in large part, attributable to a scientific system of education. While we may never know what exactly constitutes the system because of Meredith's elusiveness, we do know that Sir Austin's notions of a scientific system of education are derived from the writings of Herbert Spencer. Although Sir Austin's comprehension of the laws of evolution of intelligence is doubtless inadequate, still Spencer's arguments, for all their logical classifications and distinctions, remain idealistic and hypothetical; that is, they do not take into account individual capabilities and potentialities and problems. Spencer's healthy emphasis on relative value is weakened by a malignant and an already outdated utilitarianism especially evident in his denigration of the classics and exaltation of science.

But Spencer's reliance on utilitarianism* as the rock on which his

---

* Utilitarianism refers to a theory of ethics propounded by Jeremy Bentham, James Mill, and the latter's son, John Stuart Mill. Although each does not hold an identical theory, it is safe to generalize that the test of ethical questions was their usefulness to society. Utility was defined as the greatest happiness to the greatest number. Happiness was often equated with pleasure and quantified; Carlyle mocked utilitarianism by referring to it as a profit-and-loss philosophy, and his appellation is accurate enough to describe its failures as a system of ethics.

arguments are built extends to his arguments for science as well as those against classics. Dismissing the love of knowledge for its own sake as a reason for study, Spencer attempts to "terrorize us" into studying science. A. E. Housman's analysis of Spencer's mode of argument is worth quoting both for its penetration and its wit. Housman writes in his "Introductory Lecture" that Spencer not only shows that whatever walk of life a man pursues, knowledge of one or two sciences may be indispensable, but also

he attempts, in the case of one or two sciences, to shew that no one can neglect them with impunity. The following, for instance, is the manner in which he endeavors to terrorize us into studying geology. We may, any of us, some day, take shares in a joint-stock company; and that company may engage in mining operations; and those operations may be directed to the discovery of coal; and for want of geological information the joint-stock company may go mining for coal under the old red sandstone, where there is no coal; and then the mining operation will be fruitless, and the joint-stock company will come to grief, and where shall we be then? This is, indeed, to eat the bread of carefulness. After all, men have been known to complete their pilgrimage through this vale of tears without taking shares in a joint-stock company. But the true reply to Spencer's intimidations I imagine to be this: that the attempt to fortify man's estate against all contingencies by such precautions as these is in the first place interminable and in the second place hopeless.

Neglect of the individual and his real needs can take forms other than Sir Austin's scientific system. Tom Tulliver, in George Eliot's *The Mill on the Floss*, is subjected to the education in the classics traditionally administered to middle-class boys by the clergy. The narrator's ironic remark about Mr. Stelling's theory is equally applicable to Spencer's: "If we are to have one regimen for all minds, his seems to me as good as any other." Tom Tulliver's talents are in other areas. That their neglect is in part responsible for his failure in the world underscores in a devastatingly ironic way that his sister's failures are in part attributable to the fact that she was not offered even Mr. Stelling's misguided form of classical education, education of any intellectual sort not being considered wholly proper or necessary for young bourgeois ladies of the time.

Alternatives available to those who could not or did not wish to attend ordinary schools were instruction in the home or autodidacticism. John Stuart Mill's impressive list of early reading, that he felt "could assuredly be done by any boy or girl of average capability," is intellectually far more splendid than the systems of Stelling or Spencer, but it too, like Sir Austin's home-grown system, neglected one of the individual's needs, in this case Mill's need to cultivate and develop his feelings. The details of Mill's early education are set forth in Chapter 3 of his autobiography. His depression, resulting from a system of education which systematically ignored the emotions, and his recovery are described in the opening of the fifth chapter, a part of the autobiography widely anthologized.

The conflict between intellect and emotion that is a motif in most of the selections in this section provides much of the thematic material in *Jude the Obscure*. Hardy avers in his April, 1912, postscript to the novel that "the difficulties down to twenty or thirty years back of acquiring knowledge in letters without pecuniary means" were used for the sake of providing a "good fable for a tragedy, told for its own sake." However, Hardy does not quarrel with these readers who thought certain episodes—including those reproduced in this section —constituted "an attack on venerable institutions, and that when Ruskin College was subsequently founded it should have been called the College of Jude the Obscure."

Most of the controversies over education in the Victorian period had to take account of utilitarianism. Even Newman, who argues so eloquently in *The Idea of a University* that knowledge as its own end and that all departments of knowledge are actively complementary, is constrained to discuss utility. His major hypothesis, that the good is always useful, but the useful is not always good, commandeers the utilitarians' own clichés and arguments to attack their positions. The reader can discover for himself how Newman's ideas on education form a *via media* between the classical and scientific extremes; what may prove more difficult is to reconcile Newman's magnanimous views of a liberal education with his narrow views of the gentlemanly ends of such an education.

Huxley's "Science and Culture" and Arnold's "Literature and Science" are probably the most famous Victorian statements on education; often they are thought of as representing more or less polarized attitudes toward the relative merits of stressing science or literature in school curricula. But when the arguments and rhetorical techniques are examined carefully the essays are seen to be not at all radically diverse; in fact, there is far more agreement between Huxley and Arnold than we ordinarily expect to find. Analysis of their rhetorical devices and techniques reveals nor only considerable art and subtlety but also a basic pattern in Victorian controversy. As John D. Cooke and Lionel Stevenson have pointed out, such controversies are not rooted in personal animosity but partake of the nature of cooperative investigations.

For example, early in Huxley's essay he engages overtly in establishing for the speaker—both essays were originally lectures—the persona of a humble but experienced man more interested in peace than war. Yet, though the military metaphor unfolds slowly, it is full blown: Huxley speaks of champions, banners, and hosts. The humility of the speaker who reminds us that his opinions "may not be devoid of interest" contrasts effectively with the fact that behind the mask is Thomas Henry Huxley, a general, not a private, in the army of science.

After using the life of Sir Josiah Mason as parable, and indulging in some rather elegant literary sarcasm—the references to Shakespeare, Milton, and the Bible are useful in establishing Huxley's qualifications as at least a colonel in the literary ranks—Huxley says that he holds very strongly by two convictions: first, "that neither the discipline nor the subject matter of classical education is of such direct value to the student of physical science as to justify the expenditure of valuable time upon either"; second, "that for the purpose of attaining real culture, an exclusively scientific education is at least as useful as a purely literary one." Huxley does not begin immediately to prove or to document his convictions. First he attempts to gain sympathy and tolerance for his advocacy by pointing out that his opinions are not those of the majority. (Indeed, until the middle sixties, school and universtiy curricula were very narrowly "classical": modern topics were ignored.) Then Huxley introduces England's "chief apostle of culture," Matthew Arnold, not as an opponent but as a sort of quasi-religious statesman whose pronouncements are misused and distorted by fanatic followers. Scientifically, Huxley separates Arnold's statements into two propositions. And then, further establishing his persona as humble and tolerant, the first proposition is asserted to without reservation. Huxley argues vigorously against the second proposition, that "literature contains the materials which suffice" for that criticism of life which is the essence of culture.

His chief argument is that "our whole theory of life has long been influenced . . . by the general conceptions of the universe which have been forced upon us by physical science." Then, adopting a humanist camouflage, Huxley asserts that modern advocates of classicism are ignoring their own first principles by overlooking the Greek faith that "the free employment of reason in accordance with scientific method, is the sole method of reaching truth." (To ears accustomed to Arnold's ideas, this assertion will not sound very different from his laudatory description of the Hellenistic "disinterested curiosity," the "free play of the mind on all things.")

But Huxley has not yet proved his first conviction. He states that humanists are not the sole heirs of the "spirit of antiquity," but this does not lead him to condemn the potential benefits of a sound classical education. Rather he argues merely that the "ordinary smattering of Latin and Greek" is of no direct value to three classes of men: "those who mean to make science their serious occupation; or who intend to follow the profession of medicine; or who have to enter early on the business of life." Huxley deliberately attacks only a very extreme position: he occupies only a very narrow strip of hostile territory. The first conviction has been considerably narrowed: only one kind of classical education, and that only for three particular sets of people, has been argued to be of little direct value. As for his second conviction, Huxley again diverts the thrust of his attack from what we legitimately expected. He does not actually argue that "for the purpose of attaining real culture an exclusively scientific education is at least as effectual as an exclusively literary one," but instead that the exclusion of either brings about an undesirable "mental twist." The reader of the essay will note too the distinction between a literary education and a classical education, and Huxley's appeal to patriotism.

There is, of course, more rhetorical finesse in the essay than we have shown; nevertheless, Huxley's tactics are now more plain as is his strategy of narrowing his opposition and his real appreciation of genuine culture. More detailed study is left to the reader, for we must now examine the strategies and tactics Arnold used in defense.

"Literature and Science" begins by invoking some of Plato's ideas as representative of humanistic notions which are out of key with the exigencies of the present. Arnold seems thus to cede much ground initially, although he retains Plato's description of the aims of education. He immediately engages in combat with one of Huxley's major arguments, but before offering any answers he too establishes a persona: that of a man admittedly not widely versed in science, a simple man addressing an audience full of "sharp observers and critics" who will not be fooled by any unwarranted assumption of competence. After returning Huxley's compliments and quoting from his lectures

—and it ought to be noted that the men do not distort each other's positions by misquoting—Arnold begins an argument by definition. He says that Huxley and others mean by literature *belles lettres*, and he recalls Huxley's use of the word "smattering." That is, Arnold takes proper advantage of Huxley's modest arguments against misdirected classical educations. Arnold argues that it is merely Huxley's misinterpretation of "literature" that has led him to assert that a genuine humanism is not scientific. Both agree, then, that some ground is neutral territory: "there is . . . really no question between Professor Huxley and me as to whether knowing the great results of the modern scientific study of nature is not required as part of our culture." Arnold changes the battleground from results to processes. The fight will be conducted with the same weapons, but for different terrain.

Just as Huxley established his credentials as a humanist, so Arnold, by citing some interesting scientific knowledge, reminds us that behind the humble persona stands the knowledgeable Matthew Arnold. But Arnold will not agree that because some scientific facts are interesting and because dealing with facts provides valuable discipline, therefore training in natural sciences should be made the *main* part of education. At this point, before marshaling his strongest argument, Arnold again admits his inadequacies and cites the "ability and pugnacity" of his formidable opponents in an attempt to make his role into that of underdog.

Another major argument is predicated on the fact that there is in the majority of mankind "an impluse for relating our knowledge to our sense for conduct and our sense for beauty." After admitting that the natural sciences are not merely "instrument knowledge"—a term the reader will want to compare to Newman's definition of "useful knowledge"—Arnold argues that only to the born naturalist will the knowledge provided by natural science be satisfying, for it cannot be put into relation with our sense for conduct and our sense for beauty. Again, Arnold attacks what seemed to be one of Huxley's strong limited claims by surrounding and claiming for himself the vast remaining territory. Arnold's proofs are not so rigorous as Huxley's; his appeal is to esperience, and Huxley's is to history. Arnold succeeds, if at all, by having the audience identify themselves with the persona of the speaker: you and I, dear reader, have felt poetry and eloquence touch our emotions, and we know that the facts of science have not yet been brought home to the bosoms and businesses of men.

Availing himself of Huxley's strategy, Arnold takes up Huxley's second proposition and argues that because "literature" includes the results of scientific investigation, an exclusively literary education is less incomplete than an exclusively scientific one. And again taking advantage of Huxley's modest claims, Arnold agrees that for the majority of mankind an education in humane letters is more beneficial than one in natural sciences.

As he reminds us he promised to do, Arnold provides two arguments showing that English literature, or modern literature alone, is not sufficient to provide true culture. By returning to an initial contention, Arnold not only unifies his essay but reminds us that Huxley retreated from his convictions. Arnold's strategy is clear enough: he will occupy all the ground Huxley thought it good strategy to surrender, thus emphasizing the modesty of his opponent's gains. At the same time, the modest persona of the speaker and his appeal to personal experience rather than to history modify the aggressiveness of Arnold's claims.

The foregoing analysis shows important differences in the rhetorical techniques of the two men, but more importantly it demonstrates that their positions on the relative merits of science and literature are not very different at all, and it shows too that they share not only certain rhetorical devices but a deep concern for the advancement of culture, and that in all these ways, they are representative of Victorian controversy.

1. HUXLEY:

"Science and Culture"

Thomas Henry Huxley (1825–1895) is the subject of Cyril Bibby's *T. H. Huxley: Scientist, Humanist, and Educator*; the subtitle is an accurate reflection of the man's interests. Leonard Huxley's *Life and Letters* (2 vols., New York, 1900) is another good source of information. William Irvine's *Apes, Angels, and Victorians* (New York, 1955) is well worth consulting.

"Science and Culture" was a speech presented at the opening of a science college in Birmingham in 1880. It is analyzed extensively in the introduction to this section.

Six years ago, as some of my present hearers may remember, I had the privilege of addressing a large assemblage of the inhabitants of this city, who had gathered together to do honor to the memory of their famous townsman, Joseph Priestly; and, if any satisfaction attaches to posthumous glory, we may hope that the *manes* of the burnt-out philosopher were then finally appeased.

No man, however, who is endowed with a fair share of common sense, and not more than a fair share of vanity, will identify either contemporary or posthumous fame with the highest good; and Priestley's life leaves no doubt that he, at any rate, set a much higher value upon the advancement of knowledge, and the promotion of that freedom of thought which is at once the cause and the consequence of intellectual progress.

Hence I am disposed to think that, if Priestley could be amongst us today, the occasion of our meeting would afford him even greater pleasure than the proceedings which celebrated the centenary of his chief discovery. The kindly heart would be moved, the high sense of social duty would be satisfied, by the spectacle of well-earned wealth neither squandered in tawdry luxury and vainglorious show, nor scattered with the careless charity which blesses neither him that gives nor him that takes, but expended in the execution of a well-considered plan for the aid of present and future generations of those who are willing to help themselves.

We shall all be of one mind thus far. But it is needful to share Priestley's keen interest in physical science; and to have learned, as he had learned, the value of scientific training in fields of inquiry apparently far remote from physical science; in order to appreciate, as he would have appreciated, the value of the noble gift which Sir Josiah Mason has bestowed upon the inhabitants of the Midland district.

For us children of the nineteenth century, however, the establishment of a college under the conditions of Sir Josiah Mason's Trust, has a significance apart from any which it could have possessed a hundred years ago. It appears to be an indication that we are reaching the crisis of the battle, or rather of the long series of battles, which have been fought over education in a campaign which began long before Priestley's time, and will probably not be finished just yet.

In the last century, the combatants were the champions of ancient literature on the one side and those of modern literature on the other; but, some thirty years ago, the contest became complicated by the appearance of a third army, ranged round the banner of physical science.

I am not aware that anyone has authority to speak in the name of this new host. For it must be admitted to be somewhat of a guerrilla force, composed largely of irregulars, each of whom fights pretty much for his own hand. But the impressions of a full private, who has seen a good deal of service in the ranks, respecting the present position of affairs and the conditions of a permanent peace, may not be devoid of interest; and I do not know that I could make a better use of the present opportunity than by laying them before you.

From the time that the first suggestion to introduce physical science into ordinary education was timidly whispered, until now, the advocates of scientific education have met with opposition of two kinds. On the one hand, they have been pooh-poohed by the men of business who pride themselves on being the representatives of practicality; while, on the other hand, they have been excommunicated by the classical scholars, in their capacity of Levites in charge of the ark of culture and monopolists of liberal education.

The practical men believed that the idol whom they worship—rule of thumb—has been the source of the past prosperity, and will suffice for the future welfare of the arts and manufactures. They were of opinion that science is speculative rubbish; that theory and practice have nothing to do with one another; and that the scientific habit of mind is an impediment, rather than an aid, in the conduct of ordinary affairs.

I have used the past tense in speaking of the practical men—for although they were very formidable thirty years ago, I am not sure that the pure species has not been extirpated. In fact, so far as mere argument goes, they have been subjected to such a *feu d'enfer* that it is a miracle if any have escaped. But I have remarked that your typical practical man has an unexpected resemblance to one of Milton's angels. His spiritual wounds, such as are inflicted by logical weapons, may be as deep as a well and as wide as a church door, but beyond shedding a few drops of ichor, celestial or otherwise, he is no whit the worse. So, if any of these opponents be left, I will not waste time in vain repetition of the demonstrative eidence of the practical value of science; but knowing that a parable will sometimes penetrate where syllogisms fail to effect an entrance, I will offer a story for their consideration.

Once upon a time, a boy, with nothing to depend upon but his own vigorous nature. was thrown into the thick of the struggle for existence in the midst of a great manufacturing population. He seems to have had a hard fight, inasmuch as, by the time he was thirty years of age. his total disposable funds amounted to twenty pounds. Nevertheless, middle life found him giving proof of his comprehension of the practical problems he had been roughly called upon to solve, by a career of remarkable prosperity.

Finally, having reached old age with its well-earned surroundings of "honor, troops of friends," the hero of my story bethought himself of those who were making a like start in life, and how he could stretch out a helping hand to them.

After long and anxious reflection this successful practical man of business could devise nothing better than to provide them with the means of obtaining "sound, extensive, and practical scientific knowledge." And he devoted a large part of his wealth and five years of incessant work to this end.

I need not point the moral of a tale which, as the solid and spacious fabric of the Scientific College assures us, is no fable, nor can anything which I could say intensify the force of this practical answer to practical objections.

We may take it for granted then, that, in the opinion of those best qualified to judge, the diffusion of thorough scientific education is an absolutely essential condition of industrial progress; and that the college which has been opened today will confer an inestimable boon upon those whose livelihood is to be gained by the practice of the arts and manufactures of the district.

The only question worth discussion is, whether the conditions, under which the work of the college is to be carried out, are such as to give it the best possible chance of achieving permanent success.

Sir Josiah Mason, without doubt most wisely, has left very large freedom of action to the trustees, to whom he proposes ultimately to commit the administration of the college, so that they may be able to adjust its arrangements in accordance with the changing conditions of the future. But, with respect to three points, he has laid most explicit injunctions upon both administrators and teachers.

Party politics are forbidden to enter into the minds of either, so far as the work of the college is concerned; theology is as sternly banished from its precincts; and finally, it is especially declared that the college shall make no provision for "mere literary instruction and education."

It does not concern me at present to dwell upon the first two injunctions any longer than may be needful to express my full conviction of their wisdom. But the third prohibition brings us face to face with those other opponents of scientific education, who are by no means in the moribund condition of the practical man, but alive, alert, and formidable.

It is not impossible that we shall hear this express exclusion of "literary instruction and education" from a college which, nevertheless, professes to give a high and efficient education, sharply criticized. Certainly the time was that the Levites of culture would have sounded their trumpets against its walls as against an educational Jericho.

How often have we not been told that the study of physical science is incompetent to confer culture; that it touches none of the higher problems of life; and, what is worse, that the continual devotion to scientific studies tends to generate a narrow and bigoted belief in the applicability of scientific methods to the search after truth of all kinds? How frequently one has reason to observe that no reply to a troublesome argument tells so well as calling its author a 'mere scientific specialist." And, as I am afraid it is not permissable to speak of this form of opposition to scientific education in the past tense, may we not expect to be told that this, not only omission, but prohibition, of "mere literary instruction and education" is a patent example of scientific narrow-mindedness?

I am not acquainted with Sir Josiah Mason's reasons for the action which he has taken; but if, as I apprehend is the case, he refers to the ordinary classical course of our schools and universities by the name of "mere literary instruction and education," I venture to offer sundry reasons of my own in support of that action.

For I hold very strongly by two convictions. The first is that neither the discipline nor the subject-matter of classical education is of such direct value to the student of physical science as to justify the expenditure of valuable time upon either; and the second is, that for the purpose of attaining real culture, an exclusively scientific education is at least as effectual as an exclusively literary education.

I need hardly point out to you that these opinions, especially the latter, are diametrically opposed to those of the great majority of educated Englishmen, influenced as they are by school and university traditions. In their belief, culture is obtainable only by a liberal education; and a liberal education is synonymous, not merely with education and instruction in literature, but in one particular form of literature, namely, that of Greek and Roman antiquity. They hold that the man who has learned Latin and Greek, however little, is educated; while he who is versed in other branches of knowledge, however deeply, is a more or less respectable specialist, not admissible into the cultured caste. The stamp of the educated man, the university degree, is not for him.

I am too well acquainted with the generous catholicity of spirit, the true sympathy with scientific thought, which pervades the writings of our chief apostle of culture to identify him with these opinions; and yet one may cull from one and another of those epistles to the Philistines, which so much delight all who do not answer to that name, sentences which lend them some support.

Mr. Arnold tells us that the meaning of culture is "to know the best that has been thought and said in the world." It is the criticism of life contained in literature. That criticism regards "Europe as being, for intellectual and spiritual purposes, one great confederation, bound to a joint action and working to a common result; and whose members have, for their common outfit, a knowledge of Greek, Roman, and Eastern antiquity, and of one another. Special, local, and temporary advantages being put out of account, that modern nation will in the intellectual and spiritual sphere make most progress, which most thoroughly carries out this program. And what is that but saying that we too, all of us, as individuals, the more thoroghly we carry it out, shall make the more progress?"

We have here to deal with two distinct propositions. The first, that a criticism of life is the essence of culture; the second, that literature contains the materials which suffice for the construction of such criticism.

I think that we must all assent to the first proposition. For culture certainly means something quite different from learning or technical skill. It implies the possession of an ideal, and the habit of critically estimating the value of things by comparison with a theoretic standard. Perfect culture should supply a complete theory of life, based upon a clear knowledge alike of its possibilities and of its limitations.

But we may agree to all this, and yet strongly dissent from the assumption that literature alone is competent to supply this knowledge. After having learned all that Greek, Roman and Eastern antiquity have thought and said, and all that modern literatures have to tell us, it is not self-evident that we have laid a sufficiently broad and deep foundation for that criticism of life which constitutes culture.

Indeed, to anyone acquainted with the scope of physical science, it is not at all evident. Considering progress only in the "intellectual and spiritual sphere," I find myself wholly unable to admit that either nations or individuals will really advance, if their common outfit draws nothing from the stores of physical science. I should say that an army, without weapons of precision and with no particular base of operations, might more hopefully enter upon a campaign on the Rhine, than a man, devoid of a knowledge of what physical science has done in the last century, upon a criticism of life.

When a biologist meets with an anomaly, he instinctively turns to the study of development to clear it up. The rationale of contradictory opinions may with equal confidence be sought in history.

It is, happily, no new thing that Englishmen should employ their wealth in building and endowing institutions for educational purposes, But, five or six hundred years ago, deeds of foundation expressed or implied conditions as nearly as possible contrary to those which have been thought expedient by Sir Josiah Mason. That is to say, physical science was practically ignored, while a certain literary training was enjoined as a means to the acquirement of knowledge which was essentially theological.

The reason of this singular contradiction between the actions of men alike animated by a strong and disinterested desire to promote the welfare of their fellows, is easily discovered.

At that time, in fact, if anyone desired knowledge beyond such as could be obtained by his own observation, or by common conversation, his first necessity was to learn the Latin language, inasmuch as all the higher knowledge of the western world was contained in works written in that language. Hence, Latin grammar, with logic and rhetoric, studied through Latin, were the fundamentals of education. With respect to the substance of the knowledge imparted through this channel, the Jewish and Christian Scriptures, as interpreted and supplemented by the Romish Church, were held to contain a complete and infallibly true body of information.

Theological dicta were, to the thinkers of those days, that which the axioms and definitions of Euclid are to the geometers of these. The business of the philosophers of the Middle Ages was to deduce from the data furnished by the theologians, conclusions in accordance with ecclesiastical decrees. They were allowed the high privilege of showing, by logical process, how and why that which the Church said was true, must be true. And if their demonstrations fell short of or exceeded this limit, the Church was maternally ready to check their aberrations; if need were by the help of the secular arm.

Between the two, our ancestors were furnished with a compact and complete criticism of life. They were told how the world began and how it would end; they learned that all material existence was but a base and insignificant blot upon the fair face of the spiritual world, and that nature was, to all intents and purposes, the playground of the devil; they learned that the earth is the center of the visible universe, and that man is the cynosure of things terrestrial; and more especially was it inculcated that the course of nature had no fixed order, but that it could be, and constantly was, altered by the agency of innumerable spiritual beings, good and bad, according as they were moved by the deeds and prayers of men. The sum and substance of the whole doctrine was to produce the conviction that the only thing really worth knowing in this world was how to secure that place in a better which, under certain conditions, the Church promised.

Our ancestors had a living belief in this theory of life, and acted upon it in their dealings with education, as in all other matters. Culture meant saintliness—after the fashion of the saints of those days; the education that led to it was, of necessity, theological; and the way to theology lay through Latin.

That the study of nature—further than was requisite for the satisfaction of everyday wants—should have any bearing on human life
was far from the thoughts of men thus trained. Indeed, as nature had
been cursed for man's sake, it was an obvious conclusion that those
who meddled with nature were likely to come into pretty close contact with Satan. And, if any borh scientific investigator followed his
instincts, he might safely reckon upon earning the reputation, and
probably upon suffering the fate, of a sorcerer.

Had the western world been left to itself in Chinese isolation, there
is no saying how long this state of things might have endured. But,
happily, it was not left to itself. Even earlier than the thirteenth century, the development of Moorish civilization in Spain and the great
movement of the Crusades had introduced the leaven which, from
that day to this, has never ceased to work. At first, through the inter-
mediation of Arabic translations, afterwards by the study of the ori-
ginals, the western nations of Europe became acquainted with the
writings of the ancient philosophers and poets, and, in time, with the
whole of the vast literature of antiquity.

Whatever there was of high intellectual aspiration or dominant
capacity in Italy, France, Germany, and England, spent itself for centuries in taking possession of the rich inheritance left by the dead
civilizations of Greece and Rome. Marvelously aided by the invention
of printing, classical learning spread and flourished. Those who possessed it prided themselves on having attained the highest culture then
within the reach of mankind.

And justly. For, saving Dante on his solitary pinnacle, there was no
figure in modern literature at the time of the Renascence to compare
with the men of antiquity; there was no art to complete with their
sculpture; there was no physical science but that which Greece had
created. Above all, there was no other example of perfect intellectual
freedom—of the unhesitating acceptance of reason as the sole guide
to truth and the supreme arbiter of conduct.

The new learning necessarily soon exerted a profound influence
upon education. The language of the monks and schoolmen seemed
little better than gibberish to scholars fresh from Virgil and Cicero,
and the study of Latin was placed upon a new foundation. Moreover,
Latin itself ceased to afford the sole key to knowledge. The student
who sought the highest thought of antiquity, found only a second-
hand reflection of it in Roman literature, and turned his face to the
full light of the Greeks. And after a battle, not altogether dissimilar to

that which is at present being fought over the teaching of physical science, the study of Greek was recognized as an essential element of all higher education.

Thus the Humanists, as they were called, won the day; and the great reform which they effected was of incalculable service to mankind. But the Nemesis of all reformers is finality; and the reformers of education, like those of religion, fell into the profound, however common, error of mistaking the beginning for the end of the work of reformation.

The representatives of the Humanists, in the nineteenth century, take their stand upon classical education as the sole avenue to culture, as firmly as if we were still in the age of Renascence. Yet, surely, the present intellectual relations of the modern and the ancient worlds are profoundly different from those which obtained three centuries ago. Leaving aside the existence of a great and characteristically modern literature, of modern painting, and, especially, of modern music, there is one feature of the present state of the civilized world which separates it more widely from the Renascence than the Renascence was separated from the Middle Ages.

This distinctive character of our own times lies in the vast and constantly increasing part which is played by natural knowledge. Not only is our daily life shaped by it, not only does the prosperity of millions of men depend upon it, but our whole theory of life has long been influenced, consciously or unconsciously, by the general conceptions of the universe which have been forced upon us by physical science.

In fact, the most elementary acquaintance with the results of scientific investigation shows us that they offer a broad and striking contradiction to the opinion so implicitly credited and taught in the Middle Ages.

The notions of the beginning and the end of the world entertained by our forefathers are no longer credible. It is very certain that the earth is not the chief body in the material universe, and that the world is not subordinated to man's use. It is even more certain that nature is the expression of a definite order with which nothing interferes, and that the chief business of mankind is to learn that order and govern themselves accordingly. Moreover this scientific "criticism of life" presents itself to us with different credentials from any other. It appeals not to authority, nor to what anybody may have thought or said, but to nature. It admits that all our interpretations of natural fact are more or less imperfect and symbolic, and bids the learner seek for truth not among words but among things. It warns us that the assertion which outstrips evidence is not only a blunder but a crime.

The purely classical education advocated by the representatives of the Humanists in our day, gives no inkling of all this. A man may be a better scholar than Erasmus, and know no more of the chief causes of the present intellectual fermentation than Erasmus did. Scholarly and pious persons, worthy of all respect, favor us with allocutions upon the sadness of the antagonism of science to their medieval way of thinking, which betray an ignorance of the first principles of scientific investigation, an incapacity for understanding what a man of science means by veracity, and an unconsciousness of the weight of established scientific truths, which is almost comical.

There is no great force in the *tu quoque* argument, or else the advocates of scientific education might fairly enough report upon the modern Humanists that they may be learned specialists, but that they possess no such sound foundation for a criticism of life as deserves the name of culture. And, indeed, if we were disposed to be cruel, we might urge that the Humanists have brought this reproach upon themselves, not because they are too full of the spirit of the ancient Greek, but because they lack it.

The period of the Renascence is commonly called that of the "Revival of Letters," as if the influences then brought to bear upon the mind of Western Europe had been wholly exhausted in the field of literature. I think it is very commonly forgotten that the revival of science, effected by the same agency, although less conspicuous, was not less momentous.

In fact, the few scattered students of nature of that day picked up the clue to her secrets exactly as it fell from the hands of the Greeks a thousand years before. The foundations of mathematics were so well laid by them, that our children learn their geometry from a book written for the schools of Alexandria two thousand years ago Modern astronomy is the natural continuation and development of the work of Hipparchus and of Ptolemy; modern physics of that of Democritus and of Archimedes; it was long before modern biological science outgrew the knowledge bequeathed to us by Aristotle, by Theophrastus, and by Galen.

We cannot know all the best thoughts and sayings of the Greeks unless we know what they thought about natural phenomena. We cannot fully apprehend their criticism of life unless we understand the extent to which that criticism was affected by scientific conceptions. We falsely pretend to be the inheritors of their culture, unless we are penetrated, as the best minds among them were, with an unhesitating faith that the free employment of reason, in accordance with scientific method, is the sole method of reaching truth.

Thus I venture to think that the pretensions of our modern Humanists to the possession of the monopoly of culture and to the exclusive inheritance of the spirit of antiquity must be abated, if not abandoned. But I should be very sorry that anything I have said should be taken to imply a desire on my part to depreciate the value of classical education, as it might be and as it sometimes is. The native capacities of mankind vary no less than their opportunities; and while culture is one, the road by which one man may best reach it is widely different from that which is most advantageous to another. Again, while scientific education is yet inchoate and tentative, classical education is thoroughly well organized upon the practical experience of generations of teachers. So that, given ample time for learning and estimation for ordinary life, or for a literary career, I do not think that a young Englishman in search of culture can do better than follow the course usually marked our for him, supplementing its deficiencies by his own efforts.

But for those who mean to make science their serious occupation; or who intend to follow the profession of medicine; or who have to enter early upon the business of life; for all these, in my opinion, classical education is a mistake; and it is for this reason that I am glad to see "mere literary education and instruction" shut out from the curriculum of Sir Josiah Mason's College, seeing that its inclusion would probably lead to the introduction of the ordinary smattering of Latin and Greek.

Nevertheless, I am the last person to question the importance of genuine literary education, or to suppose that intellectual culture can be complete without it. An exclusively scientific training will bring about a mental twist as surely as an exclusively literary training. The value of the cargo does not compensate for a ship's being out of trim; and I should be sorry to think that the Scientific College would turn out none but lopsided men.

There is no need, however, that such a catastrophe should happen. Instruction in English, French, and German is provided, and thus the three greatest literatures of the modern world are made accessible to the student.

French and German, and especially the latter language, are absolutely indispensable to those who desire full knowledge in any department of science. But even supposing that the knowledge of these languages acquired is not more than sufficient for purely scientific purposes, every Englishman has, in his native tongue, an almost perfect instrument of literary expression; and, in his own literature, models of every kind of literary excellance. If an Englishman cannot get literary culture out of his Bible, his Shakespeare, his Milton, neither, in my belief, will the profoundest study of Homer and Sophocles, Virgil and Horace, give it to him.

Thus, since the constitution of the college makes sufficient provision for literary as well as for scientific education, and since artistic instruction is also contemplated, it seems to me that a fairly complete culture is offered to all who are willing to take advantage of it.

But I am not sure that at this point the "practical" man, scotched but not slain, may ask what all this talk about culture has to do with an institution, the object of which is defined to be "to promote the prosperity of the manufactures and the industry of the country." He may suggest that what is wanted for this end is not culture, nor even a purely scientific discipline, but simply a knowledge of applied science.

I often wish that this phrase, "applied science," had never been invented. For it suggests that there is a sort of scientific knowledge of direct practical use, which can be studied apart from another sort of scientific knowledge, which is of no practical utility, and which is termed "pure science." But there is no more complete fallacy than this. What people call applied science is nothing but the application of pure science to particular classes of problems. It consists of deductions from those general principles, established by reasoning and observation, which constitute pure science. No one can safely make these deductions until he has a firm grasp of the principles; and he can obtain that grasp only by personal experience of the operations of observation and of reasoning on which they are founded.

Almost all the processes employed in the arts and manufactures fall within the range either of physics or of chemistry. In order to improve them, one must thoroughly understand them; and no one has a chance of really understanding them, unless he has obtained that mastery of principles and that habit of dealing with facts, which is given by long-continued and well-directed purely scientific training in the physical and the chemical laboratory. So that there really is no question as to the necessity of purely scientific discipline, even if the work of the college were limited by the narrowest interpretation of its stated aims.

And, as to the desirableness of a wider culture than that yielded by science alone, it is to be recollected that the improvement of manufacturing processes is only one of the conditions which contribute to the prosperity of industry. Industry is a means and not an end; and mankind work only to get something which they want. What that something is depends partly on their innate, and partly on their acquired, desires.

If the wealth resulting from prosperous industry is to be spent upon the gratification of unworthy desires, if the increasing perfection of manufacturing processes is to be accompanied by an increasing debasement of those who carry them on, I do not see the good of industry and prosperity.

Now it is perfectly true that men's views of what is desirable depend upon their characters; and that the innate proclivities to which we give that name are not touched by any amount of instruction. But it does not follow that even mere intellectual education may not, to an indefinite extent, modify the practical manifestation of the characters of men in their actions, by supplying them with motives unknown to the ignorant. A pleasure-loving character will have pleasure of some sort; but, if you give him choice, he may prefer pleasures which do not degrade him to those which do. And this choice is offered to every man, who possesses in literary or artistic culture a never-failing source of pleasures, which are neither withered by age, nor staled by custom, nor embittered in the recollection by the pangs of self-reproach.

If the institution opened today fulfills the intention of its founder, the picked intelligences among all classes of the population of this district will pass through it. No child born in Birmingham, henceforward, if he have the capacity to profit by the opportunities offered to him, first in the primary and other schools, and afterwards in the Scientific College, need fail to obtain, not merely the instruction, but the culture most appropriate to the conditions of his life.

... The prosperity of industry depends not merely upon the improvement of manufacturing processes, not merely upon the ennobling of the individual character, but upon a third condition, namely, a clear understanding of the conditions of social life, on the part of both the capitalist and the operative, and their agreement upon common principles of social action. They must learn that social phenomena are as much the expression of natural laws as any others; that no

social arrangements can be permanent unless they harmonize with
the requirements of social statics and dynamics; and that, in the nature
of things, there is an arbiter whose decisions execute themselves.

But this knowledge is only to be obtained by the application of the
methods of investigation adopted in physical researches to the investigation of the phenomena of society. Hence, I confess, I should like to
see one addition made to the excellent scheme of education propounded for the college, in the shape of provision for the teaching of
sociology. For though we are all agreed that partly politics are to have
no place in the instruction of the college; yet in this country, practically governed as it is now by universal suffrage, every man who does
his duty must exercise political functions. And, if the evils which are
inseparable from the good of political liberty are to be checked, if the
perpetual oscillation of nations between anarchy and despotism is to
be replaced by the steady march of self-restraining freedom; it will be
because men will gradually bring themselves to deal with political, as
they now deal with scientific questions; to be as ashamed of undue
haste and partisan prejudice in the one case as in the other; and to
believe that the machinery of society is at least as delicate as that of a
spinning-jenny, and as little likely to be improved by the meddling of
those who have not taken the trouble to master the principles of its
action.

2. ARNOLD:
"Literature and Science"

Matthew Arnold (1822–1888) is the subject of a recent study
by G. R. Stange, *Matthew Arnold: The Poet as Humanist*. Lionel Trilling's
Matthew Arnold (1949) is the best introductory study. The most important
biography is Louis Bonnerot's *Essai de Biographie Psychologique* published
in Paris in 1947. *The Poetical Works* (Oxford, 1950), edited by C. B. Tinker
and H. F. Lowry, is standard, as is R. H. Super's edition of the *Complete
Prose Works*, still being published by the University of Michigan.

"Literature and Science" was delivered as a lecture during Arnold's
American tour in 1883. Some of its rhetorical excellence is pointed out in
the introduction to this section.

Practical people talk with a smile of Plato and of his absolute ideas; and it is impossible to deny that Plato's ideas do often seem unpractical and unpracticable, and especially when one views them in connexion with the life of a great work-a-day world like the United States. The necessary staple of the life of such a world Plato regards with disdain; handicraft and trade and the working professions he regards with disdain; but what becomes of the life of an industrial modern community if you take handicraft and trade and the working professions out of it? The base mechanic arts and handicrafts, says Plato, bring about a natural weakness in the principle of excellence in a man, so that he cannot govern the ignoble growths in him, but nurses them, and cannot understand fostering any other. Those who exercise such arts and trades, as they have their bodies, he says, marred by their vulgar businesses, so they have their souls, too, bowed and broken by them. And if one of these uncomely people has a mind to seek self-culture and philosophy, Plato compares him to a bald little tinker, who has scraped together money, and has got his release from service, and has had a bath, and bought a new coat, and is rigged out like a bridegroom about to marry the daughter of his master who has fallen into poor and helpless estate.

Nor do the working professions fare any better than trade at the hands of Plato. He draws for us an inimitable picture of the working lawyer, and of his life of bondage; he shows how this bondage from his youth up has stunted and warped him, and made him small and crooked of soul, encompassing him with difficulties which he is not man enough to rely on justice and truth as means to encounter, but has recourse, for help out of them, to falsehood and wrong. And so, says Plato, this poor creature is bent and broken, and grows up from boy to man without a particle of soundness in him, although exceedingly smart and clever in his own esteem.

One cannot refuse to admire the artist who draws these pictures. But we say to ourselves that his ideas show the influence of a primitive and obsolete order of things, when the warrior caste and the priestly caste were alone in honour, and the humble work of the world was done by slaves. We have now changed all that; the modern majesty consists in work, as Emerson declares; and in work, we may add, principally of such plain and dusty kind as the work of cultivators of the ground, handicraftsmen, men of trade and business, men of the working professions. Above all is this true in a great industrious community such as that of the United States.

Now education, many people go on to say, is still mainly governed by the ideas of men like Plato, who lived when the warrior caste and the priestly or philosophical class were alone in honour, and the really useful party of the community were slaves. It is an education fitted for persons of leisure in such a community. This education passed from Greece and Rome to the feudal communties of Europe, where also the warrior caste and the priestly caste were alone held in honour, and where the really useful and working part of the community, though not nominally slaves as in the pagan world, were practically not much better off than slaves, and not more seriously regarded. And how absurd it is, people end by saying, to inflict this education upon an industrious modern community, where very few indeed are persons of leisure, and the mass to be considered has not leisure, but is bound, for its own great good, and for the great good of the world at large, to plain labour and to industrial pursuits, and the education in question tends necessarily to make men dissatisfied with these pursuits and unfitted for them!

That is what is said. So far I must defend Plato, as to plead that his view of education and studies is in the general, as it seems to me, sound enough, and fitted for all sorts and conditions of men, whatever their pursuits may be. "An intelligent man," says Plato, "will prize those studies which result in his soul getting soberness, righteousness, and wisdom, and will less value the others." I cannot consider *that* a bad desription of the aim of education, and of the motives which should govern us in the choice of studies, whether we are preparing ourselves for a hereditary seat in the English House of Lords or for the pork trade in Chicago.

Still I admit that Plato's world was not ours, that his scorn of trade and handicraft is fantastic, that he had no conception of a great industrial community such as that of the United States, and that such a community must and will shape its education to suit its own needs. If the usual education handed down to it from the past does not suit it, it will certainly before long drop this and try another. The usual education in the past has been mainly literary .The question is whether the studies which were long supposed to be the best for all of us are practically the best now; whether others are not better. The tyranny of the past, many think, weighs on us injuriously in the predominace given to letters in education. The question is raised whether, to meet the needs of our modern life, the predominance ought not now to pass from letters to science; and naturally the question is nowhere raised with more energy than here in the United States. . . .

I am going to ask whether the present movement for ousting letters from their old predominance in education, and for transferring the predominance in education to the natural sciences, whether this brisk and flourishing movement ought to prevail, and whether it is likely that in the end it really will prevail. An objection may be raised which I will anticipate. My own studies have been almost wholly in letters, and my visits to the field of the natural sciences have been very slight and inadequate, although those sciences have always strongly moved my curiosity. A man of letters, it will perhaps be said, is not competent to discuss the comparative merits of letters and natural science as means of education. To this objection I reply, first of all, that his incompetence, if he attempts the discussion but is really incompetent for it, will be abundantly visible; nobody will be taken in; he will have plenty of sharp observers and critics to save mankind from that danger. But the line I am going to follow is, as you will soon discover, so extremely simple, that perhaps it may be followed without failure even by one who for a more ambitious line of discussion would be quite incompetent.

Some of you may possibly remember a phrase of mine which has been the object of a good deal of comment; an observation to the effect that in our culture, the aim being *to know ourselves and the world*, we have, as the means to this end, *to know the best which has been thought and said in the world*. A man of science, who is also an excellent writer and the very prince of debaters, Professor Huxley, in a discourse at the opening of Sir Josiah Mason's college at Birmingham, laying hold of this phrase, expanded it by quoting some more words of mine, which are these: "The civilised world is to be regarded as now being, for intellectual and spitual purposes, one great confederation, bound to a joint action and working to a common result; and whose members have for their proper outfit a knowledge of Greek, Roman, and Eastern antiquity, and of one another. Special local and temporary advantages being put out of account, that modern nation will in the intellectual and spiritual sphere make most progress, which most thoroughly carries out this programme."

Now on my phrase, thus enlarged, Professor Huxley remarks that when I speak of the above-mentioned knowledge as enabling us to know ourselves and the world, I assert *literature* to contain the materials which suffice for thus making us know ourselves and the world. But it is not by any means clear, says he, that after having learnt all which ancient and modern literatures have to tell us, we have laid a sufficiently broad and deep foundation for that criticism of life, that knowledge of ourselves and the world, which constitutes culture. On the contrary, Professor Huxley declares that he finds himself "wholly unable to admit that either nations or individuals will really advance, if their outfit draws nothing from the stories of physical science. An army without weapons of precision, and with no particular base of operations, might more hopefully enter upon a campaign on the Rhine, than a man, devoid of a knowledge of what physical science has done in the last century, upon a criticism of life."

This shows how needful it is for those who are to discuss any matter together, to have a common understanding as to the sense of the terms they employ—how needful, and how difficult. What Professor Huxley says, implies just the reproach which is so often brought against the study of *belles lettres*, as they are called: that the study is an elegant one, but slight and ineffectual; a smattering of Greek and Latin and other ornamental things, of little use for anyone whose object is to get at truth, and to be a practical man. . . .

But when we talk of knowing Greek and Roman antiquity, for instance, which is the knowledge people have called the humanities, I for my part mean a knowledge which is something more than a superficial humanism, mainly decorative. "I call all teaching *scientific*," says Wolf, the critic of Homer, "which is systematically laid out and followed up to its original sources. For example: a knowledge of classical antiquity is scientific when the remains of classical antiquity are correctly studied in the original languages." There can be no doubt that Wolf is perfectly right; that all learning is scientific which is systematically laid out and followed up to its original sources, and that a genuine humanism is scientific.

When I speak of knowing Greek and Roman antiquity, therefore, as a help to knowing ourselves and the world, I mean more than a knowledge of so much vocabulary, so much grammar, so many portions of authors in the Greek and Latin languages. I mean knowing the Greeks and Romans, and their life and genius, and what they were and did in the world; what we get from them, and what is its value. That, at least, is the ideal; and when we talk of endeavouring to know Greek and Roman antiquity, as a help to knowing ourselves and the world, we mean endeavouring so to know them as to satisfy this ideal, however much we may still fall short of it.

The same also as to knowing our own and other modern nations, with the like aim of getting to understand ourselves and the world. To know the best that has been thought and said by the modern nations, is to know, says Professor Huxley, "only what modern *literatures* have to tell us; it is the criticism of life contained in modern literature." And yet "the distinctive character of our times," he urges, "lies in the vast and constantly increasing part which is played by natural knowledge." And how, therefore, can a man, devoid of knowledge of what physical science has done in the last century, enter hopefully upon a criticism of modern life?

Let us, I say, be agreed about the meaning of the terms we are using. I talk of knowing the best which has been thought and uttered in the world; Professor Huxley says this means knowing *literature*. Literature is a large word; it may mean everything written with letters or printed in a book. Euclid's *Elements* and Newton's *Principia* are thus literature. All knowledge that reaches us through books is literature. But by literature Professor Huxley means *belles lettres*. He means to make me say, that knowing the best which has been thought and said by the modern nations is knowing their *belles lettres* and no more. And this is no sufficient equipment, he argues, for a criticism of modern life. But as I do not mean, by knowing ancient Rome, knowing merely more or less of Latin *belles lettres*, and taking no account of Rome's military, and political, and legal, and administrative work in the world; and as, by knowing ancient Greece, I understand knowing her as the giver of Greek art, and the guide to a free and right use of reason and to scientific method, and the founder of our mathematics and physics and astronomy and biology—I understand knowing her as all this, and not merely knowing certain Greek poems, and histories, and treatises, and speeches—so as to the knowledge of modern nations also. By knowing modern nations, I mean not merely knowing their *belles lettres*, but knowing also what has been done by such men as Copernicus, Galileo, Newton, Darwin. "Our ancestors learned," says Professor Huxley, "that the earth is the centre of the visible universe, and that man is the cynosure of things terrestrial; and more especially was it inculcated that the course of nature had no fixed order, but that it could be, and constantly was, altered." "But for us now," continues Professor Huxley, "the notions of the beginning and the end of the world entertained by our forefathers are no longer credible. It is very certain that the earth is not the chief body in the material universe, and that the world is not subordinated to man's use. It is even more certain that nature is the expression of a definite order, with which noting interferes." "And yet," he cries, "the purely classical education advocated by the representatives of the humanists in our day gives no inkling of all this."

In due place and time I will just touch upon that vexed question of classical education; but at present the question is as to what is meant by knowing the best which modern nations have thought and said. It is not knowing their *belles lettres* merely which is meant. To know Italian *belles lettres* is not to know Italy, and to know English *belles lettres* is not to know England. Into knowing Italy and England there comes a great deal more, Galileo and Newton amongst it. The reproach of being a superficial humanism, a tincture of *belles lettres*, may attach rightly enough to some other disciplines; but to the particular discipline recommended when I proposed knowing the best that has been thought and said in the world, it does not apply. In that best I certainly include what in modern times has been thought and said by the great observers and knowers of nature.

There is, therefore, really no question between Professor Huxley and me as to whether knowing the great results of the modern scietific study of nature is not required as a part of our culture, as well as knowing the products of literature and art. But to follow the processes by which those results are reached, ought, say the friends of physical science, to be made the staple of education for the bulk of mankind. And here there does arise a question between those whom Professor Huxley calls with playful sarcasm "the Levites of culture," and those whom the poor humanist is sometimes apt to regard as its Nebuchadnezzars.

The great results of the scientific investigation of nature we are agreed upon knowing, but how much of our study are we bound to give to the processes by which those results are reached? The results have their visible bearing on human life. But all the processes, too, all the items of fact, by which those results are reached and established, are interesting. All knowledge is interesting to a wise man, and the knowledge of nature is interesting to all men. It is very interesting to know, that, from the albuminous white of the egg, the chick in the egg gets the materials for its flesh, bones, blood, and feathers; while, from the fatty yolk of the egg, it gets the heat and energy which enable it at length to break its shell and begin the world. It is less interesting, perhaps, but still it is interesting, to know that when a taper burns, the wax is converted into carbonic acid and water. Moreover, it is quite true that the habit of dealing with facts, which is given by the study of nature, is, as the friends of physical science praise it for being, an excellent discipline. The appeal, in the study of nature, is constantly to observation and experiment; not only is it said that the thing is so, but we can be made to see that it is so. Not only does a man tell us that when a taper burns the wax is converted into carbonic acid and water, as a man may tell us, if he likes, that Charon is punting his ferry-boat on the river Styx, or that Victor Hugo is a sublime poet, or Mr. Gladstone the most admirable of statesmen; but we are made to see that the conversion into carbonic acid and water does actually happen. This reality of natural knowledge it is, which makes the friends of physical science contrast it, as a knowledge of things, with the humanist's knowledge, which is, say they, a knowledge of words. And hence Professor Huxley is moved to lay it down that, "for the purpose of attaining real culture, an exclusively scientific education is at least as effectual as an exclusively literary education." And a certain President of the Section for Mechanical Science in the British Association is, in Scripture phrase, "very bold," and declares that if a man, in his mental training, "has substituted literature and history for natural science, he has chosen the less useful alternative." But whether we go these lengths or not, we must all admit that in natural science the habit gained of dealing with facts is a most valuable discipline, and that every one should have some experience of it.

More than this, however, is demanded by the reformers. It is proposed to make the training in natural science the main part of education, for the great majority of mankind at any rate. And here, I confess, I part company with the friends of physical science, with whom up to this point I have been agreeing. In differing from them, however, I wish to proceed with the utmost caution and diffidence. The smallness of my own acquaintance with the disciplines of natural science is ever before my mind, and I am fearful of doing these disciplines an injustice. The ability and pugnacity of the partisans of natural science make them formidable persons to contradict. The tone of tentative inquiry, which befits a being of dim faculties and bounded knowledge, is the tone I would wish to take and not to depart from. At present it seems to me, that those who are for giving to natural knowledge, as they call it, the chief place in the education of the majority of mankind, leave one important thing out of their account: the constitution of human nature. But I put this forward on the strength of some facts not at all recondite, very far from it; facts capable of being stated in the simplest possible fashion, and to which, if I so state them, the man of science will, I am sure, be willing to allow their due weight.

Deny the facts altogether, I think, he hardly can. He can hardly deny, that when we set ourselves to enumerate the powers which go to the building up of human life, and say that they are the power of conduct, the power of intellect and knowledge, the power of beauty, and the power of social life and manners,—he can hardly deny that this scheme, though drawn in rough and plain lines enough, and not pretending to scientific exactness, does yet give a fairly true representation of the matter. Human nature is built up by these powers; we have the need for them all. When we have rightly met and adjusted the claims of them all, we shall then be in a fair way for getting soberness and righteousness, with wisdom. This is evident enough, and the friends of physical science would admit it.

But perhaps they may not have sufficiently observed another thing: namely, that the several powers just mentioned are not isolated, but there is, in the generality of mankind, a perpetual tendency to relate them one to another in divers ways. With one such way of relating them I am particularly concerned now. Following our instinct for intellect and knowledge, we acquire pieces of knowledge; and presently, in the generality of men, there arises the desire to relate these pieces of knowledge to our sense for conduct, to our sense for beauty,—and there is weariness and dissatisfaction if the desire is baulked. Now in this desire lies, I think, the strength of that hold which letters have upon us.

All knowledge is, as I said just now, interesting; and even items of knowledge which from the nature of the case cannot well be related, but must stand isolated in our thoughts, have their interest. Even lists of exceptions have their interest. If we are studying Greek accents, it is interesting to know that *pais* and *pas*, and some other monosyllables of the same form of declension, do not take the circumflex upon the last syllable of the genitive plural, but vary, in this respect, from the common rule. If we are studying physiology, it is interesting to know that the pulmonary artery carries dark blood and the pulmonary vein carries bright blood, departing in this respect from the common rule for the division of labour between the viens and the arties. But every one knows how to seek naturally to combine the pieces of our knowledge together, to bring them under general rules, to relate them to principles; and how unsatisfactory and tiresome it would be to go on for ever learning lists of exceptions, or accumulating items of fact which must stand isolated.

Well, that same need of relating our knowledge, which operates here within the sphere of our knowledge itself, we shall find operating, also, outside that sphere. We experience, as we go on learning and knowing, —the vast majority of us experience,—the need of relating what we have learnt and known to the sense which we have in us for conduct, to the sense which we have in us for beauty.

A certain Greek prophetess of Mantineia in Arcadia, Diotima by name, once explained to the philosopher Socrates that love, and impulse, and bent of all kinds, is, in fact, nothing else but the desire in men that good should for ever be present to them. This desire for good, Diotima assured Socrates, is our fundamental desire, of which fundamental desire every impluse in us is only some one particular form. And therefore this fundamental desire it is, I suppose,—this desire in men that good should be for ever present to them,—which acts in us when we feel the impulse for relating our knowledge to our sense for conduct and to our sense for beauty. At any rate, with men in general the instinct exists. Such is human nature. And the instinct, it will be admitted, is innocent, and human nature is preserved by our following the lead of its innocent instincts. Therefore, in seeking to gratify this instinct in question, we are following the instinct of self-preservation in humanity.

But, no doubt, some kinds of knowledge cannot be made to directly serve the instinct in question, cannot be directly related to the sense for beauty, to the sense for conduct. These are instrument-knowledges; they lead on to other knowledges, which can. A man who passes his life in instrument knowledges is a specialist. They may be invaluable as instruments to something beyond, for those who have the gift thus to employ them; and they may be disciplines in themselves wherein it is useful for every one to have some schooling. But it is inconceivable that the generality of men should pass all their mental life with Greek accents or with formal logic. My friend Professor Sylvester, who is one of the first mathematicians in the world, holds transcendental doctrines as to the virtue of mathematics, but those doctrines are not for common men. In the very Senate House and heart of our English Cambridge I once ventured, though not without an apology for my profaneness, to hazard the opinion that for the majority of mankind a little of mathematics, even, goes a long way. Of course this is quite consistent with their being of immense importance as an instrument to something else; but it is the few who have the aptitude for thus using them, not the bulk of mankind.

The natural sciences do not, however, stand on the same footing with these instrument-knowledges. Experience shows us that the generality of men will find more interest in learning that, when a taper burns, the wax is converted into carbonic acid and water, or in learning the explanation of the phenomenon of dew, or in learning how the circulation of the blood is carried on, than they find in learning that the genitive plural of *pais* and *pas* does not take the circumflex on the termination. And one piece of natural knowledge is added to another, and others are added to that, and at last we come to propositions so interesting as Mr Darwin's famous proposition that "our ancestor was a hairy quadruped furnished with a tail and pointed ears, probably arboreal in his habits." Or we come to propositions of such reach and magnitude as those which Professor Huxley delivers, when he says that the notions of our forefathers about the beginning and the end of the world were all wrong, and that nature is the expression of a definite order with which nothing interferes.

Interesting, indeed, these results of science are, important they are, and we should all of us be acquainted with them. But what I now wish you to mark is, that we are still, when they are propounded to us and we receive them, we are still in the sphere of intellect and knowledge. And for the generality of men there will be found, I say, to arise, when they have duly taken in the proposition that their ancestor was "a hairy quadruped furnished with a tail and pointed ears, probably arboreal in his habits," there will be found to arise an invincible desire to relate this proposition to the sense in us for conduct, and to the sense in us for beauty. But this the men of science will not do for us, and will hardly even profess to do. They will give us other pieces of knowledge, other facts, about other animals and their ancestors, or about plants, or about stones, or about stars; and they may finally bring us to those great "general conceptions of the universe, which are forced upon us all," says Professor Huxley, "by the progress of physical science." But still it will be *knowledge* only which they give us; knowledge not put for us into relation with our sense for conduct, our sense for beauty, and touched with emotion by being so put; not thus put for us, and therefore, to the majority of mankind, after a certain while, unsatisfying, wearying.

Not to the born naturalist, I admit. But what do we mean by a born naturalist? We mean a man in whom the zeal for observing nature is so uncommonly strong and eminent, that it marks him off from the bulk of mankind. Such a man will pass his life happily in collecting natural knowledge and reasoning upon it, and will ask for nothing, or hardly anything, more. I have heard it said that the sagacious and admirable naturalist whom we lost not very long ago, Mr. Darwin, once owned to a friend that for his part he did not experience the necessity for two things which most men find so necessary to them —religion and poetry; science and the domestic affections, he thought, were enough. To a born naturalist, I can well understand that this should seem so. So absorbing is his occupation with nature, so strong his love for his occupation, that he goes on acquiring natural knowledge and reasoning upon it, and has little time or inclination for thinking about getting it related to the desire in man for conduct, the desire in man for beauty. He relates it to them for himself as he goes along, so far as he feels the need; and he draws from the domestic affections all the additional solace necessary. But then Darwins are extremely rare. Another great and admirable master of natural knowledge, Faraday, was a Sandemanian. That is to say, he related his knowledge to his instinct for conduct and to his instinct for beauty, by the aid of that respectable Scottish sectary, Robert Sandeman. And so strong, in general, is the demand of religion and poetry to have their share in a man, to associate themselves with his knowing, and to relieve and rejoice it, that, probably, for one man amongst us with the disposition to do as Darwin did in this respect, there are at least fifty with the disposition to do as Faraday.

Education lays hold upon us, in fact, by satisfying this demand. Professor Huxley holds up to scorn medieval education, with its neglect of the knowledge of nature, its poverty even of literary studies, its formal logic devoted to "showing how and why that which the Church said was true and must be true." But the great medieval Universities were not brought into being, we may be sure, by the zeal for giving a jejune and contemptible education. Kings have been their nursing fathers, and queens have been their nursing mothers, but not for this. The medieval Universities came into being, because the supposed knowledge, delivered by Scripture and the Church, so deeply engaged men's hearts, by so simply, easily, and powerfully relating itself to their desire for conduct, their desire for beauty. All other knowledge was dominated by this supposed knowledge and was subordinated to it, because of the surpassing strength of the hold which it gained upon the affections of men, by allying itself profoundly with their sense for conduct, their sense for beauty.

But now, says Professor Huxley, conceptions of the universe fatal to the notions held by our forefathers have been forced upon us by physical science. Grant to him that they are thus fatal, that the new conceptions must and will soon become current everywhere, and that every one will finally perceive them to be fatal to the beliefs of our forefathers. The need of humane letters, as they are truly called, because they serve the paramount desire in men that good should be for ever present to them,—the need of humane letters, to establish a relation between the new conceptions, and our instinct for beauty, our instinct for conduct, is only the more visible. The Middle Age could do without humane letters, as it could do without the study of nature, because its supposed knowledge was made to engage its emotions so powerfully. Grant that the supposed knowledge disappears, its power of being made to engage the emotions will of course disappear along with it,—but the emotions themselves, and their claim to be engaged and satisfied, will remain. Now if we find by experience that humane letters have an undeniable power of engaging the emotions, the importance of humane letters in a man's training becomes not less, but greater, in proportion to the success of modern science in extirpating what it calls "medieval thinking."

Have humane letters, then, have poetry and eloquence, the power here attributed to them of engaging the emotions, and do they exercise it? And if they have it and exercise it, *how* do they exercise it, so as to exert an influence upon man's sense for conduct, his sense for beauty? Finally, even if they both can and do exert an influence upon the senses in question, how are they to relate to them the results,—the modern results,—of natural science? All these questions may be asked. First, have poetry and eloquence the power of calling out the emotions? The appeal is to experience. Experience shows that for the vast majority of men, for mankind in general, they have the power. Next, do they exercise it? They do. But then, *how* do they exercise it so as to affect man's sense for conduct, his sense for beauty? And this is perhaps a case for applying the Preacher's words: "Though a man labour to seek it out, yet he shall not find it; yea, farther, though a wise man think to know it, yet shall he not be able to find it." Why should it be one thing, in its effect upon the emotions, to say, "Patience is a virtue," and quite another thing, in its effect upon the emotions, to say with Homer, τλητὸν γὰρ Μοῖραι θυμὸν θέσαν ἀνθρώποισιν.—

"for an enduring heart have the destinies appointed to the children of men"? Why should it be one thing, in its effect upon the emotions, to say with the philosopher Spinoza, *Felicitas in eo consistit quod homo suum esse conservare potest*—"Man's happiness consists in his being able to preserve his own essence," and quite another thing, in its effect upon the emotions, to say with the Gospel, "What is a man advantaged, if he gain the whole world, and lose himself, forfeit himself?" How does this difference of effect arise? I cannot tell, and I am not much concerned to know; the important thing is that it does arise, and that we can profit by it. But how, finally, are poetry and eloquence to exercise the power of relating the modern results of natural science to man's instinct for conduct, his instinct for beauty? And here again I answer that I do not know *how* they will exercise it, but that they can and will exercise it I am sure. I do not mean that modern philosophical poets and modern philosophical moralists are to come and relate for us, in express terms, the results of modern scientific research to our instinct for conduct, our instinct for beauty. But I mean that we shall find, as a matter of experience, if we know the best that has been thought and uttered in the world, we shall find that the art and poetry and eloquence . . . have in fact not only the power of refreshing and delighting us, they have also the power,—such is the strength and worth, in essentials, of their authors' criticism of life,—they have a fortifying, and elevating, and quickening, and suggestive power, capable of wonderfully helping us to relate the results of modern science to our need for conduct, our need for beauty. Homer's conceptions of the physical universe were, I imagine, grotesque; but really, under the shock of hearing from modern science that "the world is not subordinated to man's use, and that man is not the cynosure of things terrestrial," I could, for my own part, desire no better comfort than Homer's line which I quoted just now.

τλητὸν γὰρ Μοῖραι θυμὸν θέσαν ἀνθρώποισιν.—

"for an enduring heart have the destinies appointed to the children of men!"

And the more that men's minds are cleared, the more that the results of science are frankly accepted, the more that poetry and eloquence come to be received and studied as what in truth they really are,—the criticism of life by gifted men, alive and active with extraordinary power at an unusual number of points,—so much the more will the value of humane letters, and of art also, which is an utterance having a like kind of power with theirs, be felt and acknowledged, and their place in education be secured.

Let us therefore, all of us, avoid indeed as much as possible any indivious comparison between the merits of humane letters, as means of education, and the merits of the natural sciences. But when some President of a Section for Mechanical Science insists on making the comparison, and tells us that "he who in his training has substituted literature and history for natural science has chosen the less useful alternative," let us make answer to him that the student of humane letters only, will, at least, know also the great general conceptions brought in by modern physical science; for science, as Professor Huxley says, forces them upon us all. But the student of the natural sciences only, will, by our very hypothesis, know nothing of humane letters; not to mention that in setting himself to be perpetually accumulating natural knowledge, he sets himself to do what only specialists have in general the gift for doing genially. And so he will probably be unsatisfied, or at any rate incomplete, and even more incomplete than the student of humane letters only.

I once mentioned in a school-report, how a young man in one of our English training colleges having to paraphrase the passage in *Macbeth* beginning,

"Can'st thou not minister to a mind diseased?"

turned this line into "Can you not wait upon the lunatic?" And I remarked what a curious state of things it would be, if every pupil of our national schools knew, let us say, that the moon is two thousand one hundred and sixty miles in diameter, and thought at the same time that a good paraphrase for

"Can'st thou not minister to a mind diseased?"

was, "Can you not wait upon the lunatic?" If one is driven to choose, I think I would rather have a young person ignorant about the moon's diameter, but aware that "Can you not wait upon the lunatic?" is bad, than a young person whose education had been such as to manage things the other way.

Or to go higher that the pupils of our national schools. I have in my mind's eye a member of our British Parliament who comes to travel here in America, who afterwards relates his travels, and who shows a really masterful knowledge of the geology of this great country and of its mining capabilities, but who ends by gravely suggesting that the United States should borrow a prince from our Royal Family, and should make him their king, and should create a House of Lords of great landed proprietors after the pattern of ours; and then America, he thinks, would have her future happily and perfectly secured. Surely, in this case, the President of the Section for Mechanical Science would himself hardly say that our member of Parliament, by concentrating himself upon geology and mineralogy, and so on, and not attending to literature and history, had "chosen the more useful alternative."

If then there is to be separation and option between humane letters on the one hand, and the natural sciences on the other, the great majority of mankind, all who have not exceptional and overpowering aptitudes for the study of nature, would do well, I cannot but think, to choose to be educated in humane letters rather than in the natural sciences. Letters will call out their being at more points, will make them live more.

I said that before I ended I would just touch on the question of classical education, and I will keep my word. Even if literature is to retain a large place in our education, yet Latin and Greek, say the friends of progress, will certainly have to go. Greek is the grand offender in the eyes of these gentlemen. The attackers of the established course of study think that against Greek, at any rate, they have irresistible arguments. Literature may perhaps be needed in education, they say; but why on earth should it be Greek literature? Why not French or German? Nay, "has not an Englishman models in his own literature of every kind of excellence?" As before, it is not on any weak pleadings of my own that I rely for convincing the gainsayers; it is on the constitution of human nature itself, and on the instinct of self-preservation in humanity. The instinct for beauty is set in human nature, as surely as the instinct for knowledge is set there, or the instinct for conduct. If the instinct for beauty is served by Greek literature and art as it is served by no other literature and art, we may trust to the instinct of self-preservation in humanity for keeping Greek as part of our culture. We may trust to it for even making the study of Greek more prevalent than it is now. Greek will come, I hope, some day to be studied more rationally than at present; but it will be increasingly studied as men increasingly feel the need in them for beauty, and how powerfully Greek art and Greek literature can serve this need. . . .

Defuit una mihi symmetria prisca,—"The antique symmetry was the one thing wanting to me," said Leonardo da Vinci; and he was an Italian. I will not presume to speak for the Americans, but I am sure that, in the Englishmen, the want of this admirable symmetry of the Greeks is a thousand times more great and crying than in any Italian. The results of the want show themselves most glaringly, perhaps, in our architecture, but they show themselves, also, in all our art. *Fit details strictly combined, in view of a large general result nobly conceived;* that is just the beautiful *symmetria prisca* of the Greeks, and it is just where we English fail, where all our art fails. Striking ideas we have, and well-executed details we have; but that high symmetry which, with satisfying and delightful effect, combines them, we seldom or never have. The glorious beauty of the Acropolis at Athens did not come from single fine things stuck about on that hill, a statue here, a gateway there,—no, it arose from all things being perfectly combined for a supreme total effect. What must not an Englishman feel about our deficiencies in this respect, as the sense for beauty, whereof this symmetry is an essential element, awakens and strengthens within him! what will not one day be his respect and desire for Greece and its *symmetria prisca*, when the scales drop from his eyes as he walks the London streets, and he sees such a lesson in meanness as the Strand, for instance, in its true deformity! But here we are coming to our friend Mr. Ruskin's province, and I will not intrude upon it, for he is its very sufficient guardian.

And so we at last find, it seems, we find flowing in favour of the humanities the natural and necessary stream of things, which seemed against them when we started. The "hairy quadruped furnished with a tail and pointed ears, probably arboreal in his habits," this good fellow carried hidden in his nature, apparently, something destined to develop into a necessity for humane letters. Nay, more; we seem finally to be even led to the further conclusion that our hairy ancestor carried in his nature, also a necessity for Greek.

And therefore, to say the truth, I cannot really think that humane letters are in much actual danger of being thrust out from their leading place in education, in spite of the array of authorities against them at this moment. So long as human nature is what it is, their attractions will remain irresistible. As with Greek, so with letters generally: they will some day come, we may hope, to be studied more rationally, but they will not lose their place. What will happen will rather be that there will be crowded into education other matters besides, far too many; there will be, perhaps, a period of unsettlement and confusion and false tendency; but letters will not in the end lose their leading place. If they lose it for a time, they will get it back again. We shall be brought back to them by our wants and aspirations. And a poor humanist may possess his soul in patience, neither strive nor cry, admit the energy and brilliancy of the partisans of physica lscience, and their present favour with the public, to be far greater than his own, and still have a happy faith that the nature of things works silently on behalf of the studies which he loves, and that, while we shall all have to acquaint ourselves with the great results reached by modern science, and to give ourselves as much training in its disciplines as we can conveniently carry, yet the majority of men will always require humane letters; and so much the more, as they have the more and the greater results of science to relate to the need in man for conduct, and to the need in him for beauty.

3. SPENCER:
Practical Knowledge

Herbert Spencer (1820–1903) railway engineer, editor, philosopher, and father of Social Darwinism, has not been accorded much attention recently. The standard works were published early in this century: David Duncan's *Life and Letters*, William Henry Hudson's *Herbert Spencer*, in 1908, and J. Rumney's *Spencer's Sociology*, in 1934. For Spencer's place as a nineteenth-century educational and social theorist, see the introductory essays in this volume.

"What Knowledge Is of Most Worth?" published as part of Spencer's *Essays on Education* in 1861, is symptomatic of the movement to scientific, "practical" education, which was shaping Victorian attitudes before Huxley's better-known advocacy of the cause.

Among mental as among bodily acquisitions, the ornamental comes before the useful. Not only in times past, but almost as much in our own era, that knowledge which conduces to personal well-being has been postponed to that which brings applause. In the Greek schools, music, poetry, rhetoric, and a philosophy which, until Socrates taught, had but little bearing upon action, were the dominant subjects; while knowledge aiding the arts of life had a very subordinate place. And in our own universities and schools at the present moment, the like anti- thesis holds. We are guilty of something like a platitude when we say that throughout his after-career, a boy, in nine cases out of ten, applies his Latin and Greek to no practical purposes. The remark is trite that in his shop, or his office, in managing his estate or his family, in playing his part as director of a bank or a railway, he is very little aided by this knowledge he took so many years to acquire—so little, that gener- ally the greater part of it drops out of his memory; and if he occasion- ally vents a Latin quotation, or alludes to some Greek myth, it is less to throw light on the topic in hand than for the sake of effect. If we inquire what is the real motive for giving boys a classical education, we find it to be simply conformity to public opinion. Men dress their children's minds as they do their bodies, in the prevailing fashion. As the Orinoco Indian puts on paint before leaving his hut, not with a view to any direct benefit, but because he would be ashamed to be seen without it; so, a boy's drilling in Latin and Greek is insisted on, not because of their intrinsic value, but that he may not be disgraced by being found ignorant of them—that he may have "the education of a gentleman"—the badge marking a certain social position, and bringing a consequent respect.

As, throughout life, not what we are, but what we shall be thought, is the question; so in education, the question is, not the intrinsic value of knowledge, so much as its extrinsic effects on others. And this being our dominant idea, direct utility is scarcely more regarded than by the barbarian when filing his teeth and staining his nails.

If there requires further evidence of the rude, undeveloped character of our education, we have it in the fact that the comparative worths of different kinds of knowledge have been as yet scarcely even discussed— much less discussed in a methodic way with definite results. Not only is it that no standard of relative values has yet been agreed upon; but the existence of any such standard has not been conceived in a clear manner. And not only is it that the existence of such a standard has not been clearly conceived; but the need for it seems to have been scarcely even felt. Men read books on this topic, and attend lectures on that; decide that their children shall be instructed in these branches of knowledge, and shall not be instructed in those; and all under the guidance of mere custom, or liking, or prejudice; without ever considering the enormous importance of determining in some rational way what things are really most worth learning. It is true that in all circles we hear occasional remarks on the importance of this or the other order of information. But whether the degree of its importance justifies the expenditure of the time needed to acquire it; and whether there are not things of more importance to which such time might be better devoted; are queries which, if raised at all, are disposed of quite summarily, according to personal predilections. It is true also, that now and then, we hear revived the standing controversy respecting the comparative merits of classics and mathematics. This controversy, how-ever, is carried on in an empirical manner, with no reference to an ascertained criterion; and the question at issue is insignificant when compared with the general question of which it is part. To suppose that deciding whether a mathematical or a classical education is the best, is deciding what is the proper *curriculum*, is much the same thing as to suppose that the whole of dietetics lies in ascertaining whether or not bread is more nutritive than potatoes!

The question which we contend is of such transcendent moment, is, not whether such or such knowledge is of worth, but what is its *relative* worth? When they have named certain advantages which a given course of study has secured them, persons are apt to assume that they have justified themselves: quite forgetting that the adequateness of the advantages is the point to be judged. There is, perhaps, not a subject to which men devote attention that has not *some* value. A year dili-gently spent in getting up heraldry, would very possibly give a little further insight into ancient manners and morals. Any one who should learn the distances between all the towns in England, might, in the course of his life, find one or two of the thousand facts he had acquired of some slight service when arranging a journey. Gathering together all the small gossip of a county, profitless occupation as it would be, might yet occasionally help to establish some useful fact—say, a good example of hereditary transmission. But in these cases, every one would admit that there was no proportion between the required labour and the probable benefit. No one would tolerate the proposal to devote some years of a boy's time to getting such information, at the cost of much more valuable information which he might else have got. And if here the test of relative value is appealed to and held conclusive, then should it be appealed to and held conclusive throughout. . . .

To this end, a measure of value is the first requisite. And happily, respecting the true measure of value, as expressed in general terms, there can be no dispute. Every one in contending for the worth of any particular order of information, does so by showing its bearing upon some part of life. In reply to the question—"Of what use is it?" the mathematician, linguist, naturalist, or philosopher, explains the way in which his learning beneficially influences action—saves from evil or secures good—conduces to happiness. When the teacher of writing has pointed out how great an aid writing is to success in business—that is, to the obtainment of sustenance—that is, to satisfactory living; he is held to have proved his case. And when the collector of dead facts (say a numismatist) fails to make clear any appreciable effects which these facts can produce on human welfare, he is obliged to admit that they are comparatively valueless. All then, either directly or by implication, appeal to this as the ultimate test.

How to live?—that is the essential question for us. Not how to live in the mere material sense only, but in the widest sense. The general problem which comprehends every special problem is—the right ruling of conduct in all directions under all circumstances. In what way to treat the body; in what way to treat the mind; in what way to manage our affairs; in what way to bring up a family; in what way to behave as a citizen; in what way to utilise those sources of happiness which nature supplies—how to use all our faculties to the greatest advantage of ourselves and others—how to live completely? And this being the great thing needful for us to learn, is, by consequence, the great thing which education has to teach. To prepare us for complete living is the function which education has to discharge; and the only rational mode of judging of an educational course is, to judge in what degree it discharges such function.

This test, never used in its entirety, but rarely even partially used, and used then in a vague, half conscious way, has to be applied consciously, methodically, and throughout all cases. It behoves us to set before ourselves, and ever to keep clearly in view, complete living as the end to be achieved; so that in bringing up our children we may choose subjects and methods of instruction, with deliberate reference to this end. Not only ought we to cease from the mere unthinking adoption of the current fashion in education, which has no better warrant than any other fashion; but we must also rise above that rude, empirical style of judging displayed by those more intelligent people who do bestow some care in overseeing the cultivation of their children's minds. It must not suffice simply to *think* that such or such information will be useful in after life, or that this kind of knowledge is of more practical value than that; but we must seek out some process of estimating their respective values, so that as far as possible we may positively *know* which are most deserving of attention. . . .

Our first step must obviously be to classify, in the order of their importance, the leading kinds of activity which constitute human life. They may be naturally arranged into:—1. those activities which directly minister to self-preservation; 2. those activities which, by securing the necessaries of life, indirectly minister to self-preservation; 3. those activities which have for their end the rearing and discipline of off-spring; 4. those activities which are involved in the maintenance of proper social and political relations; 5. those miscellaneous activities which fill up the leisure part of life, devoted to the gratification of the tastes and feelings.

That these stand in something like their true order of subordination, it needs no long consideration to show. . . .

We do not mean to say that these divisions are definitely separable. We do not deny that they are intricately entangled with each other, in such way that there can be no training for any that is not in some measure a training for all. Nor do we question that of each division there are portions more important than certain portions of the pre-ceding divisions: that, for instance, a man of much skill in business but little other faculty, may fall further below the standard of complete living than one of but moderate ability in money-getting but great judgment as a parent; or that exhaustive information bearing on right social action, joined with entire want of general culture in literature and the fine arts, is less desirable than a more moderate share of the one joined with some of the other. But, after making due qualifications, there still remain these broadly-marked divisions; and it still continues substantially true that these divisions subordinate one another in the foregoing order, because the corresponding divisions of life make one another *possible* in that order.

Of course the ideal of education is—complete preparation in all these divisions. But failing this ideal, as in our phase of civilisation every one must do more or less, the aim should be to maintain *a due proportion* between the degrees of preparation in each. Not exhaustive cultivation in any one, supremely important though it may be—not even an exclusive attention to the two, three, or four divisions of greatest importance; but an attention to all:—greatest where the value is greatest; less where the value is less; least where the value is least. For the average man (not to forget the cases in which peculiar aptitude for some one department of knowledge, rightly makes pursuit of that one the bread-winning occupation)—for the average man, we say, the desideratum is, a training that approaches nearest to perfection in the things which most subserve complete living, and falls more and more below perfection in the things that have more and more remote bearings on complete living.

In regulating education by this standard, there are some general considerations that should be ever present to us. The worth of any kind of culture, as aiding complete living, may be either necessary or more or less contingent. There is knowledge of intrinsic value; knowledge of quasi-intrinsic value; and knowledge of conventional value. Such facts as that sensations of numbness and tingling commonly precede paralysis, that the resistance of water to a body moving through it varies as the square of the velocity, that chlorine is a disinfectant—these, and the truths of Science in general, are of intrinsic value: they will bear on human conduct ten thousand years hence as they do now. The extra knowledge of our own language, which is given by an acquaintance with Latin and Greek, may be considered to have a value that is quasi-intrinsic: it must exist for us and for other races whose languages owe much to these sources; but will last only as long as our languages last. While that kind of information which, in our schools, usurps the name History—the mere tissue of names and dates and dead unmeaning events—has a conventional value only: it has not the remotest bearing on any of our actions; and is of use only for the avoidance of those unpleasant criticisms which current opinion passes upon its absence. Of course, as those facts which concern all mankind throughout all time must be held of greater moment than those which concern only a portion of them during a limited era, and of far greater moment than those which concern only a portion of them during the continuance of a fashion; it follows that in a rational estimate, knowledge of intrinsic worth must, other things equal, take precedence of knowledge that is of quasi-intrinsic or conventional worth.

One further preliminary. Acquirement of every kind has two values—value as *knowledge* and value as *discipline*. Besides its use for guiding conduct, the acquisition of each order of facts has also its use as mental exercise; and its effects as a preparative for complete living have to be considered under both these heads.

These, then, are the general ideas with which we must set out in discussing a *curriculum*:—Life as divided into several kinds of activity of successively decreasing importance; the worth of each order of facts as regulating these several kinds of activity, intrinsically, quasi-intrinsically, and conventionally; and their regulative influences estimated both as knowledge and discipline. . . .

We need not insist on the value of that knowledge which aids indirect self-preservation by facilitating the gaining of a livelihood. This is admitted by all; and, indeed, by the mass is perhaps too exclusively regarded as the end of education. But while every one is ready to endorse the abstract proposition that instruction fitting youths for the business of life is of high importance, or even to consider it of supreme importance; yet scarcely any inquire what instruction will so fit them. It is true that reading, writing, and arithmetic are taught with an intelligent appreciation of their uses. But when we have said this we have said nearly all. While the great bulk of what else is acquired has no bearing on the industrial activities, an immensity of information that has a direct bearing on the industrial activities is entirely passed over.

For, leaving out only some very small classes, what are all men employed in? They are employed in the production, preparation, and distribution of commodities. And on what does efficiency in the production, preparation, and distribution of commodities depend? It depends on the use of methods fitted to the respective natures of these commodities; it depends on an adequate acquaintance with their physical, chemical, or vital properties, as the case may be; that is, it depends on Science. This order of knowledge which is in great part ignored in our school-courses, is the order of knowledge underlying the right performance of those processes by which civilised life is made possible. Undeniable as is this truth, there seems to be no living consciousness of it: its very familiarity makes it unregarded. . . .

Look round the room in which you sit. If modern, probably the bricks in its walls were machine-made; and by machinery the flooring was sawn and planed, the mantel-shelf sawn and polished, the paper-hangings made and printed. The veneer on the table, the turned legs of the chairs, the carpet, the curtains, are all products of machinery. Your clothing—plain, figured, or printed—is it not wholly woven, nay, perhaps even sewed, by machinery? And the volume you are reading—

are not its leaves fabricated by one machine and covered with these words by another? Add to which that for the means of distribution over both land and sea, we are similarly indebted. And then observe that according as knowledge of mechanics is well or ill applied to these ends, comes success or failure. The engineer who miscalculates the strength of materials, builds a bridge that breaks down. The manufacturer who uses a bad machine cannot compete with another whose machine wastes less in friction and inertia. The ship-builder adhering to the old model is out-sailed by one who builds on the mechanically-justified wave-line principle. And as the ability of a nation to hold its own against other nations, depends on the skilled activity of its units, we see that on mechanical knowledge may turn the national fate. . . .

Yet one more science have we to note as bearing directly on industrial success—the Science of Society. Men who daily look at the state of the money-market; glance over prices current; discuss the probable crops of corn, cotton, sugar, wool, silk; weigh the chances of war; and from these data decide on their mercantile operations; are students of social science: empirical and blundering students it may be; but still, students who gain the prizes or are plucked of their profits, according as they do or do not reach the right conclusion. Not only the manufacturer and the merchant must guide their transactions by calculations of supply and demand, based on numerous facts, and tacitly recognising sundry general principles of social action; but even the retailer must do the like: his prosperity very greatly depending upon the correctness of his judgments respecting the future wholesale prices and the future rates of consumption. Manifestly, whoever takes part in the entangled commercial activities of a community, is vitally interested in understanding the laws according to which those activities vary.

. . . Each man who is immediately or remotely implicated in any form of industry (and few are not) has in some way to deal with the mathematical, physical, and chemical properties of things; perhaps, also, has a direct interest in biology; and certainly has in sociology. Whether he does or does not succeed well in that indirect self-preservation which we call getting a good livelihood, depends in a great degree on his knowledge of one or more of these sciences: not, it may be, a rational knowledge; but still a knowledge, though empirical. For what we call learning a business, really implies learning the science involved in it; though not perhaps under the name of science. And hence a grounding in science is of great importance, both because it prepares for all this, and because rational knowledge has an immense superiority over empirical knowledge. Moreover, not only is scientific culture requisite for each, that he may understand the *how* and the *why* of the things and processes with which he is concerned as maker or distributor; but it is often of much moment that he should understand the *how* and the *why* of various other things and processes. In this age of joint-stock undertakings, nearly every man above the labourer is interested as capitalist in some other occupation than his own; and, as thus interested, his profit or loss often depends on his knowledge of the sciences bearing on this other occupation. Here is a mine, in the sinking of which many shareholders ruined themselves, from not knowing that a certain fossil belonged to the old red sandstone, below which no coal is found. Numerous attempts have been made to construct electro-magnetic engines, in the hope of superseding steam; but had those who supplied the money understood the general law of the correlation and equivalence of forces, they might have had better balances at their bankers. Daily are men induced to aid in carrying out inventions which a mere tyro in science could show to be futile. Scarcely a locality but has its history of fortunes thrown away over some impossible project.

And if already the loss from want of science is so frequent and so great, still greater and more frequent will it be to those who hereafter lack science. Just as fast as productive processes become more scientific, which competition will inevitably make them do; and just as fast as joint-stock undertakings spread, which they certainly will; so fast must scientific knowledge grow necessary to every one.

That which our school-courses leave almost entirely out, we thus find to be that which most nearly concerns the business of life. Our industries would cease, were it not for the information which men begin to acquire, as they best may, after their education is said to be finished. And were it not for this information, from age to age accumulated and spread by unofficial means, these industries would never have existed. Had there been no teaching but such as goes on in our public schools, England would now be what it was in feudal times. That increasing acquaintance with the laws of phenomena, which has through successive ages enabled us to subjugate Nature to our needs, and in these days gives the common labourer comforts which a few centuries ago kings could not purchase, is scarcely in any degree owed to the appointed means of instructing our youth. The vital knowledge—that by which we have grown as a nation to what we are, and which now underlies our whole existence, is a knowledge that has got itself taught in nooks and corners; while the ordained agencies for teaching have been mumbling little else but dead formulas. . . .

And then the culture of the intellect—is not this, too, mismanaged in a similar manner? Grant that the phenomena of intelligence conform to laws; grant that the evolution of intelligence in a child also conforms to laws; and it follows inevitably that education cannot be rightly guided without a knowledge of these laws. To suppose that you can properly regulate this process of forming and accumulating ideas, without understanding the nature of the process, is absurd. How widely, then, must teaching as it is differ from teaching as it should be; when hardly any parents, and but few tutors, know anything about psychology. As might be expected, the established system is grievously at fault, alike in matter and in manner. While the right class of facts is withheld, the wrong class is forcibly administered in the wrong way and in the wrong order. . . .

And here we see most distinctly the vice of our educational system. It neglects the plant for the sake of the flower. In anxiety for elegance, it forgets substance. While it gives no knowledge conducive to self-preservation—while of knowledge that facilitates gaining a livelihood it gives but the rudiments, and leaves the greater part to be picked up any how in after life—while for the discharge of parental functions it makes not the slightest provision—and while for the duties of citizenship it prepares by imparting a mass of facts, most of which are irrelevant, and the rest without a key; it is diligent in teaching whatever adds to refinement, polish, éclat. Fully as we may admit that extensive acquaintance with modern languages is a valuable accomplishment, which, through reading, conversation, and travel, aids in giving a certain finish; it by no means follows that this result is rightly purchased at the cost of the vitally important knowledge sacrificed to it. Supposing it true that classical education conduces to elegance and correctness of style; it cannot be said that elegance and correctness of style are comparable in importance to a familiarity with the principles that should guide the rearing of children. Grant that the taste may be improved by reading the poetry written in extinct languages; yet it is not to be inferred that such improvement of taste is equivalent in value to an acquaintance with the laws of health. Accomplishments, the fine arts, *belles-lettres*, and all those things which, as we say, constitute the efflorescence of civilisation, should be wholly subordinate to that instruction and discipline in which civilisation rests. *As they occupy the leisure part of life, so should they occupy the leisure part of education.*

Recognising thus the true position of aesthetics, and holding that while the cultivation of them should form a part of education from its commencement, such cultivation should be subsidiary; we have now to inquire what knowledge is of most use to this end—what knowledge best fits for this remaining sphere of activity? To this question the answer is still the same as heretofore. Unexpected though the assertion may be, it is nevertheless true, that the highest Art of every kind is based on Science—that without Science there can be neither perfect production nor full appreciation. Science, in that limited acceptation current in society, may not have been possessed by various artists of high repute; but acute observers as such artists have been, they have always possessed a stock of those empirical generalisations which constitute science in its lowest phase; and they have habitually fallen far below perfection, partly because their generalisations were comparatively few and inaccurate. That science necessarily underlies the fine arts, becomes manifest, *à priori*, when we remember that art-products are all more or less representative of objective or subjective phenomena; that they can be good only in proportion as they conform to the laws of these phenomena; and that before they can thus conform, the artist must know what these laws are. . . .

We do not for a moment believe that science will make an artist. While we contend that the leading laws both of objective and subjective phenomena must be understood by him, we by no means contend that knowledge of such laws will serve in place of natural perception. Not the poet only, but the artist of every type, is born, not made. What we assert is, that innate faculty cannot dispense with the aid of organised knowledge. Intuition will do much, but it will not do all. Only when Genius is married to Science can the highest results be produced.

As we have above asserted, Science is necessary not only for the most successful production, but also for the full appreciation, of the fine arts. In what consists the greater ability of a man than of a child to perceive the beauties of a picture; unless it is in his more extended knowledge of those truths in nature or life which the picture renders? How happens the cultivated gentleman to enjoy a fine poem so much more than a boor does; if it is not because his wider acquaintance with objects and actions enables him to see in the poem much that the boor cannot see? And if, as is here so obvious, there must be some familiarity with the things represented, before the representation can be appreciated, then, the representation can be completely appreciated only when the things represented are completely understood.

And now let us not overlook the further great fact, that not only does science underlie sculpture, painting, music, poetry, but that science is itself poetic. The current opinion that science and poetry are opposed, is a delusion. It is doubtless true that as states of consciousness, cognition and emotion tend to exclude each other. And it is doubtless also true that an extreme activity of the reflective powers tends to deaden the feelings; while an extreme activity of the feelings tends to deaden the reflective powers: in which sense, indeed, all orders of activity are antagonistic to each other. But it is not true that the facts of science are unpoetical; or that the cultivation of science is necessarily unfriendly to the exercise of imagination and the love of the beautiful. On the contrary, science opens up realms of poetry where to the unscientific all is a blank. Those engaged in scientific researches constantly show us that they realise not less vividly, but more vividly, than others, the poetry of their subjects. . . .

We find, then, that even for this remaining division of human activities, scientific culture is the proper preparation. We find that aesthetics in general are necessarily based upon scientific principles; and can be pursued with complete success only through an acquaintance with these principles. We find that for the criticism and due appreciation of works of art, a knowledge of the constitution of things, or in other words, a knowledge of science, is requisite. And we not only find that science is the handmaid to all forms of art and poetry, but that, rightly regarded, science is itself poetic. . . .

Not only, however, for intellectual discipline is science the best; but also for *moral* discipline. The learning of languages tends, if anything, further to increase the already undue respect for authority. Such and such are the meanings of these words, says the teacher of the dictionary. So and so is the rule in this case, says the grammar. By the pupil these dicta are received as unquestionable. His constant attitude of mind is that of submission to dogmatic teaching. And a necessary result is a tendency to accept without inquiry whatever is established. Quite opposite is the mental tone generated by the cultivation of science. Science makes constant appeal to individual reason. Its truths are not accepted on authority alone; but all are at liberty to test them—nay, in many cases, the pupil is required to think out his own conclusions. Every step in a scientific investigation is submitted to his judgment. He is not asked to admit it without seeing it to be true. And the trust in his own powers thus produced is further increased by the uniformity with which Nature justifies his inferences when they are correctly drawn. From all which there flows that independence which is a most valuable element in character. Nor is this the only moral benefit bequeathed by scientific culture. When carried on, as it should always be, as much as possible under the form of original research, it exercises perseverance and sincerity. . . .

Lastly we have to assert—and the assertion will, we doubt not, cause extreme surprise—that the discipline of science is superior to that of our ordinary education, because of the *religious* culture that it gives. Of course we do not here use the words scientific and religious in their ordinary limited acceptations; but in their widest and highest acceptations. Doubtless, to the superstitions that pass under the name of religion, science is antagonistic; but not to the essential religion which these superstitions merely hide. Doubtless, too, in much of the science that is current, there is a pervading spirit of irreligion; but not in that true science which had passed beyond the superficial into the profound. . . .

So far from science being irreligious, as many think, it is the neglect of science that is irreligious—it is the refusal to study the surrounding creation that is irreligious. Take a humble simile. Suppose a writer were daily saluted with praises couched in superlative language. Suppose the wisdom, the grandeur, the beauty of his works, were the constant topics of the eulogies addressed to him. Suppose those who unceasingly uttered these eulogies on his works were content with looking at the outsides of them; and had never opened them, much less tried to understand them. What value should we put upon their praises? What should we think of their sincerity? Yet, comparing small things to great, such is the conduct of mankind in general, in reference to the Universe and its Cause. Nay, it is worse. Not only do they pass by without study, these things which they daily proclaim to be so wonderful; but very frequently they condemn as mere triflers those who give time to the observation of Nature—they actually scorn those who show any active interest in these marvels. We repeat, then, that not science, but the neglect of science, is irreligious. Devotion to science, is a tacit worship—a tacit recognition of worth in the things studied; and by implication in their Cause. It is not a mere lip-homage, but a homage expressed in actions—not a mere professed respect, but a respect proved by the sacrifice of time, thought, and labour.

Nor is it thus only that true science is essentially religious. It is religious, too, inasmuch as it generates a profound respect for, and an implicit faith in, those uniformities of action which all things disclose. By accumulated experiences the man of science acquires a thorough belief in the unchanging relations of phenomena—in the invariable connection of cause and consequence—in the necessity of good or evil results. Instead of the rewards and punishments of traditional belief, which people vaguely hope they may gain, or escape, in spite of their disobedience; he finds that there are rewards and punishments in the ordained constitution of things; and that the evil results of disobedience are inevitable. He sees that the laws to which we must submit are both inexorable and beneficent. He sees that in conforming to them, the process of things is ever towards a greater perfection and a higher happiness. Hence he is led constantly to insist on them, and is indignant when they are disregarded. And thus does he, by asserting the eternal principles of things and the necessity of obeying them, prove himself intrinsically religious.

Add lastly the further religious aspect of science, that it alone can give us true conceptions of ourselves and our relation to the mysteries of existence. At the same time that it shows us all which can be known, it shows us the limits beyond which we can know nothing. Not by dogmatic assertion, does it teach the impossibility of comprehending the Ultimate Cause of things; but it leads us clearly to recognise this impossibility by bringing us in every direction to boundaries we cannot cross. It realises to us in a way which nothing else can, the littleness of human intelligence in the face of that which transcends human intelligence. While towards the traditions and authorities of men its attitude may be proud, before the impenetrable veil which hides the Absolute its attitude is humble—a true pride and a true humility. Only the sincere man of science (and by this title we do not mean the mere calculator of distances, or analyser of compounds, or labeller of species; but him who through lower truths seeks higher, and eventually the highest)—only the genuine man of science, we say, can truly know how utterly beyond, not only human knowledge but human conception, is the Universal Power of which Nature, and Life, and Thought are manifestations. . . .

Thus to the question we set out with—What knowledge is of most worth?—the uniform reply is—Science. This is the verdict on all the counts. For direct self-preservation, or the maintenance of life and health, the all-important knowledge is—Science. For that indirect self-preservation which we call gaining a livelihood, the knowledge of greatest value is—Science. For the due discharge of parental functions, the proper guidance is to be found only in—Science. For that interpretation of national life, past and present, without which the citizen cannot rightly regulate his conduct, the indispensable key is—Science. Alike for the most perfect production and highest enjoyment of art in all its forms, the needful preparation is still—Science. And for purposes of discipline—intellectual, moral, religious—the most efficient study is, once more—Science. The question which at first seemed so perplexed, has become, in the course of our inquiry, comparatively simple. We have not to estimate the degrees of importance of different orders of human activity, and different studies as severally fitting us for them; since we find that the study of Science, in its most comprehensive meaning, is the best preparation for all these orders of activity. We have not to decide between the claims of knowledge of great though conventional value, and knowledge of less though intrinsic value; seeing that the knowledge which proves to be of most value in all other respects, is intrinsically most valuable: its worth is not dependent upon opinion, but is as fixed as is the relation of man to the surrounding world. Necessary and eternal as are its truths, all Science concerns all mankind for all time. Equally at present and in the remotest future, must it be of incalculable importance for the regulation of their conduct, that men should understand the science of life, physical, mental, and social; and that they should understand all other science as a key to the science of life. . . .

4. DICKENS:

Facts, the One Thing Needful

The standard life of Charles Dickens (1812–1870) is the two-volume biography by Edgar Johnson (New York, 1953), although it does not supersede the earlier *Life*, by John Forster. A critical edition of the novels, edited by John Butt and Kathleen Tillotson, is in progress; Graham Storey's three-volume Pilgrim Edition of the letters is now standard. Books emphasizing Dickens' relationship to his times include Phillip Collins' two studies, *Dickens and Crime* and *Dickens and Education*, and George Ford's *Dickens and His Readers*. Though most of Dickens' novels contain social criticism, they are not primarily social criticism.

The selection, from Book I of *Hard Times*, presents Dickens' attitude toward utilitarian education at its clearest—and most exaggerated.

"Now, what I want is, Facts. Teach these boys and girls nothing but Facts. Facts alone are wanted in life. Plant nothing else, and root out everything else. You can only form the minds of reasoning animals upon Facts: nothing else will ever be of any service to them. This is the principle on which I bring up my own children, and this is the principle on which I bring up these children. Stick to Facts, sir!"

The scene was a plain, bare, monotonous vault of a schoolroom, and the speaker's square forefinger emphasized his observations by underscoring every sentence with a line on the schoolmaster's sleeve. The emphasis was helped by the speaker's square wall of a forehead, which had his eyebrows for its base, while his eyes found commodious cellarage in two dark caves overshadowed by the wall. The emphasis was helped by the speaker's mouth, which was wide, thin, and hard set. The emphasis was helped by the speaker's voice, which was inflexible, dry, and dictatorial. The emphasis was helped by the speaker's hair, which bristled on the skirts of his bald head, a plantation of firs to keep the wind from its shining surface, all covered with knobs, like the crust of a plum pie, as if the head had scarcely warehouse room for the hard facts stored inside. The speaker's obstinate carriage, square coat, square legs, square shoulders—nay, his very neckcloth, trained to take him by the throat with an unaccommodating grasp, like a stubborn fact, as it was, all helped the emphasis.

"In this life, we want nothing but Facts, sir; nothing but Facts!"

The speaker, and the schoolmaster, and the third grown person present, all backed a little, and swept with their eyes the inclined plane of little vessels then and there arranged in order, ready to have imperial gallons of facts poured into them until they were full to the brim.

Thomas Gradgrind, sir. A man of realities. A man of facts and calculations. A man who proceeds upon the principle that two and two are four, and nothing over, and who is not to be talked into allowing for anything over. Thomas Gradgrind, sir—peremptorily Thomas—Thomas Gradgrind. With a rule and a pair of scales, and the multiplication table always in his pocket, sir, ready to weigh and measure any parcel of human nature, and tell you exactly what it comes to. It is a mere question of figures, a case of simple arithmetic. You might hope to get some other nonsensical belief into the head of George Gradgrind, or Augustus Gradgrind, or John Gradgrind, or Joseph Gradgrind (all supposititious, non-existent persons), but into the head of Thomas Gradgrind—no, sir!

In such terms Mr. Gradgrind always mentally introduced himself, whether to his private circle of acquaintance, or to the public in general. In such terms, no doubt, substituting the words "boys and girls" for "sir," Thomas Gradgrind now presented Thomas Gradgrind to the little pitchers before him, who were to be filled so full of facts.

Indeed, as he eagerly sparkled at them from the cellarage before mentioned, he seemed a kind of cannon loaded to the muzzle with facts, and prepared to blow them clean out of the regions of childhood at one discharge. He seemed a galvanizing apparatus, too, charged with a grim mechanical substitute for the tender young imaginations that were to be stormed away.

"Girl number twenty," said Mr. Gradgrind, squarely pointing with his square forefinger, "I don't know that girl. Who is that girl?"

"Sissy Jupe, sir," explained number twenty, blushing, standing up, and curtsying.

"Sissy is not a name," said Mr. Gradgrind. "Don't call yourself Sissy. Call yourself Cecilia."

"It's father as calls me Sissy, sir," returned the young girl in a trembling voice, and with another curtsy.

"Then he has no business to do it," said Mr. Gradgrind. "Tell him he mustn't. Cecilia Jupe. Let me see. What is your father?"

"He belongs to the horse-riding, if you please, sir."

Mr. Gradgrind frowned, and waved off the objectionable calling with his hand.

"We don't want to know anything about that, here. You mustn't tell us about that, here. Your father breaks horses, don't he?"

"If you please, sir, when they can get any to break, they do break horses in the ring, sir."

"You mustn't tell us about the ring, here. Very well, then. Describe your father as a horsebreaker. He doctors sick horses, I dare say?"

"Oh, yes, sir."

"Very well, then. He is a veterinary surgeon, a farrier, and horse-breaker. Give me your definition of a horse."

(Sissy Jupe thrown into the greatest alarm by this demand.)

"Girl number twenty unable to define a horse!" said Mr. Grad-grind, for the general behoof of all the little pitchers. "Girl number twenty possessed of no facts, in reference to one of the commonest of animals! Some boy's definition of a horse. Bitzer, yours."

The square finger, moving here and there, lighted suddenly on Bitzer, perhaps because he chanced to sit in the same ray of sunlight which, darting in at one of the bare windows of the intensely white-washed room, irradiated Sissy. For the boys and girls sat on the face of the inclined plane in two compact bodies, divided up the centre by a narrow interval; and Sissy, being at the corner of a row on the sunny side, came in for the beginning of a sunbeam, of which Bitzer, being at the corner of a row on the other side, a few rows in advance, caught the end. But, whereas the girl was so dark-eyed and dark-haired that she seemed to receive a deeper and more lustrous colour from the sun when it shone upon her, the boy was so light-eyed and light-haired that the self-same rays appeared to draw out of him what little colour he ever possessed. His cold eyes would hardly have been eyes, but for the short ends of lashes which, by bringing them into immediate contrast with something paler than themselves, expressed their form. His short-cropped hair might have been a mere continuation of the sandy freckles on his forehead and face. His skin was so unwholesomely deficient in the natural tinge, that he looked as though, if he were cut, he would bleed white.

"Bitzer," said Thomas Gradgrind, "your definition of a horse."

' Quadruped. Graminivorous. Forty teeth, namely twenty-four grinders, four eye-teeth, and twelve incisive. Sheds coat in the spring; in marshy countries, sheds hoofs too. Hoofs hard, but requiring to be shod with iron. Age known by marks in mouth." Thus (and much more) Bitzer.

"Now girl number twenty," said Mr. Gradgrind, "you know what a horse is." ...

"Very well," said this gentleman, briskly smiling, and folding his arms. "That's a horse. Now, let me ask you girls and boys, would you paper a room with representations of horses?"

After a pause, one half of the children cried in chorus, "Yes, sir!"

Upon which the other half, seeing in the gentleman's face that yes was wrong, cried out in chorus, "No, sir!"—as the custom is, in these examinations.

"Of course, no. Why wouldn't you?"

A pause. One corpulent slow boy, with a wheezy manner of breathing, ventured the answer, Because he wouldn't paper a room at all, but would paint it.

"You *must* paper it," said the gentleman, rather warmly.

"You must paper it," said Thomas Gradgrind, "whether you like it or not. Don't tell *us* you wouldn't paper it. What do you mean, boy?"

"I'll explain to you, then," said the gentleman, after another and a dismal pause, "why you wouldn't paper a room with representations of horses. Do you ever see horses walking up and down the sides of rooms in reality—in fact? Do you?"

"Yes, sir!" from one half. "No, sir!" from the other.

"Of course, no," said the gentleman, with an indignant look at the wrong half. "Why, then, you are not to see anywhere what you don't see in fact; you are not to have anywhere what you don't have in fact. What is called Taste is only another name for Fact."

Thomas Gradgrind nodded his approbation.

"This is a new principle, a discovery, a great discovery," said the gentleman. "Now, I'll try you again. Suppose you were going to carpet a room. Would you use a carpet having a representation of flowers upon it?"

There being a general conviction by this time that "No, sir!" was always the right answer to this gentleman, the chorus of No was very strong. Only a few feeble stragglers said Yes; among them Sissy Jupe.

"Girl number twenty," said the gentleman, smiling in the calm strength of knowledge.

Sissy blushed, and stood up.

"So you would carpet your room—or your husband's room, if you were a grown woman, and had a husband—with representations of flowers, would you?" said the gentleman. "Why would you?"

"If you please, sir, I am very fond of flowers," returned the girl.

"And is that why you would put tables and chairs upon them, and have people walking over them with heavy boots?"

"It wouldn't hurt them, sir. They wouldn't crush and wither, if you please, sir. They would be the pictures of what was very pretty and pleasant, and I would fancy——"

"Ay, ay, ay! But you mustn't fancy," cried the gentleman, quite elated by coming so happily to his point. "That's it! You are never to fancy."

"You are not, Cecilia Jupe," Thomas Gradgrind solemnly repeated, "to do anything of that kind."

"Fact, fact, fact!" said the gentleman. And "Fact, fact, fact!" repeated Thomas Gradgrind.

"You are to be in all things regulated and governed," said the gentleman, "by fact. We hope to have, before long, a board of fact, composed of commissioners of fact, who will force the people to be a people of fact, and of nothing but fact. You must discard the word Fancy altogether. You have nothing to do with it. You are not to have, in any object of use or ornament, what would be a contradiction in fact. You don't walk upon flowers in fact; you cannot be allowed to walk upon flowers in carpets. You don't find that foreign birds and butterflies come and perch upon your crockery; you cannot be permitted to paint foreign birds and butterflies upon your crockery. You never meet with quadrupeds going up and down walls; you must not have quadrupeds represented upon walls. You must use," said the gentleman, "for all these purposes, combinations and modifications (in primary colours) of mathematical figures which are susceptible of proof and demonstration. This is the new discovery. This is fact. This is taste."

5. MEREDITH:

Trial by Education

The best life of George Meredith (1828–1909) is the one by Lionel Stevenson, *The Ordeal of George Meredith* (New York, 1953); still valuable is G. M. Trevelyan's 1912 *The Poetry and Philosophy of George Meredith*, though Norman Kelvin's *A Troubled Eden: Nature and Society in the Works of George Meredith* is a more recent critical study. The works are complete in the 36-volume edition published in London in 1914.

The extracts from *The Ordeal of Richard Feverel* are those in which Meredith describes, as clearly as anywhere in the novel, the system of education to which Sir Austin subjects his son.

The gist of the System set forth: That a Golden Age, or something near it, might yet be established on our sphere, when fathers accepted their solemn responsibility, and studied human nature with a Scientific eye, knowing what a high Science it is, to live: and that, by hedging round the Youth from corruptness, and at the same time promoting his animal health, by helping him to grow, as he would, like a Tree of Eden; by advancing him to a certain moral fortitude ere the Apple-Disease was spontaneously developed, there would be seen something approaching to a perfect Man, as the Baronet trusted to make this one Son of his, after a receipt of his own.

What he exactly meant by the Apple-Disease, he did not explain: nor did the ladies ask for an explanation. Intuitively they felt hot when it was mentioned. . . .

With these intimates young Richard Feverel lived in the great House, unconscious of the tight jacket he was gathering flesh to feel. The System hung loosely on his limbs at first. The Curate of Lobourne attended to his rudimentary lessons: a Papworth being sometimes invited to Raynham to play with him, who said, he was a lucky fellow not to be sent to school, and tried to make the boy think so, for which purpose he had, perhaps, been brought over. Now and then a well-meaning friend of Sir Austin's ventured to remonstrate on the dangerous trial he was making in modelling any new plan of Education for a youth, but the Baronet was firm. He pointed to his son, and said, "Match him."

Towards his fourteenth year, however, the young Experiment began to grow exceedingly restless. The Curate of Lobourne sent in a report that Master Richard's lessons were contumaciously disregarded: that in his Latin and Greek he was retrograding: in propriety of behaviour likewise; for witness, exhibiting a broken slate and a broken window of the room set apart for his studies. Heavy Benson also laid a portentous book on the Baronet's table, found by him in Master Richard's bedroom, proving to be a Lemprière, and a rather grave sign in Sir Austin's estimation.

"What can this be?" the Baronet meditated, and referred to his Note-Book (a famous and much-feared Instrument at Raynham, which held the bare bones of THE PILGRIM'S SCRIP), wherein the youth's progressionary phases were mapped out in sections, from Simple Boyhood to the Blossoming Season, The Magnetic Age, The Period of Probation, from which, successfully passed through, he was to emerge into a Manhood worthy of Paradise. It was now Simple Boyhood; The Ante-Pomona Stage, as Adrian named it. A slate sent through a window was mere insubordination: a Lemprière in the bedroom looked like precocity,—looked like Pomona in person. Supposing the boy to be precocious, the whole System was disorganized; based as it was upon concordant Nature, after that saying of THE PILGRIM'S SCRIP:

'Health is the Body's Virtue: Truth, the Soul's; Valour springs but from the unison of these twain.'

Sir Austin consulted with his young Achates, and old Dr. Clifford, who were not so perplexed in arriving at a simple conclusion as the philosopher, and said, that the boy only wanted companions of his own age.

"Some one to rub his excessive vitality against, you mean?" asked the Baronet.

"Ay, Sir," Adrian replied. "He is now laden with that super-abundant energy which makes a fool of a man, and a scapegrace of a boy, and he wants to work it off."

"Too much Health," added the Doctor, "is inductive Disease."

"Scarcely sound. Scarcely sound," remarked the Baronet, "on that ground you tolerate much. You give human nature but a short tether. Our Virtues, then, are pigmies, Doctor, that daren't grow for fear of the sty?"

"Circe looks out for strapping fellows, I fancy," said Adrian, and closed the session with laughter.

Sir Austin continued to meditate some days, and then requested the Wise Youth's advice on a proposition conceived by him, to have a boy of Richard's age to stay with him in the house and be his comrade.

"I think your idea excellent," said Adrian, giving him all the credit of it. "And I know the very boy that will suit. Thompson, your solicitor, has a son. Poor fellow! only one, I believe, and about a dozen girls with parchment exteriors and snub noses. The whole family's a genesis of sheepskin. But they're well brought up. You might try the lad, Sir. The Thompsons stuck by my father in his Brief days." . . .

The author of the System sat in his study with old Dr. Clifford, much aggrieved.

"A boy who has no voice but mine, Doctor," he said; "whose spirit is clear to me as day—he enters another Circle of nature, and I require to be assured of his bodily well-being, and this boy, educated in the seclusion of a girl, refuses—nay, swears he will not."

"From which, my dear Sir Austin, you have to learn, that your son is no longer a child," was the Doctor's comment.

"A beautiful shamelessness is not necessarily dependent upon a state of childhood," returned the Baronet. "In a boy properly looked to, as this boy has been, there should not be the most distant sense of indelicacy in such a request. He registers revolt, too, with an oath:— The old way! The moment he breaks from me, in a moment he is like the world, and claims Cousinship with an oath for his password."

Sir Austin put a finger to his temple and stared at the fire.

"What do you attribute it to, Doctor?" he asked presently.

"The System, Sir," quietly replied the Doctor.

"Excellent!" Sir Austin exclaimed. "It is I who teach him bad language?"

"At a school," said the Doctor, "there are the two extremes: good boys, and the reverse. Your son does not see that distinction here. He is a heathen as to right and wrong. Good from instinct—not from principle: a creature of impulse. A noble lad, I admit, but—you know, I am of the old school, Sir Austin. I like boys to be boys, and mix together. Christians are not born in hermitages."

"Very well said, Doctor!" remarked the Baronet, always alive to a phrase, even in his tribulation. "A spice of the Devil, then, is necessary for a Christian?"

Dr. Clifford stroked his chin. "I don't say that," he replied. "But I don't mind saying that a fair stand-up fight with him is."

"For a boy, Doctor?"

"For a boy, Sir Austin. He can't have it out too soon."

"Listen, Doctor," said the Baronet, after turning in his chair uneasily two or three times.

"I think you none of you understand my System. My good Doctor! I am not preparing my son to avoid the fight. I know it is inevitable. I brace him for the struggle."

"By keeping him out of his element?" quoth the Doctor.

"By giving him all the advantages of Science," Sir Austin emphasized. "By training him. Our theory is the same, with this difference: that you set the struggle down at an earlier date than do I. It may be true I sacrifice two or three little advantages in isolating him at present: he will be the better fortified for his trial to come. You know my opinion, Doctor: we are pretty secure from the Serpent till Eve sides with him. I speak, of course, of a youth of good pure blood."

"I don't think the schools would harm such a youth," said the Doctor.

"The schools are corrupt!" said the Baronet.

Dr. Clifford could not help thinking there were other temptations than that one of Eve. For youths and for men, Sir Austin told him. She was the main bait: the sole to be dreaded for a youth of good pure blood: the main to resist.

Dr. Clifford inquired whether it was good for such a youth to be half a girl? Whereat Sir Austin smiled a laugh.

"You see him one instant a shamefaced girl, and the next, a head-long boy," the Doctor explained. "Is that good?"

"Yes, yes; I caught your meaning," said Sir Austin. "You suppose shame to be the property of innocence, and therefore of womankind. A wonderful double deduction!" He went into scientific particulars which would reduce the reader to greater confusion than it did the Doctor. They then fell upon the question of Richard's marrying.

"He shall not marry till he is thirty!" was the Baronet's Spartan Law.

"He need not marry at all," said Dr. Clifford. "Birth and death are natural accidents: Marriage we *can* avoid!" The Doctor had been jilted by a naughty damsel.

"On my System he must marry," said the Baronet, and again dissected the frame of man, and entered into scientific particulars: ending their colloquy: "However! I thank you, Doctor, for speaking as you think, and the proof that I know how to profit by it, is seen in my admission of the boy, Thompson, to my household. Perhaps our only difference, after all, is not a pathologic one. I acknowledge your diagnosis, but mollify the prescription. I give the poison to my son in small doses; whereas you prescribe large ones. You naturally contend with a homœopathist—Eh? You are inimical to that heresy?"

"With your permission, Sir Austin, I hate that humbug." The Doctor nodded grimly, and the Baronet laughed, in his stiff way, to have turned the tables on his staunch old adversary, calling him forth into the air to look after the boy, and inspect the preparations for his day's pleasure. . . .

"No!" cried Richard, "there's not a moment to be lost!" and as he said it, he reeled, and fell against Tom, muttering indistinctly of faint-ness, and that there was no time to lose. Tom lifted him in his arms, and got admission to the Inn. Brandy, the country's specific, was advised by host and hostess, and forced into his mouth, reviving him sufficiently to cry out, "Tom! the bell's ringing: we shall be late," after which he fell back insensible on the sofa where they had stretched him.

Excitement of blood and brain had done its work upon him. The poor youth suffered them to undress him and put him to bed, and there he lay, forgetful even of Love; a drowned weed borne onward by the tide of the hours. There his father found him.

Was the Scientific Humanist remorseful? Not he. He had looked forward to such a crisis as that point in the disease his son was the victim of, when the body would fail and give the spirit calm to conquer the malady, knowing very well that the seeds of the evil were not of the spirit. Moreover to see him, and have him, was a repose after the alarm Benson had sounded. Anxious he was, and prayerful; but with faith in the physical energy he attributed to his System. This providential stroke had saved the youth from Heaven knew what! "Mark!" said the Baronet to Lady Blandish, "when he recovers, he will not care for her."

The lady had accompanied him to the Bellingham Inn on first hearing of Richard's seizure.

"Oh! what an iron man you can be," she exclaimed, smothering her intuitions. She was for giving the boy his bauble; promising it him, at least, if he would only get well and be the bright flower of promise he once was.

"Can you look on him," she pleaded, "can you look on him, and persevere?"

It was a hard sight for this man who loved his son so deeply. The youth lay in his strange bed, straight and motionless, with fever on his cheeks, and altered eyes.

"See what you do to us!" said the Baronet, sorrowfully eyeing the bed.

"But if you lose him?" Lady Blandish whispered.

Sir Austin walked away from her, and probed the depths of his love. "The stroke will not be dealt by me," he said.

His patient serenity was a wonder to all who knew him. Indeed to have doubted and faltered now was to have subverted the glorious fabric just on the verge of completion. He believed that his son's pure strength was fitted to cope with any natural evil: that such was God's Law. To him Richard's passion was an ill incident to the ripeness of his years, and his perfect innocence; and this crisis the struggle of the poison passing out of him—not to be deplored. He was so confident that he did not even send for Dr. Bairam. Old Dr. Clifford of Lobourne was the medical attendant, who, with head-shaking, and gathering of lips, and reminiscences of ancient arguments, guaranteed to do all that leech could do in the matter. The old Doctor did admit that Richard's constitution was admirable, and answered to his prescriptions like a piano to the musician. "But," he said, at a family consultation, for Sir Austin had told him how it stood with the young man, "drugs are not much in cases of this sort. Change! That's what's wanted, and as soon as may be. Distraction! He ought to see the world, and know what he's made of. It's no use my talking, I know," added the Doctor.

"On the contrary," said Sir Austin. "I am quite of your persuasion. And the world he shall see—now."

"We have dipped him in Styx, you know, Doctor," Adrian remarked.

"But, Doctor," said Lady Blandish, "have you known a case of this sort before?"

"Never, my lady," said the Doctor, "they're not common in these parts. Country people are tolerably healthy-minded."

"But people—and country people—have died for love, Doctor?"

The Doctor had not met any of them.

"Men, or women?" inquired the Baronet.

Lady Blandish believed, mostly women.

"Ask the Doctor whether they were healthy-minded women," said the Baronet. "No! you are both looking at the wrong end. Between a highly-cultured being, and an emotionless animal, there is all the difference in the world. But of the two, the Doctor is nearer the truth. The healthy nature is pretty safe. If he allowed for organization he would be right altogether. To feel, but not to feel to excess, that is the problem."

> "*If I can't have the one I chose,*
> *To some fresh maid I will propose,*"

Adrian hummed a country ballad.

"That couplet," said Sir Austin, "exactly typifies the Doctor's hero. I think he must admire Agamemnon—eh, Doctor? Chryseïs taken from us, let us seize Bryseïs!—Children cry, but don't die, for their lumps of sugar. When they grow older, they—"

"Simply have a stronger appreciation of the sugar, and make a greater noise to obtain it," Adrian took him up, and elicited the smile which usually terminated any dispute he joined. . . .

When the young Experiment again knew the hours that rolled him onward, he was in his own room at Raynham. Nothing had changed: only a strong fist had knocked him down and stunned him, and he opened his eyes to a grey world. He had forgotten what he lived for.

He was weak, and thin, and with a pale memory of things. His functions were the same, everything surrounding him was the same: he looked upon the old blue hills, the far-lying fallows, the river, and the woods: he knew them, but they seemed to have lost recollection of him. Nor could he find in familiar human faces the secret intimacy of heretofore. They were the same faces: they nodded and smiled to him. What was lost he could not tell. Something had been knocked out of him! He was sensible of his father's sweetness of manner, and he was grieved that he could not reply to it, for every sense of shame and reproach had strangely gone. He felt very useless. In place of the fiery love for one, he now bore about a cold charity to all.

Thus in the heart of the young man died the Spring Primrose, and while it died another heart was pushing forth the Primrose of Autumn. . . .

Mrs. Berry cut the Cake. Somehow, as she sliced through it, the sweetness and hapless innocence of the bride was presented to her, and she launched into eulogies of Lucy, and clearly showed how little she regretted her conduct. She vowed that they seemed made for each other: that both were beautiful: both had spirit: both were innocent: and to part them, or make them unhappy, would be, Mrs. Berry wrought herself to cry aloud, Oh, such a pity!

Adrian listened to it as the expression of a matter-of-fact opinion. He took the huge quarter of Cake, nodded multitudinous promises, and left Mrs. Berry to bless his good heart.

"So dies the System!" was Adrian's comment in the street. "And now let prophets roar! He dies respectably in a marriage-bed, which is more than I should have foretold of the Monster. Meantime," he gave the Cake a dramatic tap, "I'll go sow nightmares."

6. ELIOT:

"School-Time"

The letters of George Eliot—Mary Ann Evans—(1819–1880) have been competently edited in seven volumes (Yale, 1954–55), by Gordon

Haight, who has edited *Adam Bede* and *Middlemarch* as well. The 1968 life by Haight does not replace the three-volume life written by her husband, J. W. Cross, in 1885–86. Recently George Eliot's reputation has undergone a revival; there are several recent, good critical studies, notably Joan Bennet's *George Eliot: Her Mind and Art* (Cambridge, 1948), Barbra Hardy's *The Novels of George Eliot: A Study in Form* (London, 1959), and W. J. Harvey's *The Art of George Eliot* (New York, 1961).

In the selection from *The Mill on the Floss*, the miller, Mr. Tulliver, has just placed his son at the Reverend Mr. Stelling's establishment, to prepare him "to be a man who will make his way in the world."

Tom, as you have observed, was never an exception among boys for ease of address; but the difficulty of enunciating a monosyllable in reply to Mr. or Mrs. Stelling was so great, that he even dreaded to be asked at table whether he would have more pudding. As to the percussion-caps, he had almost resolved, in the bitterness of his heart, that he would throw them into a neighbouring pond; for not only was he the solitary pupil, but he began even to have a certain scepticism about guns, and a general sense that his theory of life was undermined. For Mr. Stelling thought nothing of guns, or horses either, apparently; and yet it was impossible for Tom to despise Mr. Stelling as he had despised Old Goggles. If there were anything that was not thoroughly genuine about Mr. Stelling, it lay quite beyond Tom's power to detect it: it is only by a wide comparison of facts that the wisest full-grown man can distinguish well-rolled barrels from more supernal thunder.

Mr. Stelling was a well-sized, broad-chested man, not yet thirty, with flaxen hair standing erect, and large lightish-grey eyes, which were always very wide open; he had a sonorous bass voice, and an air of defiant self-confidence inclining to brazenness. He had entered on his career with great vigour, and intended to make a considerable impression on his fellow-men. The Rev. Walter Stelling was not a man who would remain among the "inferior clergy" all his life. He had a true British determination to push his way in the world. As a schoolmaster, in the first place; for there were capital masterships of grammar-schools to be had, and Mr. Stelling meant to have one of them. But as a preacher also, for he meant always to preach in a striking manner, so as to have his congregation swelled by admirers from neighbouring parishes, and to produce a great sensation whenever he took occasional duty for a brother clergyman of minor gifts. The style of preaching he had chosen was the extemporaneous, which was held little short of the miraculous in rural parishes like King's Lorton. Some passages of

Massillon and Bourdaloue, which he knew by heart, were really very effective when rolled out in Mr. Stelling's deepest tones; but as comparatively feeble appeals of his own were delivered in the same loud and impressive manner, they were often thought quite as striking by his hearers. Mr. Stelling's doctrine was of no particular school; if anything, it had a tinge of evangelicalism, for that was "the telling thing" just then in the diocese to which King's Lorton belonged. In short, Mr. Stelling was a man who meant to rise in his profession, and to rise by merit, clearly, since he had no interest beyond what might be promised by a problematic relationship to a great lawyer who had not yet become Lord Chancellor. A clergyman who has such vigorous intentions naturally gets a little into debt at starting; it is not to be expected that he will live in the meagre style of a man who means to be a poor curate all his life, and if the few hundreds Mr. Timpson advanced towards his daughter's fortune did not suffice for the purchase of handsome furniture, together with a stock of wine, a grand piano, and the laying out of a superior flower-garden, it followed in the most rigorous manner, either that these things must be procured by some other means, or else that the Rev. Stelling must go without them—which last alternative would be an absurd procrastination of the fruits of success, where success was certain. Mr. Stelling was so broad-chested and resolute that he felt equal to anything; he would become celebrated by shaking the consciences of his hearers, and he would by-and-by edit a Greek play, and invent several new readings. He had not yet selected the play, for having been married little more than two years, his leisure time had been much occupied with attentions to Mrs. Stelling; but he had told that fine woman what he meant to do some day, and she felt great confidence in her husband, as a man who understood everything of that sort.

But the immediate step to future success was to bring on Tom Tulliver during this first half-year; for, by a singular coincidence, there had been some negotiation concerning another pupil from the same neighbourhood, and it might further a decision in Mr. Stelling's favour, if it were understood that young Tulliver, who, Mr. Stelling observed in conjugal privacy, was rather a rough cub, had made prodigious progress in a short time. It was on this ground that he was severe with Tom about his lessons: he was clearly a boy whose powers would never be developed through the medium of the Latin grammar, without the application of some sternness. Not that Mr. Stelling was a harsh-tempered or unkind man—quite the contrary: he was jocose with Tom at table, and corrected his provincialisms and his deportment in the most playful manner; but poor Tom was only the more cowed and confused by this double novelty, for he had never been used to jokes at all like Mr. Stelling's; and for the first time in his life he had a painful sense that he was all wrong somehow. When Mr. Stelling said, as the roast-beef was being uncovered, "Now, Tulliver! which would you rather decline, roast-beef or the Latin for it?"—Tom, to whom in his coolest moments a pun would have been a hard nut, was thrown into a state of embarrassed alarm that made everything dim to him except the feeling that he would rather not have anything to do with Latin: of course he answered, "Roast-beef," whereupon there followed much laughter and some practical joking with the plates, from which Tom gathered that he had in some mysterious way refused beef, and, in fact, made himself appear "a silly." If he could have seen a fellow-pupil undergo these painful operations and survive them in good spirits, he might sooner have taken them as a matter of course. But there are two expensive forms of education, either of which a parent may procure for his son by sending him as solitary pupil to a clergyman: one is, the enjoyment of the reverend gentleman's undivided neglect; the other is, the endurance of the reverend gentleman's undivided attention. It was the latter privilege for which Mr. Tulliver paid a high price in Tom's initiatory months at King's Lorton. . . .

Mr. Stelling set to work at his natural method of instilling the Eton Grammar and Euclid into the mind of Tom Tulliver. This, he considered, was the only basis of solid instruction: all other means of education were mere charlatanism, and could produce nothing better than smatterers. Fixed on this firm basis, a man might observe the display of various or special knowledge made by irregularly educated people with a pitying smile: all that sort of thing was very well, but it was impossible these people could form sound opinions. In holding this conviction Mr. Stelling was not biassed, as some tutors have been, by the excessive accuracy or extent of his own scholarship; and as to his views about Euclid, no opinion could have been freer from personal partiality. Mr. Stelling was very far from being led astray by enthusiasm, either religious or intellectual: on the other hand, he had no secret belief that everything was humbug. He thought religion was a very excellent thing, and Aristotle a great authority, and deaneries and prebends useful institutions, and Great Britain the providential bulwark of Protestantism, and faith in the unseen a great support to afflicted minds: he believed in all these things, as a Swiss hotel-keeper believes in the beauty of the scenery around him, and in the pleasure it gives to artistic visitors. And in the same way Mr. Stelling believed in his method of education: he had no doubt that he was doing the very best thing for Mr. Tulliver's boy. Of course, when the miller talked of "mapping" and "summing" in a vague and diffident manner, Mr. Stelling had set his mind at rest by an assurance that he understood what was wanted; for how was it possible the good man could form any reasonable judgment about the matter? Mr. Stelling's duty was to teach the lad in the only right way—indeed, he knew no other: he had not wasted his time in the acquirement of anything abnormal.

He very soon set down poor Tom as a thoroughly stupid lad; for though by hard labour he could get particular declensions into his brain, anything so abstract as the relation between cases and terminations could by no means get such a lodgment there as to enable him to recognise a chance genitive or dative. This struck Mr. Stelling as something more than natural stupidity: he suspected obstinacy, or, at any rate, indifference; and lectured Tom severely on his want of thorough application. "You feel no interest in what you're doing sir," Mr. Stelling would say, and the reproach was painfully true. Tom had never found any difficulty in discerning a pointer from a setter, when once he had been told the distinction, and his perceptive powers were not at all deficient. I fancy they were quite as strong as those of the Rev. Mr. Stelling; for Tom could predict with accuracy what number of horses were cantering behind him, he could throw a stone right into the centre of a given ripple, he could guess to a fraction how many lengths of his stick it would take to reach across the playground, and could draw almost perfect squares on his slate without any measurement. But Mr. Stelling took no note of these things: he only observed that Tom's faculties failed him before the abstractions hideously symbolised to him in the pages of the Eton Grammar, and that he was in a state bordering on idiocy with regard to the demonstration that two given triangles must be equal—though he could discern with great promptitude and certainty the fact that they *were* equal. Whence Mr. Stelling concluded that Tom's brain, being peculiarly impervious to etymology and demonstrations, was peculiarly in need of being ploughed and harrowed by these patent implements: it was his favourite metaphor, that the classics and geometry constituted that culture of the mind which prepared it for the reception of any subsequent crop. I say nothing against Mr. Stelling's theory: if we are to have one regimen for all minds, his seems to me as good as any other. I only know it turned out as uncomfortably for Tom Tulliver as if he had been plied with cheese in order to remedy a gastric weakness which prevented him from digesting it. It is astonishing what a different result one gets by changing the metaphor! Once call the brain an intellectual stomach, and one's ingenious conception of the classics and geometry as ploughs and harrows seems to settle nothing. But then it is open to some one else to follow great authorities, and call the mind a sheet of white paper or a mirror, in which case one's knowledge of the digestive process becomes quite irrelevant. It was doubtless an ingenious idea to call the camel the ship of the desert, but it would hardly lead one far in training that useful beast. O Aristotle! if you had had the advantage of being "the freshest modern" instead of the greatest ancient, would you not have mingled your praise of metaphorical speech, as a sign of high intelligence, with a lamentation that intelligence so rarely shows itself in speech without metaphor— that we can so seldom declare what a thing is, except by saying it is something else?

Tom Tulliver, being abundant in no form of speech, did not use any metaphor to declare his views as to the nature of Latin: he never called it an instrument of torture; and it was not until he had got on some way in the next half-year, and in the Delectus, that he was advanced enough to call it a "bore" and "beastly stuff." At present, in relation to this demand that he should learn Latin declensions and conjugations, Tom was in a state of as blank unimaginativeness concerning the cause and tendency of his sufferings, as if he had been an innocent shrew-mouse imprisoned in the split trunk of an ash tree in order to cure lameness in cattle. It is doubtless almost incredible to instructed minds of the present day that a boy of twelve, not belonging strictly to "the masses," who are now understood to have the monopoly of mental darkness, should have had no distinct idea how there came to be such a thing as Latin on this earth: yet so it was with Tom. It would have taken a long while to make conceivable to him that there ever existed a people who bought and sold sheep and oxen, and transacted the everyday affairs of life, through the medium of this language, and still longer to make him understand why he should be called upon to learn it, when its connection with those affairs had become entirely latent.

7. HARDY:

Jude's Great Expectations

The official biography of Thomas Hardy (1840–1928), ostensibly written by his wife, Florence, is actually by Hardy himself (2 vols., London, 1928–30). The standard life is that by Carl J. Weber, *Hardy of Wessex* (New York, 1940). The 37-volume Mellstock edition of 1919–20 is standard, but John Crowe Ransom's 1961 edition of the *Selected Poems* is valuable. Samuel Hyne's *The Pattern of Hardy's Poetry* (Chapel Hill, 1961) and Albert Guerard's *Thomas Hardy: The Novels and Stories* (1949) are two of many recent, sound critical studies.

In the selection from *Jude the Obscure*, Jude muses about his intellectual abilities and Hardy tells us what has become of Jude's expectations.

He was in an enthusiastic mood. He seemed to see his way to living comfortably in Christminster in the course of a year or two, and knocking at the doors of one of those strongholds of learning of which he had dreamed so much. He might, of course, have gone there now, in some capacity or other, but he preferred to enter the city with a little more assurance as to means than he could be said to feel at present. A warm self-content suffused him when he considered what he had already done. Now and then as he went along he turned to face the peeps of country on either side of him. But he hardly saw them; the act was an automatic repetition of what he had been accustomed to do when less occupied; and the one matter which really engaged him was the mental estimate of his progress thus far.

"I have acquired quite an average student's power to read the common ancient classics, Latin in particular." This was true, Jude possessing a facility in that language which enabled him with great ease to himself to beguile his lonely walks by imaginary conversations therein.

"I have read two books of the Iliad, besides being pretty familiar with passages such as the speech of Phoenix in the ninth book, the fight of Hector and Ajax in the fourteenth, the appearance of Achilles unarmed and his heavenly armour in the eighteenth, and the funeral games in the twenty-third. I have also done some Hesiod, a little scrap of Thucydides, and a lot of the Greek Testament. . . . I wish there was only one dialect, all the same.

"I have done some mathematics, including the first six and the eleventh and twelfth books of Euclid; and algebra as far as simple equations.

"I know something of the Fathers, and something of Roman and English history.

"These things are only a beginning. But I shall not make much further advance here, from the difficulty of getting books. Hence I must next concentrate all my energies on settling in Christminster. Once there I shall so advance, with the assistance I shall there get, that my present knowledge will appear to me but as childish ignorance. I must save money, and I will; and one of those colleges shall open its doors to me—shall welcome whom now it would spurn, if I wait twenty years for the welcome.

"I'll be D.D. before I have done!" . . .

And then he continued to dream, and thought he might become even a bishop by leading a pure, energetic, wise, Christian life. And what an example he would set! If his income were £5,000 a year, he would give away £4,500 in one form and another, and live sumptuously (for him) on the remainder. Well, on second thoughts, a bishop was absurd. He would draw the line at an archdeacon. Perhaps a man could be as good and as learned and as useful in the capacity of archdeacon as in that of bishop. Yet he thought of the bishop again.

"Meanwhile I will read, as soon as I am settled in Christminster, the books I have not been able to get hold of here: Livy, Tacitus, Herodotus, Aeschylus, Sophocles, Aristophanes—" . . .

"—Euripides, Plato, Aristotle, Lucretius, Epictetus, Seneca, Antoninus. Then I must master other things: the Fathers thoroughly; Bede and ecclesiastical history generally; a smattering of Hebrew—I only know the letters as yet—" . . .

"—but I can work hard. I have staying power in abundance, thank God! and it is that which tells. . . . Yes, Christminster shall be my Alma Mater; and I'll be her beloved son, in whom she shall be well pleased." . . .

It being Sunday evening some villagers who had known him during his residence here were standing in a group in their best clothes. Jude was startled by a salute from one of them:

"Ye've got there right enough, then!"

Jude showed that he did not understand.

"Why, to the seat of l'arning—the 'City of Light' you used to talk to us about as a little boy! Is it all you expected of it?"

"Yes; more!" cried Jude.

"When I was there once for an hour I didn't see much in it for my part; auld crumbling buildings, half church, half almshouse, and not much going on at that."

"You are wrong, John; there is more going on than meets the eye of a man walking through the streets. It is a unique centre of thought and religion—the intellectual and spiritual granary of this country. All that silence and absence of goings-on is the stillness of infinite motion—the sleep of the spinning-top, to borrow the simile of a well-known writer."

"O, well, it med be all that, or it med not. As I say, I didn't see nothing of it the hour or two I was there; so I went in and had a pot o' beer, and a penny loaf, and a ha'porth o' cheese, and waited till it was time to come along home. You've j'ined a College by this time, I suppose?"

"Ah, no!" said Jude. "I am almost as far off that as ever."

"How so?"

Jude slapped his pocket.

"Just what we thought! Such places be not for such as you—only for them with plenty o' money."

"There you are wrong," said Jude, with some bitterness. "They are for such ones!"

Still, the remark was sufficient to withdraw Jude's attention from the imaginative world he had lately inhabited, in which an abstract figure, more or less himself, was steeping his mind in a sublimation of the arts and sciences, and making his calling and election sure to a seat in the paradise of the learned. He was set regarding his prospects in a cold northern light. He had lately felt that he could not quite satisfy himself in his Greek—in the Greek of the dramatists particularly. So fatigued was he sometimes after his day's work that he could not maintain the critical attention necessary for thorough application. He felt that he wanted a coach—a friend at his elbow to tell him in a moment what sometimes would occupy him a weary month in extracting from un-anticipative, clumsy books.

It was decidedly necessary to consider facts a little more closely than he had done of late. What was the good, after all, of using up his spare hours in a vague labour called "private study" without giving an outlook on practicabilities?

"I ought to have thought of this before," he said, as he journeyed back. "It would have been better never to have embarked in the scheme at all than to do it without seeing clearly where I am going, or what I am aiming at. . . . This hovering outside the walls of the colleges, as if expecting some arm to be stretched out from them to lift me inside, won't do! I must get special information."

The next week accordingly he sought it. What at first seemed an opportunity occurred one afternoon when he saw an elderly gentleman, who had been pointed out as the Head of a particular College, walking in the public path of a parklike enclosure near the spot at which Jude chanced to be sitting. The gentleman came nearer, and Jude looked anxiously at his face. It seemed benign, considerate, yet rather reserved. On second thoughts Jude felt that he could not go up and address him; but he was sufficiently influenced by the incident to think what a wise thing it would be for him to state his difficulties by letter to some of the best and most judicious of these old masters, and obtain their advice.

During the next week or two he accordingly placed himself in such positions about the city as would afford him glimpses of several of the most distinguished among the Provosts, Wardens, and other Heads of Houses; and from those he ultimately selected five whose physiognomies seemed to say to him that they were appreciative and far-seeing men. To these five he addressed letters, briefly stating his difficulties, and asking their opinion on his stranded situation.

When the letters were posted Jude mentally began to criticize them; he wished they had not been sent. "It is just one of those intrusive, vulgar, pushing, applications which are so common in these days," he thought. "Why couldn't I know better than address utter strangers in such a way? I may be an impostor, an idle scamp, a man with a bad character, for all that they know to the contrary. . . . Perhaps that's what I am!"

Nevertheless, he found himself clinging to the hope of some reply as to his one last chance of redemption. He waited day after day, saying that it was perfectly absurd to expect, yet expecting. . . .

Meanwhile the academic dignitaries to whom Jude had written

vouchsafed no answer, and the young man was thus thrown back entirely on himself, as formerly, with the added gloom of a weakened hope. By indirect inquiries he soon perceived clearly, what he had long uneasily suspected, that to qualify himself for certain open scholarships and exhibitions was the only brilliant course. But to do this a good deal of coaching would be necessary, and much natural ability. It was next to impossible that a man reading on his own system, however widely and thoroughly, even over the prolonged period of ten years, should be able to compete with those who had passed their lives under trained teachers and had worked to ordained lines.

The other course, that of buying himself in, so to speak, seemed the only one really open to men like him, the difficulty being simply of a material kind. With the help of his information he began to reckon the extent of this material obstacle, and ascertained, to his dismay, that, at the rate at which, with the best of furtune, he would be able to save money, fifteen years must elapse before he could be in a position to forward testimonials to the Head of a College and advance to a matriculation examination. The undertaking was hopeless.

He saw what a curious and cunning glamour the neighbourhood of the place had exercised over him. To get there and live there, to move among the churches and halls and become imbued with the *genius loci*, had seemed to his dreaming youth, as the spot shaped its charms to him from its halo on the horizon, the obvious and ideal thing to do. "Let me only get there," he had said with the fatuousness of Crusoe over his big boat, "and the rest is but a matter of time and energy." It would have been far better for him in every way if he had never come within sight and sound of the delusive precincts, had gone to some busy commercial town with the sole object of making money by his wits, and thence surveyed his plan in true perspective. Well, all that was clear to him amounted to this, that the whole scheme had burst up, like an iridescent soap-bubble, under the touch of a reasoned inquiry. He looked back at himself along the vista of his past years, and his thought was akin to Heine's:

> "Above the youth's inspired and flashing eyes
> I see the motley mocking fool's-cap rise!"

. . . He always remembered the appearance of the afternoon on which he awoke from his dream. Not quite knowing what to do with himself, he went up to an octagonal chamber in the lantern of a singularly built theatre that was set amidst this quaint and singular city. It had windows all round, from which an outlook over the whole town and its edifices could be gained. Jude's eyes swept all the views in succession, meditatively, mournfully, yet sturdily. Those buildings and their associations and privileges were not for him. From the looming roof of the great library, into which he hardly ever had time to enter, his gaze travelled on to the varied spires, halls, gables, streets, chapels, gardens, quadrangles, which composed the *ensemble* of this unrivalled panorama. He saw that his destiny lay not with these, but among the manual toilers in the shabby purlieu which he himself occupied, unrecognized as part of the city at all by its visitors and panegyrists, yet without whose denizens the hard readers could not read nor the high thinkers live. . . .

Descending to the streets, he went listlessly along till he arrived at an inn, and entered it. Here he drank several glasses of beer in rapid succession, and when he came out it was night. By the light of the flickering lamps he rambled home to supper, and had not long been sitting at table when his landlady brought up a letter that had just arrived for him. She laid it down as if impressed with a sense of its possible importance, and on looking at it Jude perceived that it bore the embossed stamp of one of the Colleges whose heads he had addressed. "*One*—at last!" cried Jude.

The communication was brief, and not exactly what he had expected; though it really was from the Master in person. It ran thus:

'BIBLIOLL COLLEGE.

'SIR,—I have read your letter with interest; and, judging from your description of yourself as a working-man, I venture to think that you will have a much better chance of success in life by remaining in your own sphere and sticking to your trade than by adopting any other course. That, therefore, is what I advise you to do. Yours faithfully,

'T. TETUPHENAY.

'To Mr. J. FAWLEY, Stone-mason.'

II

---

*Social Welfare
and the
Industrial Revolution*

OVERRIDING other considerations in the social history of early Victorian England, and in fact the focal point of most economic and political conflict, was the condition-of-England question. That is, quite simply, the widespread consciousness of division amounting to sickness in Victorian society. That division is exemplified by the subtitle of Disraeli's *Sybil*, published in 1845: *The Two Nations*. To divide England between "The Rich and The Poor" strikes us today as meaningless oversimplification, yet everywhere in Victorian literature we are confronted with the evidence that amazing disparity of income and privilege existed. That this polarization of society resulted in a sort of controversy over social welfare which persists to the present may be seen in the selections. Victorian England was the age of reform, certainly, but hardly any generalization beyond that can be made. The reform impulse, it is clear, stemmed in part from religion. Evangelicalism determined the tone of much controversy over social problems, and most Victorians felt the need for reform as a sort of moral imperative, whether they were conventionally religious or unconventionally agnostic. As the radical changes of industrialism led the Victorians to examine critically the structure of their society, they were forced into a set of attitudes that can be described only as paradoxical. They could not answer with any more clarity than we can the essential questions: what is the responsibility of society to its individual members, and how is that responsibility to be fulfilled?

The subjects apparently isolated in the title of this section are not in fact separable but may be conveniently symbolized by two events: the coming of the railroads, and the passage of the first Reform Bill. The coming of the railroad marks off quite clearly the old era from the new. The magnitude of the change which is described rather dispassionately by Smiles, and with some nostalgia by Thackeray, is conveyed most vividly by Dickens' portrayal of Staggs's Gardens: it is "the first shock of a great earthquake" which has "rent the whole neighbourhood to its centre." The reactions of the inhabitants of Staggs's Gardens, too, we may take as more representative than those of Thackeray. There the response of a single, very limited, class of people is made symbolic of that of the world at large, and it is compounded of three things: incredulity, fear and hope. The rapid growth of rail lines throughout the country—during 1836 and 1837 alone Parliament passed enabling legislation for thirty-nine new lines in Great Britain—rendered the new order all too credulous, and as it did so the attendant fear passed. But the railways also represented a significant application of technological skills to practical problems, and in the next decades were to account for marked growth throughout the economy. The eldest Toodle, we remember, is named "Biler," and Staggs's Gardens shows signs of a new life as well as the death of an old one. Yet the benefits cited by Smiles—fresh vegetables, cheap coals, quick travel—hardly contributed to a solution of recurrent economic crises in England in the first years of Victoria's reign. Large numbers of people—including the working class—in early Victorian England were no doubt better off financially than they had been; the natural impulse, however, was to try to discover why their lives were not better and more stable, but still subject to depression, even, sometimes, to the point of starvation. Mrs. Gaskell's *Mary Barton* depicts faithfully the situation of workers caught by economic forces much larger than they can comprehend. Their way of coping with it, joining the Chartist movement, seeking a political means to solution of an economic end, is characteristically Victorian.

Chartism was an ordered response by members of the working class to the failures of the reform of 1832. The Reform Act of that year genuinely altered the electorate as well as the distribution of seats in Parliament. Fifty-six of the rotten boroughs lost their representation entirely: Queen's Crawley, in Thackeray's *Vanity Fair*, with only four voting members in the constituency, is only a slight exaggeration of the usual case. Most important was that forty-two new seats were given to industrial towns, so that even though the franchise was not extended beyond the most highly paid skilled workmen, all had reason to hope that significant attention would be paid to their needs. The people as a whole had been involved in the movement for reform; popular agitation accounted in large part for its passage. But their condition did not improve.

The Chartism enunciated in the People's Charter, drawn up in 1838 by William Lovett and Francis Place, sought to remedy the defects of the Reform Act of 1832 by setting forth six demands. It called, first, for universal manhood suffrage. Of all the demands of the Chartists, this was the most important: without it, there was no insurance that Parliament would ever be responsive to their wishes. The Reform Parliament, they were convinced, had not done its job. In Carlyle's words, the Reform Members seemed "oblivious of their duty": "Surely Honourable Members ought to speak of the Condition-of-England question. . . ." But even the proposed radical extension of the franchise would have been ineffectual without the secret ballot, the second of the demands set forth by the People's Charter. One's conscience weakened considerably when open, public balloting might result in the loss of his job or home. These two demands, along with the third—for equal electoral districts—are clearly attempts to extend principles operative in the first Reform Bill. The latter three points in the Charter were a further effort to bring political power more directly to the hands of the working classes. They required, first, the abolition of the property qualification for those standing for Parliament; second, the payment of members; and finally, annual parliaments. All of these envision the entrance of members of "that great dumb toiling class" into Parliament—their eventual role as rulers of the country immediately responsible to a large, informed electorate.

The Chartists saw clearly that Parliament was to be the instrument of all change; their problem was to make it more responsive to the needs of the lower classes. The change they looked to ultimately was, of course, economic; but their response was political in nature and in motivation. Disappointment with the reforms of 1832, and with the harshness of the new Poor Law of 1834, was the objectification of their own frequently intense and cruel economic struggle. There were, it is sometimes said, as many chartisms as Chartist leaders, and this was especially so after Parliament in 1839 refused to receive the deputation carrying the first of the great Chartist petitions. This refusal brought about the temporary collapse of Chartism, and widened a split already implicit between its "physical force" and "moral force" wings. Yet the movement retained enough vitality to threaten the stability of England in 1842 and again most significantly in 1848, when "Physical Force" Feargus O'Connor, editor of the Chartist *Northern Star*, carried the movement as close to revolution as England was to come in the nineteenth century.

Chartism must be viewed, however, as only one of the courses of

Victorian controversy on critical economic and political issues. Another, equally important in the first decade of Victoria's reign, was the agitation for free trade, exemplified clearly in the Anti-Corn-Law League. Founded in the latter part of the 1830's by Richard Cobden and John Bright, the League set itself a limited, solely economic objective: to repeal the corn laws (restrictive tariffs on grain). Behind the movement, of course, was something much more important. The philosophy of laissez-faire, growing in strength in the half century since the publication of Adam Smith's *Wealth of Nations*, was to complete its triumph in the repeal of the corn laws in 1846 by Sir Robert Peel's Tory government. The League was to a marked degree the expression of the will of the Manchester school of economics. (Cobden was a Manchester merchant, the statistics collector and intellectual force of the League.) And Manchester itself, as a textile manufacturing center, was a symbol of the bourgeois. Unlike Chartism, lower class in its origins and expression, the Anti-Corn-Law League was firmly middle class. The droughts and crop failures that finally led Peel to reverse his earlier stand, and insist on the repeal of the corn laws even though it meant his end politically, might even be taken as expressions of the divine will that the days of the gentry as the locus of power be ended. For more than twenty years successive governments had decreased tariffs, but the corn laws remained as a symbol of a sort of veto power of the landed interests. Free-traders were persuaded that low taxes meant cheap bread, which meant low wages, and in turn resulted in low prices and good business.

Significantly, though, only a few years after free trade triumphed, one of the more important reforms directed at limiting the power of the manufacturer over his laborers was also passed. The Ten Hour Act, first introduced by Lord Shaftesbury in 1844 and passed in 1847, though it limited employment in factories to ten hours per day only for females and for boys under eighteen, had the practical effect of becoming the norm for all workers, and forced a system of shifts. This limitation on the right of contract, preceded by Shaftesbury's earlier Factory Act, and the 1842 Mines Act (excluding girls and women from underground work, and boys under the age of ten from the mines altogether), was to be followed shortly by more and more encroachments on property rights in the agitation for educational and public health reforms.

The great Victorian paradox, then—that in which political and social controversy finds its source—is that even while laissez-faire is supposedly the leading doctrine, the government takes an ever greater role in the social life and organizations of the time. And it does so, not despite the wishes of the middle classes, but in fulfillment of them. What we now identify as nineteenth-century liberalism, the prevailing attitude of the times, was composed of a variety of contradictions. In the selections presented here we may trace three kinds of attitudes toward the political and social problems of the Victorian era. The first of these is primarily emotional in its appeal, and is expressed by Carlyle, Ruskin, and Morris. The latter two are presented by Green and Mill, on philosophical grounds.

The emotionalism of Carlyle's rhetoric, which was to grow increasingly more furious through the *Latter-Day Pamphlets* of 1850, is in part the result of a deep conviction that industrialism is a perversion of the desirable relation between man and his employer, as well as that between the worker and his product. That conviction, implicit in *Chartism*, is the content of *Past and Present*. The microcosmic society headed by Abbot Samson is one in which the worker is content in his work because he has a sense of its usefulness—its relation to himself and to others like him. The sin of the machine is that the articles produced by the worker are no longer his, but the result of a process of which he is only a part. And since he receives no emotional satisfaction from work, only a minimal financial reward which is insufficient in a new and relatively expensive urban society, the gap between him and those who profit from his labor widens and develops into antagonism. The question was not whether some should have more and others less, but whether such marked disproportion should exist. The answer, for nearly all the Victorian reformers, was quite clearly "no." But neither Carlyle nor Ruskin, not even Morris, look to very specific reforms.

We usually think of Ruskin as little concerned in his early career with the problems posed by industrial society, yet the clear statement is there as early as 1851, in *The Stones of Venice*. "The Nature of Gothic," from that work, begins as an attempt to justify Gothic as being "not only the best, but the only *rational* architecture," but is quickly brought up short by the problem of the "perfection" of machine artistry. When noble irregularity is the express wish of God, then the precision of the machine is a signal of slavery. "The operative" himself becomes a machine—and to this "more than any other evil of the times" Ruskin traces the sickness of society: "It is not that men are ill fed, but that they have no pleasure in the work by which they make their bread, and therefore look to wealth as the only means of pleasure."

Granted, this occupies a relatively small space in "The Nature of Gothic," but it is a point essential to Ruskin's argument, and to our understanding of Ruskin as one of those Victorians on whom the prophetic mantle naturally devolved.

By the time of *Unto This Last* (1860) Ruskin was utterly convinced that "political economy"—by which he seems to mean, simply, the old Ricardian idea of man as a profit-seeking animal—was really the "dismal science" that Carlyle had described it as being. And it was so because it began with the wrong assumption, that the human being "is all skeleton." Political economy is incapable of realizing that mere self-interest requires a just price for work "rightly done." Yet something higher than self-interest, or the rules of expediency, governs human actions: a moral sense, whereby all of us know naturally the just act from the unjust one. Only when all recognize that justice includes "such affection as one man *owes* to another" will a right condition of things come about. Ruskin's assigning to the merchant one of the five most important roles in civilization increases the obligations of that class, since it, more than any other, involves large numbers of men. His duty is clear; he is invested with a distinctly paternal authority and responsibility.

Morris is clearly the follower of Ruskin in most things except prose style, but in "Art and Socialism" he looks forward to an end which Ruskin did not envision. He begins with nearly the same assumptions; the condition of England, he points out, is what might be expected after three centuries of commercial war. The landscape is blackened; machines have not lessened work—only made it meaningless. The standard of life is low, and by this Morris means not only the material gain which accrues from work but the spiritual solace of doing what is worth doing. Commerce, he points out, is a "mighty but monstrous system" which has overwhelmed England, has been elevated into a religion, and must be overturned by revolution. He holds out no clear plan to establish the new socialist state, but he is sure that the old one has failed to meet the claim all men may make on it: that it be satisfying. The closeness of the parallels among Carlyle, Ruskin, and Morris is not accidental; Ruskin and Carlyle were close associates, and the admiration of Morris for Ruskin is patent. That is not to say, however, that each learned from his earlier contemporary. Some influence was doubtless at work, but they shared a characteristic response to the social problems of their time which was highly emotional in its fervor and ultimately moral in import.

A more restrained, intellectual attitude is characteristic of both John Stuart Mill and Thomas Hill Green. Whereas Carlyle, Ruskin, and Morris look for moral alteration by a wide variety of means, both Mill and Green are concerned with determining the conditions and limitations of interference by the state in the processes of its society. Neither would deny entirely, perhaps, Ruskin's charge that political economy is wide of the mark in its assumptions about the nature of men.

Principles of Political Economy was published in 1848, and by that time Mill had moved a considerable distance from the orthodox Benthamism of his youth. Benthamism had been a free-trade philosophy, but freedom, as Mill was to point out in *On Liberty* in 1859, does not consist necessarily in leaving the individual alone to pursue his own ends. The greatest happiness for the greatest number sometimes involves deliberate legislative measures. In the selection presented here, Mill is primarily concerned with distinguishing between the necessary and the optional functions of government, and the result of his exploration is the assertion that no clear definition is possible. Very few functions might be said to be absolutely necessary, yet we all recognize that they are desirable; we admit them, and as we do we must also admit that interference by government is justified only on grounds of "general expediency." Only one kind of intervention cannot be tolerated, and that is anything which "concerns only the life . . . of the individual, and does not affect the interest of others. . . ." Mill does not mean that the individual has complete license, but that prohibitions may only be such as are justifiable in terms of the "general conscience." When government does not restrict the individual, but instead uses its powers to provide "means for fulfilling a certain end, leaving individuals free to avail themselves of different means," then it acts in its most responsible fashion.

The objections to governmental action which Mill explores in *Principles of Political Economy* are by now familiar to all of us—the growth in size and complexity of government, through bureaus and boards; the increase of its power and influence; the superior efficacy of private enterprise. "Laissez-faire," he tells us, "should be the general practice. . . ." But if "every departure from it . . . is a certain evil," it is also true that a "great good" may require intervention. Thomas Hill Green, in "Freedom of Contract," by redefining freedom, justifies more plainly than Mill the rights of government. True freedom consists not in the state of nature, but in society, where men join together to achieve common objectives. It can be enjoyed or exercised only by the security given the individual by society—or by his fellowmen. And it is in the interest of the individual to grant to others that which he himself possesses. Thus all the guarantees by society of individual rights, freedom of contract, property rights—have the ultimate purpose of contributing to "that equal development of the facilities which is the highest good for all." In a sense Green skirts a direct confrontation with Mill: it is not necessarily advisable, he says, "for the state to do all which it is justified in doing." But it is justified in doing a great many more things than Mill might have advised, because "we must take men as we find them."

Taking men as we find them might also, however, lead to other conclusions about the role of government. For the Social Darwinists, for example, true freedom consists only in the state of nature. Thus Herbert Spencer (only the most prominent among many of his persuasion) had argued against that most characteristic Victorian institution: poor relief. "A government," he says, "cannot rightly do anything more than protect." ("Protect" here does not mean economic protection, but rather those means by which society guarantees to all men equally their right to do all that they will.) Since poor laws take away from some to guarantee to others what they have not gained by their own efforts, such legislation is an intolerable incursion on individual rights.

That Spencer should feel so, given the system of poor relief in effect in 1850, is evidence of the distance between numbers of Victorians on important social questions. The Poor Law Amendment Act of 1834, built on laws extending back to the reign of Elizabeth, was looked on by its sponsors (mainly utilitarian) as an achievement as significant as the Reform Bill of 1832. It attempted to regularize the systems of relief, by appointing a Board of Commissioners, and to insure that the able-bodied poor (not the aged or infirm) earn their relief in a workhouse—hardly a socialistic scheme, one may say. And although the new law did succeed to some extent in alleviating the worst sufferings of the poor, it fell far short of its promises and was, as we have mentioned, one of the many causes of Chartism. Yet even this scheme Spencer objected to as unwarranted interference which stultified the very feeling of benevolence that government should strive to stimulate. (Voluntary support—"charity"—was one of the catchwords of the Social Darwinists.) Progress (or evolution) means a struggle within only a few ground rules set down by society.

Americans in particular, perhaps, ought to understand the conflict in

Victorian society. One or another variant of Spencer's Social Darwinism has for a long time—since the days of the "robber barons" certainly—been a popular mode in American thought. And, like the Victorians, we regard material wealth as the most certain proof of the goodness and justice of our actions; yet we remain critically aware, as they were, of our obligation to aid by some means those who—for whatever reason—have not struggled as successfully.

8.   REFORM BILLS:
Electoral Reform

The exhaustive *History of the English People in the Nineteenth Century*, by Elie Halévy (6 vols., Eng. trans. pub. 1924–48; reissued 1961), is the best single work in the field and is unlikely ever to be superseded. More restricted in its scope, but a sound source, is David Thomson's *England in the Nineteenth Century* (1950). Documents of the kind abstracted here are not readily available; for a fuller representation see *English Historical Documents*, under the general editorship of David C. Douglas. Of the volumes projected, those concerned with Victorian documents are XI and XII (Part I; Part II not yet completed).

The first Reform Bill, in 1832, though its provisions now appear to us rather restrictive, precipitated considerable controversy, and was under consideration in one form or another for more than a year before its final passage. Its passage represents a significant, though relatively slight, lessening of the influence of the landed interests.

Whereas it is expedient to take effectual measures for correcting divers abuses that have long prevailed in the choice of members to serve in the Commons House of Parliament, to deprive many inconsiderable places of the right of returning members, to grant such privilege to large, populous and wealthy towns, to increase the number of Knights of the Shire, to extend the elective franchise to many of H.M.'s subjects who have not heretofore enjoyed the same, and to diminish the expense of elections; be it therefore enacted . . . that each of the boroughs enumerated in the schedule marked (A.) to this Act annexed . . . shall from and after the end of this present Parliament cease to return any member or members to serve in Parliament.

II. . . . Each of the boroughs enumerated in the schedule marked (B.) to this Act annexed . . . shall from and after the end of this present Parliament return one member and no more to serve in Parliament.

III. . . . Each of the places named in the schedule marked (C.) to this Act annexed . . . shall for the purposes of this Act be a borough, and shall as such borough include the place or places respectively which shall be comprehended within the boundaries of such borough, as such boundaries shall be settled and described by an Act to be passed for that purpose in this present Parliament, which Act, when passed, shall be deemed and taken to be part of this Act as fully and effectually as if the same were incorporated herewith; and that each of the said boroughs named in the said schedule (C.) shall from and after the end of this present Parliament return two members to serve in Parliament.

IV. . . . Each of the places named in the schedule marked (D.) to this Act annexed . . . shall for the purposes of this Act be a borough . . . and shall . . . from and after the end of this present Parliament return one member to serve in Parliament. . . .

XIX. . . . Every male person of full age, and not subject to any legal incapacity, who shall be seised at law or in equity of any lands or tenements of copyhold or any other tenure whatever except freehold, for his own life, or for the life of another or for any lives whatsoever, or for any larger estate of the clear yearly value of not less than £10 over and above all rents and charges payable out of or in respect of the same, shall be entitled to vote in the election of a Knight or Knights of the Shire to serve in any future Parliament for the County, or for the Riding, parts, or division of the County, in which such lands or tenements shall be respectively situate.

XX. . . . Every male of full age, and not subject to any legal incapacity, who shall be entitled, either as lessee or assignee, to any lands or tenements, whether of freehold or of any other tenure whatever, for the unexpired residue, whatever it may be, of any term originally created for a period of not less than 60 years, (whether determinable on a life, or lives, or not) of the clear yearly value of not less than £10 over and above all rents and charges payable out of or in respect of the same, or for the unexpired residue, whatever it may be, of any term originally created for a period of not less than 20 years (whether determinable on a life or lives, or not) of the clear yearly value of not less than £50 over and above all rents and charges payable out of or in respect of the same, or who shall occupy as tenant any lands or tenements for which he shall be *bona fide* liable to a yearly rent of not less than £50, shall be entitled to vote in the election of a Knight or Knights of the Shire to serve in any future Parliament for the County, or for the Riding, parts or division of the County in which such lands or tenements shall be respectively situate; provided always, that no person, being only a sub-lessee, or the assignee of any under-lease, shall have a right to vote in such election in respect of any such term of 60 years or 20 years as aforesaid, unless he shall be in the actual occupation of the premises. . . .

XXIV. . . . Notwithstanding anything hereinbefore contained, no person shall be entitled to vote in the election of a Knight or Knights of the Shire to serve in any future Parliament in respect of his estate or interest as a freeholder in any house, warehouse, counting-house, shop or other building, occupied by himself, or in any land occupied by himself together with any house, warehouse, counting-house, shop or other building, such house, warehouse, counting-house, shop or other building being, either separately or jointly with the land so occupied therewith, of such value as would, according to the provisions hereinafter contained, confer on him the right of voting for any city or borough, whether he shall or shall not have actually acquired the right to vote for such city or borough in respect thereof. . . .

XXVI. . . . Notwithstanding anything hereinbefore contained, no person shall be entitled to vote in the election of a Knight or Knights of the Shire to serve in any future Parliament unless he shall have been duly registered according to the provisions hereinafter contained; and that no person shall be so registered in any year in respect of his estate or interest in any lands or tenements, as a freeholder, copyholder, customary tenant, or tenant in ancient demesne, unless he shall have been in the actual possession thereof, or in the receipt of the rents and profits thereof for his own use, for six calendar months at least next previous to the last day of July in such year, which said period of six calendar months shall be sufficient, any statute to the contrary notwithstanding; and that no person shall be so registered in any year, in respect of any lands or tenements held by him as such lessee or assignee, or as such occupier and tenant as aforesaid, unless he shall have been in the actual possession thereof, or in the receipt of the rents and profits thereof for his own use, as the case may require, for twelve calendar months next previous to the last day of July in such year: provided always that where any lands or tenements, which would otherwise entitle the owner, holder or occupier thereof to vote in any such election, shall come to any person, at any time within such respective periods of six or twelve calendar months, by descent, succession, marriage, marriage settlement, devise or promotion to any benefice in a Church, or by promotion to any office, such person shall be entitled in respect thereof to have his name inserted as a voter in the election of a Knight or Knights of the Shire in the lists then next to be made by virtue of this Act as hereinafter mentioned, and, upon his being duly registered according to the provisions hereinafter contained, to vote in such election.

XXVII. . . . In every city or borough which shall return a member or members to serve in any future Parliament, every male person of full age, and not subject to any legal incapacity, who shall occupy, within such city or borough, or within any place sharing in the election for such city or borough, as owner or tenant, any house, warehouse, counting-house, shop or other building, being either separately or jointly with any land within such city, borough, or place occupied therewith by him as owner, or occupied therewith by him as tenant under the same landlord, of the clear yearly value of not less than £10, shall, if duly registered according to the provisions hereinafter contained, be entitled to vote in the election of a member or members to serve in any future Parliament for such city or borough: provided always that no such person shall be so registered in any year unless he shall have occupied such premises as aforesaid for twelve calendar months next previous to the last day of July in such year, nor unless such person, where such premises are situate in any parish or township in which there shall be a rate for the relief of the poor, shall have been rated in respect of such premises to all rates for the relief of the poor in such parish or township made during the time of such his occupation so required as aforesaid, nor unless such person shall have paid, on or before the 20th day of July in such year, all the poor's rates and assessed taxes which shall have become payable from him in respect of such premises previously to the 6th day of April then next preceding: provided also that no such person shall be so registered in any year unless he shall have resided for six calendar months next previous to the last day of July in such year within the city or borough, or within the place sharing in the election for the city or borough, in respect of which city, borough or place respectively he shall be entitled to vote, or within seven statute miles thereof or of any part thereof. . . .

XXIX. . . . Where any premises as aforesaid, in any such city or borough, or in any place sharing in the election therewith, shall be jointly occupied by more persons than one as owners or tenants, each of such joint occupiers shall, subject to the conditions hereinbefore contained as to persons occupying premises in any such city, borough or place, be entitled to vote in the election for such city or borough, in respect of the premises so jointly occupied, in case the clear yearly value of such premises shall be of an amount which, when divided by the number of such occupiers, shall give a sum of not less than £10 for each and every such occupier, but not otherwise. . . .

XXXV. Provided nevertheless . . . that notwithstanding anything hereinbefore contained, no person shall be entitled to vote in the election of a member or members to serve in any future Parliament for any city or borough (other than a city or town being a County of itself, in the election for which freeholders or burgage tenants have a right to vote as hereinbefore mentioned) in respect of any estate or interest in any burgage tenement or freehold which shall have been acquired by such person since the 1st day of March 1831, unless the same shall have come to or been acquired by such person, since that day, and previously to the passing of this Act, by descent, succession, marriage, marriage settlement, devise or promotion to any benefice in a church, or by promotion to any office.

XXXVI. . . . No person shall be entitled to be registered in any year as a voter in the election of a member or members to serve in any future Parliament for any city or borough who shall within twelve calendar months next previous to the last day of July in such year have received parochial relief or other alms which by the law of Parliament now disqualify from voting in the election of members to serve in Parliament.

XXXVII. And whereas it is expedient to form a register of all persons entitled to vote in the election of a Knight or Knights of the Shire to serve in any future Parliament, and that for the purpose of forming such register the overseers of every parish and township should annually make out lists in the manner hereinafter mentioned; be it therefore enacted, that the overseers of the poor of every parish and township shall on the 20th day of June in the present and in every succeeding year cause to be fixed on or near the doors of all the churches and chapels within such parish or township, or if there be no church or chapel therein, then to be fixed in some public and conspicuous situation within the same respectively, a notice according to the form numbered 1, in the schedule (H.) to this Act annexed, requiring all persons who may be entitled to vote in the election of a Knight . . . of the Shire to serve in any future Parliament, in respect of any property situate wholly or in part in such parish or township, to deliver or transmit to the said overseers on or before the 20th day of July in the present and in every succeeding year a notice of their claim as such voters according to the form numbered 2, in the said schedule (H.) or to the like effect: provided always, that after the formation of the register to be made in each year, as hereinafter mentioned, no person whose name shall be upon such register for the time being shall be required thereafter to make any such claim as aforesaid, as long as he shall retain the same qualification, and continue in the same place of abode described in such register.

XXXVIII. . . . The overseer of the poor of every parish and township shall on or before the last day of July in the present year make out or cause to be made out, according to the form numbered 3, in the said schedule (H.) an alphabetical list of all persons who shall claim as aforesaid to be inserted in such list as voters in the election of a Knight or Knights of the Shire, to serve for the County, or for the Riding, parts, or division of the County wherein such parish or township lies . . . and that the said overseers shall on or before the last day of July in every succeeding year make out or cause to be made out a like list, containing the names of all persons who shall be upon the register for the time being as such voters, and also the names of all persons who shall claim as aforesaid to be inserted in such last-mentioned list as such voters: and in every list so to be made by the overseers as aforesaid the christian name and surname of every person shall be written at full length, together with the place of his abode, the nature of his qualification, and the local or other description of such lands or tenements, as the same are respectively set forth in his claim to vote, and the name of the occupying tenant, if stated in such claim: and the said overseers if they shall have reasonable cause to believe that any person so claiming as aforesaid, or whose name shall appear in the register for the time being, is not entitled to vote in the election of a Knight or Knights of the Shire for the County, or for the Riding, parts or division of the County in which their parish or township is situate, shall have power to add the words "objected to" opposite the name of every such person on the margin of such list; and the said overseers shall sign such list, and shall cause a sufficient number of copies of such list to be written or printed, and to be fixed on or near the doors of all the churches and chapels within their parish or township, or if there be no church or chapel therein, then to be fixed up in some public and conspicuous situation, within the same respectively, on the two Sundays next after such list shall have been made; and the said overseers shall likewise keep a true copy of such list, to be perused by any person without payment of any fee, at all reasonable hours during the two first weeks after such list shall have been made. . . .

The second Reform Act of 1867 for all practical purposes completed the process begun in 1832. It was entitled the Representation of the People Act. As the following selection makes clear, the act, though it did not provide specifically for universal manhood suffrage, expanded the Victorian electorate to include the vast majority of the male population.

. . . Every Man shall, in and after the Year One thousand eight hundred and sixty-eight, be entitled to be registered as a Voter, and, when registered, to vote for a Member or Members to serve in Parliament for a Borough, who is qualified as follows; (that is to say,)

1. Is of full Age, and not subject to any legal Incapacity; and
2. Is on the last Day of July in any Year, and has during the whole of the preceding Twelve Calendar Months been, an Inhabitant Occupier, as Owner or Tenant, of any Dwelling House within the Borough; and
3. Has during the Time of such Occupation been rated as an ordinary Occupier in respect of the Premises so occupied by him within the Borough to all Rates (if any) made for the Relief of the Poor in respect of such Premises; and
4. Has on or before the Twentieth Day of July in the same year *bona fide* paid an equal Amount in the Pound to that payable by other ordinary Occupiers in respect of all Poor Rates that have become payable by him in respect of the said Premises up to the preceding Fifth Day of January:

Provided that no Man shall under this Section be entitled to be registered as a Voter by reason of his being a joint Occupier of any Dwelling House.

4. Every Man shall, in and after the Year One thousand eight hundred and sixty-eight, be entitled to be registered as a Voter, and, when registered, to vote for a Member or Members to serve in Parliament for a Borough, who is qualified as follows; (that is to say,)

1. Is of full Age, and not subject to any legal Incapacity; and
2. As a Lodger has occupied in the same Borough separately and as sole Tenant for the Twelve Months preceding the last Day of July in any Year the same Lodgings, such Lodgings being part of one and the same Dwelling House, and of a clear yearly Value, if let unfurnished, of Ten Pounds or upwards; and

3. Has resided in such Lodgings during the Twelve Months immediately preceding the last day of July, and has claimed to be registered as a Voter at the next ensuing Registration of Voters.

5. Every Man shall, in and after the Year One thousand eight hundred and sixty-eight, be entitled to be registered as a Voter, and, when registered, to vote for a Member or Members to serve in Parliament for a County, who is qualified as follows: (that is to say,)

1. Is of full Age, and not subject to any legal Incapacity, and is seised at Law or in Equity of any Lands or Tenements of Freehold, Copyhold, or any other Tenure whatever, for his own Life, or for the Life of another, or for any Lives whatsoever, or for any larger Estate of the clear yearly Value of not less than Five Pounds over and above all Rents and Charges payable out of or in respect of the same, or who is entitled, either as Lessee or Assignee, to any Lands or Tenements of Freehold or of any other Tenure whatever, for the unexpired Residue, whatever it may be, of any Term originally created for a Period of not less than Sixty Years (whether determinable on a Life or Lives or not), of the clear yearly Value of not less than Five Pounds over and above all Rents and Charges payable out of or in respect of the same:

Provided that no Person shall be registered as a Voter under this Section unless he has complied with the Provisions of the Twenty-sixth Section of . . . [The Reform Act of 1832, see p. 100.]

6. Every Man shall, in and after the Year One thousand eight hundred and sixty-eight, be entitled to be registered as a Voter, and, when registered, to vote for a Member or Members to serve in Parliament for a County, who is qualified as follows; (that is to say,)

1. Is of full Age, and not subject to any legal Incapacity; and

2. Is on the last Day of July in any Year, and has during the Twelve Months immediately preceding been the Occupier, as Owner or Tenant, of Lands or Tenements within the County of the rateable Value of Twelve Pounds or upwards; and

3. Has during the Time of such Occupation been rated in respect to the Premises so occupied by him to all Rates (if any) made for the Relief of the Poor in respect of the said Premises; and

4. Has on or before the Twentieth Day of July in the same Year paid all Poor Rates that have become payable by him in respect of the said Premises up to the preceding Fifth Day of January. . . .

The Ballot Act of 1872 represents the achievement of one of the most important demands of the Chartist movement. No doubt it contributed as much as the broadening of the electorate to the formation of a more truly representative government in Victorian England.

. . . 2. In the case of a poll at an election the votes shall be given by ballot. The ballot of each voter shall consist of a paper (in this Act called a ballot paper) showing the names and description of the candidates. Each ballot paper shall have a number printed on the back, and shall have attached a counterfoil with the same number printed on the face. At the time of voting, the ballot paper shall be marked on both sides with an official mark, and delivered to the voter within the polling station, and the number of such voter on the register of voters shall be marked on the counterfoil, and the voter having secretly marked his vote on the paper, and folded it up so as to conceal his vote, shall place it in a closed box in the presence of the officer presiding at the polling station (in this Act called "the presiding officer") after having shown to him the official mark at the back.

Any ballot paper which has not on its back the official mark, or on which votes are given to more candidates than the voter is entitled to vote for, or on which anything, except the said number on the back, is written or marked by which the voter can be identified, shall be void and not counted.

After the close of the poll the ballot boxes shall be sealed up, so as to prevent the introduction of additional ballot papers, and shall be taken charge of by the returning officer, and that officer shall, in the presence of such agents, if any, of the candidates as may be in attendance, open the ballot boxes, and ascertain the result of the poll by counting the votes given to each candidate, and shall forthwith declare to be elected the candidates or candidate to whom the majority of votes have been given, and return their names to the Clerk of the Crown in Chancery. The decision of the returning officer as to any question arising in respect of any ballot paper shall be final, subject to reversal on petition questioning the election or return.

Where an equality of votes is found to exist between any candidates at an election for a county or borough, and the addition of a vote would entitle any of such candidates to be declared elected, the returning officer, if a registered elector of such county or borough, may give such additional vote, but shall not in any other case be entitled to vote at an election for which he is returning officer.

9. SMILES:

The Railway and Progress

Samuel Smiles (1812–1904) has since his death been almost entirely neglected aside from references to his famous *Self-Help*. The chief of his works, which have never been collected, is the *Lives of the Engineers* (5 vols., 1874). Shortly after his death T. B. Green published the only bio-graphy, *The Life and Work of Dr. Samuel Smiles* (1904); it should be read in conjunction with Smiles' *Autobiography* (1905).

The selection is from *The Life of George Stephenson, Railway Engineer*, Chapter XXV, "Advance of Public Opinion in Favour of Railways." Stephenson may be taken, as Smiles makes clear, as the most exemplary of a breed of men who were to revolutionize England's industry in the nineteenth century.

The Grand Junction Railway was an important link in the new system of communication between London and the manufacturing districts of Lancashire. This line was projected as early as the year 1824, at the time when the Liverpool and Manchester Railway was under discussion. Mr. Stephenson then published a report on the subject. Surveys were made, and plans were deposited. The canal pro-prietors and landowners opposed the bill, and it was thrown out on standing orders. The application was renewed in 1826, with no better result, the local opposition proving too strong for the promoters; and they at length determined to wait the issue of the Liverpool and Man-chester project. In 1830 the surveys of a new line, in two divisions, were made by Mr. Locke and Mr. Rastrick, under the direction of Mr. Stephenson; but the bill for the promotion of the northern portion having been rejected, that for the latter portion was withdrawn; and the act authorising the construction of the Grand Junction Railway was not obtained until the session of 1833. By that time the promoters of railways had acquired the art of "conciliating" the landlords. The process was a very expensive one, but the bill was carried without parliamentary opposition, and the works were immediately proceeded with.

Notwithstanding the decisive success of the Liverpool and Manchester project, the prejudices against railways and railway-travelling
continued very strong. Their advantages were already fully known to
the inhabitants of those districts through which they passed, for they
had experienced their practical benefits in substantial reductions in the
price of coal, in the carriage of merchandise of all kinds, and in the
cheap and rapid transit of their persons from place to place. The Liverpool and Manchester Railway was regarded as a national wonder from
the first; and strangers resorted to Lancashire from all quarters, to
witness the trains and to travel in the wake of the locomotive. To
witness a railway train some five-and-twenty years ago was an event in
one's life.

But people at a distance did not see railways and railway travelling
in the same light. The farther off, and the greater the ignorance which
prevailed as to their modes of working, the greater, of course, was the
popular alarm. The towns of the south only followed the example of
Northampton when they howled down the railways. It was proposed
to carry a line through Kent, by the populous county town of Maidstone. But a public meeting was held to oppose the project; and the
railway had not a single supporter amongst the townspeople. The railway, when at length formed through Kent, passed Maidstone at a
distance; but in a few years the Maidstone burgesses, like those of
Northampton, became clamorous for a railway, and a branch was
formed for their accommodation. Again, in a few years, they com-
plained that the route was circuitous, as they had compelled it to be;
consequently another and shorter line was formed to bring Maidstone
into more direct communication with the metropolis. In like manner
the London and Bristol (afterwards the Great Western) Railway was
vehemently opposed by the people of the towns through which the line
was projected to pass; and when the bill was thrown out by the Lords—
after 30,000*l.* had been expended by the promoters,—the inhabitants of
Eton assembled under the presidency of the Marquis of Chandos, to
rejoice and congratulate themselves and the country on the defeat of
the measure. . . .

Railways had thus, like most other great social improvements, to
force their way against the fierce antagonism of united ignorance and
prejudice. Public-spirited obstructives were ready to choke the invention at its birth, on the ground of the general good. The forcible
invasion of property—the intrusion of public roads into private

domains—the noise and nuisance caused by locomotives, and the danger of fire to the adjoining property, were dwelt upon *ad nauseam*. The lawlessness of navvies was a source of great terror to quiet villages. Then the breed of horses would be destroyed; country innkeepers would be ruined; posting towns would become depopulated; the turnpike roads would be deserted; and the institution of the English Stage-coach, with its rosy gilled coachman and guard, known to every buxom landlady at roadside country inns, would be destroyed for ever. Fox-covers and game-preserves would be interfered with; agricultural communication destroyed; land thrown out of cultivation; landowners and farmers alike reduced to beggary; the poor rates increased in consequence of the numbers of labourers thrown out of employment by the railways; and all this in order that Liverpool, Manchester, and Birmingham manufacturers, merchants, and cotton-spinners, might establish a monstrous monopoly in railroads! However, there was always this consolation to wind up with,—that the canals would beat the railroads, and that, even when the latter were made, the public would not use them, nor trust either their persons or their goods to the risks of railway accidents and explosions. They would thus prove only monuments of the folly of their projectors, whom they must inevitably involve in ruin and disaster.

It is but just to add, that there were many men of intelligence, neither prejudiced nor personally interested in opposing railways, who anticipated their ultimate failure. Mr. Macculloch, in his "Dictionary of Commerce," article "Railway," published some years after the opening of the Liverpool and Manchester line, said: "We doubt much whether there be many more situations in the kingdom where it would be prudent to establish a railway." And a writer in *Frazer's Magazine* for April, 1838, shortly before the opening of the entire line of railway communication between London, Manchester, and Liverpool, writing of the Stockton and Darlington line, observed: "The horse has since given way to inanimate power, which, after all, will be laid aside from the enormous expense of keeping the engines and roads in repair. . . . Since a greater speed (than fifteen miles an hour for passengers and seven miles for goods) would eat up all the profits, it is evident that the greater velocity of the Fire-snorters required at present, will eventually, like the dogs of Actæon, destroy their masters."

Sanitary objections were also urged in opposition to railways, and many wise doctors strongly inveighed against tunnels. Sir Anthony Carlisle insisted that "tunnels would expose healthy people to colds, catarrhs, and consumption." The noise, the darkness, and the dangers of tunnel travelling were depicted in all their horrors. Worst of all, however, was "the destruction of the atmospheric air," as Dr. Lardner termed it. Elaborate calculations were made by that gentleman to prove that the provision of ventilating shafts would be altogether insufficient to prevent the dangers arising from the combustion of coke, producing carbonic acid gas, which, in large quantities, was fatal to life. He showed, for instance, that in the proposed Box Tunnel, on the Great Western Railway, the passage of a load of 100 tons would deposit about 3090 lbs. of noxious gases, incapable of supporting life! Here was an uncomfortable prospect of suffocation for passengers between London and Bristol. But steps were adopted to allay these formidable sources of terror. Solemn documents, in the form of certificates, were got up and published, signed by several of the most distinguished physicians of the day, attesting the perfect wholesomeness of tunnels, and the purity of the air in them. Perhaps they went further than was necessary in alleging, what certainly subsequent experience has not verified, that the atmosphere of the tunnel was "dry, of an agreeable temperature, and free from smell." Mr. Stephenson declared his conviction that a tunnel twenty miles long could be worked safely, and without more danger to life than a railway in the open air; but, at the same time, he admitted that tunnels were nuisances, which he endeavoured to avoid wherever practicable.

When it was found that railways must and would be made, and that all the evidence brought to bear against them was likely to fail, claimants for compensation made their appearance in great numbers, and on all conceivable grounds. Claimants for compensation on account of residential injury were the most numerous and exorbitant. There were claims for injury to building land, injury to farms, and injury to fields. Immense claims for "severance" were set up, and often more money was extorted for cutting off the corner of a field than the entire field was worth. One ingenious claimant demanded compensation on the ground that his cows would give less milk in consequence of the formation of the railway; another, because his horses would be frightened at the noise of the trains, and kick each other. Then bridges, occupation roads, level crossings, were demanded—only to be sold again, in many cases, to the Company for substantial considerations.

Meanwhile, the legislature took no directing part in the matter; but allowed the public to scramble for railways as they best could. The private companies, to whom the extension of the railway system was abandoned by the government, were not only met with preliminary obstructions in all ways; but when they reached Parliament with their bills, they were mercilessly robbed. The costs of obtaining railway bills were frightful,—fees to parliamentary officials, fees to parliamentary agents and counsel, fees to witnesses, and other enormous expenses incident to the protracted contests conducted before the committees of both Houses. Thus, the London and Birmingham Act cost 72,868*l.*; the Great Western, 88,710*l.*; and the Acts of some railways of more recent date cost much greater sums. More money was thus wasted in parliamentary expenses than would have sufficed to form an efficient system of trunk lines throughout the kingdom.

The *vis inertiæ* of the legislature was, however, eventually overcome; and, by dint of repeated pressure from without, carried on at great cost, the railway system was gradually extended. Parliament could not disregard the urgent and repeated petitions of the commercial towns of the north for improved postal communication. But the legislature was dragged on; it did not by any means aspire to guide or to direct. It even lagged far behind. Whilst associations of private persons, mostly belonging to the trading classes, were endeavouring to force on the adoption of railways, the English Lords and Commons,—unlike the government of Belgium, which early adopted the railway system,— occupied themselves in discussing the improvement of the turnpike-roads, and in voting rewards to Mr. Macadam and his sons. The country gentlemen determined to mend and patch up the old roads as well as they could. The macadamised system was fast becoming effete, but they did not know it. The surprising performances of the "Rocket" at Rainhill* opened their eyes to the significance of the locomotive engine; but they could not yet rise above the idea of a macadamised road, and hence they hailed the proposal to apply the locomotive to turnpikes. In the year 1831 the House of Commons appointed a committee to inquire into and report upon—not the railway system—but the applicability of the steam carriage to travelling on common roads. Before this committee, Mr. Trevethick, Mr. Goldsworthy Gurney, Nathaniel Ogle, and other supporters of the common-road system, were examined; and the committee were so satisfied with their evidence that

* In October, 1829, George Stephenson's locomotive, "Rocket," won a competition against four other locomotives and at the same time changed men's minds about the supposed advantages of a fixed-engine system. The "Rocket" hauled thirteen tons seventy miles at an average speed of fifteen miles per hour. This speed was "three times greater than one of the judges of the competition had declared to be the limit of possibility."

they reported decidedly in favour of the road-locomotive system. Though Railways were ignored, yet the steam carriage was recognised.

But there are limits to the wisdom even of a parliamentary committee. Although many trials of steam carriages were made by Sir Charles Dance, Mr. Hancock, Mr. Gurney, Sir James Anderson, and others, and though the House of Commons had reported in their favour, Mr. Stephenson's first verdict pronounced upon them many years before— that they could never successfully compete with locomotive engines on railroads, nor even with horses on common roads—was fully borne out by the result; for the steam-carriage projects, after ruining many speculators and experimenters, were at length abandoned in favour of railways, which extended in all directions. Another attempt was, however, made in 1836, in favour of the common-road locomotive system; when a bill was passed through the House of Commons to repeal the acts imposing prohibitory tolls on steam carriages. When the bill went into the Lords, it was referred to a committee, who took evidence on the subject at great length. Many witnesses were examined in support of steam carriages, including Mr. Gurney, Mr. Hancock, and others, who strongly testified to their economy and efficiency.

Their lordships then called before them Mr. Stephenson, whose experience as a locomotive engineer entitled him to be heard on such a subject. His evidence was so strong and conclusive, that it could not fail to have great weight with their lordships, and, in their report to the House, they said, "It appears that some experienced engineers, after a careful examination of the expense attendant upon it (the common-road steam carriage), have been induced to abandon all hopes of its success as a profitable undertaking. It is probable, therefore, that any encouragement on the part of the legislature would only give rise to wild speculations, ruinous to those engaging in them, and to experiments dangerous to the public." However unjust the prohibitory tolls on steam carriages might be, there is no doubt that the decision of the Committee as to the impracticability of the steam-carriage system was correct; and that there was no hope of its ever competing successfully on common roads with the locomotive railway. The highest speed which the promoters promised was ten miles an hour; but this would no longer satisfy the public requirements, now that the Liverpool and Manchester Railway had demonstrated the practicability and the safety of regular travelling at thirty and forty miles an hour. The House of Commons' prophecy that "a railway could never enter into successful competition with a canal, and that, even with the best locomotive engine, the average rate would be but three miles and a half per hour," was now laughed at, because so ludicrously at variance with every-day facts.

The opening of the great main line of railroad communication between London, Liverpool, and Manchester, in 1838, shortly proved the fallaciousness of the rash prophecies promulgated by the opponents of railways. The proprietors of the canals were astounded by the fact that, notwithstanding the immense traffic conveyed by rail, their own traffic and receipts continued to increase; and that, in common with other interests, they fully shared in the expansion of trade and commerce which had been so effectually promoted by the extension of the railway system. The cattle-owners were equally amazed to find the price of horse-flesh increasing with the extension of railways, and that the number of coaches running to and from the new railway stations gave employment to a greater number of horses than under the old stage-coach system. Those who had prophesied the decay of the metropolis, and the ruin of the suburban cabbage-growers, in consequence of the approach of railways to London, were also disappointed. For, whilst the new roads let citizens out of London, they let country people in. Their action, in this respect, was centripetal as well as centrifugal. Tens of thousands who had never seen the metropolis could now visit it expeditiously and cheaply. And Londoners who had never visited the country, or but rarely, were enabled, at little cost of time or money, to see green fields and clear blue skies, far from the smoke and bustle of town. If the dear suburban-grown cabbages became depreciated in value, there were truck-loads of fresh-grown country cabbages to make amends for the loss: in this case, the "partial evil" was a far more general good. The food of the metropolis became rapidly improved, especially in the supply of wholesome meat and vegetables. And then the price of coals—an article which, in this country, is as indispensable as daily food to all classes—was greatly reduced. What a blessing to the metropolitan poor is described in this single fact! And George Stephenson was not only the inventor of the system of internal communication, by which coals were made cheaper in London, but he was also the originator of the now gigantic trade in coal conveyed to the metropolis by railway. From the first, he discovered its value, doubtless with a shrewd estimate of its profits. . . .

The prophecies of ruin and disaster to landlords and farmers were equally confounded by the opening of the London and Birmingham

Railway. The agricultural communications, so far from being "destroyed," as had been predicted, were immensely improved. The farmers were enabled to buy their coals, lime and manure, for less money; whilst they obtained a readier access to the best markets for their stock and farm produce.

Landlords also found that they could get higher rents for farms situated near a railway, than at a distance from one. Hence they became clamorous for "sidings." They felt it to be a grievance to be placed at a distance from a station. After a railway had been once opened, not a landlord would consent to have the line taken from him. Owners who had fought the promoters before Parliament, and compelled them to pass their domains at a distance, at a vastly increased expense in tunnels and deviations, now petitioned for branches and nearer station accommodation. Those who held property near the large towns, and had extorted large sums as compensation for the anticipated deterioration in the value of their building land, found a new demand for it springing up at greatly advanced prices. Land was now advertised for sale, with the attraction of being "near a railway station."

The prediction that, even if railways were made, the public would not use them, was also completely falsified by the results. The ordinary mode of fast travelling for the middle classes had heretofore been by mail coach and stage coach. Those who could not afford to pay the high prices charged for such conveyances went by waggon, and the poorer classes trudged on foot. George Stephenson was wont to say that he hoped to see the day when it would be cheaper for a poor man to travel by railway than to walk; and not many years passed before his expectation was fulfilled. In no country in the world is Time worth more money than in England; and by saving time—the criterion of distance—the railway proved a great benefactor to men of industry in all classes. Many deplored the inevitable downfall of the old stage-coach system. There was to be an end of that delightful variety of incident usually attendant on a journey by road. The rapid scamper across a fine country on the outside of the four-horse "Express" or "Highflyer"; the seat on the box beside Jehu, or the equally coveted place near the facetious guard behind; the journey amid open green fields, through smiling villages, and fine old towns, where the stage stopped to change horses and the passengers to dine,—was all very delightful in its way; and many regretted that this old-fashioned and pleasant style of travelling was about to pass away. But it had its dark side also. Any one who remembers the journey by stage from Manchester to London will associate it with recollections and sensations of not unmixed delight. To be perched for twenty hours, exposed to all weathers, on the outside of a coach, trying in vain to find a soft seat— sitting now with the face to the wind, rain, or sun, and now with the back—without any shelter such as the commonest penny-a-mile parliamentary train now daily provides,—was a miserable undertaking, looked forward to with horror by many whose business called them to travel frequently between the provinces and the metropolis. Nor were the inside passengers more agreeably accommodated. To be closely packed up in a little, inconvenient, straight-backed vehicle, where the cramped limbs could not be in the least extended, or the wearied frame indulge in any change of posture, was felt by many to be a terrible thing. Then there were the constantly recurring demands, not always couched in the politest terms, for an allowance to the driver every two or three stages, and to the guard every six or eight; and if the gratuity did not equal their expectations, growling and open abuse were not unusual. These *désagrémens*, together with the exactions practised on travellers by innkeepers, seriously detracted from the romance of stage-coach travelling; and there was a general disposition on the part of the public to change the system for a better.

The avidity with which the public at once availed themselves of the railways proved that this better system had been discovered. Notwithstanding the reduction of the coach fares between London and Birmingham to one-third of their previous rate, the public preferred travelling by the railway. They saved in time, and they saved in money, taking the whole expenses into account. In point of comfort there could be no doubt as to the infinite superiority of the railway carriage. But there remained the question of safety, which had been a great bugbear with the early opponents of railways, and was made the most of by the coach proprietors to deter the public from using them. It was predicted that trains of passengers would be blown to pieces, and that none but fools would entrust their persons to the conduct of an explosive machine such as the locomotive. It appeared, however, that during the first eight years not fewer than five millions of passengers had been conveyed along the Liverpool and Manchester Railway, and of this vast number only two persons had lost their lives by accident. During the same period, the loss of life by the upsetting of stage coaches had been immensely greater in proportion. The public were not slow, therefore, to detect the fact, that travelling by railways was greatly safer than travelling by common roads; and in all districts penetrated by railways, the coaches were very shortly taken off from want of support.

It was some time, however, before the more opulent classes, who could afford to post to town in aristocratic style, became reconciled to railway travelling. The old families did not relish the idea of being conveyed in a train of passengers, of all ranks and conditions, in which the shopkeeper and the peasant were carried along at the same speed as the duke and the baron—the only difference being in price. It was another deplorable illustration of the levelling tendencies of the age. It put an end to that gradation of rank in travelling, which was one of the few things left, by which the nobleman could be distinguished from the Manchester manufacturer and bagman. So, for a time, many of the old families sent forward their servants and luggage by railway, and condemned themselves to jog along the old highway in the accustomed family chariot, dragged by country post-horses. But the superior comfort of the railway shortly recommended itself to even the oldest families; posting went out of date; post-horses were with difficulty to be had along even the great high-roads; and nobles and servants, manufacturers and peasants, alike shared in the comfort, the convenience, and the despatch of railway travelling.

It was long before the late Duke of Wellington would trust himself behind a locomotive. The fatal accident to Mr. Huskisson, which had happened before his eyes, contributed to prejudice him strongly against railways, and it was not until the year 1843 that he performed his first trip on the South-western Railway, in attendance upon her Majesty. Prince Albert had for some time been accustomed to travel by railway alone; but in 1842, the Queen began to make use of the same mode of conveyance between Windsor and London; after which the antipathies of even the most prejudiced were effectually set at rest.

10.   THACKERAY:

Stage-Coach vs. Railroad

The works of William Makepeace Thackeray (1811–1863) are available in two good editions: the Centenary Biographical Edition (26 vols.,

1910–26), with introductions by his daughter, Anne Thackeray Ritchie, and the Oxford Edition (17 vols., 1908), edited by George Saintsbury. *The Letters and Private Papers* have been collected and edited by Gordon N. Ray (4 vols., 1945–46). Ray is also the author of the definitive, critical biography, *Thackeray* (2 vols., 1955–58). Worthwhile criticism is also in Ray's *The Buried Life* (1952), and Geoffrey Tillotson, *Thackeray the Novelist* (1954; reissued 1963).

The Roundabout Papers is a series of informal essays which appeared in *The Cornhill* magazine while Thackeray was its editor. "De Juventute," from which the selection is taken, is one of the most famous of those papers.

The vision has disappeared off the silver, the images of youth and the past are vanishing away! We who have lived before railways were made, belong to another world. In how many hours could the Prince of Wales drive from Brighton to London, with a light carriage built expressly, and relays of horses longing to gallop the next stage? Do you remember Sir Somebody, the coachman of the Age, who took our half-crown so affably? It was only yesterday; but what a gulf between now and then! *Then* was the old world. Stage-coaches, more or less swift, riding-horses, pack-horses, highwaymen, knights in armour, Norman invaders, Roman legions, Druids, Ancient Britons painted blue, and so forth—all these belong to the old period. I will concede a halt in the midst of it, and allow that gunpowder and printing tended to modernize the world. But your railroad starts the new era, and we of a certain age belong to the new time and the old one. We are of the time of chivalry as well as the Black Prince or Sir Walter Manny. We are of the age of steam. We have stepped out of the old world on to "Brunel's" vast deck, and across the waters *ingens patet telius*. Towards what new continent are we wending? to what new laws, new manners, new politics, vast new expanses of liberties unknown as yet, or only surmised? I used to know a man who had invented a flying-machine. "Sir," he would say, "give me but five hundred pounds, and I will make it. It is so simple of construction that I tremble daily lest some other person should light upon and patent my discovery." Perhaps faith was wanting; perhaps the five hundred pounds. He is dead, and somebody else must make the flying-machine. But that will only be a step forward on the journey already begun since we quitted the old world. There it lies on the other side of yonder embankments. You young folks have never seen it; and Waterloo is to you no more than Agincourt, and George IV than Sardanapalus. We elderly people have lived in that præriailroad world, which has passed into limbo and vanished from under us. I tell you it was firm under our feet once, and not long ago. They have raised those railroad embankments up, and shut off the old world that was behind them. Climb up that bank on which the irons are laid, and look to the other side—it is gone. There *is* no other side. Try and catch yesterday. Where is it? Here is a *Times* newspaper, dated Monday 26th, and this is Tuesday 27th. Suppose you deny there was such a day as yesterday?

We who lived before railways, and survive out of the ancient world, are like Father Noah and his family out of the Ark. The children will gather round and say to us patriarchs, "Tell us, grandpapa, about the old world." And we shall mumble our old stories; and we shall drop off one by one; and there will be fewer and fewer of us, and these very old and feeble. There will be but ten præailroadites left: then three—then two—then one—then 0! If the hippopotamus had the least sensibility (of which I cannot trace any signs either in his hide or his face), I think he would go down to the bottom of his tank, and never come up again. Does he not see that he belongs to bygone ages, and that his great hulking barrel of a body is out of place in these times? What has he in common with the brisk young life surrounding him? In the watches of the night, when the keepers are asleep, when the birds are on one leg, when even the little armadillo is quiet, and the monkeys have ceased their chatter,—he, I mean the hippopotamus, and the elephant, and the long-necked giraffe, perhaps may lay their heads together and have a colloquy about the great silent antediluvian world which they remember, where mighty monsters floundered through the ooze, crocodiles basked on the banks, and dragons darted out of the caves and waters before men were made to slay them. We who lived before railways are antediluvians—we must pass away. We are growing scarcer every day; and old—old—very old relics of the times when George was still fighting the Dragon.

11. DICKENS:
The Railroad in Staggs's Gardens

For bibliographical information on Charles Dickens, see head-note to Selection 4. The present selection, from Chapter 6 of *Dombey and*

Son, describes the area in which Polly Toodles (young Paul Dombey's wet nurse and surrogate mother) resides.

The first shock of a great earthquake had, just at that period, rent the whole neighbourhood to its centre. Traces of its course were visible on every side. Houses were knocked down; streets broken through and stopped; deep pits and trenches dug in the ground; enormous heaps of earth and clay thrown up; buildings that were undermined and shaking, propped by great beams of wood. Here, a chaos of carts, overthrown and jumbled together, lay topsy-turvy at the bottom of a steep un-natural hill; there, confused treasures of iron soaked and rusted in something that had accidentally become a pond. Everywhere were bridges that led nowhere; thoroughfares that were wholly impassable; Babel towers of chimneys, wanting half their height; temporary wooden houses and enclosures, in the most unlikely situations; carcases of ragged tenements, and fragments of unfinished walls and arches, and piles of scaffolding, and wildernesses of bricks, and giant forms of cranes, and tripods straddling above nothing. There were a hundred thousand shapes and substances of incompleteness, wildly mingled out of their places, upside down, burrowing in the earth, aspiring in the air, mouldering in the water, and unintelligible as any dream. Hot springs and fiery eruptions, the usual attendants upon earthquakes, lent their contributions of confusion to the scene. Boiling water hissed and heaved within dilapidated walls; whence, also, the glare and roar of flames came issuing forth; and mounds of ashes blocked up rights of way, and wholly changed the law and custom of the neighbourhood.

In short, the yet unfinished and unopened Railroad was in progress; and, from the very core of all this dire disorder, trailed smoothly away, upon its mighty course of civilisation and improvement.

But as yet, the neighbourhood was shy to own the Railroad. One or two bold speculators had projected streets; and one had built a little, but had stopped among the mud and ashes to consider farther of it. A bran-new Tavern, redolent of fresh mortar and size, and fronting nothing at all, had taken for its sign The Railway Arms; but that might be rash enterprise—and then it hoped to sell drink to the workmen. So, the Excavators' House of Call had sprung up from a beer-shop; and the old-established Ham and Beef Shop had become the Railway Eating House, with a roast leg of pork daily, through interested motives of a similar immediate and popular description. Lodging-house keepers were favourable in like manner; and for the like reasons were not to be trusted. The general belief was very slow. There were frowzy fields, and cow-houses, and dunghills, and dustheaps, and ditches, and gardens, and summer-houses, and carpet-beating grounds, at the very door of the Railway. Little tumuli of oyster shells in the oyster season, and of lobster shells in the lobster season, and of broken crockery and faded cabbage leaves in all seasons, encroached upon its high places. Posts, and rails, and old cautions to trespassers, and backs of mean houses, and patches of wretched vegetation, stared it out of countenance. Nothing was the better for it, or thought of being so. If the miserable waste ground lying near it could have laughed, it would have laughed it to scorn, like many of the miserable neighbours.

Staggs's Gardens was uncommonly incredulous. It was a little row of houses, with little squalid patches of ground before them, fenced off with old doors, barrel staves, scraps of tarpaulin, and dead bushes; with bottomless tin kettles and exhausted iron fenders, thrust into the gaps. Here, the Staggs's Gardeners trained scarlet beans, kept fowls and rabbits, erected rotten summer-houses (one was an old boat), dried clothes, and smoked pipes. Some were of opinion that Staggs's Gardens derived its name from a deceased capitalist, one Mr. Staggs, who had built it for his delectation. Others, who had a natural taste for the country, held that it dated from those rural times when the antlered herd, under the familiar denomination of Staggses, had resorted to its shady precincts. Be this as it may, Staggs's Gardens was regarded by its population as a sacred grove not to be withered by railroads; and so confident were they generally of its long outliving any such ridiculous inventions, that the master chimney-sweeper at the corner, who was understood to take the lead in the local politics of the Gardens, had publicly declared that on the occasion of the Railroad opening, if ever it did open, two of his boys should ascend the flues of his dwelling, with instructions to hail the failure with derisive jeers from the chimney-pots.

12.   CARLYLE:

"Condition-of-England" Question

Thomas Carlyle (1795–1881) has long been an interesting and controversial figure. The earliest of biographies, by his disciple J. A. Froude, remains invaluable: *Thomas Carlyle: History of His Life in London* (2 vols., 1884) and *Thomas Carlyle: History of the First Forty Years of His Life* (2 vols., 1882). The standard biography is now that by D. A. Wilson (6 vols., 1923–34). The most complete edition of Carlyle's works is the Centenary Edition (30 vols., 1896–99), edited by H. D. Trail. Valuable criticisms are: Emery Neff, *Carlyle* (1932), C. F. Harrold, *Carlyle and German Thought* (1934), and John Holloway, *The Victorian Sage* (1953).

Chartism (the first chapter of which is reprinted here) was originally intended as an article for one of the reviews, but was withdrawn as too inflammatory and later published separately as a book.

A feeling very generally exists that the condition and disposition of the Working Classes is a rather ominous matter at present; that something ought to be said, something ought to be done, in regard to it. And surely, at an epoch of history when the "National Petition" carts itself in wagons along the streets, and is presented "bound with iron hoops, four men bearing it," to a Reformed House of Commons; and Chartism numbered by the million and half, taking nothing by its iron-hooped Petition, breaks out into brickbats, cheap pikes, and even into sputterings of conflagration, such very general feeling cannot be considered unnatural! To us individually this matter appears, and has for many years appeared, to be the most ominous of all practical matters whatever; a matter in regard to which if something be not done, something will *do* itself one day, and in a fashion that will please nobody. The time is verily come for acting in it; how much more for consultation about acting in it, for speech and articulate inquiry about it!

We are aware that, according to the newspapers, Chartism is extinct; that a Reform Ministry has "put down the chimera of Chartism"

124   THE VICTORIAN MIND

in the most felicitous effectual manner. So say the newspapers;—
and yet, alas, most readers of newspapers know withal that it is
indeed the "chimera" of Chartism, not the reality, which has been
put down. The distracted incoherent embodiment of Chartism, whereby
in late months it took shape and became visible, this has been put
down; or rather has fallen down and gone asunder by gravitation and
law of nature: but the living essence of Chartism has not been put
down. Chartism means the bitter discontent grown fierce and mad,
the wrong condition therefore or the wrong disposition, of the Working
Classes of England. It is a new name for a thing which has had many
names, which will yet have many. The matter of Chartism is weighty,
deep-rooted, far-extending; did not begin yesterday; will by no means
end this day or to-morrow. Reform Ministry, constabulary rural
police, new levy of soldiers, grants of money to Birmingham; all
this is well, or is not well; all this will put down only the embodiment
or "chimera" of Chartism. The essence continuing, new and ever
new embodiments, chimeras madder or less mad, have to continue.
The melancholy fact remains, that this thing known at present by the
name Chartism does exist; has existed; and, either "put down," into
secret treason, with rusty pistols, vitriol-bottle and match-box, or openly
brandishing pike and torch (one knows not in which case *more* fatal-
looking), is like to exist till quite other methods have been tried with
it. What means this bitter discontent of the Working Classes? Whence
comes it, whither goes it? Above all, at what price, on what terms,
will it probably consent to depart from us and die into rest? These are
questions. . . .

Delirious Chartism will not have raged entirely to no purpose,
as indeed no earthly thing does so, if it have forced all thinking men
of the community to think of this vital matter, too apt to be over-
looked otherwise. Is the condition of the English working people
wrong; so wrong that rational working men cannot, will not, and
even should not rest quiet under it? A most grave case, complex
beyond all others in the world; a case wherein Botany Bay, constabulary rural police, and such like, will avail but little. Or is the discontent
itself mad, like the shape it took? Not the condition of the working
people that is wrong; but their disposition, their own thoughts, beliefs
and feelings that are wrong? This too were a most grave case, little
less alarming, little less complex than the former one. In this case too,
where constabulary police and mere rigor of coercion seems more at

home, coercion will by no means do all, coercion by itself will not even do much. If there do exist general madness of discontent, then sanity and some measure of content must be brought about again—not by constabulary police alone. When the thoughts of a people, in the great mass of it, have grown mad, the combined issue of that people's workings will be a madness, an incoherency and ruin! Sanity will have to be recovered for the general mass; coercion itself will otherwise cease to be able to coerce.

We have heard it asked, Why Parliament throws no light on this question of the Working Classes, and the condition or disposition they are in? Truly to a remote observer of Parliamentary procedure it seems surprising, especially in late Reformed times, to see what space this question occupies in the Debates of the Nation. Can any other business whatsoever be so pressing on legislators? A Reformed Parliament, one would think, should inquire into popular discontents *before* they get the length of pikes and torches! For what end at all are men, Honorable Members and Reform Members, sent to St. Stephen's, with clamor and effort; kept talking, struggling, motioning and counter-motioning? The condition of the great body of people in a country is the condition of the country itself: this you would say is a truism in all times; a truism rather pressing to get recognized as a truth now, and be acted upon, in these times. Yet read Hansard's Debates, or the Morning Papers, if you have nothing to do! The old grand question, whether A is to be in office or B, with the innumerable subsidiary questions growing out of that, courting paragraphs and suffrages for a blessed solution of that: Canada question, Irish Appropriation question, West-India question, Queen's Bedchamber question; Game Laws, Usury Laws; African Blacks, Hill Coolies, Smithfield cattle, and Dog-carts—all manner of questions and subjects, except simply this alpha and omega of all! Surely Honorable Members ought to speak of the Condition-of-England question too. Radical Members, above all; friends of the people; chosen with effort, by the people, to interpret and articulate the dumb deep want of the people! To a remote observer they seem oblivious of their duty. Are they not there, by trade, mission, and express appointment of themselves and others, to speak for the good of the British Nation? Whatsoever great British interest can the least speak for itself, for that beyond all they are called to speak. They are either speakers for that great dumb toiling class which cannot speak, or they are nothing that one can well specify.

Alas, the remote observer knows not the nature of Parliaments: how Parliaments, extant there for the British Nation's sake, find that they are extant withal for their own sake; how Parliaments travel so naturally in their deep-rutted routine, commonplace worn into ruts axle-deep, from which only strength, insight and courageous generous exertion can lift any Parliament or vehicle; how in Parliaments, Reformed or Unreformed, there may chance to be a strong man, an original, clear-sighted, great-hearted, patient and valiant man, or to be none such;—how, on the whole, Parliaments, lumbering along in their deep ruts of commonplace, find, as so many of us otherwise do, that the ruts *are* axle-deep, and the travelling very toilsome of itself, and for the day the evil thereof sufficient! What Parliaments ought to have done in this business, what they will, can or cannot yet do, and where the limits of their faculty and culpability may lie, in regard to it, were a long investigation; into which we need not enter at this moment. What they have done is unhappily plain enough. Hitherto, on this most national of questions, the Collective Wisdom of the Nation has availed us as good as nothing whatever.

And yet, as we say, it is a question which cannot be left to the Collective Folly of the Nation! In or out of Parliament, darkness, neglect, hallucination must contrive to cease in regard to it; true insight into it must be had. How inexpressibly useful were true insight into it; a genuine understanding by the upper classes of society what it is that the under classes intrinsically mean; a clear interpretation of the thought which at heart torments these wild inarticulate souls, struggling there, with inarticulate uproar, like dumb creatures in pain, unable to speak what is in them! Something they do mean; some true thing withal, in the centre of their confused hearts,—for they are hearts created by Heaven too: to the Heaven it is clear what thing; to us not clear. Would that it were! Perfect clearness on it were equivalent to remedy of it. For, as is well said, all battle is misunderstanding; did the parties know one another, the battle would cease. No man at bottom means injustice; it is always for some obscure distorted image of a right that he contends: an obscure image diffracted, exaggerated, in the wonderfulest way, by natural dimness and selfishness; getting tenfold more diffracted by exasperation of contest, till at length it become all but irrecognizable; yet still the image of a right. Could a man own to himself that the thing he fought for was wrong, contrary to fairness and the law of reason, he would own also that it thereby stood condemned and hopeless; he could fight for it no longer. Nay independently of right, could the contending parties get but accurately to discern one another's might and strength to contend, the one would peaceably yield to the other and to Necessity; the contest in this case too were over. No African expedition now, as in the days of Herodotus, is fitted out *against the South-wind*. One expedition was satisfactory in that department. The South-wind Simoom continues blowing occasionally, hateful as ever, maddening as ever; but one expedition was enough. Do we not all submit to Death? The highest sentence of the law, sentence of death, is passed on all of us by the fact of birth; yet we live patiently under it, patiently undergo it when the hour comes. Clear undeniable right, clear undeniable might: either of these once ascertained puts an end to battle. All battle is a confused experiment to ascertain one and both of these.

What are the rights, what are the mights of the discontented Working Classes in England at this epoch? He were an Œdipus, and deliverer from sad social pestilence, who could resolve us fully! For we may say beforehand, The struggle that divides the upper and lower in society over Europe, and more painfully and notably in England than elsewhere, this too is a struggle which will end and adjust itself as all other struggles do and have done, by making the right clear and the might clear; not otherwise than by that. Meantime, the questions, Why are the Working Classes discontented; what is their condition, economical, moral, in their houses and their hearts, as it is in reality and as they figure it to themselves to be; what do they complain of; what ought they, and ought they not to complain of?—these are measurable questions; on some of these any common mortal, did he but turn his eyes to them, might throw some light. Certain researches and considerations of ours on the matter, since no one else will undertake it, are now to be made public. The researches have yielded us little, almost nothing; but the considerations are of old date, and press to have utterance. We are not without hope that our general notion of the business, if we can get it uttered at all, will meet some assent from many candid men.

13. RUSKIN:

"The Roots of Honour"

The best edition of *The Works* of John Ruskin (1819–1900) is
that edited by E. T. Cook and A. D. O. Wedderburn (39 vols., 1902–12). A
valuable biography (among many available) is *The Life of John Ruskin*
(2 vols., 1911) by E. T. Cook. Useful criticism may be found in *John Ruskin:
An Introduction to Further Study of His Life and Work*, by R. H. Wilensky,
although there is no single, standard critical source.

Unto This Last, as the introduction to this section makes clear, is perhaps
Ruskin's definitive, most emphatic, statement on the social problems of
industrialization. The selection is from the first essay of this work, entitled
"The Roots of Honour."

1. Among the delusions which at different periods have possessed
themselves of the minds of large masses of the human race, perhaps
the most curious—certainly the least creditable—is the modern *soi-
disant* science of political economy, based on the idea that an advantageous code of social action may be determined irrespectively of the
influence of social affection.

Of course, as in the instances of alchemy, astrology, witchcraft,
and other such popular creeds, political economy has a plausible idea
at the root of it. "The social affections," says the economist, "are
accidental and disturbing elements in human nature; but avarice and
the desire of progress are constant elements. Let us eliminate the
inconstants, and, considering the human being merely as a covetous
machine, examine by what laws of labour, purchase, and sale, the
greatest accumulative result in wealth is obtainable. Those laws once
determined, it will be for each individual afterwards to introduce as
much of the disturbing affectionate element as he chooses, and to
determine for himself the result on the new conditions supposed."

2. This would be a perfectly logical and successful method of
analysis, if the accidentals afterwards to be introduced were of the
same nature as the powers first examined. Supposing a body in motion

to be influenced by constant and inconstant forces, it is usually the simplest way of examining its course to trace it first under the persistent conditions, and afterwards introduce the causes of variation. But the disturbing elements in the social problem are not of the same nature as the constant ones; they alter the essence of the creature under examination the moment they are added; they operate, not mathematically, but chemically, introducing conditions which render all our previous knowledge unavailable. We made learned experiments upon pure nitrogen, and have convinced ourselves that it is a very manageable gas: but, behold! the thing which we have practically to deal with is its chloride; and this, the moment we touch it on our established principles, sends us and our apparatus through the ceiling.

3. Observe, I neither impugn nor doubt the conclusion of the science, if its terms are accepted. I am simply uninterested in them, as I should be in those of a science of gymnastics which assumed that men had no skeletons. It might be shown, on that supposition, that it would be advantageous to roll the students up into pellets, flatten them into cakes, or stretch them into cables; and that when these results were effected, the re-insertion of the skeleton would be attended with various inconveniences to their constitution. The reasoning might be admirable, the conclusions true, and the science deficient only in applicability. Modern political economy stands on a precisely similar basis. Assuming, not that the human being has no skeleton, but that it is all skeleton, it founds an ossifiant theory of progress on this negation of a soul; and having shown the utmost that may be made of bones, and constructed a number of interesting geometrical figures with death's-head and humeri, successfully proves the inconvenience of the reappearance of a soul among these corpuscular structures. I do not deny the truth of this theory: I simply deny its applicability to the present phase of the world.

4. The inapplicability has been curiously manifested during the embarrassment caused by the late strikes of our workmen. Here occurs one of the simplest cases, in a pertinent and positive form, of the first vital problem which political economy has to deal with (the relation between employer and employed); and, at a severe crisis, when lives in multitudes and wealth in masses are at stake, the political economists are helpless—practically mute: no demonstrable solution of the difficulty can be given by them, such as may convince or calm the opposing parties. Obstinately the masters take one view of the

matter; obstinately the operatives another; and no political science can set them at one.

5. It would be strange if it could, it being not by "science" of any kind that men were ever intended to be set at one. Disputant after disputant vainly strives to show that the interests of the masters are, or are not, antagonistic to those of the men; none of the pleaders ever seeming to remember that it does not absolutely or always follow that the persons must be antagonistic because their interests are. If there is only a crust of bread in the house, and mother and children are starving, their interests are not the same. If the mother eats it, the children want it; if the children eat it, the mother must go hungry to her work. Yet it does not necessarily follow that there will be "antagonism" between them, that they will fight for the crust, and that the mother, being strongest, will get it, and eat it. Neither, in any other case, whatever the relations of the persons may be, can it be assumed for certain that, because their interests are diverse, they must necessarily regard each other with hostility, and use violence or cunning to obtain the advantage.

6. Even if this were so, and it were as just as it is convenient to consider men as actuated by no other moral influences than those which affect rats or swine, the logical conditions of the question are still indeterminable. It can never be shown generally either that the interests of master and labourer are alike, or that they are opposed; for, according to circumstances, they may be either. It is, indeed, always the interest of both that the work should be rightly done, and a just price obtained for it; but, in the division of profits, the gain of one may or may not be the loss of the other. It is not the master's interest to pay wages so low as to leave the men sickly and depressed, nor the workman's interest to be paid high wages if the smallness of the master's profits hinders him from enlarging his business, or conducting it in a safe and liberal way. A stoker ought not to desire high pay if the company is too poor to keep the engine-wheels in repair.

7. And the varieties of circumstances which influence these reciprocal interests are so endless, that all endeavour to deduce rules of action from balance of expediency is in vain. And it is meant to be in vain. For no human actions ever were intended by the Maker of men to be guided by balances of expediency, but by balances of justice. He has therefore rendered all endeavours to determine expediency futile for evermore. No man ever knew, or can know, what will be the ultimate result to himself, or to others, of any given line of conduct. But every

man may know, and most of us do know, what is a just and unjust act. And all of us may know also, that the consequences of justice will be ultimately the best possible, both to others and ourselves, though we can neither say what *is* best, nor how it is likely to come to pass.

I have said balances of justice, meaning, in the term justice, to include affection—such affection as one man *owes* to another. All right relations between master and operative, and all their best interests, ultimately depend on these.

8. We shall find the best and simplest illustration of the relations of master and operative in the position of domestic servants.

We will suppose that the master of a household desires only to get as much work out of his servants as he can, at the rate of wages he gives. He never allows them to be idle; feeds them as poorly and lodges them as ill as they will endure, and in all things pushes his requirements to the exact point beyond which he cannot go without forcing the servant to leave him. In doing this, there is no violation on his part of what is commonly called "justice." He agrees with the domestic for his whole time and service, and takes them;—the limits of hardship in treatment being fixed by the practice of other masters in his neighbourhood; that is to say, by the current rate of wages for domestic labour. If the servant can get a better place, he is free to take one, and the master can only tell what is the real market value of his labour, by requiring as much as he will give.

This is the politico-economical view of the case, according to the doctors of that science; who assert that by this procedure the greatest average of work will be obtained from the servant, and therefore the greatest benefit to the community, and through the community, by reversion, to the servant himself.

That, however, is not so. It would be so if the servant were an engine of which the motive power was steam, magnetism, gravitation, or any other agent or calculable force. But he being, on the contrary, an engine whose motive power is a Soul, the force of this very peculiar agent, as an unknown quantity, enters into all the political economist's equations, without his knowledge, and falsifies every one of their results. The largest quantity of work will not be done by this curious engine for pay, or under pressure, or by help of any kind of fuel which may be applied by the chaldron. It will be done only when the motive force, that is to say, the will or spirit of the creature, is brought to its greatest strength by its own proper fuel: namely, by the affections. . . .

13. The first question is, ... how far it may be possible to fix the rate of wages, irrespectively of the demand for labour.

Perhaps one of the most curious facts in the history of human error is the denial by the common political economist of the possibility of thus regulating wages; while, for all the important, and much of the unimportant, labour on the earth, wages are already regulated.

We do not sell our prime-ministership by Dutch auction; nor, on the decease of a bishop, whatever may be the general advantages of simony, do we (yet) offer his diocese to the clergyman who will take the episcopacy at the lowest contract. We (with exquisite sagacity of political economy!) do indeed sell commissions; but not openly, generalships: sick, we do not inquire for a physician who takes less than a guinea; litigious, we never think of reducing six-and-eightpence to four-and-sixpence; caught in a shower, we do not canvass the cabmen, to find one who values his driving at less than sixpence a mile.

It is true that in all these cases there is, and in every conceivable case there must be, ultimate reference to the presumed difficulty of the work, or number of candidates for the office. If it were thought that the labour necessary to make a good physician would be gone through by a sufficient number of students with the prospect of only half-guinea fees, public consent would soon withdraw the unnecessary half-guinea. In this ultimate sense, the price of labour is indeed always regulated by the demand for it; but so far as the practical and immediate administration of the matter is regarded, the best labour always has been, and is, as *all* labour ought to be, paid by an invariable standard.

14. "What!" the reader, perhaps, answers amazedly: "pay good and bad workmen alike?"

Certainly. The difference between one prelate's sermons and his successor's—or between one physician's opinion and another's—is far greater, as respects the qualities of mind involved, and far more important in result to you personally, than the difference between good and bad laying of bricks (though that is greater than most people suppose). Yet you pay with equal fee, contentedly, the good and bad workmen upon your soul, and the good and bad workmen upon your body; much more may you pay, contentedly, with equal fees, the good and bad workmen upon your house.

"Nay, but I choose my physician and (?) my clergyman, thus indicating my sense of the quality of their work." By all means, also, choose your bricklayer; that is the proper reward of the good workman, to be "chosen." The natural and right system respecting all labour is, that it should be paid at a fixed rate, but the good workman employed, and the bad workman unemployed. The false, unnatural, and destructive system is when the bad workman is allowed to offer his work at half-price, and either take the place of the good, or force him by his competition to work for an inadequate sum.

15. This equality of wages, then, being the first object towards which we have to discover the directest available road, the second is, . . . that of maintaining constant numbers of workmen in employment, whatever may be the accidental demand for the article they produce.

I believe the sudden and extensive inequalities of demand, which necessarily arise in the mercantile operations of an active nation, constitute the only essential difficulty which has to be overcome in a just organization of labour.

The subject opens into too many branches to admit of being investigated in a paper of this kind; but the following general facts bearing on it may be noted.

The wages which enable any workman to live are necessarily higher, if his work is liable to intermission, than if it is assured and continuous; and however severe the struggle for work may become, the general law will always hold, that men must get more daily pay if, on the average, they can only calculate on work three days a week than they would require if they were sure of work six days a week. Supposing that a man cannot live on less than a shilling a day, his seven shillings he must get, either for three days' violent work, or six days' deliberate work. The tendency of all modern mercantile operations is to throw both wages and trade into the form of a lottery, and to make the workman's pay depend on intermittent exertion, and the principal's profit on dexterously used chance. . . .

19. Now, there can be no question but that the tact, foresight, decision, and other mental powers, required for the successful management of a large mercantile concern, if not such as could be compared with those of a great lawyer, general, or divine, would at least match the general conditions of mind required in the subordinate officers of a ship, or of a regiment, or in the curate of a country parish. If, therefore, all the efficient members of the so-called liberal professions are still, somehow, in public estimate of honour, preferred before the

head of a commercial firm, the reasons must lie deeper than in the measurement of their several powers of mind.

And the essential reason for such preference will be found to lie in the fact that the merchant is presumed to act always selfishly. His work may be very necessary to the community; but the motive of it is understood to be wholly personal. The merchant's first object in all his dealings must be (the public believe) to get as much for himself, and leave as little to his neighbour (or customer) as possible. Enforcing this upon him, by political statute, as the necessary principle of his action; recommending it to him on all occasions, and themselves reciprocally adopting it, proclaiming vociferously, for law of the universe, that a buyer's function is to cheapen, and a seller's to cheat,—the public, nevertheless, involuntarily condemn the man of commerce for his compliance with their own statement, and stamp him forever as belonging to an inferior grade of human personality.

20. This they will find, eventually, they must give up doing. They must not cease to condemn selfishness; but they will have to discover a kind of commerce which is not exclusively selfish. Or, rather, they will have to discover that there never was, or can be, any other kind of commerce; that this which they have called commerce was not commerce at all, but cozening; and that a true merchant differs as much from a merchant according to laws of modern political economy, as the hero of the *Excursion* from Autolycus. They will find that commerce is an occupation which gentlemen will every day see more need to engage in, rather than in the businesses of talking to men, or slaying them; that, in true commerce, as in true preaching, or true fighting, it is necessary to admit the idea of occasional voluntary loss;—that sixpences have to be lost, as well as lives, under a sense of duty; that the market may have its martyrdoms as well as the pulpit; and trade its heroisms, as well as war.

May have—in the final issue, must have—and only has not had yet, because men of heroic temper have always been misguided in their youth into other fields; not recognizing what is in our days, perhaps, the most important of all fields; so that, while many a zealous person loses his life in trying to teach the form of a gospel, very few will lose a hundred pounds in showing the practice of one.

21. The fact is, that people never have had clearly explained to them the true functions of a merchant with respect to other people. I should like the reader to be very clear about this.

Five great intellectual professions, relating to daily necessities of life, have hitherto existed—three exist necessarily, in every civilized nation:—

The Soldier's profession is to *defend* it.

The Pastor's to *teach* it.

The Physician's to *keep it in health*.

The Lawyer's to *enforce justice* in it.

The Merchant's to *provide* for it.

And the duty of all these men is, on due occasion, to *die* for it.

"On due occasion," namely:—

The Soldier, rather than leave his post in battle.

The Physician, rather than leave his post in plague.

The Pastor, rather than teach Falsehood.

The Lawyer, rather than countenance Injustice.

The Merchant—What is *his* "due occasion" of death?

22. It is the main question for the merchant, as for all of us. For, truly, the man who does not know when to die, does not know how to live.

Observe, the merchant's function (or manufacturer's, for in the broad sense in which it is here used the word must be understood to include both) is to provide for the nation. It is no more his function to get profit for himself out of that provision than it is a clergyman's function to get his stipend. The stipend is a due and necessary adjunct, but not the object, of his life, if he be a true clergyman, any more than his fee (or honorarium) is the object of life to a true physician. Neither is his fee the object of life to a true merchant. All three, if true men, have a work to be done irrespective of fee—to be done even at any cost, or for quite the contrary of fee; the pastor's function being to teach, the physician's to heal, and the merchant's, as I have said, to provide. That is to say, he has to understand to their very root the qualities of the thing he deals in, and the means of obtaining or producing it; and he has to apply all his sagacity and energy to the producing or obtaining it in perfect state, and distributing it at the cheapest possible price where it is most needed.

And because the production or obtaining of any commodity involves necessarily the agency of many lives and hands, the merchant becomes in the course of his business the master and governor of large masses of men in a more direct, though less confessed way, than a military officer or pastor; so that on him falls, in great part, the responsibility for the kind of life they lead; and it becomes his duty, not only to be always considering how to produce what he sells, in the purest and cheapest forms, but how to make the various employments involved in the production or transference of it, most beneficial to the men employed.

23. And as into these two functions, requiring for their right exercise the highest intelligence, as well as patience, kindness, and tact, the merchant is bound to put all his energy, so for their just discharge he is bound, as soldier or physician is bound, to give up, if need be, his life, in such way as it may be demanded of him. Two main points he has in his providing function to maintain: first, his engagements (faithfulness to engagements being the real root of all possibilities, in commerce); and, secondly, the perfectness and purity of the thing provided; so that, rather than fail in any engagement, or consent to any deterioration, adulteration, or unjust and exorbitant price of that which he provides, he is bound to meet fearlessly any form of distress, poverty, or labour, which may, through maintenance of these points, come upon him.

24. Again: in his office as governor of the men employed by him, the merchant or manufacturer is invested with a distinctly paternal authority and responsibility. In most cases, a youth entering a commercial establishment is withdrawn altogether from home influence; his master must become his father, else he has, for practical and constant help, no father at hand: in all cases the master's authority, together with the general tone and atmosphere of his business, and the character of the men with whom the youth is compelled in the course of it to associate, have more immediate and pressing weight than the home influence, and will usually neutralize it either for good or evil; so that the only means which the master has of doing justice to the men employed by him is to ask himself sternly whether he is dealing with such subordinate as he would with his own son, if compelled by circumstances to take such a position.

Supposing the captain of a frigate saw it right, or were by any chance obliged, to place his own son in the position of a common sailor; as he would then treat his son, he is bound always to treat every one of the men under him. So, also, supposing the master of a manufactory saw it right, or were by any chance obliged, to place his own son in the position of an ordinary workman; as he would then treat his son, he is bound always to treat every one of his men. This is the only effective, true, or practical RULE which can be given on this point of political economy.

And as the captain of a ship is bound to be the last man to leave his ship in case of wreck, and to share his last crust with the sailors in case of famine, so the manufacturer, in any commercial crisis or distress, is bound to take the suffering of it with his men, and even to take more of it for himself than he allows his men to feel; as a father would in a famine, shipwreck, or battle, sacrifice himself for his son.

25. All which sounds very strange: the only real strangeness in the matter being, nevertheless, that it should so sound. For all this is true, and that not partially nor theoretically, but everlastingly and practically: all other doctrine than this respecting matters political being false in premises, absurd in deduction, and impossible in practice, consistently with any progressive state of national life; all the life which we now possess as a nation showing itself in the resolute denial and scorn, by a few strong minds and faithful hearts, of the economic principles taught to our multitudes, which principles, so far as accepted, lead straight to national destruction. . . .

14. MORRIS:
Art and Commerce

For William Morris (1834–1896) May Morris' *Collected Works* in 24 volumes (London, 1910–15) is standard. His daughter also edited *William Morris, Artist, Writer, Socialist: Unpublished and Hitherto Inaccessible Writings*, published by Oxford University Press in 1936. The official life was written by J. W. MacKail in two volumes published by Longmans in 1922. Edward Thompson's *William Morris, Romantic to Revolutionary* (New York, 1962), and Margaret Grennan's *William Morris, Medievalist and Revolutionary*, are reliable sources. The range of Morris' interests and talents are delineated in the subtitles of the books listed.

Morris' lecture "Art and Socialism" is another example of the Victorian concern to integrate the diverse and rapid currents of nineteenth-century life. The talk was delivered in 1884 to the Secular Society of Leicester and printed in *The Commonwealth* the next year.

My friends, I want you to look into the relation of Art to Commerce, using the latter word to express what is generally meant by it; namely, that system of competition in the market which is indeed the only form which most people nowadays suppose that Commerce can take. Now whereas there have been times in the world's history when Art held the supremacy over Commerce; when Art was a good deal, and Commerce, as we understand the word, was a very little; so now on the contrary it will be admitted by all, I fancy, that Commerce has become of very great importance and Art of very little. I say this will be generally admitted, but different persons will hold very different opinions not only as to whether this is well or ill, but even as to what it really means when we say that Commerce has become of supreme importance and that Art has sunk into an unimportant matter.

Allow me to give you my opinion of the meaning of it: which will lead me on to ask you to consider what remedies should be applied for curing the evils that exist in the relations between Art and Commerce. Now to speak plainly it seems to me that the supremacy of Commerce (as we understand the word) is an evil, and a very serious one; and I should call it an unmixed evil but for the strange continuity of life which runs through all historical events, and by means of which the very evils of such and such a period tend to abolish themselves. For to my mind it means this: that the world of modern civilization in its haste to gain a very inequitably divided material prosperity has entirely suppressed popular Art; or in other words that the greater part of the people have no share in Art, which as things now are must be kept in the hands of a few rich or well-to-do people, who we may fairly say need it less and not more than the laborious workers. Nor is that all the evil, nor the worst of it; for the cause of this famine of Art is that whilst people work throughout the civilized world as laboriously as ever they did, they have lost, in losing an Art which was done by and for the people, the natural solace of their labour; a solace which they once had, and always should have; the opportunity of expressing their own thoughts to their fellows by means of that very labour, by means of that daily work which nature or long custom, a second nature, does indeed require of them, but without meaning that it should be an unrewarded and repulsive burden. But, through a strange blindness and error in the civilization of these latter days, the world's work, almost all of it, the work some share of which should have been the helpful companion of every man, has become even such a burden, which every man, if he could, would shake off. I have said that people work no less laboriously than they ever did; but I should have said that they work more laboriously. The wonderful machines which in the hands of just and foreseeing men would have been used to minimize repulsive labour and to give pleasure, or in other words added life, to the human race, have been so used on the contrary that they have driven all men into mere frantic haste and hurry, thereby destroying pleasure, that is life, on all hands: they have, instead of lightening the labour of the workmen, intensified it, and thereby added more weariness yet to the burden which the poor have to carry.

Nor can it be pleaded for the system of modern civilization that the mere material or bodily gains of it balance the loss of pleasure which it has brought upon the world; for as I hinted before those gains have been so unfairly divided that the contrast between rich and poor has been fearfully intensified, so that in all civilized countries, but most of all in England, the terrible spectacle is exhibited of two peoples living street by street and door by door, people of the same blood, the same tongue, and at least nominally living under the same laws, but yet one civilized and the other uncivilized. All this I say is the result of the system that has trampled down Art, and exalted Commerce into a sacred religion; and it would seem is ready, with the ghastly stupidity which is its principal characteristic, to mock the Roman satirist for his noble warning by taking it in inverse meaning, and now bids us all for the sake of life to destroy the reasons for living.

And now in the teeth of this stupid tyranny I put forward a claim on behalf of labour enslaved by Commerce, which I know no thinking man can deny is reasonable, but which if acted on would involve such a change as would defeat Commerce; that is, would put Association instead of Competition, Social Order instead of Individualist Anarchy. Yet I have looked at this claim by the light of history and my own conscience, and it seems to me so looked at to be a most just claim, and that resistance to it means nothing short of a denial of the hope of civilization. This then is the claim: *It is right and necessary that all men should have work to do which shall be worth doing, and be of itself pleasant to do; and which should be done under such conditions as would make it neither over-wearisome nor over-anxious.* Turn that claim about as I may, think of it as long as I can, I cannot find that it is an exorbitant claim; yet again I say if Society would or could admit it, the face of the world would be changed; discontent and strife and dishonesty would be ended. To feel that we were doing work useful to others and pleasant to ourselves, and that such work and its due reward could not fail us! What serious harm could happen to us then? And the price to be paid for so making the world happy is Revolution: Socialism instead of the Laissez faire.

How can we of the middle classes help to bring such a state of things about: a state of things as nearly as possible the reverse of the present state of things? The reverse; no less than that. For first, THE WORK MUST BE WORTH DOING: think what a change that would make in the world! I tell you I feel dazed at the thought of the immensity of work which is undergone for the making of useless things. It would be an instructive day's work for any one of us who is strong enough to walk through two or three of the principal streets of London on a week-day, and take accurate note of everything in the shop windows which is embarrassing or superfluous to the daily life of a serious man. Nay, the most of these things no one, serious or unserious, wants at all; only a foolish habit makes even the lightest-minded of us suppose that he wants them, and to many people even of those who buy them they are obvious encumbrances to real work, thought, and pleasure. But I beg you to think of the enormous mass of men who are occupied with this miserable trumpery, from the engineers who have had to make the machines for making them, down to the hapless clerks who sit daylong year after year in the horrible dens wherein the whole-sale exchange of them is transacted, and the shopmen who, not daring to call their souls their own, retail them amidst numberless insults which they must not resent, to the idle public which doesn't want them, but buys them to be bored by them and sick to death of them. I am talking of the merely useless things; but there are other matters not merely useless, but actively destructive and poisonous, which command a good price in the market; for instance, adulterated food and drink. Vast is the number of slaves whom competitive Commerce employs in turning out infamies such as these. But quite apart from them there is an enormous mass of labour which is just merely wasted; many thousands of men and women making Nothing with terrible and inhuman toil which deadens the soul and shortens mere animal life itself.

All these are the slaves of what is called luxury, which in the modern sense of the word comprises a mass of sham wealth, the invention of competitive Commerce, and enslaves not only the poor people who are compelled to work at its production, but also the foolish and not over happy people who buy it to harass themselves with its encumbrance. Now if we are to have popular Art, or indeed Art of any kind,

we must at once and for all be done with this luxury; it is the sup-
planter, the changeling of Art; so much so that by those who know of
nothing better it has even been taken for Art, the divine solace of human
labour, the romance of each day's hard practice of the difficult art of
living. But I say Art cannot live beside it, nor self-respect in any class
of life. Effeminacy and brutality are its companions on the right hand
and the left. This, first of all, we of the well-to-do classes must get rid
of if we are serious in desiring the new birth of Art: and if not, then
corruption is digging a terrible pit of perdition for society, from which
indeed the new birth may come, but surely from amidst of terror,
violence, and misery. . . .

Do not think it a little matter to resist this monster of folly; to
think for yourselves what you yourselves really desire, will not only
make men and women of you so far, but may also set you thinking
of the due desires of other people, since you will soon find when you
get to know a work of art, that slavish work is undesirable. And here
furthermore is at least a little sign whereby to distinguish between a
rag of fashion and a work of art: whereas the toys of fashion when the
first gloss is worn off them do become obviously worthless even to the
frivolous, a work of art, be it never so humble, is long-lived; we never
tire of it; as long as a scrap hangs together it is valuable and instructive
to each new generation. All works of art in short have the property
of becoming venerable amidst decay; and reason good, for from the
first there was a soul in them, the thought of man, which will be visible
in them so long as the body exists in which they were implanted.

And that last sentence brings me to considering the other side of
the necessity for labour only occupying itself in making goods that
are worth making. Hitherto we have been thinking of it only from the
user's point of view; even so looked at it was surely important enough;
yet from the other side, as to the producer, it is far more important
still. For I say again that in buying these things

'Tis the lives of men you buy!

Will you from mere folly and thoughtlessness make yourselves
partakers of the guilt of those who compel their fellowmen to labour
uselessly? For when I said it was necessary for all things made to be
worth making, I set up that claim chiefly on behalf of Labour; since
the waste of making useless things grieves the workman doubly.
As part of the public he is forced into buying them, and the more
part of his miserable wages is squeezed out of him by an universal

kind of truck system; as one of the producers he is forced into making
them, and so into losing the very foundations of that pleasure in daily
work which I claim as his birthright; he is compelled to labour joy-
lessly at making the poison which the truck system compels him to
buy. So that the huge mass of men who are compelled by folly and greed
to make harmful and useless things are sacrificed to Society. I say that
this would be terrible and unendurable even though they were sacrificed
to the good of Society, if that were possible; but if they are sacrificed
not for the welfare of Society but for its whims, to add to its degradation, what do luxury and fashion look like then? On one side ruinous
and wearisome waste leading through corruption to corruption on to
complete cynicism at last, and the disintegration of all Society; and
on the other side implacable oppression destructive of all pleasure
and hope in life, and leading—witherwards? . . .

Surely there are some of you who long to be free; who have been
educated and refined, and had your perceptions of beauty and order
quickened only that they might be shocked and wounded at every
turn by the brutalities of competitive Commerce; who have been
so hunted and driven by it that, though you are well-to-do, rich even
maybe, you have now nothing to lose from social revolution: love
of art, that is to say of the true pleasure of life, has brought you to
this, that you must throw in your lot with that of the wage-slave of
competitive Commerce; you and he must help each other and have
one hope in common, or you at any rate will live and die hopeless and
unhelped. You who long to be set free from the oppression of the
money-grubbers hope for the day when you will be compelled to be
free!
Meanwhile, if otherwise that oppression has left us scarce any work
to do worth doing, one thing at least is left us to strive for, the raising
of the standard of life where it is lowest, where it is low: that will put
a spoke in the wheel of the triumphant car of competitive Commerce.
Nor can I conceive of anything more likely to raise the standard of
life than the convincing some thousands of those who live by labour
of the necessity of their supporting the second part of the claim I
have made for Labour: namely, THAT THEIR WORK SHOULD
BE OF ITSELF PLEASANT TO DO. If we could but convince
them that such a strange revolution in Labour as this would be of
infinite benefit not to them only, but to all men; and that it is so right
and natural that for the reverse to be the case, that most men's work

should be grievous to them, is a mere monstrosity of these latter days, which must in the long run bring ruin and confusion on the society that allows it—if we could but convince them, then indeed there would be chance of the phrase Art of the People being something more than a mere word. At first sight, indeed, it would seem impossible to make men born under the present system of Commerce understand that labour may be a blessing to them: not in the sense in which the phrase is sometimes preached to them by those whose labour is light and easily evaded: not as a necessary task laid by nature on the poor for the benefit of the rich: not as an opiate to dull their sense of right and wrong, to make them sit down quietly under their burdens to the end of time, blessing the squire and his relations: all this they could understand our saying to them easily enough, and sometimes would listen to it I fear with at least a show of complacency, if they thought there were anything to be made out of us thereby. But the true doctrine that labour should be a real tangible blessing in itself to the working man, a pleasure even as sleep and strong drink are to him now: this one might think it hard indeed for him to understand, so different as it is from anything which he has found labour to be.

Nevertheless, though most men's work is only borne as a necessary evil like sickness, my experience as far as it goes is, that whether it be from a certain sacredness in handiwork which does cleave to it even under the worst circumstances, or whether it be that the poor man who is driven by necessity to deal with things which are terribly real, when he thinks at all on such matters, thinks less conventionally than the rich; whatever it may be, my experience so far is that the working man finds it easier to understand the doctrine of the claim of Labour to pleasure in the work itself than the rich or well-to-do man does. Apart from any trivial words of my own, I have been surprised to find, for instance, such a hearty feeling towards John Ruskin among working-class audiences: they can see the prophet in him rather than the fantastic rhetorician, as more superfine audiences do. That is a good omen, I think, for the education of times to come. But we who somehow are so tainted by cynicism, because of our helplessness in the ugly world which surrounds and presses on us, cannot we somehow raise our own hopes at least to the point of thinking that what hope glimmers on the millions of the slaves of Commerce is something better than a mere delusion, the false dawn of a cloudy midnight with which 'tis only the moon that struggles? Let us call to mind that there yet remain monuments in the world which show us that all human labour was not always a grief and a burden to men. Let us think of the mighty and lovely architecture, for instance, of mediæval Europe: of the buildings raised before Commerce had put the coping-stone on the edifice of tyranny by the discovery that fancy, imagination, sentiment, the joy of creation, and the hope of fair fame, are marketable articles too precious to be allowed to men who have not the money to buy them, to mere handicraftsmen and day-labourers. Let us remember there was a time when men had pleasure in their daily work, but yet, as to other matters, hoped for light and freedom even as they do now: their dim hope grew brighter, and they watched its seeming fulfilment drawing nearer and nearer, and gazed so eagerly on it that they did not note how the ever watchful foe, oppression, had changed his shape and was stealing from them what they had already gained in the days when the light of their new hope was but a feeble glimmer: so they lost the old gain, and for lack of it the new gain was changed and spoiled for them into something not much better than loss.

Betwixt the days in which we now live and the end of the Middle Ages, Europe has gained freedom of thought, increase of knowledge, and huge talent for dealing with the material forces of nature; comparative political freedom withal and respect for the lives of civilized men, and other gains that go with these things: nevertheless I say deliberately that if the present state of society is to endure, she has bought these gains at too high a price in the loss of the pleasure in daily work which once did certainly solace the mass of men for their fears and oppressions: the death of Art was too high a price to pay for the material prosperity of the middle classes. . . .

Now once more I will say that we well-to-do people, those of us who love Art, not as a toy, but as a thing necessary to the life of man, as a token of his freedom and happiness, have for our best work the raising of the standard of life among the people; or in other words, establishing the claim I made for Labour, which I will now put in a different form, that we may try to see what chiefly hinders us from making that claim good and what are the enemies to be attacked. Thus then I put the claim again: *Nothing should be made by man's labour which is not worth making, or which must be made by labour degrading to the makers.*

Simple as that proposition is, and obviously right as I am sure it must seem to you, you will find, when you come to consider the matter, that it is a direct challenge to the death to the present system of labour in civilized countries. That system, which I have called competitive Commerce, is distinctly a system of war; that is, of waste and destruction, or you may call it gambling if you will; the point of it being that under it whatever a man gains he gains at the expense of some other man's loss. Such a system does not and cannot heed whether the matters it makes are worth making; it does not and cannot heed whether those who make them are degraded by their work: it heeds one thing and only one, namely what it calls making a profit; which word has come to be used so conventionally that I must explain to you what it really means, to wit, the plunder of the weak by the strong. Now I say of this system, that it is of its very nature destructive of Art, that is to say of the happiness of life. Whatever consideration is shown for the life of the people in these days, whatever is done which is worth doing, is done in spite of the system and in the teeth of its maxims; and most true it is that we do all of us tacitly at least admit that it is opposed to all the highest aspirations of mankind.

Do we not know, for instance, how those men of genius work who are the salt of the earth, without whom the corruption of Society would long ago have become unendurable? The poet, the artist, the man of science, is it not true that in their fresh and glorious days, when they are in the heyday of their faith and enthusiasm, they are thwarted at every turn by Commercial War, with its sneering question "Will it pay?" Is it not true that when they begin to win worldly success, when they become comparatively rich, in spite of ourselves they seem to us tainted by the contact with the commercial world? Need I speak of great schemes that hang about neglected; of things most necessary to be done, and so confessed by all men, that no one can seriously set a hand to because of the lack of money; while if it be a question of creating or stimulating some foolish whim in the public mind, the satisfaction of which will breed a profit, the money will come in by the ton? Nay, you know what an old story it is of the wars bred by Commerce in search of new markets, which not even the most peaceable of statesmen can resist; an old story and still it seems for ever new, and now become a kind of grim joke, at which I would rather not laugh if I could help it, but am even forced to laugh from a soul laden with anger.

And all that mastery over the powers of nature which the last hundred years or less have given us: what has it done for us under this system? In the opinion of John Stuart Mill, it was doubtful if all the mechanical inventions of modern times have done anything to lighten the toil of labour: be sure there is no doubt that they were not made for that end, but to make a profit. Those almost miraculous machines, which if orderly forethought had dealt with them might even now be speedily extinguishing all irksome and unintelligent labour, leaving us free to raise the standard of skill of hand and energy of mind in our workmen, and to produce afresh that loveliness and order which only the hand of man guided by his soul can produce; what have they done for us now? Those machines of which the civilized world is so proud, has it any right to be proud of the use they have been put to by commercial war and waste?

I do not think exultation can have a place here: commercial war has made a profit of these wonders; that is to say it has by their means bred for itself millions of unhappy workers, unintelligent machines as far as their daily work goes, in order to get cheap labour, to keep up its exciting but deadly game for ever. Indeed that labour would have been cheap enough, cheap to the commercial war generals, and deadly dear to the rest of us, but for the seeds of freedom which valiant men of old have sowed amongst us to spring up in our own day into Chartism and Trades Unionism and Socialism, for the defence of order and a decent life. Terrible would have been our slavery, and not of the working classes alone, but for these germs of the change which must be. Even as it is, by the reckless aggregation of machine-workers and their adjoints in the great cities and the manufacturing districts, it has kept down life amongst us and keeps it down to a miserably low standard; so low that any standpoint for improvement is hard even to think of. By the means of speedy communication which it has created, and which should have raised the standard of life by spreading intelligence from town to country, and widely creating modest centres of freedom of thought and habits of culture; by the means of the railways and the like, it has gathered to itself fresh recruits for the reserve army of competing lack-alls on which its gambling gains so much depend, stripping the countryside of its population, and extinguishing all reasonable hope and life in the lesser towns.

Nor can I, an artist, think last or least of the outward effects which betoken this rule of the wretched anarchy of commercial war. Think of the spreading sore of London swallowing up with its loathsomeness field and wood and heath without mercy and without hope, mocking our feeble efforts to deal even with its minor evils of smoke-laden sky and befouled river: the black horror and reckless squalor of our manufacturing districts, so dreadful to the senses which are unused to them that it is ominous for the future of the race that any man can live among it in intolerable cheerfulness: nay, in the open country itself the thrusting aside by miserable jerry-built brick and slate of the solid grey dwellings that are still scattered about, fit emblems in their cheery but beautiful simplicity of the yeomen of the English field, whose destruction at the hands of the as yet young commercial war was lamented so touchingly by the high-minded More and valiant Latimer. Everywhere in short the change from old to new involves one certainty, whatever else may be doubtful, a worsening of the aspect of the country.

This is the condition of England: of England the country of order, peace, and stability, the land of common sense and practicality; the country to which all eyes are turned of those whose hope is for the continuance and perfection of modern progress. There are countries in Europe whose aspect is not so ruined outwardly, though they may have less of material prosperity, less widespread middle-class wealth to balance the squalor and disgrace I have mentioned: but if they are members of the great commercial whole, through the same mill they have got to go, unless something should happen to turn aside the triumphant march of War Commercial before it reaches the end. That is what three centuries of Commerce have brought that hope to, which sprang up when feudalism began to fall to pieces. What can give us the dayspring of a new hope? What, save general revolt against the tyranny of commercial war? The palliatives over which many worthy people are busying themselves now are useless: because they are but unorganised partial revolts against a vast wide-spreading grasping organization which will, with the unconscious instinct of a plant, meet every attempt at bettering the condition of the people with an attack on a fresh side; new machines, new markets, wholesale emigration, the revival of grovelling superstitions, preachments of thrift to lack-alls, of temperance to the wretched; such things as these will baffle at every turn all partial revolts against the monster we of the middle classes have created for our own undoing.

I will speak quite plainly on this matter, though I must say an ugly word in the end if I am to say what I think. The one thing to be done is to set people far and wide to think it possible to raise the standard of life. If you think of it, you will see clearly that this means stirring up general discontent. And now to illustrate that I turn back to my blended claim for Art and Labour, that I may deal with the third clause in it: here is the claim again: *It is right and necessary that all men should have work to do: First, Work worth doing; Second, Work of itself pleasant to do; Third, Work done under such conditions as would make it neither over-wearisome nor over-anxious.*

With the first and second clauses, which are very nearly related to each other, I have tried to deal already. They are as it were the soul of the claim for proper labour; the third clause is the body without which that soul cannot exist. I will extend it in this way, which will indeed partly carry us over ground already covered: *No one who is willing to work should ever fear want of such employment as would earn for him all due necessaries of mind and body.* All due necessaries: what are the due necessaries for a good citizen? First, honourable and fitting work: which would involve giving him a chance of gaining capacity for his work by due education; also, as the work must be worth doing and pleasant to do, it will be found necessary to this end that his position be so assured to him that he cannot be compelled to do useless work, or work in which he cannot take pleasure.

The second necessity is decency of surroundings: including 1. good lodging; 2. ample space; 3. general order and beauty. That is: 1. Our houses must be well built, clean, and healthy. 2. There must be abundant garden space in our towns, and our towns must not eat up the fields and natural features of the country; nay, I demand even that there be left waste spaces and wilds in it, or romance and poetry, that is Art, will die out amongst us. 3. Order and beauty means that not only our houses must be stoutly and properly built, but also that they be ornamented duly: that the fields be not only left for cultivation, but also that they be not spoilt by it any more than a garden is spoilt: no one for instance to be allowed to cut down, for mere profit, trees whose loss would spoil a landscape: neither on any pretext should people be allowed to darken the daylight with smoke, to befoul rivers, or to degrade any spot of earth with squalid litter and brutal wasteful disorder.

The third necessity is leisure. You will understand that in using that word I imply first that all men must work for some portion of the day, and secondly that they have a positive right to claim a respite from that work: the leisure they have a right to claim must be ample enough to allow them full rest of mind and body: a man must have time for serious individual thought, for imagination, for dreaming even, or the race of men will inevitably worsen. Even of the honourable and fitting work of which I have been speaking, which is a whole heaven asunder from the forced work of the capitalist system, a man must

not be asked to give more than his fair share; or men will become un-
equally developed, and there will still be a rotten place in society. . . .

When will the time come when honest and clear-seeing men will
grow sick of all this chaos of waste, this robbing of Peter to pay Paul,
which is the essence of commercial war? When shall we band together
to replace the system whose motto is "The devil take the hindmost"
with a system whose motto shall be really and without qualification
"One for all and all for one?" Who knows but the time may be at
hand, but that we now living may see the beginning of that end which
shall extinguish luxury and poverty? when the upper, middle, and lower
classes shall have melted into one class, living contentedly a simple
and happy life? That is a long sentence to describe the state of things
which I am asking you to help to bring about: the abolition of slavery
is a shorter one and means the same thing. You may be tempted to
think the end not worth striving for on the one hand, or on the other
to suppose, each one of you, that it is so far ahead that nothing serious
can be done towards it in our own time, and that you may as well
therefore sit quiet and do nothing. Let me remind you how only the
other day in the lifetime of the youngest of us many thousand men of
our own kindred gave their lives on the battle-field to bring to a happy
ending a mere episode in the struggle for the abolition of slavery:
they are blessed and happy, for the opportunity came to them, and
they seized it and did their best, and the world is the wealthier for it:
and if such an opportunity is offered to us shall we thrust it from us
that we may sit still in ease of body, in doubt, in disease, of soul?
These are the days of combat: who can doubt that as he hears all round
him the sounds that betoken discontent and hope and fear in high and
low, the sounds of awakening courage and wakening conscience?
These, I say, are the days of combat, when there is no external peace
possible to an honest man; but when for that very reason the internal
peace of a good conscience founded on settled convictions is the easier
to win, since action for the cause is offered us.

Or will you say that here in this quiet, constitutionally governed
country of England there is no opportunity for action offered to us?
If we were in gagged Germany, in gagged Austria, in Russia where
a word or two might land us in Siberia or the prison of the fortress of
Peter and Paul; why then, indeed—Ah! my friends, it is but a poor
tribute to offer on the tombs of the martyrs of liberty, this refusal to
take the torch from their dying hands! Is it not of Goethe it is told,

that on hearing one say he was going to America to begin life again, he replied: "Here is America, or nowhere?" So for my part I say: "Here is Russia, or nowhere." To say the governing classes in England are not afraid of freedom of speech, therefore let us abstain from speaking freely, is a strange paradox to me. Let us on the contrary press in through the breach which valiant men have made for us: if we hang back we make their labours, their sufferings, their deaths, of no account. Believe me, we shall be shown that it is all or nothing: or will any one here tell me that a Russian moujik is in a worse case than a sweating tailor's wage-slave? Do not let us deceive ourselves, the class of victims exists here as in Russia. There are fewer of them? Maybe; then are they of themselves more helpless, and so have more need of our help.

And how can we of the middle classes, we the capitalists, and our hangers-on, help them? By renouncing our class, and on all occasions when antagonism rises up between the classes casting in our lot with the victims: with those who are condemned at the best to lack of education, refinement, leisure, pleasure, and renown; and at the worst to a life lower than that of the most brutal of savages in order that the system of competitive Commerce may endure. There is no other way: and this way, I tell you plainly, will in the long run give us plentiful occasion for self-sacrifice without going to Russia. I feel sure that in this assembly there are some who are steeped in discontent with the miserable anarchy of the century of Commerce: to them I offer a means of renouncing their class by supporting Socialist propaganda in joining the Democratic Federation, which I have the honour of representing before you, and which I believe is the only body in this country which puts forward constructive Socialism as its programme. . . .

15. MILL:
Proper Functions of Government

John Stuart Mill (1806–1873), philosopher and economist, is the subject of an excellent, recent biography by Michael St. John Packe (New York, 1954). A definitive edition is being published by the University of

Toronto Press, in which Frances E. Mineka's *The Earlier Letters* in two volumes is available. J. J. Coss has edited the *Autobiography* (New York, 1944). An important recent book is Thomas Wood's *Poetry and Philosophy: A Study in the Thought of John Stuart Mill* (London, 1961).

This selection by Mill* (Book V, Chapter 1, *Principles of Political Economy*) is typical of his writings in its balance and delicacy. Mill characteristically examines in detail each alternative he can posit, drawing sane and subtle distinctions never becoming dogmatic or shrill, though never forsaking his first principles.

1. [*Necessary and optional of government functions distinguished*] One of the most disputed questions both in political science and in practical statesmanship at this particular period, relates to the proper limits of the functions and agency of governments. At other times it has been a subject of controversy how governments should be constituted, and according to what principles and rules they should exercise their authority; but it is now almost equally a question, to what departments of human affairs that authority should extend. And when the tide sets so strongly towards changes in government and legislation, as a means of improving the condition of mankind, this discussion is more likely to increase than to diminish in interest. On the one hand, impatient reformers, thinking it easier and shorter to get possession of the government than of the intellects and dispositions of the public, are under a constant temptation to stretch the province of government beyond due bounds: while, on the other, mankind have been so much accustomed by their rulers to interference for purposes other than the public good, or under an erroneous conception of what that good requires, and so many rash proposals are made by sincere lovers of improvement, for attempting, by compulsory regulation, the attainment of objects which can only be effectually or only usefully compassed by opinion and discussion, that there has grown up a spirit of resistance *in limine* to the interference of government, merely as such, and a disposition to restrict its sphere of action within the narrowest bounds. From differences in the historical development of different nations, not necessary to be here dwelt upon, the former excess, that of exaggerating the province of government prevails most, both in theory and in practice, among the Continental nations, while in England the contrary spirit has hitherto been predominant.

* From *Collected Works of John Stuart Mill*, Vol. III, *Principles of Political Economy*, Bladen and Robson, eds. (University of Toronto Press, 1965). Reprinted by permission.

The general principles of the question, in so far as it is a question of principle, I shall make an attempt to determine in a later chapter of this Book: after first considering the effects produced by the conduct of government in the exercise of the functions universally acknowledged to belong to it. For this purpose, there must be a specification of the functions which are either inseparable from the idea of a government, or are exercised habitually and without objection by all governments; as distinguished from those respecting which it has been considered questionable whether governments should exercise them or not. The former may be termed the *necessary*, the latter the *optional*, functions of government. By the term optional it is not meant to imply, that it can ever be a matter of indifference, or of arbitrary choice, whether the government should or should not take upon itself the functions in question; but only that the expediency of its exercising them does not amount to necessity, and is a subject on which diversity of opinion does or may exist.

2. [*Multifarious character of the necessary functions of government*] In attempting to enumerate the necessary functions of government, we find them to be considerably more multifarious than most people are at first aware of, and not capable of being circumscribed by those very definite lines of demarcation, which, in the inconsiderateness of popular discussion, it is often attempted to draw round them. We sometimes, for example, hear it said that governments ought to confine themselves to affording protection against force and fraud: that, these two things apart, people should be free agents, able to take care of themselves, and that so long as a person practises no violence or deception, to the injury of others in person or property, legislators and governments are in no way called on to concern themselves about him. But why should people be protected by their government, that is, by their own collective strength, against violence and fraud, and not against other evils, except that the expediency is more obvious? If nothing, but what people cannot possibly do for themselves, can be fit to be done for them by government, people might be required to protect themselves by their skill and courage even against force, or to beg or buy protection against it, as they actually do where the government is not capable of protecting them: and against fraud every one has the protection of his own wits. But without further anticipating the discussion of principles, it is sufficient on the present occasion to consider facts.

Under which of these heads, the repression of force or of fraud, are we to place the operation, for example, of the laws of inheritance? Some such laws must exist in all societies. It may be said, perhaps, that in this matter government has merely to give effect to the disposition which an individual makes of his own property by will. This, however, is at least extremely disputable; there is probably no country by whose laws the power of testamentary disposition is perfectly absolute. And suppose the very common case of there being no will: does not the law, that is, the government, decide on principles of general expediency, who shall take the succession? and in case the successor is in any manner incompetent, does it not appoint persons, frequently officers of its own, to collect the property and apply it to his benefit? There are many other cases in which the government undertakes the administration of property, because the public interest, or perhaps only that of the particular persons concerned, is thought to require it. This is often done in case of litigated property; and in cases of judicially declared insolvency. It has never been contended that in doing these things, a government exceeds its province.

Nor is the function of the law in defining property itself, so simple a thing as may be supposed. It may be imagined, perhaps, that the law has only to declare and protect the right of every one to what he has himself produced, or acquired by the voluntary consent, fairly obtained, of those who produced it. But is there nothing recognised as property except what has been produced? Is there not the earth itself, its forests and waters, and all other natural riches, above and below the surface? These are the inheritance of the human race, and there must be regulations for the common enjoyment of it. What rights, and under what conditions, a person shall be allowed to exercise over any portion of this common inheritance, cannot be left undecided. No function of government is less optional than the regulation of these things, or more completely involved in the idea of civilized society.

Again, the legitimacy is conceded of repressing violence or treachery; but under which of these heads are we to place the obligation imposed on people to perform their contracts? Non-performance does not necessarily imply fraud; the person who entered into the contract may have sincerely intended to fulfil it: and the term fraud, which can scarcely admit of being extended even to the case of voluntary breach of contract when no deception was practised, is certainly not applicable when the omission to perform is a case of negligence. Is it no part of the duty of governments to enforce contracts? Here the doctrine of non-interference would no doubt be stretched a little, and it would be said, that enforcing contracts is not regulating the affairs of individuals at the pleasure of government, but giving effect to their own expressed desire. Let us acquiesce in this enlargement of the restrictive theory, and take it for what it is worth. But governments do not limit their concern with contracts to a simple enforcement. They take upon themselves to determine what contracts are fit to be enforced. It is not enough that one person, not being either cheated or compelled, makes a promise to another. There are promises by which it is not for the public good that persons should have the power of binding themselves. To say nothing of engagements to do something contrary to law, there are engagements which the law refuses to enforce, for reasons connected with the interest of the promiser, or with the general policy of the state. A contract by which a person sells himself to another as a slave, would be declared void by the tribunals of this and of most other European countries. There are few nations whose laws enforce a contract for what is looked upon as prostitution, or any matrimonial engagement of which the conditions vary in any respect from those which the law has thought fit to prescribe. But when once it is admitted that there are any engagements which for reasons of expediency the law ought not to enforce, the same question is necessarily opened with respect to all engagements. Whether, for example, the law should enforce a contract to labour, when the wages are too low or the hours of work too severe: whether it should enforce a contract by which a person binds himself to remain, for more than a very limited period, in the service of a given individual: whether a contract of marriage, entered into for life, should continue to be enforced against the deliberate will of the persons, or of either of the persons, who entered into it. Every question which can possibly arise as to the policy of contracts, and of the relations which they establish among human beings, is a question for the legislator; and one which he cannot escape from considering, and in some way or other deciding.

Again, the prevention and suppression of force and fraud afford appropriate employment for soldiers, policemen, and criminal judges; but there are also civil tribunals. The punishment of wrong is one business of an administration of justice, but the decision of disputes is another. Innumerable disputes arise between persons, without *mala fides* on either side, through misconception of their legal rights, or from not being agreed about the facts, on the proof of which those rights are legally dependent. It is not for the general interest that the

State should appoint persons to clear up these uncertainties and termi-
nate these disputes? It cannot be said to be a case of absolute necessity.
People might appoint an arbitrator, and engage to submit to his decision; and they do so where there are no courts of justice, or where the
courts are not trusted, or where their delays and expenses, or the
irrationality of their rules of evidence, deter people from resorting to
them. Still, it is universally thought right that the State should establish
civil tribunals; and if their defects often drive people to have recourse
to substitutes, even then the power held in reserve of carrying the case
before a legally constituted court, gives to the substitutes their principal
efficacy.

Not only does the State undertake to decide disputes, it takes precautions beforehand that disputes may not arise. The laws of most
countries lay down rules for determining many things, not because
it is of much consequence in what way they are determined, but in
order that they may be determined somehow, and there may be no
question on the subject. The law prescribes forms of words for many
kinds of contract, in order that no dispute or misunderstanding may
arise about their meaning: it makes provision that if a dispute does
arise, evidence shall be procurable for deciding it, by requiring that
the document be attested by witnesses and executed with certain
formalities. The law preserves authentic evidence of facts to which
legal consequences are attached, by keeping a registry of such facts;
as of births, deaths, and marriages, of wills and contracts, and of
judicial proceedings. In doing these things, it has never been alleged
that government oversteps the proper limits of its functions.

Again, however wide a scope we may allow to the doctrine that
individuals are the proper guardians of their own interests, and that
government owes nothing to them but to save them from being interfered with by other people, the doctrine can never be applicable to
any persons but those who are capable of acting in their own behalf.
The individual may be an infant, or a lunatic, or fallen into imbecility.
The law surely must look after the interests of such persons. It does not
necessarily do this through officers of its own. It often devolves the
trust upon some relative or connexion. But in doing so is its duty
ended? Can it make over the interests of one person to the control
of another, and be excused from supervision, or from holding the
person thus trusted, responsible for the discharge of the trust?

There is a multitude of cases in which governments, with general
approbation, assume powers and execute functions for which no reason

can be assigned except the simple one, that they conduce to general convenience. We may take as an example, the function (which is a monopoly too) of coining money. This is assumed for no more recondite purpose than that of saving to individuals the trouble, delay, and expense of weighing and assaying. No one, however, even of those most jealous of state interference, has objected to this as an improper exercise of the powers of government. Prescribing a set of standard weights and measures is another instance. Paving, lighting, and cleansing the streets and thoroughfares, is another; whether done by the general government, or as is more usual, and generally more advisable, by a municipal authority. Making or improving harbours, building lighthouses, making surveys in order to have accurate maps and charts, raising dykes to keep the sea out, and embankments to keep rivers in, are cases in point.

Examples might be indefinitely multiplied without intruding on any disputed ground. But enough has been said to show that the admitted functions of government embrace a much wider field than can easily be included within the ring-fence of any restrictive definition, and that it is hardly possible to find any ground of justification common to them all, except the comprehensive one of general expediency; nor to limit the interference of government by any universal rule, save the simple and vague one, that it should never be admitted but when the case of expediency is strong.

16. GREEN:
Limiting Laissez-Faire

Thomas Hill Green (1836–1882) is now known as one of the foremost of the Oxford Hegelians, but it was as an Oxford don that he exerted his greatest influence. His impact on Liberal thought is the subject of a recent study by Melvin Richter, *The Politics of Conscience* (1964). Another recent work, *The Social Philosophy of English Idealism*, by A. J. M. Milne (1962) discusses Green's philosophy with less specific reference to its political implications. *The Works* of Green were edited in three volumes (1885–88) by his friend R. L. Nettleship. Nettleship's memoir, included in *Works*, is a standard biographical source.

Like Mill, with whom he must be compared, Green is subtle and comprehensive, positing and examining many alternatives. Though their premises differ widely, the careful reader of this selection from *Liberal Legislation and Freedom of Contract* will remark a similarity not only of methods but also of a position reminiscent of the controversies of Arnold and Huxley.

Our political history since the first reform act naturally falls into three divisions. (1) The first, beginning with the reform of parliament, and extending to Sir R. Peel's administration is marked by the struggle of free society against close privileged corporations. Its greatest achievement was the establishment of representative municipal governments in place of the close bodies which had previously administered the affairs of our cities and boroughs; a work which after an interval of nearly half a century we hope shortly to see extended to the rural districts. Another important work was the overhauling the immense charities of the country, and the placing them under something like adequate public control. And the natural complement of this was the removal of the grosser abuses in the administration of the church, the abolition of pluralities and sinecures, and the reform of cathedral chapters. In all this, while there was much that contributed to the freedom of our civil life, there was nothing that could possibly be construed as an interference with the rights of the individual. No one was disturbed in doing what he would with his own. Even those who had fattened on abuses had their vested interests duly respected, for the house of commons then as now had "quite a passion for compensation." (2) With the ministry of Sir R. Peel began the struggle of society against monopolies; in other words, the liberation of trade. Some years later Mr. Gladstone, in his famous budgets, was able to complete the work which his master began, and it is now some twenty years since the last vestige of protection for any class of traders or producers disappeared. The taxes on knowledge, as they were called, followed the taxes on food, and since most of us grew up there has been no exchangeable commodity in England except land—no doubt a large exception—of which the exchange has not been perfectly free.

The realisation of complete freedom of contract was the special object of this reforming work. It was to set men at liberty to dispose of what they had made their own that the free-trader worked. He only interfered to prevent interference. He would put restraint on no man in doing anything that did not directly check the free dealing of some one in something else. (3) But of late reforming legislation has taken, as I have pointed out, a seemingly different direction. It has not at any rate been so readily identifiable with the work of liberation. In certain respects it has put restraints on the individual in doing what he will with his own. And it is noticeable that this altered tendency begins, in the main, with the more democratic parliament of 1868. It is true that the earlier factory acts, limiting as they do by law the conditions under which certain kinds of labour may be bought and sold, had been passed some time before. The first approach to an effectual factory act dates as far back as the time of the first reform act, but it only applied to the cotton industry, and was very imperfectly put in force. It aimed at limiting the hours of labour for children and young persons. Gradually the limitations of hours came to be enforced, other industries were brought under the operation of the restraining laws, and the same protection extended to women as to young persons. But it was only alongside of the second reform act in 1867 that an attempt was made by parliament to apply the same rule to every kind of factory and workshop; only later still, in the first parliament elected partly by household suffrage, that efficient measures were taken for enforcing the restraints which previous legislation had in principle required. Improvements and extensions in detail have since been introduced, largely through the influence of Mr. Mundella, and now we have a system of law by which, in all our chief industries except the agricultural, the employment of children except as half-timers is effectually prevented, the employment of women and young persons is effectually restricted to ten hours a day, and in all places of employment health and bodily safety have all the protection which rules can give them.

If factory regulation had been attempted, though only in a piecemeal way, some time before we had a democratic house of commons, the same cannot be said of educational law. It was the parliament elected by a more popular suffrage in 1868 that passed, as we know, the first great education act. That act introduced compulsory schooling. It left the compulsion, indeed, optional with local school-boards, but compulsion is the same in principle, is just as much compulsion by the state, whether exercised by the central government or delegated by that government to provincial authorities. The education act of 1870 was a wholly new departure in English legislation, though Mr. Forster was wise enough to proceed tentatively, and leave the adoption of compulsory bye-laws to the discretion of school-boards. It was so just as much as if he had attempted at once to enforce compulsory attendance through the action of the central government. The principle was established once for all that parents were not to be allowed to do as they willed with their children, if they willed either to set them to work or to let them run wild without elementary education. Freedom of contract in respect of all dealings with the labour of children was so far limited.

I need not trouble you with recalling the steps by which the principle of the act of 1870 has since been further applied and enforced. It is evident that in the body of school and factory legislation which I have noticed we have a great system of interference with freedom of contract. The hirer of labour is prevented from hiring it on terms to which the person of whom he hires it could for the most part have been readily brought to agree. If children and young persons and women were not ready in many cases, either from their own wish, or under the influence of parents and husbands, to accept employment of the kind which the law prohibits, there would have been no occasion for the prohibition. It is true that adult men are not placed directly under the same restriction. The law does not forbid them from working as long hours as they please. But I need not point out here that in effect the prevention of the employment of juvenile labour beyond certain hours, amounts, at least in the textile industries, to the prevention of the working of machinery beyond those hours. It thus indirectly puts a limit on the number of hours during which the manufacturer can employ his men. And if it is only accidentally, so to speak, that the hiring of men's labour is interfered with by the half-time and ten hours' system, the interference on grounds of health and safety is as direct as possible. The most mature man is prohibited by law from contracting to labour in factories, or pits, or workshops, unless certain rules for the protection of health and limb are complied with. In like manner he is prohibited from living in a house which the sanitary inspector pronounces unwholesome. The free sale or letting of a certain kind of commodity is thereby prevented. Here, then, is a great system of restriction, which yet hardly any impartial person wishes to see reversed; which many of us wish to see made more complete. Perhaps, however, we have never thoroughly considered the principles on which we approve it. It may be well, therefore, to spend a short time in ascertaining those principles. We shall then be on surer ground in approaching those more difficult questions of legislation which must shortly be dealt with, and of which the settlement is sure to be resisted in the name of individual liberty.

We shall probably all agree that freedom, rightly understood, is the greatest of blessings; that its attainment is the true end of all our effort as citizens. But when we thus speak of freedom, we should consider carefully what we mean by it. We do not mean merely freedom from restraint or compulsion. We do not mean merely freedom to do as we like irrespectively of what it is that we like. We do not mean a freedom that can be enjoyed by one man or one set of men at the cost of a loss of freedom to others. When we speak of freedom as something to be so highly prized, we mean a positive power or capacity of doing or enjoying something worth doing or enjoying, and that, too, something that we do or enjoy in common with others. We mean by it a power which each man exercises through the help or security given him by his fellow-men, and which he in turn helps to secure for them. When we measure the progress of a society by its growth in freedom, we measure it by the increasing development and exercise on the whole of those powers of contributing to social good with which we believe the members of the society to be endowed; in short, by the greater power on the part of the citizens as a body to make the most and best of themselves. Thus, though of course there can be no freedom among men who act not willingly but under compulsion, yet on the other hand the mere removal of compulsion, the mere enabling a man to do as he likes, is in itself no contribution to true freedom. In one sense no man is so well able to do as he likes as the wandering savage. He has no master. There is no one to say him nay. Yet we do not count him really free, because the freedom of savagery is not strength, but weakness. The actual powers of the noblest savage do not admit of comparison with those of the humblest citizen of a law-abiding state. He is not the slave of man, but he is the slave of nature. Of compulsion by natural necessity he has plenty of experience, though of restraint by society none at all. Nor can he deliver himself from that compulsion except by submitting to this restraint. So to submit is the first step in true freedom, because the first step towards the full exercise of the faculties with which man is endowed. But we rightly refuse to recognise the highest development on the part of an exceptional individual or exceptional class, as an advance towards the true freedom of man, if it is founded on a refusal of the same opportunity to other men. The powers of the human mind have probably never attained such force and keenness, the proof of what society can do for the individual has never been so strikingly exhibited, as among the small groups of men who possessed civil privileges in the small republics of antiquity. The whole framework of our political ideas, to say nothing of our philosophy, is derived from them. But in them this extraordinary efflorescence of the privileged class was accompanied by the slavery of the multitude. That slavery was the condition on which it depended, and for that reason it was doomed to decay. There is no clearer ordinance of that supreme reason, often dark to us, which governs the course of man's affairs, than that no body of men should in the long run be able to strengthen itself at the cost of others' weakness. The civilisation and freedom of the ancient world were shortlived because they were partial and exceptional. If the ideal of true freedom is the maximum of power for all members of human society alike to make the best of themselves, we are right in refusing to ascribe the glory of freedom to a state in which the apparent elevation of the few is founded on the degradation of the many, and in ranking modern society, founded as it is on free industry, with all its confusion and ignorant licence and waste of effort, above the most splendid of ancient republics.

If I have given a true account of that freedom which forms the goal of social effort, we shall see that freedom of contract, freedom in all the forms of doing what one will with one's own, is valuable only as a means to an end. That end is what I call freedom in the positive sense: in other words, the liberation of the powers of all men equally for contributions to a common good. No one has a right to do what he will with his own in such a way as to contravene this end. It is only through the guarantee which society gives him that he has property at all, or, strictly speaking, any right to his possessions. This guarantee is founded on a sense of common interest. Every one has an interest in securing to every one else the free use and enjoyment and disposal of his possessions, so long as that freedom on the part of one does not interfere with a like freedom on the part of others, because such freedom contributes to that equal development of the faculties of all which is the highest good for all. This is the true and the only justification of rights of property. Rights of property, however, have been and are claimed which cannot be thus justified. We are all now agreed that men cannot rightly be the property of men. The institution of property being only justifiable as a means to the free exercise of the social capabilities of all, there can be no true right to property of a kind which debars one class of men from such free exercise altogether.

We condemn slavery no less when it arises out of a voluntary agreement on the part of the enslaved person. A contract by which any one agreed for a certain consideration to become the slave of another we should reckon a void contract. Here, then, is a limitation upon freedom of contract which we all recognise as rightful. No contract is valid in which human persons, willingly or unwillingly, are dealt with as commodities, because such contracts of necessity defeat the end for which alone society enforces contracts at all.

Are there no other contracts which, less obviously perhaps but really, are open to the same objection? In the first place, let us consider contracts affecting labour. Labour, the economist tells us, is a commodity exchangeable like other commodities. This is in a certain sense true, but it is a commodity which attaches in a peculiar manner to the person of man. Hence restrictions may need to be placed on the sale of this commodity which would be unnecessary in other cases, in order to prevent labour from being sold under conditions which make it impossible for the person selling it ever to become a free contributor to social good in any form. This is most plainly the case when a man bargains to work under conditions fatal to health, *e.g.* in an unventilated factory. Every injury to the health of the individual is, so far as it goes, a public injury. It is an impediment to the general freedom; so much deduction from our power, as members of society, to make the best of ourselves. Society is, therefore, plainly within its right when it limits freedom of contract for the sale of labour, so far as is done by our laws for the sanitary regulations of factories, workshops, and mines. It is equally within its right in prohibiting the labour of women and young persons beyond certain hours. If they work beyond those hours, the result is demonstrably physical deterioration; which, as demonstrably, carries with it a lowering of the moral forces of society. For the sake of that general freedom of its members to make the best of themselves, which it is the object of civil society to secure, a prohibition should be put by law, which is the deliberate voice of society, on all such contracts of service as in a general way yield such a result. The purchase or hire of unwholesome dwellings is properly forbidden on the same principle. Its application to compulsory education may not be quite so obvious, but it will appear on a little reflection. Without a command of certain elementary arts and knowledge, the individual in modern society is as effectually crippled as by the loss of a limb or a broken constitution. He is not free to develop his faculties. With a view to securing such freedom among its members it is as certainly within the province of the state to prevent children from growing up in that kind of ignorance which practically excludes them from a free career in life, as it is within its province to require the sort of building and drainage necessary for public health.

Our modern legislation then with reference to labour, and education, and health, involving as it does manifold interference with freedom of contract, is justified on the ground that it is the business of the state, not indeed directly to promote moral goodness, for that, from the very nature of moral goodness, it cannot do, but to maintain the conditions without which a free exercise of the human faculties is impossible. It does not indeed follow that it is advisable for the state to do all which it is justified in doing. We are often warned nowadays against the danger of over-legislation; or, as I heard it put in a speech of the present home secretary in days when he was sowing his political wild oats, of "grandmotherly government." There may be good ground for the warning, but at any rate we should be quite clear what we mean by it. The outcry against state interference is often raised by men whose real objection is not to state interference but to centralisation, to the constant aggression of the central executive upon local authorities. As I have already pointed out, compulsion at the discretion of some elected municipal board proceeds just as much from the state as does compulsion exercised by a government office in London. No doubt, much needless friction is avoided, much is gained in the way of elasticity and adjustment to circumstances, by the independent local administration of general laws; and most of us would agree that of late there has been a dangerous tendency to override municipal discretion by the hard and fast rules of London "departments." But centralisation is one thing: over-legislation, or the improper exercise of the power of the state, quite another. It is one question whether of late the central government has been unduly trenching on local government, and another question whether the law of the state, either as administered by central or by provincial authorities, has been unduly interfering with the discretion of individuals. We may object most strongly to advancing centralisation, and yet wish that the law should put rather more than less restraint on those liberties of the individual which are a social nuisance. But there are some political speculators whose objection is not merely to centralisation, but to the extended action of law altogether. They think that the individual ought to be left much more to himself than has of late been the case. Might not our people, they ask, have been trusted to learn in time for themselves to eschew unhealthy dwellings, to refuse dangerous and degrading employment, to get their children the schooling necessary for making their way in the world? Would they not for their own comfort, if not from more chivalrous feeling, keep their wives and daughters from overwork? Or, failing this, ought not women, like men, to learn to protect themselves? Might not all the rules, in short, which legislation of the kind we have been discussing is intended to attain, have been attained without it; not so quickly, perhaps, but without tampering so dangerously with the independence and self-reliance of the people?

Now, we shall probably all agree that a society in which the public health was duly protected, and necessary education duly provided for, by the spontaneous action of individuals, was in a higher condition than one in which the compulsion of law was needed to secure these ends. But we must take men as we find them. Until such a condition of society is reached, it is the business of the state to take the best security it can for the young citizens' growing up in such health and with so much knowledge as is necessary for their real freedom. In so doing it need not at all interfere with the independence and self-reliance of those whom it requires to do what they would otherwise do for themselves. . . . But it was not their case [that of the self-sufficient man] that the laws we are considering were especially meant to meet. It was the overworked women, the ill-housed and untaught families, for whose benefit they were intended. And the question is whether without these laws the suffering classes could have been delivered quickly or slowly from the condition they were in. Could the enlightened self-interest of benevolence of individuals, working under a system of unlimited freedom of contract, have ever brought them into a state compatible with the free development of the human faculties? No one considering the facts can have any doubt as to the answer to this question. Left to itself, or to the operation of casual benevolence, a degraded population perpetuates and increases itself. Read any of the authorised accounts, given before royal or parliamentary commissions, of the state of the labourers, especially of the women and children, as they were in our great industries before the law was first brought to bear on them, and before freedom of contract was first interfered with in them. Ask yourself what chance there was of a generation, born and bred under such conditions, ever contracting itself out of them. Given a certain standard of moral and material well-being, people may be trusted not to sell their labour, or the labour of their children, on terms which would not allow that standard to be maintained. But with large masses of our population, until the laws we have been considering took effect, there was no such standard. There was nothing on their part, in the way either of self-respect or established demand for comforts, to prevent them from working and living, or from putting their children to work and live, in a way in which no one who is to be a healthy and free citizen can work and live. No doubt there were many high-minded employers who did their best for their workpeople before the days of state-interference, but they could not prevent less scrupulous hirers of labour from hiring it on the cheapest terms. It is true that cheap labour is in the long run dear labour, but it is so only in the long run, and eager traders do not think of the long run. If labour is to be had under conditions incompatible with the health or decent housing or education of the labourer, there will always be plenty of people to buy it under those conditions, careless of the burden in the shape of rates and taxes which they may be laying up for posterity. Either the standard of well-being on the part of the sellers of labour must prevent them from selling their labour under those conditions, or the law must prevent it. With a population such as ours was forty years ago, and still largely is, the law must prevent it and continue the prevention for some generations, before the sellers will be in a state to prevent it for themselves.

17. TENNYSON:
"The Steam Threshing Machine"

The life of Charles Tennyson Turner (1808–1879), who collaborated with his younger brother Alfred in *Poems by Two Brothers*, is available in Harold Nicolson's *Tennyson's Two Brothers* (New York, 1947). His *Collected Sonnets, Old and New*, was edited by Hallam Tennyson in 1898. Poems like these show admirably the Victorian concern about the destruction of nature by machinery and, perhaps, the difficulty of writing good, non-hortatory poetry on such subjects.

THE STEAM THRESHING MACHINE

WITH THE STRAW CARRIER

Flush with the pond the lurid furnace burned
At eve, while smoke and vapor filled the yard;
The floomy winter sky was dimly starred,
The fly-wheel with a mellow murmur turned;
While, ever rising on its mystic stair
In the dim light, from secret chambers borne,
The straw of harvest, severed from the corn,
Climbed, and fell over, in the murky air.
I thought of mind and matter, will and law,
And then of him, who set his stately seal
Of Roman words on all the forms he saw
Of old-world husbandry; *I* could but feel
With what a rich precision *he* would draw
The endless ladder, and the booming wheel!

CONTINUED

Did any seer of ancient time forebode
This mighty engine, which we daily see
Accepting our full harvests, like a god,
With clouds about his shoulders—it might be
Some poet-husbandman, some lord of verse,
Old Hesiod, or the wizard Mantuan,
Who catalogued in rich hexameters
The rake, the roller, and the mystic van;
Or else some priest of Ceres, it might seem,
Who witnessed, as he trod the silent fane,
The notes and auguries of coming change,
Of other ministrants in shrine and grange—
The sweating statue, and her sacred wain
Low-booming with the prophecy of steam!

18.   BROWNING:
"The Cry of the Children"

Elizabeth Barrett Browning (1806–1861), wife of Robert Browning and minor poetess enthusiastic for a variety of social reforms, has attracted little critical attention. The standard edition of her works is that edited by Charlotte Porter and Helen A. Clarke (6 vols., 1900). Her *Letters* were edited by F. G. Kenyon (2 vols., 1897). The most noteworthy recent biography is Gardner B. Taplin, *The Life of Elizabeth Barrett Browning* (1957).

"The Cry of the Children" (one of many poems reflecting a Victorian enthusiasm for reform) was published in 1843, and helped to make Elizabeth Barrett a popular poet while Robert Browning was yet obscure.

"Φεῦ, φεῦ, τί προσδέρκεσθέ μ' ὄμμασιν, τέκνα."—*Medea*

Do you hear the children weeping, O my brothers,
    Ere the sorrow comes with years?
They are leaning their young heads against their mothers,
    And *that* cannot stop their tears.
The young lambs are bleating in the meadows,
    The young birds are chirping in the nest,
The young fawns are playing with the shadows,
    The young flowers are blowing toward the west—
But the young, young children, O my brothers,
    They are weeping bitterly!
They are weeping in the playtime of the others,
    In the country of the free. . . .

Alas, alas, the children! they are seeking
    Death in life, as best to have;
They are binding up their hearts away from breaking,
    With a cerement from the grave.

Go out, children, from the mine and from the city,
   Sing out, children, as the little thrushes do;
Pluck your handfuls of the meadow-cowslips pretty.
   Laugh aloud, to feel your fingers let them through!
But they answer, "Are your cowslips of the meadows
      Like our weeds anear the mine?
Leave us quiet in the dark of the coal-shadows,
      From your pleasures fair and fine!

"For oh," say the children, "we are weary,
      And we cannot run or leap;
If we cared for any meadows, it were merely
      To drop down in them and sleep.
Our knees tremble sorely in the stooping,
   We fall upon our faces, trying to go;
And, underneath our heavy eyelids drooping
   The reddest flower would look as pale as snow.
For, all day, we drag our burden tiring
      Through the coal-dark, underground;
Or, all day, we drive the wheels of iron
      In the factories, round and round.

"For all day the wheels are droning, turning;
      Their wind comes in our faces,
Till our hearts turn, our heads with pulses burning,
      And the walls turn in their places;
Turns the sky in the high window, blank and reeling,
   Turns the long light that drops adown the wall,
Turn the black flies that crawl along the ceiling—
   All are turning, all the day, and we with all.
And all day the iron wheels are droning,
      And sometimes we could pray,
'O ye wheels' (breaking out in a mad moaning),
      'Stop! be silent for today!' "

Aye, be silent! Let them hear each other breathing
      For a moment, mouth to mouth!
Let them touch each other's hands, in a fresh wreathing
      Of their tender human youth!
Let them feel that this cold metallic motion
   Is not all the life God fashions or reveals;

Let them prove their living souls against the notion
    That they live in you, or under you, O wheels!
Still, all day, the iron wheels go onward,
    Grinding life down from its mark;
And the children's souls, which God is calling sunward,
    Spin on blindly in the dark.

Now tell the poor young children, O my brothers,
    To look up to Him and pray;
So the blessed One who blesseth all the others,
    Will bless them another day,
They answer, "Who is God that He should hear us,
    While the rushing of the iron wheels is stirred?
When we sob aloud, the human creatures near us
    Pass by, hearing not, or answer not a word.
And *we* hear not (for the wheels in their resounding)
    Strangers speaking at the door—
Is it likely God, with angels singing round Him,
    Hears our weeping any more?

"Two words, indeed, of praying we remember,
    And at midnight's hour of harm,
'Our Father,' looking upward in the chamber,
    We say softly for a charm.
We know no other words except 'Our Father,'
    And we think that, in some pause of angels' song,
God may pluck them with the silence sweet to gather,
    And hold both within His right hand which is strong.
'Our Father!' If He heard us, He would surely
    (For they call Him good and mild)
Answer, smiling down the steep world very purely,
    'Come and rest with me, my child.'

"But no!" say the children, weeping faster,
    "He is speechless as a stone;
And they tell us, of His image is the master
    Who commands us to work on.
Go to!" say the children—"up in Heaven,
    Dark, wheellike, turning clouds are all we find.
Do not mock us; grief has made us unbelieving—
    We look up for God, but tears have made us blind."

Do you hear the children weeping and disproving,
    O my brothers, what ye preach?
For God's possible is taught by His world's loving,
    And the children doubt of each.

And well may the children weep before you!
    They are weary ere they run;
They have never seen the sunshine, nor the glory
    Which is brighter than the sun.
They know the grief of man, without its wisdom;
    They sink in man's despair, without its calm;
Are slaves, without the liberty in Christdom,
    Are martyrs, by the pang without the palm;
Are worn as if with age, yet unretrievingly
    The harvest of its memories cannot reap—
Are orphans of the earthly love and heavenly.
    Let them weep! let them weep!

They look up with their pale and sunken faces,
    And their look is dread to see,
For they mind you of their angels in high places,
    With eyes turned on Deity.
"How long," they say, "how long, O cruel nation,
    Will you stand, to move the world, on a child's heart—
Stifle down with a mailèd heel its palpitation,
    And tread onward to your throne amid the mart?
Our blood splashes upward, O gold-heaper,
    And your purple shows your path!
But the child's sob in the silence curses deeper
    Than the strong man in his wrath."

19. HOPKINS:

"God's Grandeur"

Because Hopkins' sonnet (written in 1877, published in 1918) is not primarily a didactic poem on the evils of the industrial revolution, it serves well as a paradigm by which we can measure the success of poetry more deliberately and overtly directed toward nonliterary goals. A finer poem on the subject is difficult to imagine. For bibliographic information on Hopkins, see headnote, Selection 37.

The world is charged with the grandeur of God.
It will flame out, like shining from shook foil;
It gathers to a greatness, like the ooze of oil
Crushed. Why do men then now not reck his rod?
Generations have trod, have trod, have trod;
And all is seared with trade; bleared, smeared with toil;
And wears man's smudge and shares man's smell—the soil
Is bare now, nor can foot feel, being shod.
And for all this, nature is never spent;
There lives the dearest freshness deep down things;
And though the last lights off the black West went
Oh, morning, at the brown brink eastward, springs—
Because the Holy Ghost over the bent
World broods with warm breast and with ah! bright wings.

III

Religion

I N SPEAKING of the struggle among Victorian Christians about the nature and function of their religion, or of the struggle between Christianity and the forces of unbelief or disbelief, one is likely to fall easily into familiar generalizations. There were, as we have been told, three groups within the established Church of England—the Low, Broad, and High churches; there were, too, the dissenting sects and the Catholics, and it is true that generally they played the roles that the historian ascribes to them. The High Church was traditionally allied with the gentry and aristocracy, the Low Church with the rising middle class; both disagreed with the Broad Church about the relationship between church and state, and about the role of the church in nineteenth-century society. We know, too, something of the Oxford Movement—how it began, what it led to, the consternation caused by Newman's conversion. And in part from our own experience we sense how scientific discovery, especially the forceful presentation of evolutionary theory, affected the religious sensibilities of the Victorians. The more closely one examines such generalizations, however, the more he comes to see the diversity of Victorian religious opinion, and to recognize that Victorian disputes about religion are always closely tied to controversies in the fields of education, science, social welfare, and even art.

For more than a hundred years, even at the turn of the century, the Church of England had been the state religion, not seriously threatened by the wishes or tastes of the sovereign or the governing classes. The Corporation and Test Acts, passed in the reign of Charles II, remained in force and effectively barred nonconformists of any stripe from positions of authority either governmental or ecclesiastical. Yet the Church of England also found its supremacy increasingly threatened throughout the eighteenth century, particularly by the force of Methodism. The followers of Wesley promised that grace was available to all men, without the intermediacy of a priest ordained by the church; it held forth the possibility of a close personal, emotional relationship between the worshiper and God. Its religious individualism was directly contrasted to the attitudes of the established church toward grace and salvation. Furthermore, the Anglican priesthood at its upper levels had degenerated into a sinecure for younger sons of the aristocracy and gentry. Members of the hierarchy were nearly always related to the great families, and they frequently derived great incomes from their position. Throughout its administrative structure the Anglican Church was an inefficient and therefore ineffective patchwork, and clergy at the parish level—those in direct contact with the people— were frequently ill-prepared or careless in attending to their duties. Finally, the church did not come to grips with the problem of the shift in population which was concomitant to the growth of industrialism. The urban masses simply did not have churches to attend; when they attended at all no doubt they derived greater meaning from a nonconformist chapel.

Clearly the Anglican Church felt the threat, for it sought a number of times to bring Wesley back into the church in which he had been an ordained minister. Among nonconformist sects the Wesleyan had always been closest to the Church of England in its structure and in its conservative political attitudes, and it was a sort of Wesleyan Methodism among members of the church that resulted in the formation of a "party"—the Evangelicals, or Low Church—of which Wilberforce was an important member. Their ties with the dogma of both Methodism and the Established Church were loose enough to allow free association with either group; more important, they avoided theological confrontation in the interests of a greater end, philanthropy and reform.

The Evangelicals shared loosely with the Protestant dissenting sects the doctrine of justification by faith (divinely dispensed grace), but they simultaneously held that good works were both desirable and necessary. A vital religion is primarily, then, one characterized by zeal for reform. This earnestness was sometimes marked by a real narrowness, as we may see in the Sabbatarianism so stringently enforced in the first half of the nineteenth century. Just as often, however, one finds the Evangelicals allied with "liberal" interests, and sometimes with groups entirely outside religion—all in the interest of reform.

By 1833, when agitation by the Clapham Sect (wealthy Evangelicals devoted to philanthropic causes) led to the abolition of slavery by Parliament, the force of the original Evangelical movement within the Church of England had been spent. In internal reform of the Church, as well as in broader social reforms, the minority group of Evangelicals had again and again taken the lead. Perhaps because it allied itself so often with what Keble calls "fashionable liberalism" its force as a movement within the Church was weakened. It pointed to a need for internal reform, and accomplished some, but it did not adequately convince the High Church of its necessity. It chose political action as an important means to reform of both society and the Anglican Church, and therefore contributed to the crisis to which Keble's sermon is a response.

The advertisement to the first edition of the "Sermon on National Apostasy" is dated July 22, 1833, eight days after the sermon had been delivered. In that advertisement Keble points out that what he had feared had come to pass: "the Apostolical Church in this realm is henceforth only to stand, in the eye of the State, as one sect among many, depending, for any preeminence she may still appear to retain, merely upon the accident of her having a strong party in the country." What had happened was that in July Parliament passed, after very lengthy debate, an Irish Church Bill which suppressed ten Irish sees by uniting them with others more thickly populated with Anglicans, and revised the means by which the clergy was to be supported. Since the Church was the Apostolical Church, its episcopate was of divine origin, and to abolish bishoprics by Parliamentary action was counter to the doctrine of the apostolical succession. In short, the very life of the Church of England was threatened. This threat Keble saw as the result of a lapse of conscience on the part of Christian legislators: they, particularly, are responsible for insuring the position of "His Holy Church, established among us for the salvation of our souls." Another, even more dangerous, signal of apostasy was the "liberal" principle of toleration. Certainly no supporter of the Church of England could overlook the fact that the toleration which had led, four years before, to Catholic emancipation, was behind this attack on the position of the Established Church. Irish members of Commons had led the fight for the Church Reform Bill, and the Duke of Wellington, already a traitor in the eyes of the Church for his role in bringing about Catholic emancipation, guided the bill through the House of Lords. No greater danger to the principles of "submission and order" on which the Anglican Church rested could be conceived. The question was now, as Keble says in his advertisement, what line of conduct ought the true Anglican to follow? And especially, "what answer can we make henceforth to the partisans of the Bishop of Rome, when they taunt us with being a mere Parliamentarian Church?"

In the months immediately following Keble's sermon, the Oxford Movement began to attempt an answer to those questions. To meet the threat from within and without it was necessary to establish on firmer ground the fact of the Anglican Church as the one true apostolic church, and it attempted to do so by showing that inconsistencies between liturgy and the Thirty-nine Articles were only apparent, and that in fact doctrine could be legitimately derived only from close study of the liturgy. Since it was the liturgy which appeared most "Romanistic" to those liberal reformers outside the Oxford group, the movement carried from its beginning a sort of stigma. The *Tracts for the Times*, begun late in 1833, devoted themselves to establishing the validity of doctrines (as reflected in ritual) which had become obsolete or passed from the consciousness of the majority of the celebrants of the Anglican communion.

From the beginning Newman was among the foremost controversialists of the movement, and in 1837 published what was thought of as the definitive treatise on the Church of England as the middle way—the famous Via Media—"The Prophetical Office of the Church viewed relatively to Romanism and Popular Protestanism." The book had been intended primarily as a reply to Wiseman, the Catholic leader who had won so many converts. Eight years later, Newman himself became one of those converts. Though he did so with as little notice as he could, he had made himself so conspicuous by his opinions that reaction was inevitable. He was not the first member of the Oxford Movement, nor the last, to go over to Rome. But his final defection was startling to those who had hoped that the Tractarians could avoid the extreme toward which they seemed to be tending. The movement had offered hope that vitality might be restored the church by emphasis on its emotional potential as a eucharistic body. When it failed, momentum passed out of the High Church and into another party—the Broad Church, led by people like Thomas Arnold and Charles Kingsley. Suspiciously like the old Evangelicals, the Latitudinarians were concerned that Christianity be made active in the lives of individuals. At its extreme it became the Christian Socialism preached by Kingsley in his novels, but whatever form it took it was characterized by an impatience with questions of mere dogma which had at best only a tangential relationship to the practice of a Christian life. In particular it would object to the niceties of phraseology and the logic-chopping of Tractarianism at its most argumentative. The conversion of Newman to Catholicism was naturally regarded as the necessary end of flirting with Romish practices and, further, as a proof of the dishonesty of a mind which could let itself be trapped by such devices.

The controversy between Newman and Kingsley which is presented here, and which was to culminate in the publication of Newman's *Apologia* in the spring of 1864, focuses on that very question. In his review of Froude's *History of England* Kingsley had reproached Catholicism, and Newman in particular, for playing fast and loose with the truth. The charge, as is pointed out in the first of the installments of the *Apologia*, printed here, was based on Newman's remark that a lie is frequently "the nearest approach to truth." We are now, perhaps, inclined to accept as valid Newman's claim that as a hyperbole the remark conveys an essential truth, and that Kingsley simply could not understand Newman's argument. And although Newman protests that he does not believe malice to be one of Kingsley's motives, the reader of "What, Then, Does Dr. Newman Mean?" is likely to be inclined to think otherwise. The debate between them appears to be conducted on intellectual grounds, but it is informed by what looks very much like personal animosity on Kingsley's Part. Certainly the two had never met, yet Kingsley's distaste for the doctrine and practices of Catholicism centers on Newman alone. The argument of his pamphlet proceeds vigorously, but one has also the feeling that Kingsley willfully misunderstood Newman. (One way of understanding his attitude is to remember that Kingsley was himself very strongly attracted by the Oxford Movement in earlier days; he was, then, fighting not only Newman and Catholicism but a weakness within himself.) Ultimately Newman had the better of the argument, since the total weight of the *Apologia* either crushed or made irrelevant Kingsley's objections, as well as forestalling any significant future criticism.

The quarrel between Newman and Kingsley, whatever its broad implications, does not adequately set forth the state of religion in the middle of Victoria's reign. Even if it was not simply a doctrinal quibble, it is nevertheless true that both share common assumptions about the necessity of Christian belief. That belief was shaken by forces that presented a much greater threat than any present within Christianity itself. Sir Charles Lyell's geological discoveries as early as the 1830's presented clear proof that the biblical account of creation could not be accepted literally, and the evolutionary theory set forth in the *Origin of Species* in 1859 further threatened scriptural revelation. In addition, German biblical scholars added to the threat, though Strauss' *Das Leben Jesu*, a popular work, was not translated into English until 1846 by George Eliot. We are inclined to forget, too, that Edward Pusey, one of the founders of the Oxford Movement, and its leader after Newman's conversion, was one of the first biblical critics in England. These forces of doubt coalesced in the publication in 1860 of *Essays and Reviews*, essays in biblical criticism by seven Anglicans. Bishop John W. Colenso, though not among those, nevertheless illustrates the sort of response called forth from the ordinary churchman by the critical spirit. The authors of *Essays and Reviews* had been condemned by an ecclesiastical court, but as Colenso tells us in his Preface, he was brought, largely by his experience as a missionary, "face to face with questions, which caused . . . some uneasiness in former days." For a while he had "laid the ghosts" by accepting explanations he felt false. The practical applications of Christianity were more important. Finally, however, he was forced to the realization that the Mosaic narrative could not be *"historically true."* The italics are Colenso's, and important in clarifying his willingness to accept any explanation but a historical one. Despite this disclaimer, Colenso was tried for heresy shortly after the appearance in 1862 of his *Critical Examination of the Pentateuch.*

Implicit in the approach of Colenso, or that of the authors of *Essays and Reviews*, is a wish to purify what has been handed down to us as revelation, but also to defend the moral system which is fostered by Christianity. A somewhat different route to the same end was taken by James Martineau in *Types of Ethical Theory*. As a Unitarian minister, Martineau was heavily influenced in his youth by the determinism of Benthamite utilitarianism. He became, however (in Leslie Stephen's phrase), the "champion of theism"; in his Preface to the first edition of *Types of Ethical Theory** Martineau indicates that "it was the irresistible pleading of the moral consciousness which first drove him to rebel against the limits of the merely scientific conception." What was convincing and sound as an ethical system for Martineau (and for the philosophers and theologians whom he influenced) was unlikely to find a wider audience.

Inevitably orthodoxy was emerging from controversy second best, but the open contest always in some degree lagged behind individual consciousness of the failure of religion. Arthur Hugh Clough is typi-

---

* Space limitations forestall inclusion of a selection from the writings of Martineau.

cally taken as exemplary of the divided Victorian mind—earnest for belief, yet persuaded that total belief was impossible. In Clough it motivated resignation from his fellowship, since he could no longer subscribe to the Thirty-nine Articles, and issued sometimes in the mild cynicism of poems like "The Latest Decalogue." A more accurate measure of the mood, though, is found in Arnold's letters to Clough, where the impossibility of specific belief is contrasted to the necessity of moral law. For many Victorians—George Eliot is perhaps an extreme example—the only belief possible was a rather general ethic entirely separate from supernatural sanction. But at the same time the ordinary Victorian was extremely suspicious of such people, who were regarded, Huxley says, as "Infidels."

As "Agnosticism and Christianity" makes clear, the basis of Huxley's attitude is complete intellectual honesty. Accustomed to dealing with the fixed counters of scientific study, and disliking anything "unknowable," the only reasonable procedure is to admit lack of knowledge—to be an agnostic. Huxley is more than careful to plead that agnosticism is not to be equated with immorality, that "all that is best in the ethics of the modern world" is a development from Judeo-Christian tradition. The controversy between gnostics and agnostics is really no contest for Huxley, since the premises of the two attitudes toward religious knowledge are entirely different. His defense of the agnostic attitude is conducted accordingly: a straightforward explanation, contrasted to the narrowness characteristic, he implies, of the Christian apologist.

A similar attitude is expressed in Bradlaugh's *Plea for Atheism:* "Heresey [*i.e.*, agnosticism or atheism], in the eyes of the believer, is highest criminality. . . ." The arguments of Huxley and Bradlaugh, different as they were, are at various points strikingly similar. "Atheism" and "agnosticism" seem to be almost interchangeable terms, and Huxley might well agree with Bradlaugh's declaration that "by conduct founded on knowledge of the laws of existence" evil can be avoided or prevented. Exactly what Bradlaugh means by "the laws of existence" is not clear; no doubt he would agree with Huxley's scientific understanding of them, but his argument against theism is entirely on philosophical grounds. He demonstrates effectively the limitations of both of the usual theistic arguments. Most of us are more familiar with Huxley than Bradlaugh; Huxley's essays are widely read, while Bradlaugh seems something of a curiosity. Yet as a controversialist Bradlaugh was widely known in the last half of the nineteenth century. His editorship of the free-thought weekly, *National Reformer*, as well as his election to Parliament (where he consistently refused to take his oath on the Bible and finally gained the right for himself as well as others merely to affirm rather than swear a Bible oath), made him a conspicuous figure, as important for our understanding of Victorian controversy as the better-known Huxley.

The same status might be claimed for Annie Besant, though certainly she achieved greater notoriety than Bradlaugh. Bradlaugh had lost his belief rather early in life; only after six years of marriage to an Anglican clergyman was Mrs. Besant convinced that Christianity (and of course, her marriage) was impossible for her. Her *Gospel of Atheism* (1877) is indicative of how far, in her own case, the pendulum swung away from conventional belief, and the suddenness of the reaction foreshadows her equally violent plunge into the theosophical doctrines of Madame Blavatsky, early in the 1890's. In the interim she had been closely associated at first with Bradlaugh (she was for a number of years joint editor of the *National Reformer*), but grew away from him as she came closer to socialism. When she joined the Fabian Society in 1885 she broke, for all practical purposes, with the secularism of which she had already made a career. That her involvement with socialism had a basically religious intent becomes clear in the selection "Theosophy Applied to Social Problems." The need of all men is "for happiness and for conditions favourable to his evolution"—by which she means specifically spiritual evolution to oneness with God, the basic mystical notion of theosophy. Society then has a clear duty to its members, and its duty as defined by Mrs. Besant is to provide socialistic means to a religious end. The closeness of the theosophical mysticism to Eastern religions—especially Hinduism—is not accidental, as the chapter on "Theosophy as Religion" witnesses. That theosophy should also be considered as a science, however, is a little startling, and may be taken as evidence of the importance of the scientific mode of thought among the Victorians.

If in some respects Mrs. Besant's socialism calls to mind William Morris' ideas, or her mysticism recalls that of Carlyle in *Sartor Resartus* and *Past and Present*, we may be led to realize that the diversity of Victorian religious dialogue, though real, was addressed to problems which we find recurring in all areas of study.

20. KEBLE:

"National Apostasy"

John Keble (1792–1866), though famous in his own day as a Christian poet, has not received critical attention in the twentieth century. His works have not been collected, but are listed in an appendix to W. Locke's *John Keble, A Biography* (1892). A biography worth mention is that by Sir J. T. Coleridge: *A Memoir of the Rev. John Keble* (2 vols., rev. 1869). His place in the Oxford Movement is narrated in *The Church Revival* (1914), by S. Baring-Gould.

The sermon entitled "National Apostasy," delivered in 1833, is the first of the major documents of the Oxford Movement. It is included in the collection of *Sermons, Academical and Occasional*.

SERMON

VI

1 SAMUEL xii. 23.

As for me, God forbid that I should sin against the Lord in ceasing to pray for you: but I will teach you the good and the right way.

On public occasions, such as the present, the minds of Christians naturally revert to that portion of Holy Scripture, which exhibits to us the will of the Sovereign of the world in more immediate relation to the civil and national conduct of mankind. We naturally turn to the Old Testament, when public duties, public errors, and public dangers, are in question. And what in such cases is natural and obvious, is sure to be more or less right and reasonable. Unquestionably it is a mistaken theology, which would debar Christian nations and statesmen from the instruction afforded by the Jewish Scriptures, under a notion, that the circumstances of that people were altogether peculiar and unique, and therefore irrelevant to every other case. True, there is hazard of misapplication, as there is whenever men teach by example. There is peculiar hazard, from the sacredness and delicacy of the subject; since dealing with things supernatural and miraculous as if they were ordinary human precedents, would be not only unwise, but profane. But these hazards are more than counterbalanced by the absolute certainty, peculiar to this history, that what is there commended was right, and what is there blamed, wrong. And they would be effectually obviated, if men would be careful to keep in view this caution:—suggested every where, if I mistake not, by the manner in which the Old Testament is quoted in the New:—that, as regards reward and punishment, God dealt formerly with the Jewish people in a manner analogous to that in which He deals now, not so much with Christian nations, as with the souls of individual Christians.

Let us only make due allowances for this cardinal point of difference, and we need not surely hesitate to avail ourselves, as the time may require, of those national warnings, which fill the records of the elder Church: the less so, as the discrepancy lies rather in what is revealed of God's providence, than in what is required in the way of human duty. Reward and punishments may be dispensed, visibly at least, with a less even hand; but what tempers, and what conduct, God will ultimately reward and punish—this is a point which cannot be changed: for it depends not on our circumstances, but on His essential, unvarying Attributes.

I have ventured on these few general observations, because the impatience with which the world endures any remonstrance on religious grounds, is apt to shew itself most daringly, when the Law and the Prophets are appealed to. Without any scruple or ceremony, men give us to understand that they regard the whole as obsolete: thus taking the very opposite ground to that which was preferred by the same class of persons two hundred years ago; but, it may be feared, with much the same purpose and result. Then, the Old Testament was quoted at random for every excess of fanatical pride and cruelty: now, its authority goes for nothing, however clear and striking the analogies may be, which appear to warrant us in referring to it. The two extremes, as usual, meet; and in this very remarkable point: that they both avail themselves of the supernatural parts of the Jewish revelation to turn away attention from that, which they, of course, most dread and dislike in it: its authoritative confirmation of the plain dictates of conscience in matters of civil wisdom and duty. . . .

What are the symptoms, by which one may judge most fairly, whether or no a nation, as such, is becoming alienated from God and Christ?

And what are the particular duties of sincere Christians, whose lot is cast by Divine Providence in a time of such dire calamity?

The conduct of the Jews, in asking for a king, may furnish an ample illustration of the first point: the behaviour of Samuel, then and afterwards, supplies as perfect a pattern of the second, as can well be expected from human nature.

I. The case is at least possible, of a nation, having for centuries acknowledged, as an essential part of its theory of government, that, as a Christian nation, she is also a part of Christ's Church, and bound, in all her legislation and policy, by the fundamental rules of that Church—the case is, I say, conceivable, of a government and people, so constituted, deliberately throwing off the restraint, which in many respects such a principle would impose on them, nay, disavowing the principle itself; and that, on the plea, that other states, as flourishing or more so in regard of wealth and dominion, do well enough without it. Is not this desiring, like the Jews, to have an earthly king over them, when the Lord their God is their King? Is it not saying in other words, "We will be as the heathen, the families of the countries," the aliens to the Church of our Redeemer?

To such a change, whenever it takes place, the immediate impulse will probably be given by some pretence of danger from without—such as, at the time now spoken of, was furnished to the Israelites by an incursion of the children of Ammon; or by some wrong or grievance in the executive government, such as the malversation of Samuel's sons, to whom he had deputed his judicial functions. Pretences will never be hard to find; but, in reality, the movement will always be traceable to the same decay or want of faith, the same deficiency in Christian resignation and thankfulness, which leads so many, as individuals, to disdain and forfeit the blessings of the Gospel. Men not impressed with religious principle attribute their ill success in life,—the hard times they have to struggle with,—to any thing rather than their own ill-desert: and the institutions of the country, ecclesiastical and civil, are always at hand to bear the blame of whatever seems to be going amiss. . . .

The charge might perhaps surprise many of them, just as, in other times and countries, the impatient patrons of innovation are surprised, at finding themselves rebuked on religious grounds. Perhaps the Jews pleaded the express countenance, which the words of their Law, in one place, seemed, by anticipation, to lend to the measure they were urging. And so, in modern times, when liberties are to be taken, and the intrusive passions of men to be indulged, precedent and permission, or what sounds like them, may be easily found and quoted for every thing. But Samuel, in God's name, silenced all this, giving them to understand, that in His sight the whole was a question of motive and purpose, not of ostensible and colourable argument;—in His sight, I say, to Whom we, as well as they, are nationally responsible for much more than the soundness of our deductions as matter of disputation, or of law; we are responsible for the meaning and temper in which we deal with His Holy Church, established among us for the salvation of our souls.

These, which have been hitherto mentioned as omens and tokens of an Apostate Mind in a nation, have been suggested by the portion itself of sacred history, to which I have ventured to direct your attention. There are one or two more, which the nature of the subject, and the palpable tendency of things around us, will not allow to be passed over.

One of the most alarming, as a symptom, is the growing indifference, in which men indulge themselves, to other men's religious sentiments. Under the guise of charity and toleration we are come almost to this pass; that no difference, in matters of faith, is to disqualify for our approbation and confidence, whether in public or domestic life. Can we conceal it from ourselves, that every year the practice is becoming more common, of trusting men unreservedly in the most delicate and important matters, without one serious inquiry, whether they do not hold principles which make it impossible for them to be loyal to their Creator, Redeemer, and Sanctifier? Are not offices conferred, partnerships formed, intimacies courted,—nay, (what is almost too painful to think of,) do not parents commit their children to be educated, do they not encourage them to intermarry, in houses, on which Apostolical Authority would rather teach them to set a mark, as unfit to be entered by a faithful servant of Christ?

I do not now speak of public measures only or chiefly; many things of that kind may be thought, whether wisely or no, to become from time to time necessary, which are in reality as little desired by those who lend them a seeming concurrence, as they are, in themselves, undesirable. But I speak of the spirit which leads men to exult in every step of that kind; to congratulate one another on the supposed decay of what they call an exclusive system.

Very different are the feelings with which it seems natural for a true Churchman to regard such a state of things, from those which would arise in his mind on witnessing the mere triumph of any given set of adverse opinions, exaggerated or even heretical as he might deem them. He might feel as melancholy,—he could hardly feel so indignant.

But this is not a becoming place, nor are these safe topics, for the indulgence of mere feeling. The point really to be considered is, whether, according to the coolest estimate, the fashionable liberality of this generation be not ascribable, in a great measure, to the same temper which led the Jews voluntarily to set about degrading themselves to a level with the idolatrous Gentiles? And, if it be true any where, that such enactments are forced on the Legislature by public opinion, is APOSTASY too hard a word to describe the temper of that nation?

The same tendency is still more apparent, because the fair gloss of candour and forbearance is wanting, in the surly or scornful impatience often exhibited, by persons who would regret passing for unbelievers, when Christian motives are suggested, and checks from Christian principles attempted to be enforced on their public conduct. I say, "their public conduct," more especially; because in that, I know not how, persons are apt to be more shameless, and readier to avow the irreligion that is in them;—amongst other reasons, probably, from each feeling that he is one of a multitude, and fancying, therefore, that his responsibility is divided.

For example:—whatever be the cause, in this country of late years, (though we are lavish in professions of piety,) there has been observable a growing disinclination, on the part of those bound by VOLUNTARY OATHS, to whatever reminds them of their obligation; a growing disposition to explain it all away. We know what, some years ago, would have been thought of such uneasiness, if betrayed by persons officially sworn, in private, legal, or commercial life. If there be any subjects or occasions, now, on which men are inclined to judge of it more lightly, it concerns them deeply to be quite sure, that they are not indulging or encouraging a profane dislike of God's awful Presence; a general tendency, as a people, to leave Him out of all their thoughts.

They will have the more reason to suspect themselves, in proportion as they see and feel more of that impatience under pastoral authority, which our Saviour Himself has taught us to consider as a never-failing symptom of an unchristian temper. "He that heareth you, heareth Me; and he that despiseth you, despiseth Me." Those words of divine truth put beyond all sophistical exception, what common sense would lead us to infer, and what daily experience teaches;—that disrespect to the Successors of the Apostles, as such, is an unquestionable symptom of enmity to Him, who gave them their commission at first, and has pledged Himself to be with them for ever. Suppose such disrespect general and national, suppose it also avowedly grounded not on any fancied tenet of religion, but on mere human reasons of popularity and expediency, either there is no meaning at all in these emphatic declarations of our Lord, or that nation, how highly soever she may think of her own religion and morality, stands convicted in His sight of a direct disavowal of His Sovereignty.

To this purpose it may be worth noticing, that the ill-fated chief, whom God gave to the Jews, as the prophet tells us, in His anger, and whose disobedience and misery were referred by himself to his "fearing the people, and obeying their voice," whose conduct, therefore, may be fairly taken as a sample of what public opinion was at that time supposed to require—his first step in apostasy was, perhaps, an intrusion on the sacrificial office, certainly an impatient breach of his engagement with Samuel, as the last and greatest of his crimes was persecuting David, whom he well knew to bear God's special commission. God forbid, that any Christian land should ever, by her prevailing temper and policy, revive the memory and likeness of Saul, or incur a sentence of reprobation like his. But if such a thing should be, the crimes of that nation will probably begin in infringement on Apostolical Rights; she will end in persecuting the true Church; and in the several stages of her melancholy career, she will continually be led on from bad to worse by vain endeavours at accommodation and compromise with evil. Sometimes toleration may be the word, as with Saul when he spared the Amalekites; sometimes state security, as when he sought the life of David; sometimes sympathy with popular feeling, as appears to have been the case, when violating solemn treaties, he attempted to exterminate the remnant of the Gibeonites, in his zeal for the children of Israel and Judah. Such are the sad but obvious results of separating religious resignation altogether from men's notions of civil duty.

II. But here arises the other question, on which it was proposed to say a few words; and with a view to which, indeed, the whole subject must be considered, if it is to lead to any practical improvement. What should be the tenor of their conduct, who find themselves cast on such times of decay and danger? How may a man best reconcile his allegiance to God and his Church with his duty to his country, that country, which now, by the supposition, is fast becoming hostile to the Church, and cannot therefore long be the friend of God?

Now in proportion as any one sees reason to fear that such is, or soon may be, the case in his own land, just so far may he see reason to be thankful, especially if he be called to any national trust, for such a complete pattern of his duty, as he may find in the conduct of Samuel. That combination of sweetness with firmness, of consideration with energy, which constitutes the temper of a perfect public man, was never perhaps so beautifully exemplified. He makes no secret of the bitter grief and dismay, with which the resolution of his countrymen had filled him. He was prepared to resist it at all hazards, had he not received from God Himself directions to give them their own way; protesting, however, in the most distinct and solemn tone, so as to throw the whole blame of what might ensue on their wilfulness. Having so protested, and found them obstinate, he does not therefore at once forsake their service, he continues discharging all the functions they had left him, with a true and loyal, though most heavy, heart. "God forbid that I should sin against the Lord in ceasing to pray for you: but I will teach you the good and the right way."

Should it ever happen (which God avert, but we cannot shut our eyes to the danger) that the Apostolical Church should be forsaken, degraded, nay trampled on and despoiled by the State and people of England, I cannot conceive a kinder wish for her, on the part of her most affectionate and dutiful children, than that she may, consistently, act in the spirit of this most noble sentence; nor a course of conduct more likely to be blessed by a restoration to more than her former efficiency. In speaking of the Church, I mean, of course, the laity, as well as the clergy in their three orders,—the whole body of Christians united, according to the will of Jesus Christ, under the Successors of the Apostles. It may, by God's blessing, be of some use, to shew how, in the case supposed, the example of Samuel might guide her collectively, and each of her children individually, down even to minute details of duty.

The Church would, first of all, have to be constant, as before, in INTERCESSION. No despiteful usage, no persecution, could warrant her in ceasing to pray, as did her first fathers and patterns, for the State, and all who are in authority. That duty once well and cordially performed, all other duties, so to speak, are secured. Candour, respectfulness, guarded language,—all that the Apostle meant, in warning men not to "speak evil of dignities," may then, and then only, be practised, without compromise of truth and fortitude, when the habit is attained of praying as we ought for the very enemies of our precious and holy cause.

The constant sense of God's presence and consequent certainty of final success, which can be kept up no other way, would also prove an effectual bar against the more silent but hardly less malevolent feeling, of disgust, almost amounting to misanthropy, which is apt to lay hold on sensitive minds, when they see oppression and wrong triumphant on a large scale. The custom of interceding, even for the wicked, will keep the Psalmist's reasoning habitually present to their thoughts: "Fret not thyself because of the ungodly, neither be thou envious against the evil doers: for they shall soon be cut down like the grass, and be withered even as the green herb . . . Leave off from wrath, and let go displeasure: fret not thyself, else shalt thou be moved to do evil."

Thus not only by supernatural aid, which we have warrant of God's word for expecting, but even in the way of natural consequence, the first duty of the Church and of Churchmen, INTERCESSION, sincerely practised, would prepare them for the second;—which, following the words of Samuel as our clue, we may confidently pronounce to be REMONSTRANCE. "I will teach you the good and the right way." REMONSTRANCE, calm, distinct, and persevering, in public and in private, direct and indirect, by word, look, and demeanour, is the unequivocal duty of every Christian, according to his opportunities, when the Church landmarks are being broken down.

Among laymen, a deep responsibility would appear to rest on those particularly, whose profession leads them most directly to consider the boundaries of the various rights and duties, which fill the space of civilized Society. The immediate machinery of change must always pass through their hands; and they have also very great power in forming and modifying public opinion. The very solemnity of this day may remind them, even more than others, of the close amity which must ever subsist between equal justice and pure religion; Apostolical religion, more especially, in proportion to her superior truth and exactness. It is an amity, made still more sacred, if possible, in the case of the Church and Law of England, by historical recollections, associations and precedents, of the most engaging and ennobling cast. . . .

After all, the surest way to uphold or restore our endangered Church, will be for each of her anxious children, in his own place and station, to resign himself more thoroughly to his God and Saviour in those duties, public and private, which are not immediately affected by the emergencies of the moment: the daily and hourly duties, I mean, of piety, purity, charity, justice. It will be a consolation understood by every thoughtful Churchman, that let his occupation be, apparently, never so remote from such great interests, it is in his power, by doing all as a Christian, to credit and advance the cause he has most at heart; and what is more, to draw down God's blessing upon it. . . .

21. KINGSLEY:
Rejoinder to Newman

Charles Kingsley (1819–1875) had a diverse career as clergyman, novelist and social reformer. *The Life and Works of Charles Kingsley* (19 vols., 1901–3) includes in the first four volumes *His Letters and Memories of His Life*, edited by Mrs. Kingsley. For criticism, three sources are commendable: M. F. Thorp, *Charles Kingsley* (1937), Louis Cazamian, *Le Roman social en Angleterre* (1903), and Cazamian's *Kingsley: le socialisme chr. tien* (1904).

This selection from " 'What, Then, Does Dr. Newman Mean?' A Reply to a Pamphlet Lately Published by Dr. Newman," prompted Newman's *Apologia pro Vita Sua*, surely the most famous of all Victorian religious statements. Kingsley's "Reply," though not so famous, deserves attention as an example of Broad Church concern for an immediately relevant religion.

Dr. Newman has made a great mistake. He has published a correspondence between himself and me, with certain "Reflexions" and a title-page, which cannot be allowed to pass without a rejoinder.

Before commenting on either, I must give a plain account of the circumstances of the controversy, which seem to have been misunderstood in several quarters. In the January number of *Macmillan's Magazine*, I deliberately and advisedly made use of these words:—

"Truth, for its own sake, had never been a virtue with the Roman "clergy. Father Newman informs us that it need not, and, on the "whole, ought not to be; that cunning is the weapon which Heaven "has given to the saints wherewith to withstand the brute male force "of the wicked world which marries and is given in marriage." This accusation I based upon a considerable number of passages in Dr. Newman's writings, and especially on a sermon entitled "Wisdom and Innocence," and preached by Dr. Newman as Vicar of St. Mary's, and published as No. XX. of his "Sermons on Subjects of the Day."

Dr. Newman wrote, in strong but courteous terms, to Messrs. Macmillan and Co. complaining of this language as a slander. I at once took the responsibility on myself, and wrote to Dr. Newman.

I had been informed (by a Protestant) that he was in weak health, that he wished for peace and quiet, and was averse to controversy; I therefore felt some regret at having disturbed him: and this regret was increased by the moderate and courteous tone of his letters, though they contained, of course, much from which I differed. I addressed to him the following letter, of which, as I trust every English gentleman will feel, I have no reason to be ashamed:—

REVEREND SIR,

I have seen a letter of yours to Mr. Macmillan, in which you complain of some expressions of mine in an article in the January number of *Macmillan's Magazine*.

That my words were just, I believed from many passages of your writings; but the document to which I expressly referred was one of your sermons on "Subjects of the Day," No. XX. in the volume published in 1844, and entitled "Wisdom and Innocence."

It was in consequence of that sermon that I finally shook off the strong influence which your writings exerted on me, and for much of which I still owe you a deep debt of gratitude.

I am most happy to hear from you that I mistook (as I understand from your letter) your meaning; and I shall be most happy, on your showing me that I have wronged you, to retract my accusation as publicly as I have made it.

I am, Rev. Sir,
Your faithful servant,
CHARLES KINGSLEY.

I received a very moderate answer from Dr. Newman, and a short correspondence ensued, which ended in my inserting in the February number of *Macmillan's Magazine* the following apology:—

RELIGION   193

To the Editor of "MACMILLAN'S MAGAZINE."

SIR,

In your last number I made certain allegations against the teaching of Dr. John Henry Newman, which I thought were justified by a sermon of his, entitled "Wisdom and Innocence" (Sermon XX. of "Sermons bearing on Subjects of the Day"). Dr. Newman has, by letter, expressed in the strongest terms his denial of the meaning which I have put upon his words. It only remains, therefore, for me to express my hearty regret at having so seriously mistaken him.

Yours faithfully,

CHARLES KINGSLEY.

My object had been throughout to avoid war, because I thought Dr. Newman wished for peace. I therefore dropped the question of the meaning of "many passages of his writings," and confined myself to the sermon entitled "Wisdom and Innocence," simply to give him an opportunity of settling the dispute on that one ground.

But whether Dr. Newman lost his temper, or whether he thought that he had gained an advantage over me, or whether he wanted a more complete apology than I chose to give, whatever, I say, may have been his reasons, he suddenly changed his tone of courtesy and dignity for one of which I shall only say that it shows sadly how the atmosphere of the Romish priesthood has degraded his notions of what is due to himself; and when he published (as I am much obliged to him for doing) the whole correspondence, he appended to it certain reflexions, in which he attempted to convict me of not having believed the accusation which I had made.

There remains for me, then, nothing but to justify my mistake, as far as I can.

I am, of course, precluded from using the sermon entitled "Wisdom and Innocence" to prove my words. I have accepted Dr. Newman's denial that it means what I thought it did; and Heaven forbid that I should withdraw my word once given, at whatever disadvantage to myself. But more, I am informed by those from whose judgment on such points there is no appeal, that "*en hault courage*" and strict honour, I am also precluded, by the terms of my explanation, from using any other of Dr. Newman's past writings to prove my assertion. I have declared Dr. Newman to have been an honest man up to the 1st of February, 1864. It was, as I shall show, only Dr. Newman's fault that I ever thought him to be anything else. It depends entirely on Dr. Newman whether he shall sustain the reputation which he has so recently acquired. If I give him thereby a fresh advantage in this argument, he is most welcome to it. He needs, it seems to me, as many advantages as possible. But I have a right, in self-justification, to put before the public so much of that sermon, and of the rest of Dr. Newman's writings, as will show why I formed so harsh an opinion of them and him, and why I still consider that sermon (whatever may be its meaning) as most dangerous and misleading. And I have a full right to do the same by those "many passages of Dr. Newman's writings" which I left alone at first, simply because I thought that Dr. Newman wished for peace.

First, as to the sermon entitled "Wisdom and Innocence." It must be remembered always that it is not a Protestant, but a Romish sermon. It is occupied entirely with the attitude of "the world" to "Christians" and "the Church." By the world appears to be signified, especially, the Protestant public of these realms. What Dr. Newman means by Christians, and the Church, he has not left in doubt; for in the preceding sermon (XIX. p. 328) he says: "But, if the truth must be spoken, "what are the humble monk, and the holy nun, and other regulars, as "they are called, but Christians after the very pattern given us in "Scripture? What have they done but this—continue in the world the "Christianity of the Bible? Did our Saviour come on earth suddenly, "as He will one day visit, in whom would He see the features of the "Christians He and His apostles left behind them, but in them? Who "but these give up home and friends, wealth and ease, good name and "liberty of will, for the kingdom of heaven? Where shall we find the "image of St. Paul, or St. Peter, or St. John, or of Mary the mother of "Mark, or of Philip's daughters, but in those who, whether they "remain in seclusion, or are sent over the earth, have calm faces, and "sweet plaintive voices, and spare frames, and gentle manners, and "hearts weaned from the world, and wills subdued; and for their "meekness meet with insult, and for their purity with slander, and for "their gravity with suspicion, and for their courage with cruelty . . ." This is his definition of Christians. And in the sermon itself he sufficiently defines what he means by "the Church" in two "notes" of her character, which he shall give in his own words (Sermon XX. p. 346):— "What, for instance, though we grant that sacramental confession, and "the celibacy of the clergy do tend to consolidate the body politic in "the relation of rulers and subjects, or, in other words, to aggrandize "the priesthood? for how can the Church be one body without such "relation?" . . .

Monks and nuns the only perfect Christians; sacramental confession and the celibacy of the clergy notes of the Church; the laity in relation to the clergy of subjects to rulers. What more? If I, like others, on the strength of Dr. Newman's own definitions, gave to his advice to Christians concerning "wisdom," "prudence," "silence," the meaning which they would have in the mouth of a Romish teacher—St. Alfonso da Liguori, for instance—whom can Dr. Newman blame for the mistake, save himself?

But to the sermon itself; the text of which is from Matthew x. 16. It begins by stating that the Church has been always helpless and persecuted, in proportion to its purity. Dr. Newman then asks, how Christians are to defend themselves if they might not fight? and answers, "They were allowed the arms, that is, the arts, of the defence-less." He shows how the weaker animals are enabled to defend themselves by various means, among which he enumerates "natural cunning, which enables them to elude or even to destroy their enemies." He goes on to show how the same holds good in our own species, in the case of "a captive, effeminate race"; of "slaves"; of "ill-used and oppressed children"; of the "subjects of a despot." "They exercise the inalienable "right of self-defence in such methods as they best may; only, since "human nature is unscrupulous, guilt or innocence is all the same to "them, if it works their purpose."

He goes on to point out the analogy between these facts and the conduct fit for Christians. "The servants of Christ are forbidden to defend "themselves by violence; but they are not forbidden other means: "direct means are not allowed, but others are even commanded. For "instance, foresight, 'beware of men': avoidance, 'when they persecute "you in one city, flee into another': prudence and skill, as in the text, " 'Be ye wise as serpents.' "

The mention of the serpent reminds him of the serpent in Paradise; and he says, "Considering that the serpent was chosen by the enemy of "mankind as the intrument of his temptations in Paradise, it is very "remarkable that Christ should choose it as the pattern of wisdom for "His followers. It is as if He appealed to the whole world of sin, and "to the bad arts by which the feeble gain advantages over the strong. "It is as if He set before us the craft and treachery, the perfidy of the "slave, and bade us extract a lesson even from so great an evil. It is as "if the more we are forbidden violence, the more we are exhorted to

"prudence; as if it were our bounden duty to rival the wicked in endow-
"ments of mind, and to excel them in their exercise."

Dr. Newman then goes on to assert, that "if there be one reproach
more than another which has been cast upon" the Church, "it is that of
fraud and cunning." He quotes the imputations of craftiness and
deceitfulness thrown upon St. Paul, and even of "deceit" upon our
Lord himself. He then says that "Priestcraft has ever been considered
the badge, and its imputation is a kind of note, of the Church." He
asserts that the accusation has been, save in a few exceptions, un-
founded; and that "the words 'craft' and 'hypocrisy' are "but the
"version of 'wisdom' and 'harmlessness' in the language of the world."
"It is remarkable, however, that not only is harmlessness the corrective
"of wisdom, securing it against the corruption of craft and deceit, as
"stated in the text: but innocence, simplicity, implicit obedience to
"God, tranquillity of mind, contentment, these and the like virtues
"are in themselves a sort of wisdom; I mean, they produce the same
"results as wisdom, because God works for those who do not work for
"themselves; and thus they especially incur the charge of craft at the
"hands of the world, because they pretend to so little, yet effect so much.
"This circumstance admits dwelling on."

He then goes on to mention seven heads:—

"First, sobriety, self-restraint, control of word and feeling, which
"religious men exercise, have about them an appearance of being
"artificial, because they are not natural; and of being artful, because
"artificial"; and adds shortly after, that "those who would be holy
"and blameless, the sons of God, find so much in the world to unsettle
"and defile them, that they are necessarily forced upon a strict self-
"restraint, lest they should receive injury from such intercourse with
"it as is unavoidable; and this self-restraint is the first thing which makes
"holy persons seem wanting in openness and manliness." Next he
points out that "religious men are a mystery to the world; and being a
"mystery, they will in mere self-defence be called by the world myster-
"ious, dark, subtle, designing." Next, that "it is very difficult to make
"the world understand the difference between an outward obedience
"and an inward assent." He then instances the relations between the
early Christians and the heathen magistrates; and adds, that "when
"religious men outwardly conform, on the score of duty, to the powers
"that be, the world is easily led into the mistake that they have re-
"nounced their opinions, as well as submitted their actions; and it feels
"or affects surprise, to find that their opinions remain; and it considers,

"or calls this, an inconsistency, or a duplicity": with more to the same purpose.

Next, the silent resignation of Christians is set forth as a cause of the world's suspicion; and "so is their confidence, in spite of their "apparent weakness, their cause will triumph."

Another cause of the world's suspicion is, the unexpected success of religious men.

Another, that the truth has in itself the power of spreading, without instruments, "making the world impute" to secret management that uniformity, which is nothing but the echo of the One Living and True Word.

Another, that when Christians prosper, contrary to their own expectations, "it looks like deceit to show surprise, and to disclaim the work themselves."

And lastly, because God works for Christians, and they are successful, when they only mean to be dutiful. "But what duplicity does the world "think it, to speak of conscience, or honour, or propriety, or delicacy, "or to give other tokens of personal motives, when the event seems to "show that a calculation of results has been the actuating principle at "bottom. It is God who designs, but His servants seem designing. . . ."

Dr. Newman then goes on to point out how "Jacob is thought "worldly wise in his dealings with Laban, whereas he was a 'plain man,' "simply obedient to the angel." . . . "Moses is sometimes called saga-"cious and shrewd in his measures or his law, as if wise acts might not "come from the source of wisdom." . . . "Bishops have been called "hypocritical in submitting and yet opposing themselves to the civil "power, in a matter of plain duty, if a popular movement was the "consequence; and then hypocritical again if they did their best to "repress it. And, in like manner, theological doctrines or ecclesiastical "usages are styled politic if they are but salutary; as if the Lord of the "Church, who has willed her sovereignty, might not effect it by secon-"dary causes. What, for instance, though we grant that sacramental "confession and the celibacy of the clergy do tend to consolidate the "body politic in the relation of rulers and subjects, or, in other words, "to aggrandise the priesthood? For how can the Church be one body "without such relation; and why should not He, who has decreed that "there should be unity, take measures to secure it?"

The reason of these suspicions on the part of the world is then stated to be, that "men do not like to hear of the interposition of Providence "in the affairs of the world; and they invidiously ascribe ability and "skill to His agents, to escape the thought of an Infinite Wisdom and an "Almighty Power. . . ."

The sermon then closes with a few lines of great beauty, in that style which has won deservedly for Dr. Newman the honour of being the most perfect orator of this generation; but they have no reference to the question in hand, save the words, "We will glory in what they disown."

I have tried conscientiously to give a fair and complete digest of this, to me, very objectionable and dangerous sermon. I have omitted no passage in which Dr. Newman guards himself against the conclusions which I drew from it; and none, I verily believe, which is required for the full understanding of its general drift. I have abstained from all comment as I went on, in order not to prejudice the minds of my readers. But I must now turn round and ask, whether the mistake into which Dr. Newman asserts me to have fallen was not a very reasonable one; and whether the average of educated Englishmen, in reading that sermon, would not be too likely to fall into the same? I put on it, as I thought, the plain and straightforward signification. I find I am wrong; and nothing is left for me but to ask, with some astonishment, What, then, did the sermon mean? Why was it preached? To insinuate that a Church which had sacramental confession and a celibate clergy was the only true Church? Or to insinuate that the admiring young gentlemen who listened to him stood to their fellow-countrymen in the relation of the early Christians to the heathen Romans? Or that Queen Victoria's Government was to the Church of England what Nero's or Diocletian's was to the Church of Rome? It may have been so. I know that men used to suspect Dr. Newman—I have been inclined to do so myself—of writing a whole sermon, not for the sake of the text or of the matter, but for the sake of one single passing hint—one phrase, one epithet, one little barbed arrow which, as he swept magnificently past on the stream of his calm eloquence, seemingly unconscious of all presences, save those unseen, he delivered unheeded, as with his fingertip, to the very heart of an initiated hearer, never to be withdrawn again. I do not blame him for that. It is one of the highest triumphs of oratoric power, and may be employed honestly and fairly, by any person who has the skill to do it honestly and fairly. But then—Why did he entitle his sermon "Wisdom and Innocence"?

What, then, could I think that Dr. Newman meant? I found a preacher bidding Christians imitate, to some undefined point, the "arts" of the basest of animals and of men, and even of the Devil himself. I found him, by a strange perversion of Scripture, insinuating that St. Paul's conduct and manner were such as naturally to bring down on him the reputation of being a crafty deceiver. I found him —horrible to have to say it—even hinting the same of One greater than St. Paul. I found him denying or explaining away the existence of that priestcraft which is a notorious fact to every honest student of history; and justifying (as far as I can understand him) that double-dealing by which prelates, in the middle age, too often played off alternately the sovereign against the people and the people against the sovereign, careless which was in the right, as long as their own power gained by the move. I found him actually using of such (and, as I thought, of himself and his party likewise) the words, "They yield outwardly; to "assent inwardly were to betray the faith. Yet they are called deceitful "and double-dealing, because they do as much as they can, and not "more than they may." I found him telling Christians that they will always seem "artificial," and "wanting in openness and manliness;" that they will always be "a mystery" to the world, and that the world will always think them rogues; and bidding them glory in what the world (*i.e.* the rest of their fellow countrymen) disown, and say with Mawworm, "I like to be despised."

Now how was I to know that the preacher, who had the reputation of being the most acute man of his generation, and of having a specially intimate acquaintance with the weaknesses of the human heart, was utterly blind to the broad meaning and the plain practical result of a sermon like this, delivered before fanatic and hot-headed young men, who hung upon his every word? That he did not foresee that they would think that they obeyed him, by becoming affected, artificial, sly, shifty, ready for concealments and equivocations? That he did not foresee that they, hearing his words concerning priestcraft and double-dealing, and being engaged in the study of the Mediæval Church, would consider the same chicanery allowed to them which they found practised but too often by the Mediæval Church? or even go to the Romish casuists, to discover what amount of cunning did or did not come under Dr. Newman's one passing warning against craft and deceit? In a word, that he did not foresee that the natural result of the sermon on the minds of his disciples would be, to make them suspect that truth was not a virtue for its own sake, but only for the sake of the spread of "catholic opinions," and the "salvation of their own souls;" and that cunning was the weapon which Heaven had allowed to them to defend themselves against the persecuting Protestant public?

All England stood round in those days, and saw that this would be the outcome of Dr. Newman's teaching. How was I to know that he did not see it himself?

And as a fact, his teaching had this outcome. Whatever else it did, it did this. In proportion as young men absorbed it into themselves, it injured their straightforwardness and truthfulness. The fact is notorious to all England. It spread misery and shame into many an English home. The net practical result of Dr. Newman's teachings on truthfulness cannot be better summed up than by one of his own disciples, Mr. Ward, who, in his "Ideal of a Christian Church," page 382, say thus:—

"Candour is rather an intellectual than a moral virtue, and by no "means either universally or distinctively characteristic of the saintly "mind."

Dr. Newman ought to have told his disciple, when he wrote those words, that he was on the highroad to the father of lies; and he ought to have told the world, too, that such was his opinion; unless he wished it to fall into the mistake into which I fell—namely, that he had wisdom enough to know the practical result of his words, and therefore meant what they seemed to say.

Dr. Newman has nothing to blame for that mistake, save his own method. If he would (while a member of the Church of England) persist (as in this sermon) in dealing with matters dark, offensive, doubtful, sometimes actually forbidden, at least according to the notions of the great majority of English Churchmen; if he would always do so in a tentative, paltering way, seldom or never letting the world know how much he believed, how far he intended to go; if, in a word, his method of teaching was a suspicious one, what wonder if the minds of men were filled with suspicions of him? What wonder if they said of him (as he so naïvely, in one of his letters, expresses his fear that they will say again), "Dr. Newman has the skill of a great "master of verbal fence, who knows, as well as any man living, how to "insinuate a doctrine without committing himself to it?" If he told the world, as he virtually does in this sermon, "I know that my conduct "looks like cunning; but it is only the 'arts' of the defenceless:" what "wonder if the world answered, "No. It is what it seems. That is just "what we call cunning; a habit of mind which, once indulged, is certain "to go on from bad to worse, till the man becomes—like too many of "the mediaeval clergy who indulged in it—utterly untrustworthy." Dr. Newman, I say, has no one to blame but himself. The world is not so blind but that it will soon find out an honest man if he will take the trouble of talking and acting like one. No one would have suspected him to be a dishonest man, if he had not perversely chosen to assume a style which (as he himself confesses) the world always associates with dishonesty. . . .

I go on now to other works of Dr. Newman, from which (as I told him in my first letter) I had conceived an opinion unfavourable to his honesty.

I shall be expected to adduce, first and foremost, the too-notorious No. 90 of "Tracts for the Times." I shall not do so. On reading that tract over again, I have been confirmed in the opinion which I formed of it at first, that, questionable as it was, it was not meant to be consciously dishonest; that some few sayings in it were just and true; that many of its extravagances were pardonable, as the natural fruit of a revulsion against the popular cry of those days, which called on clergymen to interpret the Articles only in their Calvinistic sense, instead of including under them (as their wise framers intended) not only the Calvinistic, but the Anglican form of thought. There were pages in it which shocked me, and which shock me still. I will instance the commentaries on the 5th, on the 7th, on the 9th, and on the 12th Articles; because in them Dr. Newman seemed to me trying to make the Articles say the very thing which (I believe) the Articles were meant not to say. But I attributed to him no intentional dishonesty. The fullest licence of interpretation should be given to every man who is bound by the letter of a document. The *animus imponentium* should be heard of as little as possible, because it is almost certain to become merely the *animus interpretantium*. And more: Every excuse was to be made for a man struggling desperately to keep himself in what was, in fact, his right place, to remain a member of the Church of England, where Providence had placed him, while he felt himself irresistibly attracted towards Rome. But I saw in that tract a fearful danger for the writer. It was but too probable, that if he continued to demand of that subtle brain of his, such *tours de force* as he had all but succeeded in performing, when he tried to show that the Article against "the sacrifice of masses" "did not speak against the mass itself," he would surely end in one or other of two misfortunes. He would either destroy his own sense of honesty—*i.e.* conscious truthfulness—and become a dishonest person; or he would destroy his common sense—*i.e.* unconscious truthfulness, and become the slave and puppet seemingly of his own logic, really of his own fancy, ready to believe anything, however preposterous, into which he could, for the moment, argue himself. I thought, for years past, that he had become the former; I now see that he has become the latter.

I beg pardon for saying so much about myself. But this is a personal matter between Dr. Newman and me, and I say what I say simply to show, not Dr. Newman, but my fellow-Protestants, that my opinion of him was not an "impulsive" or "hastily-formed one." I know his writings of old, and now. But I was so far just to him, that No. 90, which made all the rest of England believe him a dishonest man, had not the same effect on me.

22. NEWMAN:
On Kingsley

The *Apologia* of John Henry, Cardinal Newman (1801–1890), has been edited many times, notably by Wilfred Ward (1913), C. F. Harrold (1947), A. Dwight Culler (1956), and David DeLaura (1967). The standard life is Ward's (2 vols., 1912). The letters and diaries of the leader of the Oxford Movement are being edited by C. S. Dessain and V. F. Blehl. Walter Houghton's *The Art of Newman's Apology* (New Haven, 1945) is a fine study. The published correspondence between Kingsley and Newman serves to emphasize a certain paranoid self-consciousness in Newman that is concealed in his *Apologia* and to mitigate the clumsy harshness of Kingsley's pamphlet, "What, Then, Does Dr. Newman Mean?"

DR. NEWMAN TO THE REV. CHARLES KINGSLEY

The Oratory, January 17, 1864

Reverend Sir,

Since you do no more than announce to me your intention of inserting in Macmillan's Magazine the letter, a copy of which you are so good as to transcribe for me, perhaps I am taking a liberty in making any remarks to you upon it. But then, the very fact of your showing it to me seems to invite criticism; and so sincerely do I wish to bring this painful matter to an immediate settlement, that, at the risk of being officious, I avail myself of your courtesy to express the judgement which I have carefully formed upon it.

I believe it to be your wish to do me such justice as is compatible with your duty of upholding the consistency and quasi-infallibility which is necessary for a periodical publication; and I am far from expecting any thing from you which would be unfair to Messrs. Macmillan and Co. Moreover, I am quite aware, that the reading public, to whom your letter is virtually addressed, cares little for the wording of an explanation, provided it be made aware of the fact that an explanation has been given.

Nevertheless, after giving your letter the benefit of both these considerations, I am sorry to say I feel it my duty to withhold from it the approbation which I fain would bestow.

Its main fault is, that, quite contrary to your intention, it will be understood by the general reader to intimate; that I have been confronted with definite extracts from my works, and have laid before you my own interpretations of them. Such a proceeding I have indeed challenged, but have not been so fortunate as to bring about.

But besides, I gravely disapprove of the letter as a whole. The grounds of this dissatisfaction will be best understood by you, if I place in parallel columns its paragraphs, one by one, and what I conceive will be the popular reading of them.

This I proceed to do.

> I have the honour to be,
>
> Reverend Sir,
>
> Your obedient Servant,
>
> (*Signed*) John H. Newman

Mr. Kingsley's Letter	*Unjust, but too probable, popular rendering of it*
1. Sir—In your last number I made certain allegations against the teaching of the Rev. Dr. Newman, which were founded on a Sermon of his, entitled "Wisdom and Innocence," preached by him as Vicar of St. Mary's, and published in 1844.	

2. Dr. Newman has, by letter, expressed in the strongest terms his denial of the meaning which I have put upon his words.

2. I have set before Dr. Newman, as he challenged me to do, extracts from his writings, and he has affixed to them what he conceives to be their legitimate sense, to the denial of that in which I understood them.

3. No man knows the use of words better than Dr. Newman; no man, therefore, has a better right to define what he does, or does not, mean by them.

3. He has done this with the skill of a great master of verbal fence, who knows, as well as any man living, how to insinuate a doctrine without committing himself to it.

4. It only remains, therefore, for me to express my hearty regret at having so seriously mistaken him, and my hearty pleasure at finding him on the side of truth, in this or any other matter.

4. However, while I heartily regret that I have so seriously mistaken the sense which he assures me his words were meant to bear, I cannot but feel a hearty pleasure also, at having brought him, for once in a way, to confess that after all truth is a Christian virtue.

REV. CHARLES KINGSLEY TO DR. NEWMAN

Eversley Rectory, January 18, 1864

Reverend Sir,

I do not think it probable that the good sense and honesty of the British Public will misinterpret my apology, in the way in which you expect.

Two passages in it, which I put in in good faith and good feeling, may, however, be open to such a bad use, and I have written to Messrs. Macmillan to omit them; viz. the words, "No man knows the use of words better than Dr. Newman;" and those, "My hearty pleasure at finding him in the truth (*sic*) on this or any other matter."

As to your Art. 2, it seems to me, that, by referring publicly to the Sermon on which my allegations are founded, I have given, not only you, but every one an opportunity of judging of their injustice. Having done this, and having frankly accepted your assertion that I was mistaken, I have done as much as one English gentleman can expect from another.

I have the honour to be,
Reverend Sir,
Your obedient Servant,
(*Signed*) Charles Kingsley

MR. KINGSLEY'S METHOD OF DISPUTATION

[Published as a Pamphlet, Thursday, April 21, 1864]

I cannot be sorry to have forced Mr. Kingsley to bring out in fulness his charges against me. It is far better that he should discharge his thoughts upon me in my lifetime, than after I am dead. Under the circumstances I am happy in having the opportunity of reading the worst that can be said of me by a writer who has taken pains with his work and is well satisfied with it. I account it a gain to be surveyed from without by one who hates the principles which are nearest to my heart, has no personal knowledge of me to set right his misconceptions of my doctrine, and who has some motive or other to be as severe with me as he can possibly be.

And first of all, I beg to compliment him on the motto in his Title-page; it is felicitous. A motto should contain, as in a nutshell, the contents, or the character, or the drift, or the *animus* of the writing to which it is prefixed. The words which he has taken from me are so apposite as to be almost prophetical. There cannot be a better illustration than he thereby affords of the aphorism which I intended them to convey. I said that it is not more than an hyperbolical expression to say that in certain cases a lie is the nearest approach to truth. Mr. Kingsley's pamphlet is emphatically one of such cases as are contemplated in that proposition. I really believe, that his view of me is about as near an approach to the truth about my writings and doings, as he is capable of taking. He has done his worst towards me; but he has also done his best. So far well; but, while I impute to him no malice, I unfeignedly think, on the other hand, that, in his invective against me, he as faithfully fulfils the other half of the proposition also.

This is not a mere sharp retort upon Mr. Kingsley, as will be seen, when I come to consider directly the subject, to which the words of his motto relate. I have enlarged on that subject in various passages of my publications; I have said that minds in different states and circumstances cannot understand one another, and that in all cases they must be instructed according to their capacity, and, if not taught step by step, they learn only so much the less; that children do not apprehend the thoughts of grown people, nor savages the instincts of civilization, nor blind men the perceptions of sight, nor pagans the doctrines of Christianity, nor men the experiences of Angels. In the same way, there are people of matter-of-fact, prosaic minds, who cannot take in the fancies of poets; and others of shallow, inaccurate minds, who cannot take in the ideas of philosophical inquirers. In a Lecture of mine I have illustrated this phenomenon by the supposed instance of a foreigner, who, after reading a commentary on the principles of English Law, does not get nearer to a real apprehension of them than to be led to accuse Englishmen of considering that the Queen is impeccable and infallible, and that the Parliament is omnipotent.

Mr. Kingsley has read me from beginning to end in the fashion in which the hypothetical Russian read Blackstone; not, I repeat, from malice, but because of his intellectual build. He appears to be so constituted as to have no notion of what goes on in minds very different from his own, and moreover to be stone-blind to his ignorance. A modest man or a philosopher would have scrupled to treat with scorn and scoffing, as Mr. Kingsley does in my own instance, principles and convictions, even if he did not acquiesce in them himself, which had been held so widely and for so long,—the beliefs and devotions and customs which have been the religious life of millions upon millions of Christians for nearly twenty centuries,—for this in fact is the task on which he is spending his pains. Had he been a man of large or cautious mind, he would not have taken it for granted that cultivation must lead every one to see things precisely as he sees them himself. But the narrow-minded are the more prejudiced by very reason of their narrowness. The Apostle bids us "in malice be children, but in understanding be men." I am glad to recognize in Mr. Kingsley an illustration of the first half of this precept; but I should not be honest, if I ascribed to him any sort of fulfilment of the second.

I wish I could speak as favourably either of his drift or of his method of arguing, as I can of his convictions. As to his drift, I think its ultimate point is an attack upon the Catholic Religion. It is I indeed, whom he is immediately insulting,—still, he views me only as a representative, and on the whole a fair one, of a class or caste of men, to whom, conscious as I am of my own integrity, I ascribe an excellence superior to mine. He desires to impress upon the public mind the conviction that I am a crafty, scheming man, simply untrustworthy; that, in becoming a Catholic, I have just found my right place; that I do but justify and am properly interpreted by the common English notion of Roman casuists and confessors; that I was secretly a Catholic when I was openly professing to be a clergyman of the Established Church; that so far from bringing, by means of my conversion, when at length it openly took place, any strength to the Catholic cause, I am really a burden to it—an additional evidence of the fact, that to be a pure, german, genuine Catholic, a man must be either a knave or a fool.

These last words bring me to Mr. Kingsley's method of disputation, which I must criticize with much severity;—in his drift he does but follow the ordinary beat of controversy, but in his mode of arguing he is actually dishonest.

He says that I am either a knave or a fool, and (as we shall see by and by) he is not quite sure which, probably both. He tells his readers that on one occasion he said that he had fears I should "end in one or other of two misfortunes." "He would either," he continues, "destroy his own sense of honesty, i.e. conscious truthfulness—and become a dishonest person; or he would destroy his common sense, i.e. unconscious truthfulness, and become the slave and puppet seemingly of his own logic, really of his own fancy . . . I thought for years past that he had become the former; I now see that he has become the latter." Again, "When I read these outrages upon common sense, what wonder if I said to myself, 'This man cannot believe what he is saying?'" Such has been Mr. Kingsley's state of mind till lately, but now he considers that I am possessed with a spirit of "almost boundless silliness," of "simple credulity, the child of scepticism," of "absurdity," of a "self-deception which has become a sort of frantic honesty." And as to his fundamental reason for this change, he tells us, he really does not know what it is. However, let the reason be what it will, its upshot is intelligible enough. He is enabled at once, by this professed change of judgment about me, to put forward one of these alternatives, yet to keep the other in reserve;—and this he actually does. He need not commit himself to a definite accusation against me, such as requires definite proof and admits of definite refutation; for he has two strings to his bow;—when he is thrown off his balance on the one leg, he can recover himself by the use of the other. If I demonstrate that I am not a knave, he may exclaim, "Oh, but you are a fool!" and when I demonstrate that I am not a fool, he may turn round and retort, "Well, then, you are a knave." I have no objection to reply to his arguments in behalf of either alternative, but I should have been better pleased to have been allowed to take them one at a time.

But I have not yet done full justice to the method of disputation, which Mr. Kingsley thinks it right to adopt. Observe this first:— He means by a man who is "silly" not a man who is to be pitied, but a man who is to be *abhorred*. He means a man who is not simply weak and incapable, but a moral leper; a man who, if not a knave, has every thing bad about him except knavery; nay, rather, has together with every other worst vice, a spice of knavery to boot. *His* simpleton is one who has become such, in judgment for his having once been a knave. *His* simpleton is not a born fool, but a self-made idiot, one who has drugged and abused himself into a shameless depravity; one, who, without any misgiving or remorse, is guilty of drivelling superstition, of reckless violation of sacred things, of fanatical excesses, of passionate inanities, of unmanly audacious tyranny over the weak, meriting the wrath of fathers and brothers. This is that milder judgment, which he seems to pride himself upon as so much charity; and, as he expresses it, he "does not know" why. This is what he really meant in his letter to me of January 14, when he withdrew his charge of my being dishonest. He said, "The *tone* of your letters, even more than their language, makes me feel, *to my very deep pleasure*,"—what? that you have gambled away your reason, that you are an intellectual sot, that you are a fool in a frenzy. And in his Pamphlet, he gives us this explanation why he did not say this to my face, viz. that he had been told that I was "in weak health," and was "averse to controversy." He "felt some regret for having disturbed me."

But I pass on from these multiform imputations, and confine myself to this one consideration, viz. that he has made any fresh imputation upon me at all. He gave up the charge of knavery; well and good: but where was the logical necessity of his bringing another? I am sitting at home without a thought of Mr. Kingsley; he wantonly breaks in upon me with the charge that I had "*informed*" the world "that Truth for its own sake *need not* and on the whole *ought not to be* a virtue with the Roman clergy." When challenged on the point he cannot bring a fragment of evidence in proof of his assertion, and he is convicted of

false witness by the voice of the world. Well, I should have thought
that he had now nothing whatever more to do. "Vain man!" he seems
to make answer, "what simplicity in you to think so! If you have not
broken one commandment, let us see whether we cannot convict
you of the breach of another. If you are not a swindler or forger,
you are guilty of arson or burglary. By hook or by crook you shall not
escape. Are *you* to suffer or *I*? What does it matter to you who are
going off the stage, to receive a slight additional daub upon a character
so deeply stained already? But think of me, the immaculate lover of
Truth, so observant (as I have told you) of '*hault courage* and strict
honour,'—and (aside)—'and not as this publican'—do you think I can
let you go scot free instead of myself? No; *noblesse oblige*. Go to the
shades, old man, and boast that Achilles sent you thither."

But I have not even yet done with Mr. Kingsley's method of disputation. Observe secondly:—when a man is said to be a knave or a fool,
it is commonly meant that he is *either* the one *or* the other; and that,—
either in the sense that the hypothesis of his being a fool is too absurd
to be entertained; or, again, as a sort of contemptuous acquittal of
one, who after all has not wit enough to be wicked. But this is not at
all what Mr. Kingsley proposes to himself in the antithesis which he
suggests to his readers. Though he speaks of me as an utter dotard and
fanatic, yet all along, from the beginning of his Pamphlet to the end,
he insinuates, he proves from my writings, and at length in his last
pages he openly pronounces, that after all he was right at first, in
thinking me a conscious liar and deceiver.

Now I wish to dwell on this point. It cannot be doubted, I say, that,
in spite of his professing to consider me as a dotard and driveller,
on the ground of his having given up the notion of my being a knave,
yet it is the very staple of his Pamphlet that a knave after all I must be.
By insinuation, or by implication, or by question, or by irony, or by
sneer, or by parable, he enforces again and again a conclusion which
he does not categorically enunciate.

Now it may be asked of me, "Well, why should not Mr. Kingsley
take a course such as this? It was his original assertion that Dr. Newman was a professed liar, and a patron of lies; he spoke somewhat at
random; granted; but now he has got up his references and he is
proving, not perhaps the very thing which he said at first, but something very like it, and to say the least quite as bad. He is now only
aiming to justify morally his original assertion; why is he not at liberty
to do so?"

Why should he *not* now insinuate that I am a liar and a knave! he had of course a perfect right to make such a charge, if he chose; he might have said, "I was virtually right, and here is the proof of it," but this he has not done, but on the contrary has professed that he no longer draws from my works, as he did before, the inference of my dishonesty. He says distinctly, "When I read these outrages upon common sense, what wonder if I said to myself, 'This man cannot believe what he is saying?' *I believe I was wrong*." "I said, This man has no real care for truth. Truth for its own sake is no virtue in his eyes, and he teaches that it need not be. *I do not say that now*." "I do not call this conscious dishonesty; the man who wrote that sermon *was already past the possibility* of such a sin."

Why should he *not!* because it is on the ground of my not being a knave that he calls me a fool; adding to the words just quoted, "[My readers] have fallen perhaps into the prevailing superstition that cleverness is synonymous with wisdom. They cannot believe that (as is too certain) great literary and even barristerial ability may co-exist with almost boundless silliness."

Why should he *not!* because he has taken credit to himself for that high feeling of honour which refuses to withdraw a concession which once has been made, though, (wonderful to say!) at the very time that he is recording this magnanimous resolution, he lets it out of the bag that his relinquishment of it is only a profession and a pretence; for he says: "I have accepted Dr. Newman's denial that [the Sermon] means what I thought it did; and *heaven forbid*" (oh!) "that I should withdraw my word once given, *at whatever disadvantage to myself*." Disadvantage! but nothing can be advantageous to him which is *untrue;* therefore in proclaiming that the concession of my honesty is a disadvantage to him, he thereby implies unequivocally that there is some probability still, that I am *dis*honest. He goes on, "I am informed by those from whose judgment on such points there is no appeal, the '*en hault courage*,' and strict honour, I am also *precluded*, by the *terms* of my explanation, from using any other of Dr. Newman's past writings to prove my assertion." And then, "I have declared Dr. Newman to have been an honest man up to the 1st of February, 1864; it was, as I shall show, only Dr. Newman's fault that I ever thought him to be any thing else. It depends entirely on Dr. Newman whether he shall *sustain* the reputation which he has so recently acquired," (by diploma of course from Mr. Kingsley.)

"If I give him thereby a fresh advantage in this argument, he is *most welcome* to it. He needs, it seems to me, *as many advantages as possible*."

What a princely mind! How loyal to his rash promise, how delicate towards the subject of it, how conscientious in his interpretation of it! I have no thought of irreverence towards a Scripture Saint, who was actuated by a very different spirit from Mr. Kingsley's, but somehow since I read his Pamphlet words have been running in my head, which I find in the Douay version thus; "Thou has also with thee Semei the son of Gera, who cursed me with a grievous curse when I went to the camp, but I swore to him, saying, I will not kill thee with the sword. Do not thou hold him guiltless. But thou art a wise man and knowest what to do with him, and thou shalt bring down his grey hairs with blood to hell."

Now I ask, Why could not Mr. Kingsley be open? If he intended still to arraign me on the charge of lying, why could he not say so as a man? Why must he insinuate, question, imply, and use sneering and irony, as if longing to touch a forbidden fruit, which still he was afraid would burn his fingers, if he did so? Why must he "palter in a double sense," and blow hot and cold in one breath? He first said he considered me a patron of lying; well, he changed his opinion; and as to the logical ground of this change, he said that, if any one asked him what it was, he could only answer that *he really did not know*. Why could not he change back again, and say he did not know why? He had quite a right to do so; and then his conduct would have been so far straightforward and unexceptionable. But no;—in the very act of professing to believe in my sincerity, he takes care to show the world that it is a profession and nothing more. That very proceeding which he lays to my charge, (whereas I detest it,) of avowing one thing and thinking another, that proceeding he here exemplifies himself; and yet, while indulging in practices as offensive as this, he ventures to speak of his sensitive admiration of "hault courage and strict honour!" "I forgive you, Sir Knight," says the heroine in the Romance, "I forgive you as a Christian." "That means," said Wamba, "that she does not forgive him at all." Mr. Kingsley's word of honour is about as valuable as in the jester's opinion was the Christian charity of Rowena. But here we are brought to a further specimen of Mr. Kingsley's method of disputation, and having duly exhibited it, I shall have done with him.

It is his last, and he has intentionally reserved it for his last. Let it be recollected that he professed to absolve me from his original charge of dishonesty up to February 1. And further, he implies that, *at the time when he was writing,* I had not *yet* involved myself in any fresh acts suggestive of that sin. He says that I have had a great *escape* of conviction, that he hopes I shall take warning, and act more cautiously. "It depends entirely," he says, "on *Dr. Newman, whether* he shall *sustain* the reputation which he has so recently acquired." Thus, in Mr. Kingsley's judgment. I was *then,* when he wrote these words, *still* innocent of dishonesty, for a man cannot sustain what he actually has not got; *only he could not be sure of my future.* Could not be sure! Why at this very time he had already noted down valid proofs, as he thought them, that I *had* already forfeited the character which he contemptuously accorded to me. He had cautiously said *"up to* February 1st," *in order* to reserve the Title-page and last three pages of my Pamphlet, which were not published till February 12th, and out of these four pages, which he had *not* whitewashed, he had *already* forged charges against me of dishonesty at the very time that he implied that as yet there was nothing against me. When he gave me that plenary condonation, as it seemed to be, he had already done his best that I should never enjoy it. He knew well at p. 27, what he meant to say at pp. 58 and 59. At best indeed I was only out upon ticket of leave; but that ticket was a pretence; he had made it forfeit when he gave it. But he did not say so at once, first, because between p. 27 and p. 58 he meant to talk a great deal about my idiocy and my frenzy, which would have been simply out of place, had he proved me too soon to be a knave again; and next, because he meant to exhaust all those insinuations about my knavery in the past, which "strict honour" did not permit him to countenance, in order thereby to give colour and force to his direct charges of knavery in the present, which "strict honour" *did* permit him to handsel. So in the fifth act he gave a start, and found to his horror that, in my miserable four pages, I had committed the "enormity" of an "economy," which in matter of fact he had got by heart before he began the play. Nay, he suddenly found two, three, and (for what he knew) as many as four profligate economies in that Title-page and those Reflections, and he uses the language of distress and perplexity at this appalling discovery.

Now why this *coup de théâtre?* The reason soon breaks on us. Up to February 1, he could not categorically arraign me for lying, and therefore could not involve me, (as was so necessary for his case,) in the popular abhorrence which is felt for the casuists of Rome: but, as soon as ever he could openly and directly pronounce (saving his "hault courage and strict honour") that I am guilty of three or four new economies, then at once I am made to bear, not only my own sins, but the sins of other people also, and, though I have been condoned the knavery of my antecedents, I am guilty of the knavery of a whole priesthood instead. So the hour of doom for Semei is come, and the wise man knows what to do with him—he is down upon me with the odious names of "St. Alfonso da Liguori," and "Scavini" and "Neyraguet," and "the Romish moralists," and their "compeers and pupils," and I am at once merged and whirled away in the gulph of notorious quibblers, and hypocrites, and rogues.

But we have not even yet got at the real object of the stroke, thus reserved for his *finale*. I really feel sad for what I am obliged now to say. I am in warfare with him, but I wish him no ill;—it is very difficult to get up resentment towards persons whom one has never seen. It is easy enough to be irritated with friends or foes, *vis-à-vis;* but, though I am writing with all my heart against what he has said of me, I am not conscious of personal unkindness towards himself. I think it necessary to write as I am writing, for my own sake, and for the sake of the Catholic Priesthood; but I wish to impute nothing worse to Mr. Kingsley than that he has been furiously carried away by his feelings. But what shall I say of the upshot of all this talk of my economies and equivocations and the like? What is the precise *work* which it is directed to effect? I am at war with him; but there is such a thing as legitimate warfare: war has its laws; there are things which may fairly be done, and things which may not be done. I say it with shame and with stern sorrow;—he has attempted a great transgression; he has attempted (as I may call it) to *poison the wells*. I will quote him and explain what I mean.

"Dr. Newman tries, by cunning sleight-of-hand logic, to prove that I did not believe the accusation when I made it. Therein he is mistaken. I did believe it, and I believed also his indignant denial. But when he goes on to ask with sneers, why I should believe his denial, if I did not consider him trustworthy in the first instance? I can only answer, I really do not know. There is a *great deal* to be said for *that* view, *now that* Dr. Newman has become (one must needs suppose) *suddenly* and *since* the 1st of February, 1864, a convert to the *economic* views of St. Alfonso da Liguori and his compeers. I am *henceforth* in doubt and *fear*, as much as any honest man can be, *concerning every word* Dr. Newman may write. *How can I tell that I shall not be the dupe of some cunning equivocation*, of one of the three kinds laid down as permissible by the blessed Alfonso da Liguori and his pupils, even when confirmed by an oath, because 'then we do not deceive our neighbour, but allow him to deceive himself?' . . . It is admissible, therefore, to use words and sentences which have a double signification, and leave the hapless hearer to take which of them he may choose. *What proof have I, then, that by 'mean it? I never said it!' Dr. Newman does not signify,* I did not say it, but I did mean it?"

Now these insinuations and questions shall be answered in their proper places; here I will but say that I scorn and detest lying, and quibbling, and double-tongued practice, and slyness, and cunning, and smoothness, and cant, and pretence, quite as much as any Protestants hate them; and I pray to be kept from the snare of them. But all this is just now by the bye; my present subject is Mr. Kingsley; what I insist upon here, now that I am bringing this portion of my discussion to a close, is this unmanly attempt of his, in his concluding pages, to cut the ground from under my feet;—to poison by anticipation the public mind against me, John Henry Newman, and to infuse into the imaginations of my readers, suspicion and mistrust of every thing that I may say in reply to him. This I call *poisoning the wells*. . . .

Well, I can only say, that, if his taunt is to take effect, I am but wasting my time in saying a word in answer to his foul calumnies; and this is precisely what he knows and intends to be its fruit. I can hardly get myself to protest against a method of controversy so base and cruel, lest in doing so, I should be violating my self-respect and self-possession; but most base and most cruel it is. We all know how our imagination runs away with us, how suddenly and at what a pace;— the saying "Caesar's wife should not be suspected," is an instance of what I mean. The habitual prejudice, the humour of the moment, is the turning-point which leads us to read a defence in a good sense or a bad. We interpret it by our antecedent impressions. The very same sentiments, according as our jealousy is or is not awake, or our aversion stimulated, are tokens of truth or of dissimulation and pretence. There is a story of a sane person being by mistake shut up in the wards of a Lunatic Asylum, and that, when he pleaded his cause to some strangers visiting the establishment, the only remark he elicited in answer was, "How naturally he talks! you would think he was in his senses." Controversies should be decided by the reason; is it legitimate warfare to appeal to the misgivings of the public mind and to its dislikings? Any how, if Mr. Kingsley is able thus to practise upon my readers, the more I succeed, the less will be my success. If I am natural, he will tell them, "Ars est celare artem;" if I am convincing, he will suggest that I am an able logician; if I show warmth, I am acting the indignant innocent; if I am calm, I am thereby detected as a smooth hypocrite; if I clear up difficulties, I am too plausible and perfect to be true. The more triumphant are my statements, the more certain will be my defeat.

So will it be if Mr. Kingsley succeeds in his manoeuvre; but I do not for an instant believe that he will. Whatever judgment my readers eventually form of me from these pages, I am confident that they will believe me in what I shall say in the course of them. I have no misgiving at all, that they will be ungenerous or harsh with a man who has been so long before the eyes of the world; who has so many to speak of him from personal knowledge; whose natural impulse it has ever been to speak out; who has ever spoken too much rather than too little; who would have saved himself many a scrape, if he had been wise enough to hold his tongue; who has ever been fair to the doctrines and arguments of his opponents; who has never slurred over facts and reasonings which told against himself; who has never given his name or authority to proofs which he thought unsound, or to testimony which he did not think at least plausible; who has never shrunk from confessing a fault when he felt that he had committed one; who has ever consulted for others more than for himself; who has given up much that he loved and prized and could have retained, but that he loved honesty better than name, and Truth better than dear friends.

23. COLENSO:

The Historical Accuracy of the Old Testament

John William Colenso (1814–1863), Bishop of Natal, died while his *Critical Examination of the Pentateuch* was being published (in seven parts, 1862–79). The only readily available biographical account is that in the *DNB*. See A. W. Benn, *History of English Rationalism in the Nineteenth Century* (2 vols., 1906), for a critical view of Colenso's place in the religious

tradition of his time. Colenso's demonstration of the historical inaccuracy
of large portions of the Five Books of Moses led him to be tried for heresy.
The "Introductory Remarks" given here from Colenso's first chapter clarify
the grounds of his objections.

1. The first five books of the Bible,—commonly called the Pentateuch . . . or Book of Five Volumes,—are supposed by most English
readers of the Bible to have been written by Moses, except the last
chapter of Deuteronomy, which records the death of Moses, and
which, of course, it is generally allowed, must have been added by
another hand, perhaps that of Joshua. It is believed that Moses wrote
under such special guidance and teaching of the Holy Spirit, that he
was preserved from making any error in recording such matters as
came within his own cognisance, and was instructed also in respect of
events, which took place before he was born,—before, indeed, there
was a human being on the earth to take note of what was passing. He
was in this way, it is supposed, enabled to write a true account of the
Creation. And, though the accounts of the Fall and of the Flood, as
well as of later events, which happened in the time of Abraham, Isaac,
and Jacob, may have been handed down by tradition from one generation to another, and even, some of them, perhaps, written down in
words, or represented in hieroglyphics, and Moses may, probably,
have derived assistance from these sources also in the composition of
his narrative, yet in all his statements, it is believed, he was under
such constant control and superintendence of the Spirit of God, that
he was kept from making any serious error, and certainly from writing
anything altogether untrue. We may rely with undoubting confidence—
such is the statement usually made—on the historical veracity, and
infallible accuracy, of the Mosaic narrative in all its main particulars.
Thus, Archdeacon PRATT writes, *Science and Scripture not at variance*,
p. 102:—

By the inspiration of Holy Scripture I understand, that the Scriptures were
written under the guidance of the Holy Spirit, who communicated to the writers
facts before unknown, directed them in the selection of other facts already
known, and *preserved them from error of every kind in the records they made.*

2. But, among the many results of that remarkable activity in
scientific enquiry of every kind, which, by God's own gift, distinguishes
the present age, this also must be reckoned, that attention and labour
are now being bestowed, more closely and earnestly than ever before,
to search into the real foundations for such a belief as this. As the

Rev. A. W. HADDAN has well said, (*Replies to Essays and Reviews, p. 349,*)—

It is a time when religious questions are being sifted with an apparatus of knowledge, and with faculties and a temper of mind, seldom, if ever, before brought to bear upon them. The entire creation of new departments of knowledge, such as philology,—the discovery of things before absolutely unknown, of the physical history of the globe,—the rising from the grave, as it were, of whole periods of history contemporary with the Bible, through newly found or newly interpreted monuments,—the science of manuscripts and of settling texts,—all these, and many more that might be named, embrace in themselves a whole universe of knowledge bearing upon religion, and specially upon the Bible, to which our fathers were utter strangers. And beyond all these is the change in the very spirit of thought itself, equally great, and equally appropriate to the conditions of the present conflict,—the transformation of history by the critical weighing of evidence, by the separation from it of the subjective and the mythical, by the treatment of it in a living and real way,—*the advance in Biblical Criticism, which has undoubtedly arisen from the more thorough application to the Bible of the laws of human criticism.*

3. This must, in fact, be deemed, undoubtedly, *the* question of the present day, upon the reply to which depend vast and momentous interests. The time is to come, as I believe, in the Providence of God, when this question can no longer be put by,—when it must be resolutely faced, and the whole matter fully and freely examined, if we would be faithful servants of the God of Truth. Whatever the result may be, it is our bounden duty to 'buy the truth' at any cost, even at the sacrifice, if need be, of much, which we have hitherto held to be most dear and precious. . . .

4. For myself, I have become engaged in this enquiry, from no wish or purpose of my own, but from the plain necessities of my position as a Missionary Bishop. I feel, however, that I am only drawn in with the stream, which in this our age is setting steadily in this direction, and swelling visibly from day to day. What the end may be, God only, the God of Truth, can foresee. Meanwhile, believing and trusting in His guidance, I have launched my bark upon the flood, and am carried along by the waters. . . .

7. But my labours, as a translator of the Bible, and a teacher of intelligent catechumens, have brought me face to face with questions, from which I had hitherto shrunk, but from which, under the circumstances, I felt it would be a sinful abandonment of duty any longer to turn away. I have, therefore, as in the sight of God Most High, set

myself deliberately to find the answer to such questions, with, I trust and believe, a sincere desire to know the Truth, as God wills us to know it, and with a humble dependence on that Divine Teacher, who alone can guide us into that knowledge, and help us to use the light of our minds aright. The result of my enquiry is this, that I have arrived at the conviction,—as painful to myself at first, as it may be to my reader, though painful now no longer under the clear shining of the Light of Truth,—that the Pentateuch, as a whole, cannot possibly have been written by Moses, or by any one acquainted personally with the facts which it professes to describe, and, further, that the (so-called) Mosaic narrative, by whomsoever written, and though imparting to us, as I fully believe it does, revelations of the Divine Will and Character, cannot be regarded as *historically true*.

8. Let it be observed that I am not here speaking of a number of petty variations and contradictions, such as, on closer examination, are found to exist throughout the books, but which may be in many cases sufficiently explained, by alleging our ignorance of all the circumstances of the case, or by supposing some misplacement, or loss, or corruption, of the original manuscript, or by suggesting that a later writer has inserted his own gloss here and there, or even whole passages, which may contain facts or expressions at variance with the true Mosaic Books, and throwing an unmerited suspicion upon them. However perplexing such contradictions are, when found in a book which is believed to be divinely infallible, yet a humble and pious faith will gladly welcome the aid of a friendly criticism, to relieve it in this way of its doubts. I can truly say that I would do so heartily myself. . . .

10. But I wish to repeat here most distinctly that my reason, for no longer receiving the Pentateuch as historically true, is not that I find insuperable difficulties with regard to the *miracles*, or supernatural *revelations* of Almighty God, recorded in it, but solely that I cannot, as a true man, consent any longer to shut my eyes to the absolute, palpable, self-contradictions of the narrative. The notion of miraculous or supernatural interferences does not present to my own mind the difficulties which its seems to present to some. I could believe and receive the miracles of Scripture heartily, if only they were authenticated by a veracious history; though, if this is not the case with the Pentateuch, any miracles, which rest on such an unstable support, must necessarily fall to the ground with it. The language, therefore, of

Prof. MANSEL, *Aids to Faith*, *p.* 9, is wholly inapplicable to the present case:—

The real question at issue, between the believer and the unbeliever in the Scripture miracles, is not whether they are established by sufficient testimony, but whether they can be established by any testimony at all.

And I must equally demur to that of Prof. BROWNE, *Aids to Faith*, *p.* 296, who, in his Essay, admirable as it is for its general candour and fairness, yet implies that doubts of the Divine Authority of any portion of the Scriptures *must*, in all or most cases, arise from 'unbelieving opinions,' while 'criticism comes afterwards.' Of course, a *thorough searching* criticism *must*, from the nature of the case, 'come afterwards.' But the 'unbelieving opinions' in my own case, and, I doubt not, in the case of many others, have been the necessary consequence of my having been led, in the plain course of my duty, to shake off the incubus of a dogmatic education, and steadily look one or two facts in the face. In my case, critical enquiry to some extent has preceded the formation of these opinions; but the one has continually reacted on the other.

11. For the conviction of the unhistorical character of the (so-called) Mosaic narrative seems to be forced upon us, by the consideration of the many absolute *impossibilities* involved in it, when treated as relating simple matters of fact, and without taking account of any argument, which throws discredit on the story merely by reason of the miracles, or supernatural appearances, recorded in it, or particular laws, speeches, and actions, ascribed in it to the Divine Being. We need only consider well the statements made in the books themselves, by whomsoever written, about matters which they profess to narrate as facts of common history,—statements, which every Clergyman, at all events, and every Sunday-School Teacher, not to say, every Christian, is surely bound to examine thoroughly, and try to understand rightly, comparing one passage with another, until he comprehends their actual meaning, and is able to explain that meaning to others. If we do this, we shall find them to contain a series of manifest contradictions and inconsistencies, which leave us, it would seem, no alternative but to conclude that main portions of the story of the Exodus, though based, probably, on some real historical foundation, yet are certainly not to be regarded as historically true.

12. The proofs, which seem to me to be conclusive on this point, I feel it to be my duty, in the service of God and the Truth, to lay before my fellow-men, not without a solemn sense of the responsibility which I am thus incurring, and not without a painful foreboding of the serious

consequences which, in many cases, may ensue from such a publication. There will be some now, as in the time of the first preaching of Christianity, or in the days of the Reformation, who will seek to turn their liberty into a 'cloke of lasciviousness.' 'The unrighteous will be unrighteous still; the filthy will be filthy still.' The heart, that is unclean and impure, will not fail to find excuse for indulging its lusts, from the notion that somehow the very principle of a living faith in GOD is shaken, because belief in the Pentateuch is shaken. But it is not so. Our belief in the Living GOD remains as sure as ever, though not the Pentateuch only, but the whole Bible, were removed. It is written on our hearts by GOD's own Finger, as surely as by the hand of the Apostle in the Bible, that 'GOD IS, and is a rewarder of them that diligently seek Him.' It is written there also, as plainly as in the Bible, that 'GOD is not mocked,'—that, 'whatsoever a man soweth, that shall he also reap,'—and that 'he that soweth to the flesh, shall of the flesh reap corruption.'

13. But there will be others of a different stamp,—meek, lowly, loving souls, who are walking daily with God, and have been taught to consider a belief in the historical veracity of the story of the Exodus an essential part of their religion, upon which, indeed, as it seems to them, the whole fabric of their faith and hope in God is based. It is not really so: the Light of God's Love did not shine less truly on pious minds, when Enoch 'walked with God' of old, though there was then no Bible in existence, than it does now. And it is, perhaps, God's Will that we shall be taught in this our day, among other precious lessons, not to build up our faith upon a Book, though it be the Bible itself, but to realise more truly the blessedness of knowing that He Himself, the Living God, our Father and Friend, is nearer and closer to us than any book can be,—that His Voice within the heart may be heard continually by the obedient child that listens for it, and *that* shall be our Teacher and Guide, in the path of duty, which is the path of life, when all other helpers—even the words of the Best of Books—may fail us.

14. In discharging, however, my present duty to God and to the Church, I trust that I shall be preserved from saying a single word that may cause *unnecessary* pain to those who now embrace with all their hearts, as a primary article of Faith, the ordinary view of Scripture Inspiration. *Pain*, I know, I must cause to some. But I feel very deeply that it behoves every one, who would write on such a subject as this, to remember how closely the belief in the historical truth of every portion

of the Bible is interwoven, at the present time, in England, with the faith of many, whose piety and charity may far surpass his own. He must beware lest, even by rudeness or carelessness of speech, he 'offend one of these little ones;' while yet he may feel it to be his duty, as I do now, to tell out plainly the truth, as God, he believes, has enabled him to see it. And that truth in the present instance, as I have said, is this, that the Pentateuch, as a whole, was not written by Moses, and that, with respect to some, at least, of the chief portions of the story, it cannot be regarded as historically true. It does not, therefore, cease to 'contain the true Word of God,' with 'all things necessary for salvation,' to be 'profitable for doctrine, reproof, correction, instruction in righteousness " It still remains an integral portion of that Book, which, whatever intermixture it may show of human elements,— of error, infirmity, passion, and ignorance,—has yet, through God's Providence, and the special working of His Spirit on the minds of its writers, been the means of revealing to us His True Name, the Name of the only Living and True God, and has all along been, and, as far as we know, will never cease to be, the mightiest instrument in the hand of the Divine Teacher, for awakening in our minds just conceptions of His Character, and of His gracious and merciful dealings with the children of men. Only we must not attempt to put into the Bible what we think *ought* to be there: we must not indulge that 'forward delusive faculty,' as Bishop BUTLER styles the 'imagination,' and lay it down for certain beforehand that God could only reveal Himself to us by means of an *infallible* Book. We must be content to take the Bible as it is, and draw from it those Lessons which it really contains. Accordingly, that which I have done, or endeavoured to do, in this book, is to make out from the Bible—at least, from the first part of it—what account it gives of itself, what it really is, what, if we love the truth, we must understand and believe it to be, what, if we will speak the truth, we must represent it to be.

24. CLOUGH:
"The Latest Decalogue"

Arthur Hugh Clough (1819–1861) is the subject of an excellent biography by Lady Katherine Chorley, *Arthur Hugh Clough: The Uncommitted Mind* (1962). His *Poems and Prose Remains* were edited by his wife in two volumes in 1869. The *Poems* are now available in an excellent edition by H. F. Lowry, A. L. P. Norrington, and F. L. Mulhauser (1952); Mulhauser is also the editor of the *Correspondence* (2 vols., 1957). W. E. Houghton's *The Poetry of Clough* (1963) is a necessary study.

Clough's earnest skepticism led him to resign his Oriel Fellowship—he could no longer subscribe to the Thirty-nine Articles, but his seriousness was often conveyed with wit and energy, as in this poem, "The Latest Decalogue" (1849).

> Thou shalt have one God only; who
> Would be at the expense of two?
> No graven images may be
> Worshipped, except the currency:
> Swear not at all; for for thy curse
> Thine enemy is none the worse:
> At church on Sunday to attend
> Will serve to keep the world thy friend:
> Honour thy parents; that is, all
> From whom advancement may befall:
> Thou shalt not kill; but need'st not strive
> Officiously to keep alive:
> Do not adultery commit;
> Advantage rarely comes of it:
> Thou shalt not steal; an empty feat,
> When it's so lucrative to cheat:
> Bear not false witness; let the lie
> Have time on its own wings to fly:
> Thou shalt not covet; but tradition
> Approves all forms of competition.

The sum of all is, thou shalt love,
If any body, God above:
At any rate shall never labour
More than thyself to love thy neighbour.

25. BRADLAUGH:
Of Atheism and Atheists

Charles Bradlaugh (1833–1891), politician and "free thought advocate," published his *Autobiography* in 1873. *The Life* (2 vols., 1894) was done by H. B. Bonner and J. M. Robertson. Interesting sidelights are also given by the *Autobiography* of Mrs. Annie Besant, with whom he was for a long time associated.

Bradlaugh was elected to Parliament in 1880 but was not seated until 1886 because he insisted on affirming his oath rather than swearing it on the Bible. His *A Few Words About the Devil, and Other Biographical Sketches and Essays* contains "A Plea For Atheism," from which this selection is taken.

It is too often the fashion with persons of pious reputation to speak in unmeasured language of Atheism as favoring immorality, and of Atheists as men whose conduct is necessarily vicious, and who have adopted atheistic views as a desperate defiance against a Deity justly offended by the badness of their lives. Such persons urge that among the proximate causes of Atheism are vicious training, immoral and profligate companions, licentious living, and the like. Dr. John Pye Smith, in his "Instructions on Christian Theology," goes so far as to declare that "nearly all the Atheists upon record have been men of extremely debauched and vile conduct." Such language from the Christian advocate is not surprising, but there are others who, professing great desire for the spread of Freethought, and with pretensions to rank among acute and liberal thinkers, declare Atheism impracticable, and its teachings cold, barren, and negative. In this brief essay I shall except to each of the above allegations, and shall endeavour to demonstrate that Atheism affords greater possibility for human happiness than any system yet based on Theism, or possible to be founded thereon, and that the lives of true Atheists must be more virtuous, because more human, than those of the believers in Deity, the humanity of the devout believer often finding itself neutralized by a faith with which it is necessarily in constant collision. The devotee piling the faggots at the *auto da fe* of a heretic, and that heretic his son, might, notwithstanding, be a good father in every respect but this. Heresy, in the eyes of the believer, is highest criminality, and outweighs all claims of family or affection.

Atheism, properly understood, is in nowise a cold, barren negative; it is, on the contrary, a hearty, fruitful affirmation of all truth, and involves the positive assertion and action of highest humanity.

Let Atheism be fairly examined, and neither condemned—its defense unheard—on the *ex parte* slanders of the professional preachers of fashionable orthodoxy, whose courage is bold enough while the pulpit protects the sermon, but whose valor becomes tempered with discretion when a free platform is afforded and discussion claimed; nor misjudged because it has been the custom to regard Atheism as so unpopular as to render its advocacy impolitic. The best policy against all prejudice is to assert firmly the verity. The Atheist does not say "There is no God," but he says, "I know not what you mean by God: I am without idea of God; the word 'God' is to me a sound conveying no clear or distinct affirmation. I do not deny God, because I can not deny that of which I have no conception, and the conception of which by its affirmer is so imperfect that he is unable to define it to me." If you speak to the Atheist of God as a creator, he answers that the conception of creation is impossible. We are utterly unable to construe it in thought as possible that the complement of existence has been either increased or diminished, much less can we conceive an absolute origination of substance. We can not conceive either, on the one hand, nothing becoming something, or on the other, something becoming nothing. The Theist who speaks of God creating the universe, must either suppose that Deity evolved it out of himself, or that he produced it from nothing. But the Theist can not regard the universe as evolution of Deity, because this would identify Universe and Deity, and be Pantheism rather than Theism. There would be no distinction of substance—in fact, no creation. Nor can the Theist regard the universe as created out of nothing, because Deity is, according to him, necessarily eternal and infinite. His existence being eternal and infinite, precludes the possibility of the conception of vacuum to be filled by the universe if created. No one can even think of any point of existence in extent or duration and say here is the point of separation between the creator and the created. Indeed, it is not possible for the Theist to imagine a beginning to the universe. It is not possible to conceive either an absolute commencement, or an absolute termination of existence; that is, it is impossible to conceive a beginning before which you have a period when the universe has yet to be: or to conceive an end, after which the universe, having been, no longer exists. It is impossible in thought to originate or annihilate the universe. The Atheist affirms that he cognizes to-day effects, that these are at the same time causes and effects—causes to the effects they precede, effects to the causes they follow. Cause is simply everything without which the effect would not result, and with which it must result. Cause is the means to an end, consummating itself in that end. The Theist who argues for creation must assert a point of time, that is, of duration, when the created did not yet exist. At this point of time either something existed or nothing; but something must have existed, for out of nothing nothing can come. Something must have existed, because the point fixed upon is that of the duration of something. This something must have been either finite or infinite; if finite, it could not have been God; and if the something were infinite, then creation was impossible, as it is impossible to add to infinite existence.

If you leave the question of creation and deal with the government of the universe, the difficulties of Theism are by no means lessened. The existence of evil is then a terrible stumbling-block to the Theist. Pain, misery, crime, poverty, confront the advocate of eternal goodness, and challenge with unanswerable potency his declaration of Deity as all-good, all-wise, and all-powerful. Evil is either caused by God, or exists independently; but it can not be caused by God, as in that case he would not be all-good; nor can it exist independently, as in that case he would not be all-powerful. Evil must either have had a beginning, or it must be eternal; but, according to the Theist, it can not be eternal, because God alone is eternal. Nor can it have had a beginning, for if it had it must either have originated in God, or outside of God; but, according to the Theist, it can not have originated in God, for he is all-good, and out of all-goodness evil can not originate; nor can evil have originated outside of God, for, according to the Theist, God is infinite, and it is impossible to go outside of or beyond infinity.

To the Atheist this question of evil assumes an entirely different aspect. He declares that evil is a result, but not a result from God or Devil. He affirms that by conduct founded on knowledge of the laws of existence it is possible to ameliorate and avoid present evil, and, as our knowledge increases, to prevent its future recurrence.

Some declare that the belief in God is necessary as a check to crime. They allege that the Atheist may commit murder, lie, or steal, without fear of any consequences. To try the actual value of this argument, it is not unfair to ask, Do Theists ever steal? If yes, then in each such theft, the belief in God and his power to punish has been inefficient as a preventive of the crime. Do Theists ever lie or murder? If yes, the same remark has further force—hell-fire failing against the lesser as against the greater crime. The fact is that those who use such an argument overlook a great truth—*i.e.*, that all men seek happiness, though in very diverse fashions. Ignorant and miseducated men often mistake the true path to happiness, and commit crime in the endeavour to obtain it. Atheists hold that by teaching mankind the real road to human happiness, it is possible to keep them from the by-ways of criminality and error. Atheists would teach men to be moral now, not because God offers as an inducement reward by and by, but because in the virtuous act itself immediate good is insured to the doer and the circle surrounding him. Atheism would preserve man from lying, stealing, murdering now, not from fear of an eternal agony after death, but because these crimes make this life itself a course of misery.

While Theism, asserting God as the creator and governor of the universe, hinders and checks man's efforts by declaring God's will to be the sole directing and controlling power, Atheism, by declaring all events to be in accordance with natural laws—that is, happening in certain ascertainable sequences—stimulates man to discover the best conditions of life, and offers him the most powerful inducements to morality. While the Theist provides future happiness for a scoundrel repentant on his death bed, Atheism affirms present and certain happiness for the man who does his best to live here so well as to have little cause for repenting hereafter.

Theism declares that God dispenses health and inflicts disease, and sickness and illness are regarded by the Theist as visitations from an angered Deity, to be borne with meekness and content. Atheism declares that physiological knowledge may preserve us from disease by preventing our infringing the law of health, and that sickness results not as the ordinance of offended Deity, but from ill-ventilated dwellings and workshops, bad and insufficient food, excessive toil, mental suffering, exposure to inclement weather, and the like—all these finding root in poverty, the chief source of crime and disease; that prayers and piety afford no protection against fever, and that if the human being be kept without food he will starve as quickly whether he be Theist or Atheist, theology being no substitute for bread. . . .

From the word "God" the Theist derives no argument in his favor; it teaches nothing, defines nothing, demonstrates nothing, explains nothing. The Theist answers that this is no sufficient objection, that there are many words which are in common use to which the same objection applies. Even admitting that this were true, it does not answer the Atheist's objection. Alleging a difficulty on the one side is not a removal of the obstacle already pointed out on the other.

The Theist declares his God to be not only immutable, but also infinitely intelligent, and says: "Matter is either essentially intelligent, or essentially non-intelligent; if matter were essentially intelligent, no matter could be without intelligence; but matter can not be essentially intelligent, because some matter is not intelligent, therefore matter is essentially non-intelligent; but there is intelligence, therefore there must be a cause for the intelligence, independent of matter; this must be an intelligent being—*i.e.*, God." The Atheist answers, I do not know what is meant, in the mouth of the Atheist, by "matter." "Matter," "substance," "existence," are three words having the same signification in the Atheist's vocabulary. It is not certain that the Theist expresses any very clear idea when he uses the words "matter" and "intelligence." Reason and understanding are sometimes treated as separate faculties, yet it is not unfair to presume that the Theist would include them both under the word intelligence. Perception is the foundation of the intellect. The perceptive faculty, or perceptive faculties, differs or differ in each animal, yet in speaking of matter that Theist uses the word "intelligence" as though the same meaning were to be understood in every case. The recollection of the perceptions is the exercise of a different faculty from the perceptive faculty, and occasionally varies disproportionately; thus an individual may have great perceptive faculties, and very little memory, or the reverse, yet memory, as well as perception, is included in intelligence. So also the faculty of comparing between two or more perceptions; the faculty of judging and the faculty of reflecting—all these are subject to the same remarks, and all these and other faculties are included in the word intelligence. We answer, then, that "God" (whatever that word may mean) can not be intelligent. He can never perceive; the act of perception results in the obtaining a new idea, but if God be omniscient his ideas have been eternally the same. He has either been always and always will be perceiving, or he has never perceived at all. But God can not have been always perceiving, because if he had he would always have been obtaining fresh knowledge, in which case he must have some time had less knowledge than now; that is he would have been less perfect; that is, he would not have been God: he can never recollect or forget, he can never compare, reflect nor judge. There can not be perfect intelligence without understanding; but following Coleridge, "understanding is the faculty of judging according to sense." The faculty of whom? Of some person, judging according to that person's senses? But has "God" senses? Is there anything beyond "God" for "God" to sensate? There can not be perfect intelligence without reason. By reason we mean that faculty or aggregation of faculties which avails itself of past experience to predetermine, more or less accurately, experience in the future, and to affirm truths which sense perceives, experiment verifies, and experience confirms. To God there can be neither past nor future, therefore to him reason is impossible. There can not be perfect intelligence without will, but has God will? If God wills, the will of the all-powerful must be irresistible; the will of the infinite must exclude all other wills.

God can never perceive. Perception and sensation are identical. Every sensation is accompanied by pleasure or pain. But God, if immutable, can neither be pleased nor pained. Every fresh sensation involves a change in mental and perhaps in physical condition. God, if immutable, can not change. Sensation is the source of all ideas, but it is only objects external to the mind which can be sensated. If God be infinite there can be no objects external to him, and therefore sensation must be to him impossible. Yet without perception where is intelligence?

God can not have memory or reason—memory is of the past, reason for the future, but to God immutable there can be no past, no future. The words, past, present, and future, imply change; they assert progression of duration. If God be immutable, to him change is impossible. Can you have intelligence destitute of perception, memory, and reason? God can not have the faculty of judgment—judgment implies in the act of judging a conjoining or disjoining of two or more thoughts, but this involves change of mental condition. To God, the immutable, change is impossible. Can you have intelligence, yet no perception, no memory, no reason, no judgment? God can not think. The law of the thinkable is that the thing thought must be separated from the thing which is not thought. To think otherwise would be to think of nothing—to have an impression with no distinguishing mark, would be to have no impression. Yet this separation implies change, and to God, immutable, change is impossible. Can you have intelligence without thought? If the Theist replies to this that he does not mean by infinite intelligence as an attribute of Deity an infinity of the intelligence found in a finite degree of humankind, then he is bound to explain, clearly and distinctly, what other "intelligence" he means, and until this be done the foregoing statements require answer.

The Atheist does not regard "substance" as either essentially intelligent or the reverse. Intelligence is the result of certain conditions of existence. Burnished steel is bright—that is, brightness is the necessity of a certain condition of existence. Alter the condition, and the characteristic of the condition no longer exists. The only essential of substance is its existence. Alter the wording of the Theist's objection. Matter is either essentially bright, or essentially non-bright. If matter were essentially bright, brightness should be the essence of all matter; but matter can not be essentially bright, because some matter is not bright, therefore matter is essentially non-bright; but there is brightness, therefore there must be a cause for this brightness independent of matter; that is, there must be an essentially bright being—*i.e.*, God.

Another Theistic proposition is thus stated: "Every effect must have a cause; the first cause universal must be eternal: *ergo*, the first cause universal must be God." This is equivalent to saying that "God" is "first cause." But what is to be understood by cause? Defined in the absolute, the word has no real value. "Cause," therefore, can not be eternal. What can be understood by "first cause?" To us the two words convey no meaning greater than would be conveyed by the phrase "round triangle." Cause and effect are correlative terms—each cause is the effect of some precedent; each effect the cause of its consequent. It is impossible to conceive existence terminated by a primal or initial cause. The "beginning," as it is phrased, of the universe, is not thought out by the Theist, but conceded without thought. To adopt the language of Montaigne, "Men make themselves believe that they believe." The so-called belief in Creation is nothing more than the prostration of the intellect on the threshold of the unknown. We can only cognize the ever-succeeding phenomena of existence as a line in continuous and eternal evolution. This line has to us no beginning; we trace it back into the misty regions of the past but a little way; and however far we may be able to journey, there is still the great beyond. Then what is meant by "universal cause?" Spinoza gives the following definition of cause, as used in its absolute signification: "By cause of itself I understand that, the essence of which involves existence, or that, the nature of which can only be considered as existent." That is, Spinoza treats "cause" absolute and "existence" as two words having the same meaning. If his mode of defining the word be contested, then it has no meaning other than its relative signification of a means to an end. "Every effect must have a cause." Every effect implies the plurality of effects, and necessarily that each effect must be finite; but how is it possible from a finite effect to logically deduce a universal, *i.e.*, infinite, cause? . . .

Every child is born into the world an Atheist; and if he grows into a Theist, his Deity differs with the country in which the believer may happen to be born, or the people among whom he may happen to be educated. The belief is the result of education or organization. Religious belief is powerful in proportion to the want of scientific knowledge on the part of the believer. The more ignorant, the more credulous. In the mind of the Theist "God" is equivalent to the sphere of the unknown; by the use of the word he answers without thought problems which might otherwise obtain scientific solution. The more ignorant the Theist, the greater his God. Belief in God is not a faith founded on reason, but a prostration of the reasoning faculties on the threshold of the unknown. Theism is worse than illogical; its teachings are not only without utility; but of itself it has nothing to teach. Separated from Christianity with its almost innumerable sects, from Mahometanism with its numerous divisions, and separated also from every other preached system, Theism is a Will-o'-the-wisp, without reality. Apart from orthodoxy, Theism is a boneless skeleton; the various mythologies give it alike flesh and bone, otherwise coherence it hath none. What does Christian Theism teach? That the first man made perfect by the all-powerful, all-wise, all-good God, was neverthless imperfect, and by his imperfection brought misery into the world, when the all-good God must have intended misery should never come. That this God made men to share this misery—men whose fault was their being what he made them. That this God begets a son, who is nevertheless his unbegotten self, and that by belief in the birth of God's eternal son, and in the death of the undying who died to satisfy God's vengeance, man may escape the consequences of the first man's error. Christian Theism declares that belief alone can save man, and yet recognizes the fact that man's belief results from teaching, by establishing missionary societies to spread the faith. Christian Theism teaches that God, though no respecter of persons, selected as his favorites one nation in preference to all others: that man can do no good of himself or without God's aid, but yet that each man has a free will; that God is all-powerful, but that few go to heaven and the majority to hell; that all are to love God, who has predestined from eternity that by far the largest number of human beings are to be burning in hell for ever.

26. BESANT:

Victorian Mysticism

Mrs. Annie Besant (1847–1933) devoted her long life to causes of one sort or another, stemming from atheism through socialism to Indian nationalism. Her works have not been collected. Her *Autobiography* (1893) narrates the story of her life through her first fascination with theosophical doctrines. Her later life as a somewhat mystic politician is unsympathetically viewed by T. M. Nair in *The Evolution of Mrs. Besant* (1918); a more balanced view is that in H. V. Lovett, *History of the Indian Nationalist Movement*, (1920).

In this selection, as in many others in *Theosophy*, we can see the nineteenth century trying to create a unified theory accounting for diverse expressions of what was felt to be the underlying harmony of creation. The selection is taken from Sections IV and V.

THEOSOPHY AS RELIGION

... Spirit, as Man, has three aspects, manifesting himself as Will, Intuition, and Intellect, in the three subtlest bodies. But the word is also used in a narrower sense, denoting the first of the three aspects, that which is manifested in the highest world of our fivefold system—the spiritual, or nirvānic, world, where his manifestation is Will, or Power. Often, also, the word is used to denote the two higher aspects by being made to include Intuition, and no objection can be raised to this. The two aspects indeed represent the "spiritual nature" of the human being, as Intellect and Mind represent his Intelligence, the

Emotions his feelings, and the Body his instrument of Action. We have seen that as this diversion marks out the four great departments of human thought—the scientific, the ethico-artistic, the philosophical, and the religious—it is therefore a convenient one. But for the sake of perfect clearness I shall use the word "Spirit" to denote the Monad clothed in an atom of the highest manifested world, and the word "Intuition" to denote him clothed in an additional atom of the next lower one.

The word "Religion" covers Man's search for God and God's answer to the searching. God's answer is His Self-revelation to the seeking Spirit who is Man. As the atmosphere surrounds us and interpenetrates us, but we remain unconscious of its presence though our very life depends on it, so the Universal Spirit surrounds and interpenetrates the particularised Spirit, and the latter knows not Him on whom his life depends:

"Closer is He than breathing, nearer than hands and feet."

"To know God" is, then, the essence of Religion, as we have seen that all religions testify; all else is subordinate, and the man who thus knows is the Mystic, the Gnostic, the Theosophist. The names are indeed borne by many, but only "those who know" can wear them in their full significance. "God is immanent in everything" is the statement of the truth in Nature which makes such knowledge possible. "God is all and in all" is the Christian way of putting the same truth; though S. Paul puts it in the future, the Mystic puts it in the present. What does it mean?

THE IMMANENCE OF GOD

It means that the essence of Religion is this recognition of God everywhere. The true Theosophist sees in each a portion of the divine Splendour. In the stability of mountains, in the might of crashing billows; in the rush of whirling winds, he sees His Strength. In the star-strewn depths of space, in the wide stretchings of deserts, he sees His Immensity. In the colours of flower-spangled meadows, in the rippling laughter of brooklets, in the green depths of forest shades, in the gleaming expanse of snowy mountain peaks, in the waving of the golden corn in the sunshine, in the silver of wavelets in the moonlight, he sees His Beauty. In the sweet shy smile of the maiden wooed in her dawning, in the eager kiss of the lover who claims her as bride, in the tender eyes of the wife as they rest on the husband, in the answering glance of the husband caressing the wife, in the laughing lips of the child joyous in play, in the warm protecting care of the father and mother, in the steadfast devotion of friend to friend, in the leal fidelity of comrade to comrade, he sees His Love. This is the "recollectedness" of the Mystic, and is the true meaning of the word mistranslated "fear" which "is the beginning of Wisdom." To realise this, and thus to know oneself to be one with God, is the aim of Theosophy, as of all true Religion. All else is means to this end.

THEOSOPHICAL TEACHINGS

The common doctrines of religions, that which has been believed everywhere, at all times, and by everyone, form the body of doctrines promulgated by Theosophy. These are: The One Existence—the One God—manifested in the universe under three Aspects ("Persons," from *persona*, a mask); the hierarchies of superhuman Beings—Devas, Angels, and Archangels; the Incarnation of Spirit in matter, of which Reincarnation is the human phase; the Law of Action and Reaction, "as a man sows, so shall he reap"; the existence of the Path to Perfection, and of divine Men; the three worlds—physical, intermediate, and heavenly—and the higher heavens; the Brotherhood of humanity. These are the leading doctrines of Universal Religion. They can all be proved to be true by the wider Science which investigates the manifested worlds, excluding none from its study so far as its instruments can reach. Hence Theosophy is everywhere the defender and helper of religions, serving each in its own domain, pointing out to each man the sufficiency of his own faith, and urging him to deepen and spiritualise his beliefs rather than to attack the forms preferred by others. It is thus a peacemaker among conflicting creeds, a carrier of goodwill, amity, and tolerance wherever it goes. Knowing that all religions come from one source, the White Brotherhood, it discourages bitterness of feeling among religionists and all virulent attacks by one on another. And hence we say of the Theosophical Society, its vehicle: "Peace is its watchword, as Truth is its aim."

THE PATH TO PERFECTION AND DIVINE MEN

This is a teaching which, though found in all religions, has dropped much out of sight in modern days, till reproclaimed in Theosophy, and may therefore be fitly sketched here. It is very fully described in Hindūism, Buddhism, Roman Catholic Christianity, and Sūfīsm (mystic Muhammadanism), and its main features are identical in all. The man who would enter the Path must recognise Unity as his aim, and this is to reached by profound devotion to God and unwearying service of Man. The first stage is named Purification in the Christian books, the Probationary or Preparatory Path in the others. The Christian name gives the negative side, the getting rid of weaknesses; the non-Christian the positive side, the acquirement of four "Qualifications"; these are: (1) Discrimination between the Real and the Unreal; (2) Dispassion, or Desirelessness as regards the Unreal; (3) the Six Jewels, or Good Conduct, comprising Self-control in Thought, Self-control in Action, Tolerance, Endurance, Confidence in the God within, and Equanimity or Balance; (4) Desire for Union, or Love. The partial but definite acquirement of these by the candidate brings him to the entrance of the Path of Illumination, to use the Christian term, of the Path of Holiness, or "the Path," to use the non-Christian. Theosophy follows the older nomenclature, which divides this Path into four stages, each entered by an "Initiation." Initiation is a definite ceremony, conducted by the Perfected Members of the White Brotherhood, under the sanction of its Head; it gives to the new Initiate an expansion of consciousness, and admits him to a definite rank in the Brotherhood; he is pledged to Service, and what is technically called "safe for ever"; that is, he cannot drop even temporarily out of evolution during its period of activity.

Each successive Initiation carries with it certain definite obligations, which must be fully discharged before the next step can be taken. The fifth Initiation "perfects" the Man, closing his human evolution. By that He becomes a liberated Spirit; He has "reached the further shore." Some of These remain on our earth, to watch over and forward human evolution; others depart to fill the various offices needed for the helping of our own and other planets, and for the general guidance of the Solar System. Those we call "Masters" are among Those who remain on our earth, and They form the fifth grade of the White Brotherhood; other ranks rise above Them, until the head of the whole Hierarchy is reached.

GOVERNMENT OF OUR WORLD

The world is divided into areas, each of which has a Master at its head, and He guides its activities, selects some men as His instruments, uses them, lays them quietly aside when useless, seeking ever to inspire, to guide, to attract, to check, but never to dominate the human will. The Great Plan must be carried out, but it is carried out by utilising free agents, who pursue certain aims which attract them, power, fame, wealth, and the rest. Where a man's aims, if carried out, will forward the Plan, opportunities to rise are placed in his way, and he obtains what he wants, ignorantly accomplishing a little bit of the Plan. "All the world's a stage, and all the men and women merely players"; but the Drama is written by the divine Playwright; men can only choose their parts, limited in their choice by the Karma they have created in their past, that includes their capacities.

Further, there are great departments in the government of the world, that includes the whole planet. The administrative department, that rules seismic changes, the raising and submerging of continents, the evolution of races, sub-races, and nations, and the like, has among its leading officials the Manus; a Manu is a typical Man, and each root-race has its Manu, embodying its type in its highest perfection. The teaching department is headed by the Bodhisattva, or Christ, the Supreme Teacher of Gods and Men; He founds religions directly or through His messengers, and places each under the protection of a Master, He Himself superintending and blessing all. When He becomes a Buddha, He leaves the earth, and is succeeded by another as Bodhisattva.

These Mighty Beings are the viceregents on our earth of the Supreme Lord, the LOGOS, or manifested God. They are "ministers of His, that do His pleasure." Thus it comes to pass that His word is guided, protected, assisted, as it slowly rolls upwards, by the long road of evolution, to His Feet.

THEOSOPHY APPLIED TO SOCIAL PROBLEMS

It may help the reader to understand the value of Theosophy in its bearing on Life, if we consider how it may be applied to the resolution of some of the more painful problems which confront us in the present state of Society. Many suggestions may be drawn from civilisations founded and ruled in the past by members of the White Brotherhood, although, under the greatly changed conditions now prevailing, new applications of the fundamental principles must be devised. The foundation of a stable Society must be Brotherhood; the need of every human being is for happiness and for conditions favourable to his evolution, and the duty of Society is to supply an environment which yields these. The birth of a human being into an organised Society gives to him a claim, and to Society a duty—the claim of a child on its parents, the duty of the parents to the child. It is this natural and proper claim of the younger on the elder that has been perverted into the aggressive doctrine of "rights"; animals, children, the sick, the ignorant, the helpless, all these have rights—the right to be kindly used, protected, nursed, taught, shielded; the strong, the grown-up, have only duties.

Organised Society exists for the happiness and the welfare of its members, and where it fails to secure these it stands *ipso facto* condemned. "Government exists only for the good of the governed." So said Pythagoras, preaching on the hill at Tauromenion, and the phrase has echoed down the centuries, and has become the watchword of those who are seeking the betterment of social conditions. . . .

Pythagoras has become the Master K. H., well known in connection with the Theosophical Society, and he speaks out the Theosophical ideal of the State—the father-mother of its citizens, the Protector of all.

*The duty of the State, of organised Society, is to secure to every one of its members at least the minimum of welfare—*of food, clothing, shelter, education, leisure—*which will enable each to develop to the full the faculties which he brought with him into the world.* There is no necessity for the existence of starvation and poverty, of overwork and absence of leisure, of lack of comfort and the means of enjoyment. Human brains are quite clever enough to plan out a social system in which every citizen should have enough for happy life; the only obstacles are selfishness and want of will. It was done long ago under the King-Initiates who ruled in the City of the Golden Gate and in Peru. It was done in the time of King Rāmachandra, as may be read in the *Rāmāyana*. It was done when the Manu ruled in the City of the Bridge. But it must be planned out by wisdom, not by ignorance, and brought about by the love and sacrifice of the higher, and not by the uprising of the lower. Mobs can make revolutions; but they cannot build a State.

PRINCIPLES OF THE NEW ORDER

Basing itself on the study of the past, Theosophy can lay down certain principles, to be worked out into details by the highly educated and experienced. The principles are: that Government should be in the hands of the Elders, *i.e.* the wisest, the most experienced, and the morally best; that the possession of ability and of power imposes the duty of service; that freedom brings happiness only to the educated and self-controlled, and that no one, so long as he is ignorant and unself-controlled, should have any share in the governing of others, and should only have such freedom as is consistent with the welfare of the community; that the life of such a one should be rendered as happy and useful as possible, under discipline until he is fit to "run alone," so that his evolution may be quickened; that co-operation, mutual aid, should be substituted for competition, mutual struggle; that the fewer resources a man has within himself, the more means of outer enjoyment should be placed within his reach by Society.

SUGGESTIONS

The suggestions which follow are the results of my own study of what has been done in the past, and of my own thought on present conditions. They are *only* suggestions, and many Theosophists might disagree with them. My only wish is to indicate a line of change consonant with Theosophical ideas. Brotherhood imperatively demands fundamental social changes, and the rapid growth of unrest, justified by the conditions of the classes that live by manual labour, will force a change ere long. The only question is whether the change shall be brought about by open-eyed wisdom or by blind suffering. At present, Society is engaged in trying the latter plan.

The land of a country should be used to support: (1) the Ruler, his Councillors, Officials of every grade, the administration of Justice, the maintenance of internal Order and of National Defence; (2) Religion, Education, Amusement, Pensions, and the care of the Sick; (3) all who are not included under (1) and (2), and who gain their livelihood by manual labour in production and distribution.

Education, free and universal, should be the only work of the period between seven and twenty-one years of age, so that the youths of both sexes should, on reaching manhood and womanhood, be ready to become dutiful and useful citizens, with their faculties well developed, so that they would be capable of leading an honourable, self-supporting and self-respecting life.

The working life—and all should work in one of the three above-named divisions—should last from twenty-one to fifty years of age, unless a shorter term should be found sufficient for the support of the nation. During the remainder of the life, the citizen should be in receipt of a pension, the result of the accumulated surplus of his working years, and therefore a repayment, not a gift; he should be free to devote himself to any pursuit he pleased.

Production and distribution should be organised by such men as make the huge fortunes now becoming so numerous, and after full provision for all concerned in the producing and distributing, the surplus profits should go to (1) and (2), chiefly to the latter. The organisation of industry should be governed by the idea that labour should be rendered as little burdensome as possible by healthy conditions and by the substitution of machinery for human beings in all unpleasant and dangerous work—mining, drainage, and the like; where unpleasant forms of human labour are necessary for the welfare of the community, the hours of labour should be shortened in proportion to the disagreeableness of the task, without any diminution of pay. If the scavenger, for instance, is to lead a human life, as much of his work as can be done by machinery should be thus performed; for the rest, his hours should be very short, his pay good—since the health of the community depends on him—and recreation, some refining and educative, some purely amusing, should be readily available within his reach. He is an active hand of Nature, helping her in her constant task of transforming the foul and the dangerous into the nourishment of new life and new beauty. He should be regarded . . . not as a drudge but as a co-worker with God. Is it said that he is coarse, repellent? So much the more shame for us, the refined and attractive, who profit by his work, and have made him what he is by our selfishness, our indifference, and our neglect.

The doctrine of Reincarnation, applied to education, leads us to see in the child an ego who has come into our care during the time of the growth of his body, to be helped in training it for the purpose for which he has returned to the earth. Recognising that in the ego himself are enshrined all the powers accumulated in past lives, and that the germs of these are planted in the new mental body, we feel the full force of Plato's famous phrase, that "All knowledge is reminiscence," and seek to draw out of the ego that which he knows, that he may stimulate the germinal mental faculties, and so impress the plastic brain. We do not regard the child-body as belonging to us, parents or teachers, but as belonging to the ego, and we see it to be our duty to help him in gaining full possession of it, to work from outside while he works from within, and to follow out any indication given by him as to the best line of study, the easiest road of progress. We give to the child the greatest liberty compatible with his physical, moral, and mental safety, and in everything try to understand and to help, not to coerce. . . .

Reincarnation, applied to the treatment of criminals and of the undeveloped class which is ever on the verge of crime, suggests a policy wholly different from that of our present Society, which gives them complete liberty to do as they like, punishes them when they commit a legal offence, restores them to liberty after a varying term of gaol, and so gives them a life of alternating freedom and imprisonment, transforming them into habitual criminals, and handing them over finally to "the divine mercy," man having failed to do any good with them.* In the light of Reincarnation I suggest that the congenital criminal is a savage, come to us as to a school, and that it is our business to treat him as the intellectual and moral baby which he is, and to restrain the wild beast in him from doing harm. These people, and the almost criminal class above them, are recognisable from birth, and they should be segregated in small special schools, given such elementary education as they can assimilate, be treated kindly and firmly, have many games, and be taught a rough form of manual labour. The teachers in these schools should be volunteers from the higher social classes, willing to teach and play with the boys, and capable of arousing in them a feeling of admiration, attachment, and loyalty, which would evoke obedience. They must be with those who are obviously their superiors if this is to be done. From these schools they should be drafted into small colonies, bright, pleasant villages, with shops, playground, music-hall, and restaurant, ruled by men of the same type as before; they should have everything to make life pleasant, except freedom to make it mischievous and miserable; these colonies would supply gangs of labourers for all the rougher kinds of work, mining, road-making, porterage, scavengering, etc., leaving the decent people now employed in these free for higher tasks. Some, the true congenital criminal, the raw savage, would remain under this kindly restraint for life, but they would go out of life far less of savages than they were when they came into it. Some would respond to the treatment, and would acquire sufficient industry and self-control to be ultimately set free. The chief difficulties would be innate rowdyism and idleness, for the criminal is a loafer, incapable of steady industry. The school would do something to improve him, and to do right would be made pleasant, while to be rowdy and idle would be made

* That which follows is the immediate treatment of the criminal as he is. We hope, later, to eliminate the type [Mrs. Besant's note].

unpleasant; "he that will not work neither shall he eat" is a sound maxim, for food is made by work and he who, being able, refuses to make it has no claim to it. Checks might be given for each hour's work, exchangeable at the shops and restaurant for the necessaries of life, and the man could do as much or as little as he liked; the equivalent in necessaries and luxuries would be at his own choice. It is only possible here to indicate the broad lines of the solution of this problem, and similar methods would be employed, *mutatis mutandis*, with girls and women of the corresponding type.

Karma, applied to the slums, would see in them magnets for the lowest types of incarnating Spirits; it would be our wisdom, as it is our duty, to get rid of these foul spots, attractive only to the most undesirable of the incoming crowd. In the light of Theosophy, it is the duty of the elders to plan out, and gradually to construct, towns of decent dwellings with sufficient interspaces, to which should be transplanted the dwellers in the slums; these poison-spots must be pulled down, and the soil, sodden with the filth of generations, should be turned into gardens; the filth will then be changed into trees and flowers, whereas to build new houses on such soil is to invite disease. Moreover, Beauty must be sought, for, as said in Section II., it is a necessity of life for all, not a luxury for the few. Beauty refines and cultivates, and reproduces itself in the forms and manners of those who live under its influences. Beauty in dress, in the home, in the town, is a crying need as an evolutionary force. It is not without significance that before the present age of machinery, when people were more surrounded by natural beauty than they are now, the clothes of the people of every class were beautiful, as they still are in the East; it is natural to man to seek to express himself in Beauty; it is only as he becomes far removed from Nature, that he accepts with indifference ugliness in clothes and surroundings. Contrast the clothes seen in our slums with those seen in an Indian village.

Volumes might be written on this theme of the application of Theosophy to life, but within our present limits the above must suffice.

IV

Science

A‍T the turn of the nineteenth century Wordsworth argued that:

The knowledge both of the poet and the man of science is pleasure, but the knowledge of the one cleaves to us as a necessary part of our existence . . . the other is a personal and individual acquisition, slow to come to us, and by no habitual and direct sympathy connecting us with our fellow beings.

The Preface to *Lyrical Ballads* continues:

If the labors of men of science should ever create any material revolution, direct or indirect, in our condition, and in the impressions which we habitually receive, the poet . . . will be ready to follow the steps of the men of science, not only in these general indirect effects, but he will be at his side, carrying sensation into the midst of the object of the science itself. The remotest discoveries of the chemist, the botanist, or the mineralogist will be as proper objects of the poet's art as any upon which it can be employed, if the time should ever come when these things shall be familiar to us, and the relations under which they are contemplated by the followers of these respective sciences shall be manifestly and palpably material to us as enjoying and suffering beings.

Eighty-two years later Matthew Arnold gave voice to what is essentially the same complaint about science. After admitting that we all need to be acquainted with the "important" and "interesting" results of science, Arnold argues that

when they are propounded to us and we receive them, we are still in the sphere of intellect and knowledge. And for the generality of man there will be found, I say, to arise, when they have duly taken in the proposition that their ancestor was "a hairy quadruped furnished with a tail and pointed ears, probably arboreal in habits," there will be found to arise an invincible desire to relate this proposition to the sense in us for conduct, and to the sense in us for beauty. But this the men of science will not do for us, and will hardly even profess to do. They will give us other pieces of knowledge, other facts, about other animals and their ancestors, or about plants, or about stones, or about stars; and they may finally bring to us those great "general conceptions of the universe, which are forced upon us all," says Professor Huxley, "by the progress of physical science." But still it will be *knowledge* only which they give us; knowledge not put for us into relation with our sense for conduct, our sense for beauty, and touched with emotion by being so put. . . .

Yet by 1882, in the life of the average citizen in Victorian England, science had had profound and emotional significance. His life was materially far more comfortable than before because of rapid advances in technology; his concept of the physical and spiritual nature of the earth on which he dwelt and the universe of which it was part had been radically challenged and shaken. Science seemed to have reduced the importance of man in and to nature from Gulliver in Lilliput, or a divinely favored Adam in Eden, to that of a type, a species, which had been lucky to survive nature's random process of natural selection: man was rather like a Gulliver in Brobdingnag who had luckily escaped the farmer's reaping hook. No longer did man occupy a fixed position in the great chain of being; rather that chain was seen as a web of relationships still being spun and woven.

One of the results of these changes was optimism. Many felt that since nature had done so well while operating randomly, then, if she were directed by man's intelligence, perfection of physical forms and social institutions was indeed an attainable goal. Another result was as emotionally charged, but negatively rather than positively. What today we would call the absurdity of man's tenure on earth was made vividly evident by the theoretical advances of scientists like Darwin. The realization that man as a species was only fortunate, not divinely protected, and that his survival was more likely due to chance than any other factor, was vastly unsettling emotionally. Anxiety became a prevalent tone and mood, and men's psyches were nearly literally torn between what their rational faculties told them was and what their religions had taught them to believe.

Relying as they did on appeals to an omniscient and ultimate authority, the High Church and Roman Catholicism gained converts eager to be told that they should believe what they longed to believe. The Evangelical movement gained strength because it too dismissed the controversies between science and religion and appealed directly to man's emotional dependencies. This is not to say that the results of science were not intelligently considered by enlightened clergymen, but rather that it seems to us likely that the average citizen was touched deeply by the processes and the results of science, that some of his habits of perception were radically altered, that they did make a manifest difference to him as an enjoying and suffering being.

As for the other part of the poets' arguments, it was not until the twentieth century that we recognized that our sense for beauty can be and is awakened by the harmonious configurations of the laws of science, that scientific and artistic creativity spring from the same kinds of mental activity, that, as Arthur Koestler has mathematically rephrased Keats' words, "beauty is a function of truth." The revolution in manners or conduct arrived sooner. "Social Darwinism" is a rationalization familiar to students of the more extreme and unscupulous uses to which the doctrine of laissez-faire was put. Further, many hedonistic excesses were excused by the uncertainties of modern life and unchecked by the fear of an inevitable accounting at the bar of divine justice.

The following selections should serve to acquaint us with two kinds of controversies. First, the divisions within the scientific community are made plain in the extracts from Huxley, Chambers, and Butler, and from the *Athenaeum's* report of the so-called Huxley-Wilberforce Debate. Comte's positivism, introduced into English thought by George Henry Lewes, has its roots in the scientific controversy as to whether luck or cunning, random selection or predestination, is ultimately the motive force behind evolutionary change.

It needs to be recalled that the idea of evolution was itself not new in 1859. What was startling, and even profoundly unsettling, was the idea that evolution had not been consistently progressive, that there had been innumerable lost types, that those that survived were "fittest" rather than "chosen" or "elected." We ought to recall too that Darwin's ideas about the descent of man were not published until 1871; that it was, in fact, the idea of natural selection that provoked controversy during the mid-Victorian period.

The impact of science on theories of education has been presented in an earlier section of this anthology. The apparent conflict between science and religion (or what Huxley would call "ecclesiasticism" not "theology") is too well known to be examined here in great detail. Probably the *Athenaeum* reporter's account of Bishop Wilberforce's attack on Darwin, an attack against the quality of his evidence and the validity of his methods, and Huxley's reply, a reply by a member

of the Church of England, will suffice to remind us that the controversies did not take place between men whose modes of thought and
feeling were entirely at variance. The problem of final causes is not
avoided; rather we are asked to consider new philosophies of causation. In Huxley's explanation of "The Darwinian Hypothesis" he
argues strenuously that the recognition of secondary causes is not dis-
respectful. Though an "immediate intervention of a higher power"
is denied (it is something Cardinal Newman constantly postulated),
the idea of secondary causation is said to reveal that the development
of species "has an order and a unity." Huxley's God is more subtle
and foresighted than most.

Although Huxley vigorously denies the validity of Chambers'
transmutation theory, his language is as shot through with religious
metaphor as is Chambers'. Consider:

> All living beings march, side by side, along the high road of development,
> and separate the later the more like they are; like people leaving church,
> who all go down the aisle, but having reached the door, some turn into the
> parsonage, others go down the village, and others part only in the next parish.

Again, a rather typical Huxleyian rhetorical turn calculated to win
churchgoers and influence humanists is the echo of Wordsworth in the
statement that "living things are formed of the same elements as the
inorganic world . . . they act and react upon it, bound by a thousand
ties of natural piety." We need only point out that despite Huxley's
scorn for *Vestiges of Creation*, the intimate connection of the organic
and inorganic is one of Chambers' major arguments.

Of course Huxley's main argument with Chambers and the Lamarc-
kians is whether species underwent planned, progressive development,
as Chambers insists, or whether "the question," as Huxley argues,
"is not transmutation or a transition of species as of the production
of forms which became permanent."

Like Huxley, Chambers argues that the history of science reveals
that "the whole of nature is a legitimate field for the exercise of our
intellectual faculties." By seeing all in relation to "cause" we will
admit that "the whole is alike worshipful." One of the most noticeable
motifs in Chambers' work is the reiteration that God's grandeur is in
no way diminished by man's perception of it, and that the results of
his investigations merely reveal a farsighted, consistent, supra-
human God.

Comte's philosophical expansion of the laws of embryological development, especially that ontogeny recapitulates phylogeny*, demonstrates how the great results of science permeated the intellectual atmosphere of the Victorian period; it also demonstrates how puny and jejune were Professor Draper's arguments against Darwin's theories. Not only does Comte's theory, as explained by Lewes†, account for natural selection; it traces the history of man in a broad, philosophical, and generally accurate manner as compared to Draper's attempt to show immutable law at work in even the minutia of man's advancement toward civilization. Even Reverend Cresswell could point out that Draper had to force the history of Greece to conform to a procrustean theory. Comte's three stages are as weakly general as Draper's are weakly specific, yet there is a psychological accuracy in the descriptions of man's theological, metaphysical, and positive stages that is not paralleled by physiological accuracy in Draper's descriptions of the stages of automatism, instinct, and intelligence.

By the time of Butler's *Luck or Cunning* we are one stage onward in the scientific argument, though Butler's thinking is not based on religious but on vaguely mystical grounds. Butler's preference for the idea of a designed natural selection rather than a fortuitous natural selection is based on the perception that "the idea underlying the old evolutionists is more in accord with the instinctive feelings we have cherished too long to be able now to disregard them than the central idea which underlies *The Origin of Species*." In another way too the selection from Butler may strike us as a falling off. Butler's wit, for example his playing with Darwin's title page, is far less graceful than Huxley's, and the nastiness of the passage we are about to quote might lead one to conclude that Butler is preaching to the converted. In calling attention to Darwin's omission of the word "accidental" from in front of "variations" Butler writes: "Mr. Darwin was a master of scientific chiaroscuro, and owes his reputation in no small measure to the judgment with which he kept his meaning dark when a less practised hand would have thrown light upon it."

One's judgment of Butler may be more charitable at the end of the

* The biological concept that the developmental stages in the life cycle of an individual parallel the evolutionary stages through which passed the phylum, or larger family of which the individual is a member.

† In *Comte's Philosophy of Science*, which unfortunately we had no space to represent.

selection we have chosen, where, for a moment, the spirit of compromise and cooperation that pervades Victorian controversies shines
through. Using Butler's own illustration, surely the likelihood of
numerous false starts in the history of telescope-making places the
entire argument in the gray area of selection wherein neither luck nor
cunning can say with certainty, *meum, tuum.*

In turning to the second kind of selection we have chosen to represent
what was provoked by scientific controversies, we find set forth in the
imaginative literature of the period not only divided attitudes about
which theory was correct, but also the emotional conflicts provoked in
sensitive men who in their own minds and hearts lived the roles of
believer and doubter. That is to say, we find that science had indeed
come home to the bosoms and businesses of men. Poets are, aren't
they, men speaking to other men?

It is something of a commonplace of literary criticism to suggest
that the poets of the Victorian period turned to the past not only
to find a brave old world but in order to comment on contemporary
problems without seeming to violate putative canons of art and without
seeming to preach. Still, it is not so common to find agreement as to
just what their criticisms were, because they are presented obliquely.

Some readers and critics argue that Tennyson's "Lucretius" is a
mordant comment on the materialism of science—whom the Gods
would destroy they first make mad. But in Lucretius' first dream and
in his final vision he not only speaks pridefully of his knowledge of
nature's entropy, but he also catalogs the horrors of having made
such a discovery, and as a result, he courts tranquillity through
suicide. The emotion revealed is the horror of realizing that the gods
too are dissoluble into atoms. The poem is more the evocation of loss
of a certain kind of faith, a naïve faith, in place of which is worship
of "the all generating powers and genial heat of nature," than it is a
denunciation of intellect. If it were the latter, then only brute passion,
not anything divine, is triumphant. However, it is not Lucretius'
passions but his reason which has destroyed the kind of world we long
to believe in. His passions do not triumph over his intellect except in an
artificially induced state of madness. We must remember that in a
dramatic monologue our sympathies are supposed to be with the
speaker—at least at first. Lucretius' reason posited, especially in lines
95 and following, a pleasant universe. He is more sinned against than
sinning, and Tennyson's pessimism may be directed toward the world
that rejects science and intellect.

An achievement as impressive as Tennyson's, though of a different order, is Browning's "Caliban upon Setebos." Caliban, half man, half monster—whom some have identified as the missing link—tries to fathom the nature of God by assuming that he is the God of nature; that is, Caliban attributes his own attitudes and modes of behavior to God. There is, perhaps, less error and a different kind of satire in the poem than we conventionally assume. Does not modern psychology tell us that, like Caliban, man created God in his own image? Second, Caliban's mockery of conventional piety, of man's attempts to placate God, and the arrogance of man's reasoning about God's motives, as these are expressed in lines 22 and following, are both perceptive and worshipful. Caliban is evidently aware that Setebos' or God's nature is as unfathomable to him as God's is to man. Caliban's vision of the Quiet may remind us of Lucretius' more pacific vision. Caliban's terror during the storm, together with his unwillingness to seem to believe in traditional ways by acting as though he believes, are double-edged irony; more than primitive religion and Calvinism are being mocked.

Arnold shows us the dilemma of modern man more clearly. As the monks in the monastery anticipate their deaths by sleeping in their caskets, Arnold waits forlornly in his desert wasteland which was once a "cloistral round." He is, like Tiresias, "throbbing between two lives," "wandering between two worlds, one dead,/ The other powerless to be born." The rationalism of the unborn world has blighted the abbey's garden, but the children are too attached to the garden that the desert once was for them to leave now: "their bent was taken long ago." It is worthy of note that though the poet's dilemma is most clearly personal in this poem, still emotional distance is achieved through the use of an extended metaphor utilizing romantic material. The distance serves the same function for Arnold that it serves for the other poets: it allows comment on the present without seeming prosaic or offending a conventionally pious audience.

Meredith's "The Woods of Westermain" posits for us an ameliorative view of evolution. Feelings of pessimism about man's fate fluctuate during the Victorian period according to how much chance and random selection are admitted to be the governing forces of evolution, whether the laws of the physical universe and society are thought of as "nature red in tooth and claw." Hardy's suggestion in "Hap" is not only that the universe does not care about man, but that it does not care either way, that man is so alone that there is not even a superior power which is hostile to him. This suggestion can be seen as leading to the impossible kind of Social Darwinism wherein all social control is abandoned. Meredith's view of evolution in the poem printed here is more optimistic. It suggests that while there is much to learn from those in whom a selfish egoism is rampant, still there is the hope that if man can unite and harmonize the three stages of evolution represented within him (stages Meredith calls Blood, Brain, and Spirit; *cf.* Comte and Draper), he can penetrate the secret of nature and "ascend to heights unmatched." Tennyson argued that man must

> arise, and fly
> The reeling faun, the sensual feast;
> Move upward, working out the beast,
> And let the ape and tiger die.

In contrast, Meredith's vision is more Lamarckian and totally humanistic:

> Each of each in sequent birth
> Blood and brain and spirit, three . . .
> Join for true felicity.
> [If] they [are] parted, then expect
> Some one sailing to be wrecked.

It should be clear now that as surely as Victorian controversies about science were revealed in the literature of the time, so too was science no longer divorced from the emotional lives of men, as some claim it had been since the early seventeenth century. The Victorian period may have been iron, but it does not seem to have been rusty too.

27. *ATHENAEUM:*
Debate on Darwin

The history and importance of *The Athenaeum* are described in L. A. Marchand's *The Athenaeum: A Mirror of Victorian Culture* (Chapel Hill, 1941).

This selection is one contemporary record of what later was seen as one of the most important public encounters of proponents and opponents of Darwin's theories. It is here presented in two reports on the meeting of the British Association for the Advancement of Science, from *The Athenaeum*; one on July 7, 1860 and the other on July 14, 1860.

REPORT OF JULY 7, 1860

'On the Final Causes of the Sexuality of Plants, with particular Reference to Mr. Darwin's Work "On the Origin of Species by Natural Selection," ' by Dr. DAUBENY.—Dr. Daubeny began by pointing out the identity between the two modes by which the multiplication of plants is brought about, the very same properties being imparted to the bud or to the graft as to the seed produced by the ordinary process of fecundation, and a new individual being in either instance equally produced. We are, therefore, led to speculate as to the final cause of the existence of sexual organs in plants, as well as in those lower animals which can be propagated by cuttings. One use, no doubt, may be the dissemination of the species; for many plants, if propagated by buds alone, would be in a manner confined to a single spot. Another secondary use is the production of fruits which afford nourishment to animals. A third may be to minister to the gratification of the senses of man by the beauty of their forms and colours. But as these ends are only answered in a small proportion of cases, we must seek further for the uses of the organs in question; and hence the author suggested that they might have been provided, in order to prevent that uniformity in the aspect of Nature, which would have prevailed if plants had been multiplied exclusively by buds. It is well known that a bud is a mere counterpart of the stock from whence it springs, so that we are always sure of obtaining the very same description of fruit by merely grafting a bud or cutting of a pear or apple tree upon another plant of the same species. On the other hand, the seed never produces an individual exactly like the plant from which it sprang; and hence, by the union of the sexes in plants, some variation from the primitive type is sure to result. Dr. Daubeny remarked that if we adopt in any degree the views of Mr. Darwin with respect to the origin of species by natural selection, the creation of sexual organs in plants might be regarded as intended to promote this specific object. Whilst, however, he gave his assent to the Darwinian hypothesis, as likely to aid us in reducing the number of existing species, he wished not to be considered as advocating it to the extent to which the author seems disposed to carry it. He rather desired to recommend to naturalists the necessity of further inquiries, in order to fix the limits within which the doctrine proposed by Mr. Darwin may assist us in distinguishing varieties from species.

Prof. HUXLEY, having been called on by the Chairman, deprecated any discussion on the general question of the truth of Mr. Darwin's theory. He felt that a general audience, in which sentiment would unduly interfere with intellect, was not the public before which such a discussion should be carried on. Dr. Daubeny had brought forth nothing new to demand or require remark.—Mr. R. DOWDEN, of Cork, mentioned, first, two instances in which plants had been disseminated by seeds, which could not be effected by buds; first, in the introduction of *Senecio squalida*, by the late Rev. W. Hincks; and, second, in the diffusion of chicory, in the vicinity of Cork, by the agency of its winged seeds. He related several anecdotes of a monkey, to show that however highly organized the Quadrumana might be, they were very inferior in intellectual qualities to the dog, the elephant and other animals. He particularly referred to his monkey being fond of playing with a hammer; but although he liked oysters as food, he never could teach him to break the oysters with his hammer as a means of indulging his appetite.—Dr. WRIGHT stated that a friend of his, who had gone out to report on the habits of the gorilla—the highest form of monkey—had observed that the female gorilla took its young to the sea-shore for the purpose of feeding them on oysters, which they broke with great facility.—Prof. OWEN wished to approach this subject in the spirit of the philosopher, and expressed his conviction that there were facts by which the public could come to some conclusion with regard to the probabilities of the truth of Mr. Darwin's theory. Whilst giving all praise to Mr. Darwin for the courage with which he had put forth his theory, he felt it must be tested by facts. As a contribution to the facts by which the theory must be tested, he would refer to the structure of the highest Quadrumana as compared with man. Taking the brain of the gorilla, it presented more differences, as compared with the brain of man, than it did when compared with the brains of the very lowest and most problematical form of Quadrumana. The deficiencies in cerebral structure between the gorilla and man were immense. The posterior lobes of the cerebrum in man presented parts which were wholly absent in the gorilla. The same remarkable differences of structure were seen in other parts of the body; yet he would especially refer to the structure of the great toe in man, which was constructed to enable him to assume the upright position; whilst in the lower monkeys it was impossible, from the structure of their feet, that they should do so. He concluded by urging on the physiologist the necessity of experiment. The chemist, when in doubt, decided his questions by experiment; and this was what was needed by the physiologist.—Prof. HUXLEY begged to be permitted to reply to Prof. Owen. He denied altogether that the difference between the brain of the gorilla and man was so great as represented by Prof. Owen, and appealed to the published dissections of Tiedemann and others. From the study of the structure of the brain of the Quadrumana, he maintained that the difference between man and the highest monkey was not so great as between the highest and the lowest monkey. He maintained also, with regard to the limbs, that there was more difference between the toeless monkeys and the gorilla than between the latter and man. He believed that the great feature which distinguished man from the monkey was the gift of speech. . . .

REPORT OF JULY 14, 1860

. . . 'On the Intellectual Development of Europe, considered with Reference to the Views of Mr. Darwin and others, that the Progression of Organisms is determined by Law,' by Prof. DRAPER, M.D., of New York.—The object of this paper was to show that the advancement of man in civilization does not occur accidentally or in a fortuitous manner, but is determined by immutable law. The author introduced his subject by recalling proofs of the dominion of law in the three great lines of the manifestation of life. First, in the successive stages of development of every individual, from the earliest rudiment to maturity; secondly, in the numberless organic forms now living contemporaneously with us, and constituting the animal series; thirdly, in the orderly appearance of that grand succession which in the slow lapse of geological time has emerged, constituting the life of the Earth, showing therefrom not only the evidences, but also proofs of the dominion of law over the world of life. In those three lines of life he established that the general principle is, to differentiate instinct from automatism, and then to differentiate intelligence from instinct. In man himself three distinct instrumental nervous mechanisms exist, and three distinct modes of life are perceptible, the automatic, the instinctive, the intelligent. They occur in an epochal order, from infancy through childhood to the more perfect state. Such holding good for the individual, it was then affirmed that it is physiologically impossible to separate the individual from the race, and that what holds good for the one holds good for the other too; and hence that man is the archetype of society, and individual development the model of social progress, and that both are under the control of immutable law: that a parallel exists between individual and national life in this, that the production, life, and death of an organic particle in the person, answers to the production, life, and death of a person in the nation. Turning from these purely physiological considerations to historical proof, and selecting the only European nation which thus far has offered a complete and completed intellectual life, Prof. Draper showed, that the characteristics of Greek mental development answer perfectly to those of individual life, presenting philosophically five well-marked ages or periods. . . . From the solutions of the four great problems of Greek philosophy, given in each of these five stages of its life, he showed that it is possible to determine the law of the variation of Greek opinion, and to establish its analogy with that of the variations of opinion in individual life. Next, passing to the consideration of Europe in the aggregate, Prof. Draper showed that it has already in part repeated these phases in its intellectual life. Its first period closes with the spread of the power of Republican Rome, the second with the foundation of Constantinople, the third with the Turkish invasion of Europe: we are living in the fourth. Detailed proofs of the correspondence of these periods to those of Greek life, and through them to those of individual life, are given in a work now printing on this subject, by the author, in America. Having established this conclusion, Prof. Draper next briefly alluded to many collateral problems or inquiries. He showed that the advances of men are due to external and not to interior influences, and that in this respect a nation is like a seed, which can only develope when the conditions are favourable, and then only in a definite way; that the time for psychical change corresponds with that for physical, and that a nation cannot advance except its material condition be touched—this having been the case throughout all Europe, as is manifested by the diminution of the blue-eyed races thereof; that all organisms and even man are dependent for their characteristics, continuance, and life on the physical conditions under which they live; that the existing apparent invariability presented by the world of organization is the direct consequence of the physical equilibrium, but that if that should suffer modification, in an instant the fanciful doctrine of the immutability of species would be brought to its proper value. . . . From his work on Physiology, published in 1856, he gave his views in support of the doctrine of the transmutation of species; the transitional forms of the animal and also the human type: the production of new ethnical elements, or nations; and the laws of their origin, duration, and death.

The announcement of this paper attracted an immense audience to the Section, which met this morning in the Library of the New Museum. The discussion was commenced by the Rev. Mr. CRESSWELL, who denied that any parallel could be drawn between the intellectual progress of man and the physical development of the lower animals. So far from the author being correct with regard to the history of Greece, its masterpieces in literature—the Iliad and Odyssey—were produced during its national infancy. The theory of intellectual development proposed was directly opposed to the known facts of the history of man.—Sir B. BRODIE stated, he could not subscribe to the hypothesis of Mr. Darwin. His primordial germ had not been demonstrated to have existed. Man had a power of self-consciousness—a principle differing from anything found in the material world, and he did not see how this could originate in lower organisms. This power of man was identical with the Divine Intelligence; and to suppose that this could originate with matter, involved the absurdity of supposing the source of Divine power dependent on the arrangement of matter.— The BISHOP OF OXFORD stated that the Darwinian theory, when tried by the principles of inductive science, broke down. The facts brought forward did not warrant the theory. The permanence of specific forms was a fact confirmed by all observation. The remains of animals, plants, and man found in those earliest records of the human race—the Egyptian catacombs, all spoke of their identity with existing forms, and of the irresistible tendency of organized beings to assume an unalterable character. The line between man and the lower animals was distinct: there was no tendency on the part of the lower animals to become the self-conscious intelligent being, man; or in man to degenerate and lose the high characteristics of his mind and intelligence. All experiments had failed to show any tendency in one animal to assume the form of the other. In the great case of the pigeons quoted by Mr. Darwin, he admitted that no sooner were these animals set free than they returned to their primitive type. Everywhere sterility attended hybridism, as was seen in the closely-allied forms of the horse and the ass. Mr. Darwin's conclusions were an hypothesis, raised most unphilosophically to the dignity of a causal theory. He was glad to know that the greatest names in science were opposed to this theory, which he believed to be opposed to the interests of science and humanity.—Prof. HUXLEY defended Mr. Darwin's theory from the charge of its being merely an hypothesis. He said, it was an explanation of phenomena in Natural History, as the undulating theory was of the phenomena of light. No one objected to that theory because an undulation of light had never been arrested and measured. Darwin's theory was an explanation of facts; and his book was full of new facts, all bearing on his theory. Without asserting that every part of the theory had been confirmed, he maintained that it was the best explanation of the origin of species which had yet been offered. With regard to the psychological distinction between man and animals; man himself was once a monad—a mere atom, and nobody could say at what moment in the history of his development he became consciously intelligent. The question was not so much one of a transmutation or transition of species, as of the production of forms which became permanent. Thus the short-legged sheep of America were not produced gradually, but originated in the birth of an original parent of the whole stock, which had been kept up by a rigid system of artificial selection.— Admiral FITZROY regretted the publication of Mr. Darwin's book, and denied Prof. Huxley's statement, that it was a logical arrangement of facts.—Dr. BEALE pointed out some of the difficulties with which the Darwinian theory had to deal, more especially those vital tendencies of allied species which seemed independent of all external agents.—Mr. LUBBOCK expressed his willingness to accept the Darwinian hypothesis in the absence of any better. He would, however, express his conviction, that time was not an essential element in these changes. Time alone produced no change.—Dr. HOOKER, being called upon by the President to state his views of the botanical aspect of the question, observed, that the Bishop of Oxford having asserted that all men of science were hostile to Mr. Darwin's hypothesis—whereas he himself was favourable to it—he could not presume to address the audience as a scientific authority. As, however, he had been asked for his opinion, he would briefly give it. In the first place, his Lordship, in his eloquent address, had, as it appeared to him, completely misunderstood Mr. Darwin's hypothesis: his Lordship intimated that this maintained the doctrine of the transmutation of existing species one into another, and had confounded this with that of the successive development of species by variation and natural selection. The first of these doctrines was so wholly opposed to the facts, reasonings, and results of Mr. Darwin's work, that he could not conceive how any one who had read it could make such a mistake—the whole book, indeed, being a protest against that doctrine. Then, again, with regard to the general phenomena of species, he understood his Lordship to affirm that these did not present characters that should lead careful and philosophical naturalists to favour Mr. Darwin's views. To this assertion Dr. Hooker's experience of the Vegetable Kingdom was diametrically opposed. He considered that at least one half of the known kinds of plants were disposable in groups, of which the species were connected by varying characters common to all in that group, and sensibly differing in some individuals only of each species; so much so that, if each group be likened to a cobweb, and one species be supposed to stand in the centre of that web, its varying characters might be compared to the radiating and concentric threads, when the other species would be represented by the points of union of these; in short, that the general characteristics of orders, genera, and species amongst plants differed in degrees only from those of varieties, and afforded the strongest countenance to Mr. Darwin's hypothesis. As regarded his own acceptation of Mr. Darwin's views, he expressly disavowed having adopted them as a creed. He knew no creeds in scientific matters. He had early begun the study of natural science under the idea that species were original creations; and it should be steadily kept in view that this was merely another hypothesis, which in the abstract was neither more nor less entitled to acceptance than Mr. Darwin's: neither was, in the present state of science, capable of demonstration, and each must be tested by its power of explaining the mutual dependence of the phenomena of life. For many years he had held to the old hypothesis, having no better established one to adopt, though the progress of botany had, in the interim, developed no new facts that favoured it, but a host of most suggestive objections to it. On the other hand, having fifteen years ago been privately made acquainted with Mr. Darwin's views, he had during that period applied these to botanical investigations of all kinds in the most distant parts of the globe, as well as to the study of some of the largest and most different Floras at home. Now, then, that Mr. Darwin had published it, he had no hesitation in publicly adopting his hypothesis, as that which offers by far the most probable explanation of all the phenomena presented by the classification, distribution, structure, and development of plants in a state of nature and under cultivation; and he should, therefore, continue to use his hypothesis as the best weapon for future research, holding himself ready to lay it down should a better be forthcoming, or should the now abandoned doctrine of original creations regain all it had lost in his experience.

28. HUXLEY:
Darwin Explained

The essay below is perhaps the finest example of the popularization of science for which Huxley is chiefly remembered. More people may know their Darwin from Huxley than from Darwin, and this 1859 selection from *Darwiniana* ("The Darwinian Hypothesis") presents clearly some of the reasons.

For bibliographical information on Huxley, see headnote, Selection 1.

The hypothesis of which the present work of Mr. Darwin is but the preliminary outline, may be stated in his own language as follows:— "Species originated by means of natural selection, or through the preservation of the favoured races in the struggle for life." To render this thesis intelligible, it is necessary to interpret its terms. In the first place, what is a species? The question is a simple one, but the right answer to it is hard to find, even if we appeal to those who should know most about it. It is all those animals or plants which have descended from a single pair of parents; it is the smallest distinctly definable group of living organisms; it is an eternal and immutable entity; it is a mere abstraction of the human intellect having no existence in nature. Such are a few of the significations attached to this simple word which may be culled from authoritative sources; and if, leaving terms and theoretical subtleties aside, we turn to facts and endeavour to gather a meaning for ourselves, by studying the things to which, in practice, the name of species is applied, it profits us little. For practice varies as much as theory. Let two botanists or two zoologists examine and describe the productions of a country, and one will pretty certainly disagree with the other as to the number, limits, and definitions of the species into which he groups the very same things. In these islands, we are in the habit of regarding mankind as of one species, but a fortnight's steam will land us in a country where divines and savants, for once in agreement, vie with one another in loudness of assertion, if not in cogency of proof, that men are of different species; and, more particularly, that the species negro is so distinct from our own that the Ten Commandments have actually no reference to him. Even in the calm region of entomology, where, if anywhere in this sinful world, passion and prejudice should fail to stir the mind, one learned coleopterist will fill ten attractive volumes with descriptions of species of beetles, nine-tenths of which are immediately declared by his brother beetle-mongers to be no species at all.

The truth is that the number of distinguishable living creatures almost surpasses imagination. At least 100,000 such kinds of insects alone have been described and may be identified in collections, and the number of separable kinds of living things is under-estimated at half a million. Seeing that most of these obvious kinds have their accidental varieties, and that they often shade into others by imperceptible degrees, it may well be imagined that the task of distinguishing between what is permanent and what fleeting, what is a species and what a mere variety, is sufficiently formidable. . . .

If, weary of the endless difficulties involved in the determination of species, the investigator, contenting himself with the rough practical distinction of separable kinds, endeavours to study them as they occur in nature—to ascertain their relations to the conditions which surround them, their mutual harmonies and discordancies of structure, the bond of union of their present and their past history, he finds himself, according to the received notions, in a mighty maze, and with, at most, the dimmest adumbration of a plan. If he starts with any one clear conviction, it is that every part of a living creature is cunningly adapted to some special use in its life. Has not his Paley told him that that seemingly useless organ, the spleen, is beautifully adjusted as so much packing between the other organs? And yet, at the outset of his studies, he finds that no adaptive reason whatsoever can be given for one-half of the peculiarities of vegetable structure. He also discovers rudimentary teeth, which are never used, in the gums of the young calf and in those of the foetal whale; insects which never bite have rudimental jaws, and others which never fly have rudimental wings; naturally blind creatures have rudimental eyes; and the halt have rudimentary limbs. So, again, no animal or plant puts on its perfect form at once, but all have to start from the same point, however various the course which each has to pursue. Not only men and horses, and cats and dogs, lobsters and beetles, periwinkles and mussels, but even the very sponges and animalcules commence their existence under forms which are essentially undistinguishable; and this is true of all the infinite variety of plants. Nay, more, all living beings march, side by side, along the high road of development, and separate the later the more like they are; like people leaving church, who all go down the aisle, but having reached the door, some turn into the parsonage, others go down the village, and others part only in the next parish. A man in his development runs for a little while parallel with, though never passing through, the form of the meanest worm, then travels for a space beside the fish, then journeys along with the bird and the reptile for his fellow travellers; and only at last, after a brief companionship with the highest of the four-footed and four-handed world, rises into the dignity of pure manhood. No competent thinker of the present day dreams of explaining these indubitable facts by the notion of the existence of unknown and undiscoverable adaptations to purpose. And we would remind those who, ignorant of the facts, must be moved by authority, that no one has asserted the incompetence of the doctrine of final causes, in its application to physiology and anatomy, more strongly than our own eminent anatomist, Professor Owen, who, speaking of such cases, says ("On the Nature of Limbs," pp. 39, 40)—"I think it will be obvious that the principle of final adaptations fails to satisfy all the conditions of the problem."

But, if the doctrine of final causes will not help us to comprehend the anomalies of living structure, the principle of adaptation must surely lead us to understand why certain living beings are found in certain regions of the world and not in others. The Palm, as we know, will not grow in our climate, nor the Oak in Greenland. The white bear cannot live where the tiger thrives, nor *vice versâ*, and the more the natural habits of animal and vegetable species are examined, the more do they seem, on the whole, limited to particular provinces. But when we look into the facts established by the study of the geographical distribution of animals and plants it seems utterly hopeless to attempt to understand the strange and apparently capricious relations which they exhibit. One would be inclined to suppose *à priori* that every country must be naturally peopled by those animals that are fittest to live and thrive in it. And yet how, on this hypothesis, are we to account for the absence of cattle in the Pampas of South America, when those parts of the New World were discovered? It is not that they were unfit for cattle, for millions of cattle now run wild there; and the like holds good of Australia and New Zealand. It is a curious circumstance, in fact, that the animals and plants of the Northern Hemisphere are not only as well adapted to live in the Southern Hemisphere as its own autochthones, but are, in many cases, absolutely better adapted, and so overrun and extirpate the aborigines. Clearly, therefore, the species which naturally inhabit a country are not necessarily the best adapted to its climate and other conditions. The inhabitants of islands are often distinct from any other known species of animal or plants (witness our recent examples from the work of Sir Emerson Tennent, on Ceylon), and yet they have almost always a sort of general family resemblance to the animals and plants of the nearest mainland. On the other hand, there is hardly a species of fish, shell, or crab common to the opposite sides of the narrow isthmus of Panama. Wherever we look, then, living nature offers us riddles of difficult solution, if we suppose that what we see is all that can be known of it.

But our knowledge of life is not confined to the existing world. Whatever their minor differences, geologists are agreed as to the vast thickness of the accumulated strata which compose the visible part of our earth, and the inconceivable immensity of the time the lapse of which they are the imperfect but the only accessible witnesses. Now, throughout the greater part of this long series of stratified rocks are scattered, sometimes very abundantly, multitudes of organic remains, the fossilised exuviae of animals and plants which lived and died while the mud of which the rocks are formed was yet soft ooze, and could receive and bury them. It would be a great error to suppose that these organic remains were fragmentary relics. Our museums exhibit fossil shells of immeasurable antiquity, as perfect as the day they were formed; whole skeletons without a limb disturbed; nay, the changed flesh, the developing embryos, and even the very footsteps of primæval organisms. Thus the naturalist finds in the bowels of the earth species as well defined as, and in some groups of animals more numerous than, those which breathe the upper air. But, singularly enough, the majority of these entombed species are wholly distinct from those that now live. Nor is this unlikeness without its rule and order. As a broad fact, the further we go back in time the less the buried species are like existing forms; and, the further apart the sets of extinct creatures are, the less they are like one another. In other words, there has been a regular succession of living beings, each younger set, being in a very broad and general sense, somewhat more like those which now live.

Such is a brief summary of the main truths which have been established concerning species. Are these truths ultimate and irresolvable facts, or are their complexities and perplexities the mere expressions of a higher law?

A large number of persons practically assume the former position to be correct. They believe that the writer of the Pentateuch was empowered and commissioned to teach us scientific as well as other truth, that the account we find there of the creation of living things is simply and literally correct, and that anything which seems to contradict it is, by the nature of the case, false. All the phenomena which have been detailed are, on this view, the immediate product of a creative fiat and, consequently, are out of the domain of science altogether.

Whether this view prove ultimately to be true or false, it is, at any rate, not at present supported by what is commonly regarded as logical proof, even if it be capable of discussion by reason; and hence we consider ourselves at liberty to pass it by, and to turn to those views which profess to rest on a scientific basis only, and therefore admit of being argued to their consequences. And we do this with the less hesitation as it so happens that those persons who are practically conversant with the facts of the case (plainly a considerable advantage) have always thought fit to range themselves under the latter category.

Since Lamarck's time, almost all competent naturalists have left speculations on the origin of species to such dreamers as the author of the "Vestiges," by whose well-intentioned efforts the Lamarckian theory received its final condemnation in the minds of all sound thinkers. Notwithstanding this silence, however, the transmutation theory, as it has been called, has been a "skeleton in the closet" to many an honest zoologist and botanist who had a soul above the mere naming of dried plants and skins. Surely, has such an one thought, nature is a mighty and consistent whole, and the providential order established in the world of life must, if we could only see it rightly, be consistent with that dominant over the multiform shapes of brute matter. But what is the history of astronomy, of all the branches of physics, of chemistry, of medicine, but a narration of the steps by which the human mind has been compelled, often sorely against its will, to recognise the operation of secondary causes in events where ignorance beheld an immediate intervention of a higher power? And when we know that living things are formed of the same elements as the inorganic world, that they act and react upon it, bound by a thousand ties of natural piety, is it probable, nay is it possible, that they, and they alone, should have no order in their seeming disorder, no unity in their seeming multiplicity, should suffer no explanation by the discovery of some central and sublime law of mutual connection?

Questions of this kind have assuredly often arisen, but it might have been long before they received such expression as would have commanded the respect and attention of the scientific world, had it not been for the publication of the work which prompted this article. Its author, Mr. Darwin, inheritor of a once celebrated name, won his spurs in science when most of those now distinguished were young men, and has for the last twenty years held a place in the front ranks of British philosophers. After a circumnavigatory voyage, undertaken solely for the love of his science, Mr. Darwin published a series of researches which at once arrested the attention of naturalists and geologists; his generalisations have since received ample confirmation and now command universal assent, nor is it questionable that they have had the most important influence on the progress of science. More recently Mr. Darwin, with a versatility which is among the rarest of gifts, turned his attention to a most difficult question of zoology and minute anatomy; and no living naturalist and anatomist has published a better monograph than that which resulted from his labours. Such a man, at all events, has not entered the sanctuary with unwashed hands, and when he lays before us the results of twenty years' investigation and reflection we must listen even though we be disposed to strike.

But, in reading his work, it must be confessed that the attention which might at first be dutifully, soon becomes willingly, given, so clear is the author's thought, so outspoken his conviction, so honest and fair the candid expression of his doubts. Those who would judge the book must read it: we shall endeavour only to make its line of argument and its philosophical position intelligible to the general reader in our own way.

The Baker Street Bazaar has just been exhibiting its familiar annual spectacle. Straight-backed, small-headed, big-barrelled oxen, as dissimilar from any wild species as can well be imagined, contended for attention and praise with sheep of half-a-dozen different breeds and styes of bloated preposterous pigs, no more like a wild boar or sow than a city alderman is like an ourang-outang. The cattle show has been, and perhaps may again be, succeeded by a poultry show, of whose crowing and clucking prodigies it can only be certainly predicated that they will be very unlike the aboriginal *Phasianus gallus*. If the seeker after animal anomalies is not satisfied, a turn or two in Seven Dials will convince him that the breeds of pigeons are quite as extraordinary and unlike one another and their parent stock, while the Horticultural Society will provide him with any number of corresponding aberrations from nature's types. He will learn with no little surprise, too, in the course of his travels, that the proprietors and producers of these animal and vegetable anomalies regard them as distinct species, with a firm belief, the strength of which is exactly proportioned to their ignorance of scientific biology, and which is the more remarkable as they are all proud of their skill in originating such "species."

On careful enquiry it is found that all these, and the many other artificial breeds or races of animals and plants, have been produced by one method. The breeder—and a skilful one must be a person of much sagacity and natural or acquired perceptive faculty—notes some slight difference, arising he knows not how, in some individuals of his stock. If he wish to perpetuate the difference, to form a breed with the peculiarity in question strongly marked, he selects such male and female individuals as exhibit the desired character, and breed from them. Their offspring are then carefully examined, and those which exhibit the peculiarity the most distinctly are selected for breeding; and this operation is repeated until the desired amount of divergence from the primitive stock is reached. It is then found that by continuing the process of selection—always breeding, that is, from well-marked forms, and allowing no impure crosses to interfere—a race may be formed, the tendency of which to reproduce itself is exceedingly strong; nor is the limit to the amount of divergence which may be thus produced known; but one thing is certain, that, if certain breeds of dogs, or of pigeons, or of horses, were known only in a fossil state, no naturalist would hesitate in regarding them as distinct species.

But in all these cases we have human interference. Without the breeder there would be no selection, and without the selection no race. Before admitting the possibility of natural species having originated in any similar way, it must be proved that there is in Nature some power which takes the place of man, and performs a selection *suâ sponte*. It is the claim of Mr. Darwin that he professes to have discovered the existence and the *modus operandi* of this "natural selection," as he terms it; and, if he be right, the process is perfectly simple and comprehensible, and irresistibly deducible from very familiar but well nigh forgotten facts.

Who, for instance, has duly reflected upon all the consequences of the marvellous struggle for existence which is daily and hourly going on among living beings? Not only does every animal live at the expense of some other animal or plant, but the very plants are at war. The ground is full of seeds that cannot rise into seedlings; the seedlings rob one another of air, light and water, the strongest robber winning the day, and extinguishing his competitors. Year after year, the wild animals with which man never interferes are, on the average, neither more nor less numerous than they were; and yet we know that the annual produce of every pair is from one to perhaps a million young; so that it is mathematically certain that, on the average, as many are killed by natural causes as are born every year, and those only escape which happen to be a little better fitted to resist destruction than those which die. The individuals of a species are like the crew of a foundered ship, and none but good swimmers have a chance of reaching the land.

Such being unquestionably the necessary conditions under which living creatures exist, Mr. Darwin discovers in them the instrument of natural selection. Suppose that in the midst of this incessant competition some individuals of a species (A) present accidental variations which happen to fit them a little better than their fellows for the struggle in which they are engaged, then the chances are in favour, not only of these individuals being better nourished than the others, but of their predominating over their fellows in other ways, and of having a better chance of leaving offspring, which will of course tend to reproduce the peculiarities of their parents. Their offspring will, by a parity of reasoning, tend to predominate over their contemporaries, and there being (suppose) no room for more than one species such as A, the weaker variety will eventually be destroyed by the new destructive influence which is thrown into the scale, and the stronger will take its place. Surrounding conditions remaining unchanged, the new variety (which we may call B)—supposed, for argument's sake, to be the best adapted for these conditions which can be got out of the original stock—will remain unchanged, all accidental deviations from the type becoming at once extinguished, as less fit for their post than B itself. The tendency of B to persist will grow with its persistence through successive generations, and it will acquire all the characters of a new species.

But, on the other hand, if the conditions of life change in any degree, however slight, B may no longer be that form which is best adapted to withstand their destructive, and profit by their sustaining, influence; in which case if it should give rise to a more competent variety (C), this will take its place and become a new species; and thus, by natural selection, the species B and C will be successively derived from A.

That this most ingenious hypothesis enables us to give a reason for many apparent anomalies in the distribution of living beings in time and space, and that it is not contradicted by the main phenomena of life and organisation appear to us to be unquestionable; and, so far, it must be admitted to have an immense advantage over any of its predecessors. But it is quite another matter to affirm absolutely either the truth or falsehood of Mr. Darwin's views at the present stage of the inquiry. Goethe has an excellent aphorism defining that state of mind which he calls "Thätige Skepsis"—active doubt. It is doubt which so loves truth that it neither dares rest in doubting, nor extinguish itself by unjustified belief; and we commend this state of mind to students of species, with respect to Mr. Darwin's or any other hypothesis, as to their origin. The combined investigations of another twenty years may, perhaps, enable naturalists to say whether the modifying causes and the selective power, which Mr. Darwin has satisfactorily shown to exist in Nature, are competent to produce all the effects he ascribes to them; or whether, on the other hand, he has been led to over-estimate the value of the principle of natural selection, as greatly as Lamarck over-estimated his *vera causa* of modification by exercise.

But there is, at all events, one advantage possessed by the more recent writer over his predecessor. Mr. Darwin abhors mere speculation as nature abhors a vacuum. He is as greedy of cases and precedents as any constitutional lawyer, and all the principles he lays down are capable of being brought to the test of observation and experiment. The path he bids us follow professes to be, not a mere airy track, fabricated of ideal cobwebs, but a solid and broad bridge of facts. If it be so, it will carry us safely over many a chasm in our knowledge, and lead us to a region free from the snares of those fascinating but barren virgins, the Final Causes, against whom a high authority has so justly warned us. "My sons, dig in the vineyard," were the last words of the old man in the fable: and, though the sons found no treasure, they made their fortunes by the grapes.

29.   CHAMBERS:
In the Beginning, and Since Then . . .

The selected works of Robert Chambers (1802–1871) were edited in seven volumes in 1897. A *Memoir* of the life of this splendid amateur historian, antiquarian, scientist, and biographer was written by his brother, William (Edinburgh, 1884). Chambers' *Vestiges of the Natural History of Creation*, published anonymously, became one of the most popular books of the nineteenth century. The Preface and portions of Chapter 1 here reprinted are from the tenth edition.

The author of this work—a private person with limited opportunities of study—first had his attention attracted to the early history of animated nature, on becoming acquainted with an outline of the Laplacian hypothesis of the solar system. Having previously been convinced that the Divine Governor of the world conducts its passing affairs by a fixed rule, to which we apply the term natural law, he was much impressed on finding reason to believe that the physical arrangements of the universe had been originated in the same manner, as it seemed to him to favour the idea of a perfect unity in the action of the One Eternal and Infinite. After this point was attained, he was not long in perceiving that the commencement of life and organization was very

unsatisfactorily accounted for by "fiats," "special miracles," "interferences," and other suggestions and figures of speech in vogue amongst
geologists. It seemed to him logically necessary that we should regard
the organic part of nature as having been instituted in the manner of
law also, though not less under the providential care of the Supreme
than the physical phenomena of the beginning, or any part of the great
pageant of nature which daily passes before our eyes, and in which we
ourselves have a place.

He had heard of the hypothesis of Lamarck; but it seemed to him
to proceed upon a vicious circle, and he dismissed it as wholly inadequate to account for the existence of the animated species. He was
not acquainted with the works of St. Hilaire, but through such treatises
on physiology as had fallen in his way, he was aware of some of the
transcendental views of that science entertained both in France and
England. With the aid of these, in conjunction with some knowledge
of the succession of fossils in the series of rock-formations, he applied
himself to the task of elucidating the Great Mystery, as it was frequently termed by men of science. He did not do so—as far as he knows
himself,—in an irreverent spirit, or with a hostile design to any form of
faith or code of morals. He viewed the inquiry as simply philosophical,
and felt assured that our conception of the divine Author of Nature
could never be truly injured by any additional insight we might gain
into His works and ways. At the same time, having no name or place
in the world to give a recommendation to his ideas, and greatly dis-
relishing the turbid waters of controversy, he resolved, if possible, to
speculate on this question as *Vox et præterea nihil*.

The difficulties of the way were great, and the guiding posts and
lights very uncertain. The first fact to be accounted for, the passage
from the inorganic to the organic, did not, however, so much embarrass
him—illustrated as it was by organic chemistry—as the means by
which all animals above the very humblest were created. The first of
any given mammalian species—how was so complicated a being to
be formed out of inorganic elements in a manner describable as
natural—how even, without ordinary maternity, were the first examples
of any such species to be nursed into maturity? After long cogitation,
the idea at length came unpromptedly into his mind—and therefore so
far was an original idea—that the ordinary phenomenon of reproduction was the key to the genesis of species. In that process—simple
because familiar to us, but in reality mysterious, because we only can
look darkly and adoringly through results to the inscrutable Agent—

we see a gradual evolution of high from low, of complicated from simple, of special from general, all in unvarying order, and therefore all natural, although all of divine ordination. Might there not have been, in those *secula seculorum* with which the geologist deals, a similar or analogous evolution of being, throwing off, as it were, the various species as it proceeded, until it rested (if it does rest) with humanity itself? The idea was of startling novelty and vastness; yet, when the mind was trained to view it steadily and coolly, it seemed to have much to recommend it. It suggested a process of a slow and gradual character, and so far was in harmony with the hypothesis of the physical arrangements of the universe. It demanded no new power or means in nature, for the changes of an embryo fell little short of the required advances from species to species. The doctrine of unity of organization; the affinities seen in lines of species; the curious fact of rudimentary organs; above all, the actual history of the course of animated nature, as revealed by the researches of the palæontologist; were all in harmony with the idea, and could be reconciled to no other of a greatly different character. The author therefore embraced the doctrine of Progressive Development as a hypothetic history of organic creation.

The work in which he embodied his views was published in 1844, with such slender hopes of success on his part, that, to ensure some attention in appropriate circles, he directed a considerable part of the impression to be given away. As is well known, the fate of the book was not to rest in obscurity or oblivion, but to be extensively read, and become the subject of much animadversion. It has never had a single declared adherent—and nine editions have been sold. Obloquy has been poured upon the nameless author from a score of sources—and his leading idea, in a subdued form, finds its way into books of science, and gives a direction to research. Professing adversaries write books in imitation of his, and, with the benefit of a few concessions to prejudice, contrive to obtain the favour denied to him. It is needless to say that the storm of opposition has never for a moment affected his original faith in the hypothesis—as how, indeed, could it, when not one of the writers on that side proved himself to have taken up a correct conception of the aim of the work, showed a power of reasoning upon it logically, or seemed capable of taking a candid view of the data on which it rests? But he has been, nevertheless, open to correction on many points which the progress of science has rendered clearer to his own mind, and accordingly the work has undergone much change. . . .

GENERAL CONSIDERATIONS

RESPECTING

THE ORIGIN OF THE ANIMATED TRIBES

... It is now to be remarked, that there is nothing in the whole series of operations displayed in inorganic geology, which may not be accounted for by the agency of the ordinary forces of nature. Those movements of subterranean force which thrust up mountain ranges and upheaved continents, stand in inextricable connexion, on the one hand, with the volcanoes which are yet belching forth lava and shaking large tracts of ground, as, on the other, with the primitive incandescent state of the earth. Those forces which disintegrated the early rocks, and of the detritus formed new beds at the bottom of seas, are still seen at work to the same effect in every part of the globe. To bring these truths the more clearly before us, it is possible to make a substance resembling basalt in a furnace; limestone and sandstone have both been formed from suitable materials in appropriate receptacles; the phenomena of cleavage have, with the aid of electricity, been simulated on a small scale, and by the same agent crystals are formed. In short, the remark which was made regarding the indifference of the cosmical laws to the scale on which they operated, is to be repeated regarding the geological. A common furnace will sometimes exemplify the operation of forces which have been concerned in the production of a Giant's Causeway; and in a sloping ploughed field after rain, we may often observe, at the lower end of a furrow, a handful of washed and neatly deposited mud or sand, capable of serving as an illustration of the way in which Nature has produced the deltas of the Nile and Ganges. In the ripple-mark on sandy beaches of the present day, we see Nature's exact repetition of the operations by which she impressed similar features on the sandstones of the carbonigenous era. Even such marks as wind-slanted rain would in our day produce on tide-deserted sands, have been read upon tablets of the ancient strata. It is the same Nature—that is to say, God through or in the manner of nature—working everywhere and in all time, causing the wind to blow, and the rain to fall, and the tide to ebb and flow, inconceivable ages before the birth of our race, as now. So also we learn from the conifers of those old ages, that there were winter and summer upon earth, before any of us lived to liken the one to all that is genial in our own nature, or to say that the other breathed no airs so unkind as man's ingratitude. Let no one suppose there is any necessary disrespect for the Creator in thus tracing his laws in their minute and familiar operations. There is in reality no true great and small, grand and familiar, in nature. Such only appear, when we thrust ourselves in as a point from which to start in judging. Let us pass, if possible, beyond immediate impressions, and see all in relation to Cause, and we shall chastenedly admit that the whole is alike worshipful.

The Creator, then, is seen to have formed our earth, and effected upon it a long and complicated series of changes, in the same manner in which we find that he conducts the affairs of nature before our living eyes: that is, *in the manner of natural law*. This is no rash or unauthorized affirmation. It is what we deduce from the calculations of a Newton and a Laplace, on the one hand; and from the industrious observation of facts by a Murchison and a Lyell, on the other. It is a point of stupendous importance in human knowledge; here at once is the whole region of the inorganic taken out of the dominion of marvel, and placed under an idea of divine regulation which we may endlessly admire and trust in.

Mixed up, however, with the geognostic changes, and apparently as a final object connected with the formation of the globe itself, there is another set of phenomena presented in the course of our history—the coming into existence, namely, of a long suite of living things, vegetable and animal, terminating in the families which we still see occupying the surface. The question arises—In what manner has this set of phenomena originated? Can we touch at and rest for a moment on the possibility of plants and animals having likewise been produced in a natural way; thus assigning immediate causes of but one character for everything revealed to our sensual observation; or are we at once to reject this idea, and remain content, either to suppose that creative power here acted in a different way, or to believe unexaminingly, that the inquiry is one beyond our powers?

Taking the last question first, I would reply, that I am extremely loath to imagine that there is anything in nature which we should, for any reason, refrain from examining. If we can infer aught from the past history of science, it is, that the whole of nature is a legitimate field for the exercise of our intellectual faculties; that there is a connexion between this knowledge and our well-being; and that, if we may judge from things once despaired of by our inquiring reason, but now made clear and simple, there is none of Nature's mysteries which we may not hopefully attempt to penetrate. To remain idly content to *presume* a various class of immediate causes for organic nature, seems to me, on this ground, equally objectionable.

With respect to the other question. The idea has several times arisen, that some natural course was observed in the production of organic things, and this even before we were permitted to attain clear conclusions regarding inorganic nature. It was always set quickly aside, as unworthy of serious consideration. The case is different now, when we have admitted law in the whole domain of the inorganic. There are even some considerations on the very threshold of the question, which appear to throw the balance of likelihood strongly on the side of natural causes, however difficult it may be to say what these causes were. The production of the organic world is, we see, mixed up with the production of the physical. It is mixed in the sense of actual connexion and dependence, and it is mixed in regard to time, for the one class of phenomena commenced, whenever the other had arrived at a point which favoured or admitted of it; life, as it were, *pressed in* as soon as there were suitable conditions, and, once it had commenced, the two classes of phenomena went on, hand in hand, together. It is surely very unlikely, *a priori*, that in two classes of phenomena, to all appearance perfectly co-ordinate, and for certain intimately connected, there should have been *two totally distinct modes of the exercise of the divine power*. Were such the case, it would form a most extraordinary, and what to philosophic consideration ought to be a most startling exception, from that which we otherwise observe of the character of the divine procedure in the universe. Further, let us consider the comparative character of the two classes of phenomena, for comparison may of course be legitimate until the natural system is admitted. The absurdities into which we should thus be led must strike every reflecting mind. The Eternal Sovereign arranges a solar or an astral system, by dispositions imparted primordially to matter; he causes, by the same majestic means, vast oceans to form and continents to rise, and all the grand meteoric agencies to proceed in ceaseless alternation, so as to fit the earth for a residence of organic beings. But when, in the course of these operations, fuci and corals are to be for the first time placed in those oceans, a change in his plan of administration is required. It is not easy to say what is presumed to be the mode of his operations. The ignorant believe the very hand of Deity to be at work. Amongst the learned, we hear of "creative fiats," "interferences," "interpositions of the creative energy," all of them very obscure phrases, apparently not susceptible of a scientific explanation, but all tending simply to this—

that the work was done in a marvellous way, and not in the way of nature. Let the contrast between the two propositions be well marked. According to the first, all is done by the continuous energy of the divine will—a power which has no regard to great or small: according to the second, there is a procedure strictly resembling that of a human being in the management of his affairs. And not only on this one occasion, but all along the stretch of geological time, this special attention is needed whenever a new family of organisms is to be introduced: a new fiat for fishes, another for reptiles, a third for birds; nay, taking up the present views of geologists as to species, such an event as the commencement of a certain cephalopod, one with a few new nodulosities and corrugations upon its shell, would, on this theory, require the particular care of that same Almighty who willed at once the whole means by which INFINITY was replenished with its worlds! . . .

The whole aim of science from the beginning has been to ascertain law; one set of phenomena after another has been brought under this conception, without our ever feeling that God was less the adorable creator of his own world. It seems strange that a stand should appear necessary at this particular point in the march of science. Perhaps if our ordinary ideas respecting natural law were more just, the difficulty might be lessened. It cannot be sufficiently impressed that the whole idea relates only to the *mode* in which the Deity has been pleased to manifest his power in the external world. It leaves the absolute fact of his authorship of and supremacy over nature, precisely where it was; only telling us that, instead of dealing with the natural world as a human being traffics with his own affairs, adjusting each circumstance to a relation with other circumstances as they emerge, in the mode befitting his finite capacity, the Creator has originally conceived, and since sustained, arrangements fitted to serve in a general sufficiency for all contingencies; himself, of course, necessarily living in all such arrangements, as the only means by which they could be, even for a moment, upheld. Were the question to be settled upon a consideration of the respective moral merits of the two theories, I would say that the latter is greatly the preferable, as it implies a far grander view of the divine power and dignity than the other. For one thing, it places the leading divine attribute of foresight in a much more sublime position. . . .

It is now to be remarked that what has been ascertained of the

actual history of organic beings upon earth, is in no respect out of harmony with this idea of their creation after the manner of law. We
have seen that these did not come at once, as they might have been
expected to do if produced by some special act, or even some special
interposition of will, on the part of the Deity. They came in a long-
extending succession, in an order, as would appear, of progressive
organization; grade following grade, till, from a humble starting-
point in both kingdoms, the highest forms were realized. Time, we see,
was an element in the evolution of Being, as it is in the reproduction
of an individual at the present day. At the beginning of geological
investigation, it was thought that some immediate external conditions
ruled the appearance of particular classes of animals at particular
times: as that the absence of dry land was the cause of the late commencement of terrestrial animals; that there being for a long time only
reptilian land vertebrata, was owing to an overcharge of the atmosphere with carbonic acid—the store from which came the chief material
of the abundant vegetation of the carbonigenous ages and so forth.
But it is now seen that the progress of the animal world was, in its
main features, independent of such circumstances. There *was* dry
land for many ages before there were any land animals. The sea
abounded in invertebrate animals, while as yet fish did not exist,
though the conditions required for the existence of both are the same.
The oolitic continents, where only reptiles roamed, could have equally
supported mammalia, for which the atmosphere was then fully fitted,
even upon the admission of the carbonic acid hypothesis, as the coal
was by that time formed; yet mammalia came not. It was supposed
at the dawn of true geology, that fresh creations of animals were
connected with great physical revolutions of the surface; as if, at
particular times, all had perished in storms of volcanic violence, and
been replaced with a wholly new fauna. This idea is likewise passing
away. It is now seen that changes in specific forms took place quietly
in the course of time, while no volcanic disturbances are traceable.
In short, it is always becoming more and more manifest that organic
progress—both the specific changes in classes formerly existing, and
the accession of new and higher classes—depended, not by any means
wholly or immediately upon external circumstances, but in great part
upon time. All this looks very unlike either special working or special
willing on the part of the Creator, but, on the contrary, very like the
simply natural procedure of things in the world of our own day.

There are some facts in the history of fossils, which it is difficult to reconcile with the idea of special creative effort, but which perfectly harmonize with that of a creation in a natural manner. It is admitted, for instance, that "the differences which exist between extinct faunas and the animals now living are *so much greater in proportion as these faunas are most ancient.*" Passing downward in the formations and backward in time, we first find species identical with the present; next, only genera; afterwards, only families or orders. These are the words of naturalists; but the truth simply is, that in early formations, animals resembled the present in broad general characters; afterwards they resembled them in characters more particular; finally, they became identical. Always as we advance, the total mass of the animal creation puts on more and more of the appearances which it now bears. . . .

30. BUTLER:
Choice or Chance in Evolution?

The Works of Samuel Butler (1835–1902), satirist, painter, biologist, and scholar, have been edited in twenty volumes by H. F. Jones and A. T. Bartholomew (London, 1919). One should read both Malcolm Muggeridge's *Earnest Atheist* (London, 1936), and P. N. Furbank's *Samuel Butler* (Cambridge, 1948). Butler's abilities as a popularizer are similar to those of Huxley, but his talent and achievement are inferior.

The selection is taken from the sixth chapter of *Luck or Cunning*, which illustrates clearly Butler's adherence to Lamarck as well as his peevishness in controversy.

According to Messrs. Darwin and Wallace, and ostensibly, I am afraid I should add, a great majority of our most prominent biologists, the view taken by Erasmus Darwin and Lamarck is not a sound one. Some organisms, indeed, are so admirably adapted to their surroundings, and some organs discharge their functions with so much appearance of provision, that we are apt to think they must owe their development to sense of need and consequent contrivance, but this opinion is fantastic; the appearance of design is delusive; what we are tempted to see as an accumulated outcome of desire and cunning, we should regard as mainly an accumulated outcome of good luck.

Let us take the eye as a somewhat crucial example. It is a seeing-machine, or thing to see with. So is a telescope; the telescope in its highest development is a secular accumulation of cunning, sometimes small, sometimes great; sometimes applied to this detail of the instrument, and sometimes to that. It is an admirable example of design; nevertheless, as I said in "Evolution Old and New," he who made the first rude telescope had probably no idea of any more perfect form of the instrument than the one he had himself invented. Indeed, if he had, he would have carried his idea out in practice. He would have been unable to conceive such an instrument as Lord Rosse's; the design, therefore, at present evidenced by the telescope was not design all on the part of one and the same person. Nor yet was it unmixed with chance; many a detail has been doubtless due to an accident or coincidence which was forthwith seized and made the best of. Luck there always has been and always will be, until all brains are opened, and all connections made known, but luck turned to account becomes design; there is, indeed, if things are driven home, little other design than this. The telescope, therefore, is an instrument designed in all its parts for the purpose of seeing, and, take it all round, designed with singular skill.

Looking at the eye, we are at first tempted to think that it must be the telescope over again, only more so; we are tempted to see it as something which has grown up little by little from small beginnings, as the result of effort well applied and handed down from generation to generation, till, in the vastly greater time during which the eye has been developing as compared with the telescope, a vastly more astonishing result has been arrived at. We may indeed be tempted to think this, but, according to Mr. Darwin, we should be wrong. Design had a great deal to do with the telescope, but it had nothing or hardly anything whatever to do with the eye. The telescope owes its development to cunning, the eye to luck, which, it would seem, is so far more cunning than cunning that one does not quite understand why there should be any cunning at all. The main means of developing the eye was, according to Mr. Darwin, not use as varying circumstances might direct with consequent slow increase of power and an occasional happy flight of genius, but natural selection. Natural selection, according to him, though not the sole, is still the most important means of its development and modification. What, then, is natural selection?

Mr. Darwin has told us this on the title-page of the "Origin of Species." He there defines it as "The Preservation of Favoured Races;" "Favoured" is "Fortunate," and "Fortunate" "Lucky;" it is plain, therefore, that with Mr. Darwin natural selection comes to "The Preservation of Lucky Races," and that he regarded luck as the most important feature in connection with the development even of so apparently purposive an organ as the eye, and as the one, therefore, on which it was most proper to insist. And what is luck but absence of intention or design? What, then, can Mr. Darwin's title-page amount to when written out plainly, but to an assertion that the main means of modification has been the preservation of races whose variations have been unintentional, that is to say, not connected with effort or intention, devoid of mind or meaning, fortuitous, spontaneous, accidental, or whatever kindred word is least disagreeable to the reader? It is impossible to conceive any more complete denial of mind as having had anything to do with organic development, than is involved in the title-page of the "Origin of Species" when its doubtless carefully considered words are studied—nor, let me add, is it possible to conceive a title-page more likely to make the reader's attention rest much on the main doctrine of evolution, and little, to use the words now most in vogue concerning it, on Mr. Darwin's own "distinctive feature."

It should be remembered that the full title of the "Origin of Species" is, "On the origin of species by means of natural selection, or the preservation of favoured races in the struggle for life." The significance of the expansion of the title escaped the greater number of Mr. Darwin's readers. Perhaps it ought not to have done so, but we certainly failed to catch it. The very words themselves escaped us—and yet there they were all the time if we had only chosen to look. We thought the book was called "On the Origin of Species," and so it was on the outside; so it was also on the inside fly-leaf; so it was on the title-page itself as long as the most prominent type was used; the expanded title was only given once, and then in smaller type; so the three big "Origins of Species" carried us with them to the exclusion of the rest.

The short and working title, "On the Origin of Species," in effect claims descent with modification generally; the expanded and technically true title only claims the discovery that luck is the main means f organic modification, and this is a very different matter. The book ought to have been entitled, "On Natural Selection, or the preservation of favoured races in the struggle for life, as the main means of the origin of species;" this should have been the expanded title, and the short title should have been "On Natural Selection.". . .

At any rate it will be admitted that Mr. Darwin did not make his title-page express his meaning so clearly that his readers could readily catch the point of difference between himself and his grandfather and Lamarck; nevertheless the point just touched upon involves the only essential difference between the systems of Mr. Charles Darwin and those of his three most important predecessors. All four writers agree that animals and plants descend with modification; all agree that the fittest alone survive; all agree about the important consequences of the geometrical ratio of increase; Mr. Charles Darwin has said more about these last two points than his predecessors did, but all three were alike cognisant of the facts and attached the same importance to them, and would have been astonished at its being supposed possible that they disputed them. The fittest alone survive; yes—but the fittest from among what? Here comes the point of divergence; the fittest from among organisms whose variations arise mainly through use and disuse? In other words, from variations that are mainly functional? Or from among organisms whose variations are in the main matters of luck? From variations into which a moral and intellectual system of payment according to results has largely entered? Or from variations which have been thrown for with dice? From variations among which, though cards tell, yet play tells as much or more? Or from those in which cards are everything and play goes for so little as to be not worth taking into account? Is "the survival of the fittest" to be taken as meaning "the survival of the luckiest" or "the survival of those who know best how to turn fortune to account"? Is luck the only element of fitness, or is not cunning even more indispensable?

Mr. Darwin has a habit, borrowed, perhaps, *mutatis mutandis*, from the framers of our collects, of every now and then adding the words "through natural selection," as though this squared everything, and descent with modification thus became his theory at once. This is not the case. Buffon, Erasmus Darwin, and Lamarck believed in natural selection to the full as much as any follower of Mr. Charles Darwin can do. They did not use the actual words, but the idea underlying them is the essence of their system. . . .

It is indeed true that the younger Darwin gave the words "natural

selection" the importance which of late years they have assumed. . . .
"In the literal sense of the word (*sic*) no doubt natural selection is a
false term," as personifying a fact, making it exercise the conscious
choice without which there can be no selection, and generally crediting
it with the discharge of functions which can only be ascribed legitimately to living and reasoning beings. Granted, however, that while
Mr. Charles Darwin adopted the expression natural selection and admitted it to be a bad one, his grandfather did not use it at all; still
Mr. Darwin did not mean the natural selection which Mr. Matthew
and those whose opinions he was epitomising meant. Mr. Darwin
meant the selection to be made from variations into which purpose
enters to only a small extent comparatively. The difference, therefore,
between the older evolutionists and their successor does not lie in the
acceptance by the more recent writer of a quasi-selective power in
nature which his predessors denied, but in the background—hidden
behind the words natural selection, which have served to cloak it—
in the views which the old and the new writers severally took of the
variations from among which they are alike agreed that a selection or
quasi-selection is made.

It now appears that there is not one natural selection, and one survival
of the fittest only, but two natural selections, and two survivals of the
fittest, the one of which may be objected to as an expression more
fit for religious and general literature than for science, but may still
be admitted as sound in intention, while the other, inasmuch as it
supposes accident to be the main purveyor of variations, has no
correspondence with the actual course of things; for if the variations
are matters of chance or hazard unconnected with any principle of
constant application, they will not occur steadily enough, throughout
a sufficient number of successive generations, nor to a sufficient number
of individuals for many generations together at the same time and
place, to admit of the fixing and permanency of modification at all.
The one theory of natural selection, therefore, may, and indeed will,
explain the facts that surround us, whereas the other will not. Mr.
Charles Darwin's contribution to the theory of evolution was not,
as is commonly supposed, "natural selection," but the hypothesis
that natural selection from variations that are in the main fortuitous
could accumulate and result in specific and generic differences.

In the foregoing paragraph I have given the point of difference
between Mr. Charles Darwin and his predecessors. Why, I wonder,
have neither he nor any of his exponents put this difference before us

in such plain words that we should readily apprehend it? Erasmus Darwin and Lamarck were understood by all who wished to understand them; why is it that the misunderstanding of Mr. Darwin's "distinctive feature" should have been so long and obstinate? Why is it that, no matter how much writers like Mr. Grant Allen and Professor Ray Lankester may say about "Mr. Darwin's master-key," nor how many more like hyperboles they brandish, they never put a succinct *résumé* of Mr. Darwin's theory side by side with a similar *résumé* of his grandfather's and Lamarck's? Neither Mr. Darwin himself, nor any of those to whose advocacy his reputation is mainly due, have done this. Professor Huxley is the man of all others who foisted Mr. Darwin most upon us, but in his famous lecture on the coming of age of the "Origin of Species" he did not explain to his hearers wherein the Neo-Darwinian theory of evolution differed from the old; and why not? Surely, because no sooner is this made clear than we perceive that the idea underlying the old evolutionists is more in accord with instinctive feelings that we have cherished too long to be able now to disregard them than the central idea which underlies the "Origin of Species."

. . . Mr. Darwin was the Gladstone of biology, and so old a scientific hand was not going to make things unnecessarily clear unless it suited his convenience. Then, indeed, he was like the man in "The Hunting of the Snark," who said, "I told you once, I told you twice, what I tell you three times is true." . . . Mr. Darwin's attitude as regards design in organism will appear from the passage about the eye already referred to, which it may perhaps be as well to quote in full. Mr. Darwin says:—

"It is scarcely possible to avoid comparing the eye to a telescope. We know that this instrument has been perfected by the long-continued efforts of the highest human intellects, and we naturally infer that the eye has been formed by a somewhat analogous process. But may not this inference be presumptuous? Have we any right to assume that the Creator works by intellectual powers like those of man? If we must compare the eye to an optical instrument, we ought in imagination to take a thick layer of transparent tissue, with a nerve sensitive to light beneath, and then suppose every part of this layer to be continually changing slowly in density, so as to separate into layers of different densities and thicknesses, placed at different distances from each other, and with the surfaces of each layer slowly changing in form. Further we must suppose that there is a power always intently watching each slight accidental alteration in the transparent layers, and carefully selecting each alteration which, under varied circumstances, may in any way, or in any degree, tend to produce a distincter image. We must suppose each new state of the instrument to be multiplied by the million, and each to be preserved till a better be produced, and then the old ones to be destroyed. In living bodies variation will cause the slight alterations, generation will multiply them almost infinitely, and natural selection will pick out with unerring skill each improvement. Let this process go on for millions on millions of years, and during each year on millions of individuals of many kinds; and may we not believe that a living optical instrument might thus be formed as superior to one of glass as the works of the Creator are to those of man?"

Mr. Darwin does not in this passage deny design, or cunning, point blank; he was not given to denying things point blank, nor is it immediately apparent that he is denying design at all, for he does not emphasize and call attention to the fact that the *variations* on whose accumulation he relies for his ultimate specific difference are accidental, and, to use his own words, in the passage last quoted, caused by *variation*. He does, indeed, in his earlier editions, call the variations "accidental," and accidental they remained for ten years, but in 1869 the word "accidental" was taken out. Mr. Darwin probably felt that the variations had been accidental as long as was desirable; and though they would, of course, in reality remain as accidental as ever, still, there could be no use in crying "accidental variations" further. If the reader wanted to know whether they were accidental or no, he had better find out for himself. Mr. Darwin was a master of what may be called scientific chiaroscuro, and owes his reputation in no small measure to the judgment with which he kept his meaning dark when a less practised hand would have thrown light upon it. There can, however, be no question that Mr. Darwin, though not denying purposiveness point blank, was trying to refer the development of the eye to the accumulation of small accidental improvements, which were not as a rule due to effort and design in any way analogous to those attendant on the development of the telescope. . . .

The hesitating feeble gait of one who fears a pitfall at every step, so easily recognisable in the "numerous, successive, slight altera-tions" . . . may be traced in many another page of the "Origin of Species" by those who will be at the trouble of comparing the several editions. It is only when this is done, and the working of Mr. Darwin's mind can be seen as though it were the twitchings of a dog's nose, that any idea can be formed of the difficulty in which he found himself involved by his initial blunder of thinking he had got a distinctive feature which entitled him to claim the theory of evolution as an original idea of his own. He found his natural selection hang round his neck like a millstone. There is hardly a page in the "Origin of Species" in which traces of the struggle going on in Mr. Darwin's mind are not discernible, with a result alike exasperating and pitiable. I can only repeat what I said in "Evolution Old and New," namely, that I find the task of extracting a well-defined meaning out of Mr. Darwin's words comparable only to that of trying to act on the advice of a lawyer who has obscured the main issue as much as he can, and whose chief aim has been to leave as many loopholes as possible for himself to escape by, if things should go wrong hereafter. Or, again, to that of one who has to construe an Act of Parliament which was originally drawn with a view to throwing as much dust as possible in the eyes of those who would oppose the measure, and which, having been found utterly unworkable in practice, has had clauses repealed up and down it till it is now in an inextricable tangle of confusion and contradiction. . . .

I have given the opinions of these contending parties in their extreme development; but they both admit abatements which bring them somewhat nearer to one another. Design, as even its most strenuous upholders will admit, is a difficult word to deal with; it is, like all our ideas, substantial enough until we try to grasp it—and then, like all our ideas, it mockingly eludes us; it is like life or death—a rope of many strands; there is design within design, and design within undesign; there is undesign within design (as when a man shuffles cards designing that there shall be no design in their arrangement), and undesign within undesign; when we speak of cunning or design in connection with organism we do not mean cunning, all cunning, and nothing but cunning, so that there shall be no place for luck; we do not mean that conscious attention and forethought shall have been bestowed upon the minutest details of action, and nothing been left to work itself out departmentally according to precedent, or as it otherwise best may according to the chapter of accidents.

So, again, when Mr. Darwin and his followers deny design and effort to have been the main purveyors of the variations whose accumulation results in specific difference, they do not entirely exclude the action of use and disuse—and this at once opens the door for cunning; nevertheless, according to Erasmus Darwin and Lamarck, the human eye and the long neck of the giraffe are alike due to the accumulation of variations that are mainly functional, and hence practical; according to Charles Darwin they are alike due to the accumulation of variations that are mainly accidental, fortuitous, spontaneous, that is to say, that cannot be reduced to any known general principle. According to Charles Darwin "the preservation of favoured," or lucky, "races" is by far the most important means of modification; according to Erasmus Darwin effort "*non sibi res sed se rebus subjungere*" is unquestionably the most potent means; roughly, therefore, there is no better or fairer way of putting the matter, than to say that Charles Darwin is the apostle of luck, and his grandfather, and Lamarck, of cunning.

31. TENNYSON:
"Lucretius"

The works of Alfred, Lord Tennyson (1809–1892), are available in many fine editions, though that by Hallam Tennyson (1913) is considered standard and includes the poet's own notes. His son's two-volume *Memoir* of 1897 should be read together with Sir Charles Tennyson's biography (New York, 1949). Further reading would include Sir Harold Nicolson's *Tennyson: Aspects of His Life, Character, and Poetry* (London, 1923) and Jerome Buckley's *Tennyson: The Growth of a Poet* (Cambridge, Mass., 1960).

"Lucretius" is one of the laureate's most important poems on the subject of science. As is suggested in the introduction, its workings are subtle and complex. They deserve and will repay close attention.

> Lucilia, wedded to Lucretius, found
> Her master cold; for when the morning flush
> Of passion and the first embrace had died
> Between them, tho' he loved her none the less,
> Yet often when the woman heard his foot

Return from pacings in the field, and ran
To greet him with a kiss, the master took
Small notice, or austerely, for—his mind
Half buried in some weightier argument,
Or fancy-borne perhaps upon the rise
And long roll of the hexameter—he past
To turn and ponder those three hundred scrolls
Left by the Teacher, whom he held divine.
She brook'd it not, but wrathful, petulant,
Dreaming some rival, sought and found a witch
Who brew'd the philtre which had power, they said,
To lead an errant passion home again.
And this, at times, she mingled with his drink,
And this destroy'd him; for the wicked broth
Confused the chemic labor of the blood,
And tickling the brute brain within the man's
Made havoc among those tender cells, and check'd
His power to shape. He loathed himself, and once
After a tempest woke upon a morn
That mock'd him with returning calm, and cried:

  "Storm in the night! for thrice I heard the rain
Rushing; and once the flash of a thunderbolt—
Methought I never saw so fierce a fork—
Struck out the streaming mountain-side, and show'd
A riotous confluence of watercourses
Blanching and billowing in a hollow of it,
Where all but yester-eve was dusty-dry.

  "Storm, and what dreams, ye holy Gods, what dreams!
For thrice I waken'd after dreams. Perchance
We do but recollect the dreams that come
Just ere the waking. Terrible: for it seem'd
A void was made in Nature; all her bonds
Crack'd; and I saw the flaring atom-streams
And torrents of her myriad universe,
Ruining along the illimitable inane,
Fly on to clash together again, and make
Another and another frame of things
For ever. That was mine, my dream, I knew it—
Of and belonging to me, as the dog

With inward yelp and restless forefoot plies
His function of the woodland; but the next!
I thought that all the blood by Sylla shed
Came driving rainlike down again on earth.
And where it dash'd the reddening meadow, sprang
No dragon warriors from Cadmean teeth,
For these I thought my dream would show to me,
But girls, Hetairai, curious in their art,
Hired animalisms, vile as those that made
The mulberry-faced Dictator's orgies worse
Than aught they fable of the quiet Gods.
And hands they mixt, and yell'd and round me drove
In narrowing circles till I yell'd again
Half-suffocated, and sprang up, and saw—
Was it the first beam of my latest day?

"Then, then, from utter gloom stood out the breasts,
The breasts of Helen, and hoveringly a sword
Now over and now under, now direct,
Pointed itself to pierce, but sank down shamed
At all that beauty; and as I stared, a fire,
The fire that left a roofless Ilion,
Shot out of them, and scorch'd me that I woke.

"Is this thy vengeance, holy Venus, thine,
Because I would not one of thine own doves,
Not even a rose, were offer'd to thee? thine,
Forgetful how my rich prooemion makes
Thy glory fly along the Italian field,
In lays that will outlast thy deity?

"Deity? nay, thy worshippers. My tongue
Trips, or I speak profanely. Which of these
Angers thee most, or angers thee at all?
Not if thou be'st of those who, far aloof
From envy, hate and pity, and spite and scorn,
Live the great life which all our greatest fain
Would follow, centred in eternal calm.

"Nay, if thou canst, O Goddess, like ourselves
Touch, and be touch'd, then would I cry to thee

To kiss thy Mavors, roll thy tender arms
Round him, and keep him from the lust of blood
That makes a steaming slaughter-house of Rome.

    "Ay, but I meant not thee; I meant not her
Whom all the pines of Ida shook to see
Slide from that quiet heaven of hers, and tempt
The Trojan, while his neatherds were abroad;
Nor her that o'er her wounded hunter wept
Her deity false in human-amorous tears;
Nor whom her beardless apple-arbiter
Decided fairest. Rather, O ye Gods,
Poet-like as the great Sicilian called
Calliope to grace his golden verse—
Ay, and this Kypris also—did I take
That popular name of thine to shadow forth
The all-generating powers and genial heat
Of Nature, when she strikes thro' the thick blood
Of cattle, and light is large, and lambs are glad
Nosing the mother's udder, and the bird
Makes his heart voice amid the blaze of flowers;
Which things appear the work of mighty Gods.

    "The Gods! and if I go *my* work is left
Unfinish'd—*if* I go. The Gods, who haunt
The lucid interspace of world and world,
Where never creeps a cloud, or moves a wind,
Nor ever falls the least white star of snow,
Nor ever lowest roll of thunder moans,
Nor sound of human sorrow mounts to mar
Their sacred everlasting calm! and such,
Not all so fine, nor so divine a calm,
Not such, nor all unlike it, man may gain
Letting his own life go. The Gods, the Gods!
If all be atoms, how then should the Gods
Being atomic not be dissoluble,
Not follow the great law? My master held
That Gods there are, for all men so believe.
I prest my footsteps into his, and meant
Surely to lead my Memmius in a train

Of flowery clauses onward to the proof
That Gods there are, and deathless. Meant? I meant?
I have forgotten what I meant; my mind
Stumbles, and all my faculties are lamed.

"Look where another of our Gods, the Sun,
Apollo, Delius, or of older use
All-seeing Hyperion—what you will—
Has mounted yonder; since he never sware,
Except his wrath were wreak'd on wretched man,
That he would only shine among the dead
Hereafter—tales! for never yet on earth
Could dead flesh creep, or bits of roasting ox
Moan round the spit—nor knows he what he sees;
King of the East altho' he seem, and girt
With song and flame and fragrance, slowly lifts
His golden feet on those empurpled stairs
That climb into the windy halls of heaven.
And here he glances on an eye new-born,
And gets for greeting but a wail of pain;
And here he stays upon a freezing orb
That fain would gaze upon him to the last;
And here upon a yellow eyelid fallen
And closed by those who mourn a friend in vain,
Not thankful that his troubles are no more.
And me, altho' his fire is on my face
Blinding, he sees not, nor at all can tell
Whether I mean this day to end myself,
Or lend an ear to Plato where he says,
That men like soldiers may not quit the post
Allotted by the Gods. But he that holds
The Gods are careless, wherefore need he care
Greatly for them, nor rather plunge at once,
Being troubled, wholly out of sight, and sink
Past earthquake—ay, and gout and stone, that break
Body toward death, and palsy, death-in-life,
And wretched age—and worst disease of all,
These prodigies of myriad nakednesses,
And twisted shapes of lust, unspeakable,
Abominable, strangers at my hearth

Not welcome, harpies miring every dish,
The phantom husks of something foully done,
And fleeting thro' the boundless universe,
And blasting the long quiet of my breast
With animal heat and dire insanity?

"How should the mind, except it loved them, clasp
These idols to herself? or do they fly
Now thinner, and now thicker, like the flakes
In a fall of snow, and so press in, perforce
Of multitude, as crowds that in an hour
Of civic tumult jam the doors, and bear
The keepers down, and throng, their rags and they
The basest, far into that council-hall
Where sit the best and stateliest of the land?

"Can I not fling this horror off me again,
Seeing with how great ease Nature can smile,
Balmier and nobler from her bath of storm,
At random ravage? and how easily
The mountain there has cast his cloudy slough,
Now towering o'er him in serenest air,
A mountain o'er a mountain,—ay, and within
All hollow as the hopes and fears of men?

"But who was he that in the garden snared
Picus and Faunus, rustic Gods? a tale
To laugh at—more to laugh at in myself—
For look! what is it? there? yon arbutus
Totters; a noiseless riot underneath
Strikes through the wood, sets all the tops quivering—
The mountain quickens into Nymph and Faun;
And here an Oread—how the sun delights
To glance and shift about her slippery sides,
And rosy knees and supple roundedness,
And budded bosom-peaks—who this way runs
Before the rest!—A satyr, a satyr, see,
Follows; but him I proved impossible;
Twy-natured is no nature. Yet he draws
Nearer and nearer, and I scan him now
Beastlier than any phantom of his kind

That ever butted his rough brother-brute
For lust or lusty blood or provender.
I hate, abhor, spit, sicken at him; and she
Loathes him as well; such a precipitate heel,
Fledged as it were with Mercury's ankle-wing,
Whirls her to me—but will she fling herself
Shameless upon me? Catch her, goat-foot! nay,
Hide, hide them, million-myrtled wilderness,
And cavern-shadowing laurels, hide! do I wish—
What?—that the bush were leafless? or to whelm
All of them in one massacre? O ye Gods,
I know you careless, yet, behold, to you
From childly wont and ancient use I call—
I thought I lived securely as yourselves—
No lewdness, narrowing envy, monkey-spite,
No madness of ambition, avarice, none;
No larger feast than under plane or pine
With neighbors laid along the grass, to take
Only such cups as left us friendly-warm,
Affirming each his own philosophy—
Nothing to mar the sober majesties
Of settled, sweet, Epicurean life.
But now it seems some unseen monster lays
His vast and filthy hands upon my will,
Wrenching it backward into his, and spoils
My bliss in being; and it was not great,
For save when shutting reasons up in rhythm,
Or Heliconian honey in living words,
To make a truth less harsh, I often grew
Tired of so much within our little life,
Or of so little in our little life—
Poor little life that toddles half an hour
Crown'd with a flower or two, and there an end—
And since the nobler pleasure seems to fade,
Why should I, beastlike as I find myself,
Not manlike end myself?—our privilege—
What beast has heart to do it? And what man,
What Roman would be dragg'd in triumph thus?
Not I; not he, who bears one name with her
Whose death-blow struck the dateless doom of kings,

When, brooking not the Tarquin in her veins,
She made her blood in sight of Collatine
And all his peers, flushing the guiltless air,
Spout from the maiden fountain in her heart.
And from it sprang the Commonwealth, which breaks
As I am breaking now!

                        "And therefore now
Let her, that is the womb and tomb of all,
Great Nature, take, and forcing far apart
Those blind beginnings that have made me man,
Dash them anew together at her will
Thro' all her cycles—into man once more,
Or beast or bird or fish, or opulent flower.
But till this cosmic order everywhere
Shatter'd into one earthquake in one day
Cracks all to pieces—and that hour perhaps
Is not so far when momentary man
Shall seem no more a something to himself,
But he, his hopes and hates, his homes and fanes,
And even his bones long laid within the grave,
The very sides of the grave itself shall pass,
Vanishing, atom and void, atom and void,
Into the unseen for ever—till that hour,
My golden work in which I told a truth
That stays the rolling Ixionian wheel,
And numbs the Fury's ringlet-snake, and plucks
The mortal soul from out immortal hell,
Shall stand. Ay, surely; then it fails at last
And perishes as I must; for O Thou,
Passionless bride, divine Tranquillity,
Yearn'd after by the wisest of the wise,
Who fail to find thee, being as thou art
Without one pleasure and without one pain,
Howbeit I know thou surely must be mine
Or soon or late, yet out of season, thus
I woo thee roughly, for thou carest not
How roughly men may woo thee so they win—
Thus—thus—the soul flies out and dies in the air."

With that he drove the knife into his side.

She heard him raging, heard him fall, ran in,
Beat breast, tore hair, cried out upon herself
As having fail'd in duty to him, shriek'd
That she but meant to win him back, fell on him,
Clasp'd, kiss'd him, wail'd. He answered, "Care not thou!
Thy duty? what is duty? Fare thee well!"

32.   BROWNING:
"Caliban Upon Setebos"

The standard biography of Robert Browning (1812–1889) is the revised edition of *The Life of Robert Browning* by W. H. Griffin and H. C. Minchin (London, 1938); a more modern approach is that taken by Beth Miller in *Robert Browning: A Portrait* (New York, 1953). *The Poetical Works* edited by Augustine Birrell in 1915 is standard. Indispensable is the only word that describes William DeVane's *A Browning Handbook* (rev. ed., New York, 1955). Robert Langbaum's *The Poetry of Experience* (New York, 1957), is important, as is E. D. H. Johnson's *The Alien Vision of Victorian Poetry* (Princeton, 1962).

The poetry of Browning, late in achieving popularity in its own day, has now achieved a prominence which overshadows—perhaps unjustly—that of his chief rival, Tennyson. The Caliban of this poem is that of Shakespeare's *The Tempest*, deformed, half-human son of the witch Sycorax, servant of Prospero and Miranda, antagonist of Ariel. The subtitle of this poem is "Natural Theology in the Island."

"Thou thoughtest that I was altogether such an one as thyself."

['Will sprawl, now that the heat of day is best,
Flat on his belly in the pit's much mire,
With elbows wide, fists clenched to prop his chin;
And, while he kicks both feet in the cool slush,
And feels about his spine small eft-things course,
Run in and out each arm, and make him laugh;
And while above his head a pompion-plant,
Coating the cave-top as a brow its eye,

Creeps down to touch and tickle hair and beard,
And now a flower drops with a bee inside,
And now a fruit to snap at, catch and crunch—
He looks out o'er yon sea which sunbeams cross
And recross till they weave a spider-web
(Meshes of fire, some great fish breaks at times),
And talks to his own self, howe'er he please,
Touching that other, whom his dam called God.
Because to talk about Him, vexes—ha,
Could He but know! and time to vex is now,
When talk is safer than in wintertime.
Moreover Prosper and Miranda sleep—
In confidence he drudges at their task,
And it is good to cheat the pair, and gibe,
Letting the rank tongue blossom into speech.]

Setebos, Setebos, and Setebos!
'Thinketh, He dwelleth i' the cold o' the moon.

'Thinketh, He made it, with the sun to match,
But not the stars; the stars came otherwise;
Only made clouds, winds, meteors, such as that;
Also this isle, what lives and grows thereon,
And snaky sea which rounds and ends the same,

'Thinketh, it came of being ill at ease;
He hated that He cannot change His cold,
Nor cure its ache. 'Hath spied an icy fish
That longed to 'scape the rock-stream where she lived,
And thaw herself within the lukewarm brine
O' the lazy sea her stream thrusts far amid,
A crystal spike 'twixt two warm walls of wave;
Only, she ever sickened, found repulse
At the other kind of water, not her life
(Green-dense and dim-delicious, bred o' the sun),
Flounced back from bliss she was not born to breathe,
And in her old bounds buried her despair,
Hating and loving warmth alike. So He.

'Thinketh, He made thereat the sun, this isle,
Trees and the fowls here, beast and creeping thing—
Yon otter, sleek-wet, black, lithe as a leech;

Yon auk, one fire-eye in a ball of foam,
That floats and feeds; a certain badger brown
He hath watched hunt with that slant white-wedge eye
By moonlight; and the pie with the long tongue
That pricks deep into oakwarts for a worm,
And says a plain word when she finds her prize,
But will not eat the ants; the ants themselves
That build a wall of seeds and settled stalks
About their hole—He made all these and more,
Made all we see, and us, in spite; how else?
He could not, Himself, make a second self
To be His mate—as well have made Himself.
He would not make what He mislikes or slights,
An eyesore to Him, or not worth His pains;
But did, in envy, listlessness, or sport,
Make what Himself would fain, in a manner, be—
Weaker in most points, stronger in a few,
Worthy, and yet mere playthings all the while,
Things He admires and mocks too—that is it.
Because, so brave, so better though they be,
It nothing skills if He begin to plague.
Look now, I melt a gourd-fruit into mash,
Add honeycomb and pods, I have perceived,
Which bite like finches when they bill and kiss—
Then, when froth rises bladdery, drink up all,
Quick, quick, till maggots scamper through my brain;
Last, throw me on my back i' the seeded thyme,
And wanton, wishing I were born a bird.
Put case, unable to be what I wish,
I yet could make a live bird out of clay;
Would not I take clay, pinch my Caliban
Able to fly?—for, there, see, he hath wings,
And great comb like the hoopoe's to admire,
And there, a sting to do his foes offense;
There, and I will that he begin to live,
Fly to yon rock-top, nip me off the horns
Of grigs high up that make the merry din,
Saucy through their veined wings, and mind me not.
In which feat, if his leg snapped, brittle clay,
And he lay stupidlike—why, I should laugh;

And if he, spying me, should fall to weep,
Beseech me to be good, repair his wrong,
Bid his poor leg smart less or grow again—
Well, as the chance were, this might take or else
Not take my fancy; I might hear his cry,
And give the manikin three sound legs for one,
Or pluck the other off, leave him like an egg,
And lessoned he was mine and merely clay.
Were this no pleasure, lying in the thyme,
Drinking the mash, with brain become alive,
Making and marring clay at will? So He.

'Thinketh, such shows nor right nor wrong in Him,
Nor kind, nor cruel; He is strong and Lord.
'Am strong myself compared to yonder crabs
That march now from the mountain to the sea;
'Let twenty pass and stone the twenty-first,
Loving not, hating not, just choosing so.
'Say, the first straggler that boasts purple spots
Shall join the file, one pincer twisted off;
'Say, this bruised fellow shall receive a worm,
And two worms he whose nippers end in red;
As it likes me each time, I do. So He.

Well then, 'supposeth He is good i' the main,
Placable if His mind and ways were guessed,
But rougher than His handiwork, be sure!
Oh, He hath made things worthier than Himself,
And envieth that, so helped, such things do more
Than He who made them! What consoles but this?
That they, unless through Him, do naught at all,
And must submit; what other use in things?
'Hath cut a pipe of pithless elder-joint
That, blown through, gives exact the scream o' the jay
When from her wing you twitch the feathers blue;
Sound this, and little birds that hate the jay
Flock within stone's throw, glad their foe is hurt.
Put case such pipe could prattle and boast forsooth,
"I catch the birds, I am the crafty thing,
I make the cry my maker cannot make

With his great round mouth; he must blow through mine!"
Would not I smash it with my foot? So He.

But wherefore rough, why cold and ill at ease?
Aha, that is a question! Ask, for that,
What knows—the something over Setebos
That made Him, or He, may be, found and fought,
Worsted, drove off, and did to nothing, perchance.
There may be something quiet o'er His head,
Out of His reach, that feels nor joy nor grief,
Since both derive from weakness in some way.
I joy because the quails come; would not joy
Could I bring quails here when I have a mind;
This Quiet, all it hath a mind to, doth.
'Esteemeth stars the outposts of its couch,
But never spends much thought nor care that way.
It may look up, work up—the worse for those
It works on! 'Careth but for Setebos
The many-handed as a cuttlefish,
Who, making Himself feared through what He does,
Looks up, first, and perceives he cannot soar
To what is quiet and hath happy life;
Next looks down here, and out of very spite
Makes this a bauble-world to ape yon real,
These goods things to match those as hips do grapes,
'Tis solace making baubles, aye, and sport.
Himself peeped late, eyed Prosper at his books
Careless and lofty, lord now of the isle;
Vexed, 'stitched a book of broad leaves, arrow-shaped,
Wrote thereon, he knows what, prodigious words;
Has peeled a wand and called it by a name;
Weareth at whiles for an enchanter's robe
The eyed skin of a supple oncelot;
And hath an ounce sleeker than youngling mole,
A four-legged serpent he makes cower and couch,
Now snarl, now hold its breath and mind his eye,
And saith she is Miranda and my wife;
'Keeps for his Ariel a tall pouch-bill crane
He bids go wade for fish and straight disgorge;
Also a sea-beast, lumpish, which he snared,

Blinded the eyes of, and brought somewhat tame,
And split its toe-webs, and now pens the drudge
In a hole o' the rock and calls him Caliban—
A bitter heart that bides its time and bites.
'Play thus at being Prosper in a way,
Taketh his mirth with make-believes. So He.

His dam held that the Quiet made all things
Which Setebos vexed only; 'holds not so.
Who made them weak, meant weakness He might vex.
Had He meant other, while His hand was in,
Why not make horny eyes no thorn could prick,
Or plate my scalp with bone against the snow,
Or overscale my flesh 'neath joint and joint,
Like an orc's armor? Aye—so spoil His sport!
He is the One now; only He doth all.

'Saith, He may like, perchance, what profits Him.
Aye, himself loves what does him good; but why?
'Gets good no otherwise. This blinded beast
Loves whoso places flesh-meat on his nose,
But, had he eyes, would want no help, but hate
Or love, just as it liked him; He hath eyes.
Also it pleaseth Setebos to work,
Use all His hands, and exercise much craft,
By no means for the love of what is worked.
'Tasteth, himself, no finer good i' the world
When all goes right, in this safe summertime,
And he wants little, hungers, aches not much,
Than trying what to do with wit and strength.
'Falls to make something; 'piled yon pile of turfs,
And squared and stuck there squares of soft white chalk,
And, with a fish-tooth, scratched a moon on each,
And set up endwise certain spikes of tree,
And crowned the whole with a sloth's skull atop,
Found dead i' the woods, too hard for one to kill.
No use at all i' the work, for work's sole sake;
'Shall some day knock it down again. So He.

'Saith He is terrible; watch His feats in proof!
One hurricane will spoil six good months' hope.

He hath a spite against me, that I know,
Just as He favors Prosper—who knows why?
So it is, all the same, as well I find.
'Wove wattles half the winter, fenced them firm
With stone and stake to stop she-tortoises
Crawling to lay their eggs here; well, one wave,
Feeling the foot of Him upon its neck,
Gaped as a snake does, lolled out its large tongue,
And licked the whole labor flat—so much for spite.
'Saw a ball flame down late (yonder it lies)
Where, half an hour before, I slept i' the shade.
Often they scatter sparkles; there is force!
'Dug up a newt He may have envied once
And turned to stone, shut up inside a stone.
Please Him and hinder this?—What Prosper does?
Aha, if He would tell me how! Not He!
There is the sport; discover how or die!
All need not die, for of the things o' the isle
Some flee afar, some dive, some run up trees.
Those at His mercy—why, they please Him most
When—when—well, never try the same way twice!
Repeat what act has pleased, He may grow wroth.
You must not know His ways, and play Him off,
Sure of the issue. 'Doth the like himself—
'Spareth a squirrel that it nothing fears
But steals the nut from underneath my thumb,
And when I threat, bites stoutly in defense;
'Spareth an urchin that, contrariwise,
Curls up into a ball, pretending death
For fright at my approach—the two ways please.
But what would move my choler more than this,
That either creature counted on its life
Tomorrow and next day and all days to come,
Saying, forsooth, in the inmost of its heart,
"Because he did so yesterday with me,
And otherwise with such another brute,
So must he do henceforth and always."—Aye?
'Would teach the reasoning couple what "must" means!
'Doth as he likes, or wherefore Lord? So He.

'Conceiveth all things will continue thus,
And we shall have to live in fear of Him
So long as He lives, keeps His strength; no change,
If He have done His best, make no new world
To please Him more, so leave off watching this—
If He surprise not even the Quiet's self
Some strange day—or, suppose, grow into it
As grubs grow butterflies; else, here are we,
And there is He, and nowhere help at all.

'Believeth with the life, the pain shall stop.
His dam held different, that after death
He doth plagued enemies and feasted friends—
Idly! He doth His worst in this our life,
Giving just respite lest we die through pain,
Saving last pain for worst—with which, an end.
Meanwhile, the best way to escape His ire
Is, not to seem too happy. 'Sees, himself,
Yonder two flies, with purple films and pink,
Bask on the pompion-bell above; kills both.
'Sees two black painful beetles roll their ball
On head and tail as if to save their lives;
Moves them the stick away they strive to clear.

Even so, 'would have Him misconceive, suppose
This Caliban strives hard and ails no less,
And always, above all else, envies Him.
Wherefore he mainly dances on dark nights,
Moans in the sun, gets under holes to laugh,
And never speaks his mind save housed as now;
Outside, 'groans, curses. If He caught me here,
O'erheard this speech, and asked "What chucklest at?"
'Would, to appease Him, cut a finger off,
Or of my three kid yearlings burn the best,
Or let the toothsome apples rot on tree,
Or push my tame beast for the orc to taste—
While myself lit a fire, and made a song
And sung it, "*What I hate, be consecrate
To celebrate Thee and Thy state, no mate
For Thee; what see for envy in poor me?*"
Hoping the while, since evils sometimes mend,

Warts rub away, and sores are cured with slime,
That some strange day, will either the Quiet catch
And conquer Setebos, or likelier He
Decrepit may doze, doze, as good as die.

[What, what? A curtain o'er the world at once!
Crickets stop hissing; not a bird—or, yes,
There scuds His raven that hath told Him all!
It was fool's play, this prattling! Ha! The wind
Shoulders the pillared dust, death's house o' the move,
And fast invading fires begin! White blaze—
A tree's head snaps—and there, there, there, there, there,
His thunder follows! Fool to gibe at Him!
Lo! 'Lieth flat and loveth Setebos!
'Maketh his teeth meet through his upper lip,
Will let those quails fly, will not eat this month
One little mess of whelks, so he may 'scape!]

33.   ARNOLD:

"Stanzas from the Grande Chartreuse"

Arnold's poetry, currently in critical disfavor for failing to fuse meter and meaning, may nevertheless strike a contemporary as more modern and relevant in matter and manner than the poetry of either Tennyson or Browning. The introductory essay to this section attempts to account for the legitimacy of this estimate in terms of the poem printed below.

For bibliographical information on Arnold, see headnote, Selection 2.

Through Alpine meadows soft-suffused
With rain, where thick the crocus blows,
Past the dark forges long disused,
The mule-track from Saint Laurent goes.
The bridge is cross'd, and slow we ride,
Through forest, up the mountain-side.

The autumnal evening darkens round,
The wind is up, and drives the rain;
While, hark! far down, with strangled sound
Doth the Dead Guier's stream complain,
Where that wet smoke, among the woods,
Over his boiling cauldron broods.

Swift rush the spectral vapours white
Past limestone scars with ragged pines,
Showing—then blotting from our sight!—
Halt—through the cloud-drift something shines!
High in the valley, wet and drear,
The huts of Courrerie appear.

Strike leftward! cries our guide; and higher
Mounts up the stony forest-way.
At last the encircling trees retire;
Look! through the showery twilight grey
What pointed roofs are these advance?—
A palace of the Kings of France?

Approach, for what we seek is here!
Alight, and sparely sup, and wait
For rest in this outbuilding near;
Then cross the sward and reach that gate.
Knock; pass the wicket! Thou art come
To the Carthusians' world-famed home.

The silent courts, where night and day
Into their stone-carved basins cold
The splashing icy fountains play—
The humid corridors behold!
Where, ghostlike in the deepening night,
Cowl'd forms brush by in gleaming white.

The chapel, where no organ's peal
Invests the stern and naked prayer—
With penitential cries they kneel
And wrestle; rising then, with bare
And white uplifted faces stand,
Passing the Host from hand to hand;

Each takes, and then his visage wan
Is buried in his cowl once more.
The cells!—the suffering Son of Man
Upon the wall—the knee-worn floor—
And where they sleep, that wooden bed,
Which shall their coffin be, when dead!

The library, where tract and tome
Not to feed priestly pride are there,
To hymn the conquering march of Rome,
Nor yet to amuse, as ours are!
They paint of souls the inner strife,
Their drops of blood, their death in life.

The garden, overgrown—yet mild,
See, fragrant herbs are flowering there!
Strong children of the Alpine wild
Whose culture is the brethren's care;
Of human tasks their only one,
And cheerful works beneath the sun.

Those halls, too, destined to contain
Each its own pilgrim-host of old,
From England, Germany, or Spain—
All are before me! I behold
The House, the Brotherhood austere!
—And what am I, that I am here?

For rigorous teachers seized my youth,
And purged its faith, and trimm'd its fire,
Show'd me the high, white star of Truth,
There bade me gaze, and there aspire.
Even now their whispers pierce the gloom:
What dost thou in this living tomb?

Forgive me, masters of the mind!
At whose behest I long ago
So much unlearnt, so much resign'd—
I come not here to be your foe!
I seek these anchorites, not in ruth,
To curse and to deny your truth;

Not as their friend, or child, I speak!
But as, on some far northern strand,
Thinking of his own Gods, a Greek
In pity and mournful awe might stand
Before some fallen Runic stone—
For both were faiths, and both are gone.

Wandering between two worlds, one dead,
The other powerless to be born,
With nowhere yet to rest my head,
Like these, on earth I wait forlorn.
Their faith, my tears, the world deride—
I come to shed them at their side.

Oh, hide me in your gloom profound,
Ye solemn seats of holy pain!
Take me, cowl'd forms, and fence me round,
Till I possess my soul again;
Till free my thoughts before me roll,
Not chafed by hourly false control!

For the world cries your faith is now
But a dead time's exploded dream;
My melancholy, sciolists say,
Is a pass'd mode, an outworn theme—
As if the world had ever had
A faith, or sciolists been sad!

Ah, if it *be* pass'd, take away,
At least, the restlessness, the pain;
Be man henceforth no more a prey
To these out-dated stings again!
The nobleness of grief is gone—
Ah, leave us not the fret alone!

But—if you cannot give us ease—
Last of the race of them who grieve
Here leave us to die out with these
Last of the people who believe!
Silent, while years engrave the brow;
Silent—the best are silent now.

Achilles ponders in his tent,
The kings of modern thought are dumb;
Silent they are; though not content,
And wait to see the future come.
They have the grief men had of yore,
But they contend and cry no more.

Our fathers water'd with their tears
This sea of time whereon we sail,
Their voices were in all men's ears
Who pass'd within their puissant hail.
Still the same ocean round us raves,
But we stand mute, and watch the waves.

For what avail'd it, all the noise
And outcry of the former men?—
Say, have their sons achieved more joys,
Say, is life lighter now than then?
The sufferers died, they left their pain—
The pangs which tortured them remain.

What helps it now, that Byron bore,
With haughty scorn which mock'd the smart,
Through Europe to the Ætolian shore
The pageant of his bleeding heart?
That thousands counted every groan,
And Europe made his woe her own?

What boots it, Shelley! that the breeze
Carried thy lovely wail away,
Musical through Italian trees
Which fringe thy soft blue Spezzian bay?
Inheritors of thy distress
Have restless hearts one throb the less?

Or are we easier, to have read,
O Obermann! the sad, stern page,
Which tells us how thou hidd'st thy head
From the fierce tempest of thine age
In the lone brakes of Fontainebleau,
Or chalets near the Alpine snow?

Ye slumber in your silent grave!—
The world, which for an idle day
Grace to your mood of sadness gave,
Long since hath flung her weeds away.
The eternal trifler breaks your spell;
But we—we learnt your lore too well!

Years hence, perhaps, may dawn an age,
More fortunate, alas! than we,
Which without hardness will be sage,
And gay without frivolity.
Sons of the world, oh, speed those years;
But, while we wait, allow our tears!

Allow them! We admire with awe
The exulting thunder of your race;
You give the universe your law,
You triumph over time and space!
Your pride of life, your tireless powers,
We laud them, but they are not ours.

We are like children rear'd in shade
Beneath some old-world abbey wall,
Forgotten in a forest-glade,
And secret from the eyes of all.
Deep, deep the greenwood round them waves,
Their abbey, and its close of graves!

But, where the road runs near the stream,
Oft through the trees they catch a glance
Of passing troops in the sun's beam—
Pennon, and plume, and flashing lance!
Forth to the world those soldiers fare,
To life, to cities, and to war!

And through the wood, another way,
Faint bugle-notes from far are borne,
Where hunters gather, staghounds bay,
Round some fair forest-lodge at morn.
Gay dames are there, in sylvan green;
Laughter and cries—those notes between!

The banners flashing through the trees
Make their blood dance and chain their eyes;
That bugle-music on the breeze
Arrests them with a charm'd surprise.
Banner by turns and bugle woo:
Ye shy recluses, follow too!

O children, what do ye reply?—
'Action and pleasure, will ye roam
Through these secluded dells to cry
And call us?—but too late ye come!
Too late for us your call ye blow,
Whose bent was taken long ago.

'Long since we pace this shadow'd nave;
We watch those yellow tapers shine,
Emblems of hope over the grave,
In the high altar's depth divine;
The organ carries to our ear
Its accents of another sphere.

'Fenced early in this cloistral round
Of reverie, of shade, of prayer,
How should we grow in other ground?
How can we flower in foreign air?
—Pass, banners, pass, and bugles, cease;
And leave our desert to its peace!'

34. MEREDITH:
"The Woods of Westermain"

Meredith's poetry is as allusive and, for the inattentive, elusive as his prose. Though not one of the major Victorian poets, Meredith's psychological inquisitiveness and acuity and his experiments with more realistic patterns of speech and thought make him one of the most important innovaters of the period.

For bibliographical information on Meredith, see headnote, Selection 5.

I

Enter these enchanted woods,
    You who dare.
Nothing harms beneath the leaves
More than waves a swimmer cleaves.
Toss your heart up with the lark,
Foot at peace with mouse and worm,
    Fair you fare.
Only at a dread of dark
Quaver, and they quit their form:
Thousand eyeballs under hoods
    Have you by the hair.
Enter these enchanted woods,
    You who dare.

II

Here the snake across your path
Stretches in his golden bath:
Mossy-footed squirrels leap
Soft as winnowing plumes of Sleep:
Yaffles on a chuckle skim
Low to laugh from branches dim:
Up the pine, where sits the star,
Rattles deep the moth-winged jar.
Each has business of his own;
But should you distrust a tone,
    Then beware.
Shudder all the haunted roods,
All the eyeballs under hoods
    Shroud you in their glare.
Enter these enchanted woods,
    You who dare.

III

Open hither, open hence,
Scarce a bramble weaves a fence,
Where the strawberry runs red,
With white star-flower overhead;
Cumbered by dry twig and cone,
Shredded husks of seedlings flown,

Mine of mole and spotted flint:
Of dire wizardry no hint,
Save mayhap the print that shows
Hasty outward-tripping toes,
Heels to terror, on the mould.
These, the woods of Westermain,
Are as others to behold,
Rich of wreathing sun and rain;
Foliage lustreful around
Shadowed leagues of slumbering sound.
Wavy tree-tops, yellow whins,
Shelter eager minikins,
Myriads, free to peck and pipe:
Would you better? would you worse?
You with them may gather ripe
Pleasures flowing not from purse.
Quick and far as Colour flies
Taking the delighted eyes,
You of any well that springs
May unfold the heaven of things;
Have it homely and within,
And thereof its likeness win,
Will you so in soul's desire:
This do sages grant t' the lyre.
This is being bird and more,
More than glad musician this;
Granaries you will have a store
Past the world of woe and bliss;
Sharing still its bliss and woe;
Harnessed to its hungers, no.
On the throne Success usurps
You shall seat the joy you feel
Where a race of water chirps,
Twisting hues of flourished steel:
Or where light is caught in hoop
Up a clearing's leafy rise,
Where the crossing deerherds troop
Classic splendours, knightly dyes.
Or, where old-eyed oxen chew
Speculation with the cud,

Read their pool of vision through,
Back to hours when mind was mud;
Nigh the knot, which did untwine
Timelessly to drowsy suns;
Seeing Earth a slimy spine,
Heaven a space for winging tons.
Farther, deeper, may you read,
Have you sight for things afield,
Where peeps she, the Nurse of seed,
Cloaked, but in the peep revealed;
Showing a kind face and sweet:
Look you with the soul you see't.
Glory narrowing to grace,
Grace to glory magnified,
Following that will you embrace
Close in arms or aëry wide.
Banished is the white Foam-born
Not from here, nor under ban
Phoebus lyrist, Phoebe's horn,
Pipings of the reedy Pan.
Loved of Earth of old they were,
Loving did interpret her;
And the sterner worship bars
None whom Song has made her stars.
You have seen the huntress moon
Radiantly facing dawn,
Dusky meads between them strewn
Glimmering like downy awn:
Argent Westward glows the hunt,
East the blush about to climb;
One another fair they front,
Transient, yet outshine the time
Even as dewlight off the rose
In the mind a jewel sows.
Thus opposing grandeurs live
Here if Beauty be their dower:
Doth she of her spirit give,
Fleetingness will spare her flower.
This is in the tune we play,
Which no spring of strength would quell;

In subduing does not slay;
Guides the channel, guards the well:
Tempered holds the young blood-heat,
Yet through measured grave accord
Hears the heart of wildness beat
Like a centaur's hoof on sward.
Drink the sense the notes infuse,
You a larger self will find:
Sweetest fellowship ensues
With the creatures of your kind.
Ay, and Love, if Love it be
Flaming over *I* and *ME*,
Love meet they who do not shove
Cravings in the van of Love.
Courtly dames are here to woo,
Knowing love if it be true.
Reverence the blossom-shoot
Fervently, they are the fruit.
Mark them stepping, hear them talk,
Goddess, is no myth inane,
You will say of those who walk
In the woods of Westermain.
Waters that from throat and thigh
Dart the sun his arrows back;
Leaves that on a woodland sigh
Chat of secret things no lack;
Shadowy branch-leaves, waters clear,
Bare or veiled they move sincere;
Not by slavish terrors tripped;
Being anew in nature dipped,
Growths of what they step on, these;
With the roots the grace of trees.
Casket-breasts they give, nor hide,
For a tyrant's flattered pride,
Mind, which nourished not by light,
Lurks the shuffling trickster sprite:
Whereof are strange tales to tell;
Some in blood writ, tombed in hell.
Here the ancient battle ends,
Joining two astonished friends,

Who the kiss can give and take
With more warmth than in that world
Where the tiger claws the snake,
Snake her tiger clasps infurled,
And the issue of their fight
Peoples lands in snarling plight.
Here her splendid beast she leads
Silken-leashed and decked with weeds
Wild as he, but breathing faint
Sweetness of unfelt constraint.
Love, the great volcano, flings
Fires of lower Earth to sky;
Love, the sole permitted, sings
Sovereignly of *ME* and *I*.
Bowers he has of sacred shade,
Spaces of superb parade,
Voiceful . . . But bring you a note
Wrangling, howsoe'er remote,
Discords out of discord spin
Round and round derisive din:
Sudden will a pallor pant
Chill at screeches miscreant;
Owls or spectres, thick they flee;
Nightmare upon horror broods;
Hooded laughter, monkish glee,
 Gaps the vital air.
Enter these enchanted woods
 You who dare.

IV

You must love the light so well
That no darkness will seem fell.
Love it so you could accost
Fellowly a livid ghost.
Whish! the phantom wisps away.
Owns him smoke to cocks of day.
In your breast the light must burn
Fed of you, like corn in quern
Ever plumping while the wheel
Speeds the mill and drains the meal.

Light to light sees little strange,
Only features heavenly new;
Then you touch the nerve of Change,
Then of Earth you have the clue;
Then her two-sexed meanings melt
Through you, wed the thought and felt.
Sameness locks no scurfy pond
Here for Custom, crazy-fond:
Change is on the wing to bud
Rose in brain from rose in blood.
Wisdom throbbing shall you see
Central in complexity;
From her pasture 'mid the beasts
Rise to her ethereal feasts,
Not, though lightning track your wit
Starward, scorning them you quit:
For be sure the bravest wing
Preens it in our common spring,
Thence along the vault to soar,
You with others, gathering more,
Glad of more, till you reject
Your proud title of elect,
Perilous even here while few
Roam the arched greenwood with you.
      Heed that snare.
Muffled by his cavern-cowl
Squats the scaly Dragon-fowl,
Who was lord ere light you drank,
And lest blood of knightly rank
Stream, let not your fair princess
Stray: he holds the leagues in stress,
      Watches keenly there.
Oft has he been riven; slain
Is no force in Westermain.
Wait, and we shall forge him curbs,
Put his fangs to uses, tame,
Teach him, quick as cunning herbs,
How to cure him sick and lame.
Much restricted, much enringed,

Much he frets, the hooked and winged,
   Never known to spare.
'Tis enough: the name of Sage
Hits no thing in nature, nought;
Man the least, save when grave Age
From yon Dragon guards his thought.
Eye him when you hearken dumb
To what words from Wisdom come.
When she says how few are by
Listening to her, eye his eye.
   Self, his name declare.
Him shall Change, transforming late,
Wonderously renovate.
Hug himself the creature may:
What he hugs is loathed decay.
Crying, slip thy scales, and slough!
Change will strip his armour off;
Make of him who was all maw,
Inly only thrilling-shrewd,
Such a servant as none saw
Through his days of dragonhood.
Days when growling o'er his bone,
Sharpened he for mine and thine;
Sensitive within alone;
Scaly as in clefts of pine.
Change, the strongest son of Life,
Has the Spirit here to wife,
Lo, their young of vivid breed
Bear the lights that onward speed,
Threading thickets, mounting glades,
Up the verdurous colonnades,
Round the fluttered curves, and down,
Out of sight of Earth's blue crown,
Whither, in her central space,
Spouts the Fount and Lure o' the chase.
Fount unresting, Lure divine!
There meet all: too late look most.
Fire in water hued as wine
Springs amid a shadowy host;
Circled: one close-headed mob,

Breathless, scanning divers heaps
Where a Heart begins to throb,
Where it ceases, slow, with leaps.
And 'tis very strange, 'tis said,
How you spy in each of them
Semblance of that Dragon red,
As the oak in bracken-stem.
And, 'tis said, how each and each:
Which commences, which subsides:
First my Dragon! doth beseech
Her who food for all provides.
And she answers with no sign;
Utters neither yea nor nay;
Fires the water hued as wine;
Kneads another spark in clay.
Terror is about her hid;
Silence of the thunders locked;
Lightnings lining the shut lid;
Fixity on quaking rocked.
Lo, you look at Flow and Drought
Interflashed and interwrought:
Ended is begun, begun
Ended, quick as torrents run.
Young Impulsion spouts to sink;
Luridness and lustre link;
'Tis your come and go of breath
Mirrored pants the Life, the Death;
Each of either reaped and sown:
Rosiest rosy wanes to crone.
See you so? your senses drift;
'Tis a shuttle weaving swift.
Look with spirit past the sense,
Spirit shines in permanence.
That is She, the view of whom
Is the dust within the tomb,
Is the inner blush above,
Look to loathe, or look to love;
Think her Lump, or know her Flame;
Dread her scourge, or read her aim;
Shoot your hungers from their nerve;

Or, in her example, serve.
Some have found her sitting grave;
Laughing, some; or, browed with sweat,
Hurling dust of fool and knave
In a hissing smithy's jet.
More it were not well to speak;
Burn to see, you need but seek.
Once beheld she gives the key
Airing every doorway, she;
Little can you stop or steer
Ere of her you are the seër,
On the surface she will witch,
Rendering Beauty yours, but gaze
Under, and the soul is rich
Past computing, past amaze.
Then is courage that endures
Even her awful tremble yours.
Then, the reflex of that Fount
Spied below, will Reason mount
Lordly and a quenchless force,
Lighting Pain to its mad source,
Scaring Fear till Fear escapes,
Shot through all its phantom shapes.
Then your spirit will perceive
Fleshly seed of fleshly sins;
Where the passions interweave,
How the serpent tangle spins
Of the sense of Earth misprised,
Brainlessly unrecognised;
She being Spirit in her clods,
Footway to the God of Gods.
Then for you are pleasures pure,
Sureties as the stars are sure:
Not the wanton beckoning flags
Which, of flattery and delight,
Wax to the grim Habit-Hags
Riding souls of men to night:
Pleasures that through blood run sane,
Quickening spirit from the brain.
Each of each in sequent birth,

Blood and brain and spirit, three
(Say the deepest gnomes of Earth),
Join for true felicity.
Are they parted, then expect
Some one sailing will be wrecked:
Separate hunting are they sped,
Scan the morsel coveted.
Earth that Triad is: she hides
Joy from him who that divides;
Showers it when the three are one
Glassing her in union.
Earth your haven, Earth your helm,
You command a double realm;
Labouring here to pay your debt,
Till your little sun shall set;
Leaving her the future task:
Loving her too well to ask.
Eglantine that climbs the yew,
She her darkest wreathes for those
Knowing her the Ever-new,
And themselves the kin o' the rose.
Life, the chisel, axe and sword,
Wield who have her depths explored:
Life, the dream, shall be their robe,
Large as air about the globe;
Life, the question, hear its cry
Echoed with concordant Why;
Life, the small self-dragon ramped,
Thrill for service to be stamped.
Ay, and over every height
Life for them shall wave a wand:
That, the last, where sits affright,
Homely shows the stream beyond.
Love the light and be its lynx,
You will track her and attain;
Read her as no cruel Sphinx
In the woods of Westermain.
Daily fresh the woods are ranged;
Glooms which otherwhere appal,
Sounded: here, their worths exchanged,

Urban joins with pastoral:
Little lost, save what may drop
Husk-like, and the mind preserves.
Natural overgrowths they lop,
Yet from nature neither swerves,
Trained or savage: for this cause:
Of our Earth they ply the laws,
Have in Earth their feeding root,
Mind of man and bent of brute.
Hear that song; both wild and ruled.
Hear it: is it wail or mirth?
Ordered, bubbled, quite unschooled?
None, and all: it springs of Earth.
O but hear it! 'tis the mind;
Mind that with deep Earth unites,
Round the solid trunk to wind
Rings of clasping parasites.
Music have you there to feed
Simplest and most soaring need.
Free to wind, and in desire
Winding, they to her attached
Feel the trunk a spring of fire,
And ascend to heights unmatched,
Whence the tidal world is viewed
As a sea of windy wheat,
Momently black, barren, rude;
Golden-brown, for harvest meet;
Dragon-reaped from folly-sown;
Bride-like to the sickle-blade:
Quick it varies, while the moan,
Moan of a sad creature strayed,
Chiefly is its voice. So flesh
Conjures tempest-flails to thresh
Good from worthless. Some clear lamps
Light it; more of dead marsh-damps.
Monster is it still, and blind,
Fit but to be led by Pain.
Glance we at the paths behind,
Fruitful sight has Westermain.
There we laboured, and in turn

Forward our blown lamps discern,
As you see on the dark deep
Far the loftier billows leap,
   Foam for beacon bear.
Hither, hither, if you will,
Drink instruction, or instil,
Run the woods like vernal sap,
Crying, hail to luminousness!
   But have care.
In yourself may lurk the trap:
On conditions they caress.
Here you meet the light invoked:
Here is never secret cloaked.
Doubt you with the monster's fry
All his orbit may exclude;
Are you of the stiff, the dry,
Cursing the not understood;
Grasp you with the monster's claws;
Govern with his truncheon-saws;
Hate, the shadow of a grain;
You are lost in Westermain:
Earthward swoops a vulture sun,
Nighted upon carrion:
Straightway venom winecups shout
Toasts to One whose eyes are out:
Flowers along the reeling floor
Drip henbane and hellebore:
Beauty, of her tresses shorn,
Shrieks as nature's maniac:
Hideousness on hoof and horn
Tumbles, yapping in her track:
Haggard Wisdom, stately once,
Leers fantastical and trips:
Allegory drums the sconce,
Impiousness nibblenips.
Imp that dances, imp that flits,
Imp o' the demon-growing girl,
Maddest! whirl with imp o' the pits
Round you, and with them you whirl
Fast where pours the fountain-rout

Out of Him whose eyes are out:
Multitudes on multitudes,
Drenched in wallowing devilry:
And you ask where you may be,
    In what reek of a lair
Given to bones and ogre-broods:
    And they yell you Where.
Enter these enchanted woods,
    You who dare.

V

Art

D URING the years which this anthology attempts to bring before modern eyes with a sense of their variety, modernity, and vitality, questions about the nature and function of art were among the most predominant. Men as distinguished as Macaulay and Bentham argued that poetry was not what the age demanded and that art should be assessed by determining the amount, not the kind, of pleasure it gave. Poetry was regarded by many as an entertainment not even affording the "superior amusement" Eliot ascribes to it. In the earlier essays, we have touched upon the ways in which some of the poets responded to the challenge: Tennyson and Browning by using the past as a vehicle to comment on the present and by competing openly with prose in poems which directly discuss the problems of modern life.

Although the poets of the Romantic period often conceived of their poetry as more accessible to the public than the poetry of the Neo-classic period, which they felt was clotted by a diction too far removed from ordinary life and lives, it is neverthless true that the reading public taking shape during the latter two-thirds of the nineteenth century was asking new and different things of its literary lions. One reason for this may be that life itself, in the form of political and social forces, impressed itself more forcibly on the lives of a more generally middle-class reading public. Be this as it may, poetry and art in general found themselves trying to perform at once two tasks that many practitioners felt were mutually exclusive. Almost all the major figures answered the call of the public who wished to know, in an Arnoldian sense, how to live, how to respond to the pressures of daily existence. But while answers were given, many of those giving them felt that they were betraying the very nature of art, which was conceived of as inhabiting a world more or less its own, governed by aesthetic laws, independent of particular social responsibilities.

While the best artists were able to keep from doing violence to art's asocial nature and materials and were able to respond to the public's demand that art perform a socially useful function, much bad hortatory "poetry" appeared. As if in response, a movement toward art for its own sake first gained momentum and, finally, the day. William Morris' address on the Pre-Raphaelite movement* tells us as much about the currents of thought affecting literature as about those affecting art. In tracing the history of the Pre-Raphaelite school, Morris properly insists on the primacy of the doctrine of naturalism; the public schooled in a tradition of artificiality mistook naturalism for monstrosity. Pre-Raphaelite paintings told stories, and they fulfilled a decorative function as well. They did these things, according to Morris, in much the same way that poetry tried to. But, as Morris also points out, modern life seemed singularly deficient in providing *beautiful* scenes to represent. In order to pay its debt to beauty, art turned to itself and to the past. Morris, unlike Arnold, argues that great ages of criticism and creativity do not always coincide, and he explains that the painters of the Pre-Raphaelite Brotherhood were held in disrepute for not providing the public what it wanted or could understand; both arguments provide documentation for our earlier generalizations about art and society and are, without forcing, applicable to literature as well as to painting.

The twin temptations facing art were to fall back to a world not only asocial but antisocial or to desert its rightful palace altogether. That art for its own sake turned out no more antisocial than it did pays tribute to art, not criticism, for it was the criticism of men like John Morley, who held very narrow definitions of art's social duties, that was largely responsible for divorcing art from society. The art that did emerge from the aesthetic movement is the great imagist and symbolist art of our century, and our criticism is the broadly human and aesthetically formal criticism adumbrated in William Michael Rossetti's defense of Swinburne against the strictures of men like Morley.

Morley's comments on Swinburne are not all of the admonitory sort; he praises the poet's "bountifulness of imagination" and "mastery of the music of verse." He praises Swinburne's "forcible and vigorous

* Unfortunately limitations of space prevented us from including Morris' "Address on the Collection of the English Pre-Raphaelite School in the City of Birmingham Museum and Art Gallery," which was delivered on Friday, October 24, 1891.

imagination" and the way in which he manipulates sound patterns with "variety and rapidity and sustention." He praises some "sweet and picturesque lines" and even finds some "perfect delicacy and beauty." What Morley finds objectionable, as he admits in his opening paragraph, may have no real place in the criticism of literature: namely, the choice of subject matter. Morley's fear is that the English public will emulate Swinburne's characters and their actions, that readers will "gradually acquire a truly delightful familiarity with unspeakable foulness." Denying that Swinburne's "tone of mind" is Grecian, Morley argues that there is but one string to his lyre, and that one, Morley suspects, may be a trick or device or habitual way of handling words rather than a genuine musical gift. No matter which, though; its function is to conceal a lack of sober thought. We shall find these charges raised again by Gerard Manley Hopkins.

Morley would seem to have a notion that "true poetic awe" or "meditation" or "things really poetical convey to man the pure and peaceful and bounteous kindly aspects of the great landscape of human life," and though at the outset he says a critic ought not impose his taste in subjects on an artist, it is precisely this and the idea of the necessity for rigid social control that form the basis of his critique. They force him to misinterpret the tone of Swinburne's best poetry, which is neither vindictive nor scornful but a profound and passionate and intense note of despair. To call the poet an apostle of a "crushing iron-shod despair" is to have missed the desperate and plaintive questioning that is a typical mode of Swinburne's poetry.

William Michael Rossetti's reply to Morley does battle primarily on literary, not social or moral, grounds, and many of his attitudes we find strikingly modern. Take for example his recognition that Swinburne "seldom writes other than dramatically" and that, consequently, we cannot attribute to the poet opinions expressed by his *dramatis personae*. Not that Rossetti sidesteps an argument; he argues that Swinburne's conception of the power that rules the universe is very close to the ideas of David Hume and that Swinburne's interest in the unresolved questions of the relationship between "ideal right" and "actual fact" vents itself in "passionate obtestations." Rossetti's arguments about the relationship between poetry and morality are similarly modern. He again separates the morals of the man from the morality of the work and he argues that poems have a sort of "absolute value" measured by the quality and amount of their imagination, conception, and execution. Rossetti further asserts that art's primary function is not to improve what is ordinarily meant by the morals of the reader but is rather a more Shelleyan and humanizing function.

Gerard Manley Hopkins, writing to Robert Bridges in 1879, also agrees that "Swinburne's genius is astonishing, but it will only do one thing." Both Morley and Rossetti would concur, but each makes different rhetorical use of the argument. Hopkins, whose technical innovations align him more nearly with Swinburne than any other Victorian poet, is acutely aware that his own poetry needs a special kind of audience, an audience not unlike the one to which Rossetti claims Swinburne appeals: "a poet for poetic students." Others of Hopkins' letters to Bridges discuss many other bones of aesthetic contention, perhaps the most obvious being ideas about art for art's sake. Those reading Hopkins for the first time are more likely to remark his ideas about a special kind of audience, and they are also likely, unfortunately, to find ironic rather than instructive his repeated pleading for intelligibility and a sense of reality and for a language that is "an elevation of ordinary, modern speech." Hopkins has little patience for decadent art. In 1889 we find him attacking Swinburne for lacking "truth," "feelings," and "adequate matter."

Rossetti keeps in view the fit audience required for Swinburne's poems: those who have the ability to discern beauty of execution. He intimates that such folk comprise the kind of qualified audience whose applause is most worth winning. But lest we should think he agrees with Morley or would agree with Hopkins, Rossetti argues that Swinburne's "conceptions are, in fact, as vivid as his expressions," and he even states that in the poet's early work the richness was more intellectual and poetic than dramatic.

More riches abound in the selection from Rossetti than we have space to comment on. But we must call attention to his sympathetic understanding of Swinburne's spiritual plight, to what Morley called the "affright" which seizes man when he finds himself suspended in the form given him by nature between the two abysms of infinity and nothingness. This terror is not unlike that expressed by Arnold in the "Stanzas from the Grande Chartreuse" and not unlike that expressed by Hopkins in the so-called "terrible sonnets," though it is more basic and passionate than Arnold's and less traditionally religious than Hopkins'. This terror posits for us the *weltenschauung* that provides the quasi-philosophical framework for Pater's *The Renaissance*.

Walter Pater's criticism is often thought to provide both an aesthetic theory to bolster the practice of the "aesthetes" and the "decadents" and also to provide a set of rationalizations for the sensual excesses of many practitioners of art for its own sake. But the shrine is not responsible for the acts of the pilgrims, Darwin is not responsible for social Darwinism, and Pater is responsible for neither the social climate nor the personal desires producing the behavior that so shocked the *fin de siècle*. In fact, Pater is, like Ruskin, an advocate of the "moral aesthetic." We can see this in *Appreciations* where he writes that the distinction between good art and great art depends in literature

not on its form but on the matter. Thackeray's *Esmond*, surely, is greater art than *Vanity Fair*, by the greater dignity of its interests. It is on the quality of the matter it informs or controls, its compass, its variety, its alliance to greater ends, on the depth of the note of revolt, or the largeness of hope in it, that the greatness of literary art depends.

The profound sense of sadness, the recognition of the ephemerality of man's existence, and the resulting yearning for concreteness characterizing the selections from Pater may be easy to burlesque; but they seem to strike one of the deepest chords of man's emotional nature. In the language and practice of T. S. Eliot, in such poems as "The Love Song of J. Alfred Prufrock" and "The Wasteland" we find the equivalent of:

Experience already reduced to a group of impressions is ringed round for each one of us by that thick wall of personality through which no real voice has even pierced on its way to us, or from us to that which we can only conjecture to be without.

As we said, such reflections are easy to burlesque, but before we turn to Oscar Wilde's deliberate distortions of Pater's ideas, we need to comment on the place of parody in Victorian literature. Imitation may be the most sincere form of flattery, but to write a good parody is to capture the essentials of an artist's matter and manner and show an understanding surpassing mere flattery. At the same time it can be a form of praise in that recognition of another's importance is tacit and the trouble it took to study another's work is manifest. The Victorian period produced a wealth of parody, perhaps because the voices of its masters were so distinct.

But parody embodies controversy and disagreement too. The fact that it criticizes overtly and praises covertly, amusing us all the while, can be taken as emblematic of Victorian controversy. Not campaigns of mutual extermination but cooperative investigations into the nature of truth is the spirit of most Victorian controversy, as we have quoted from John Cooke and Lionel Stevenson. The parodies and burlesques in the discussions of art should remind us that to think of the Victorians as always profoundly earnest is an egregious error; their wit and humor deserve more attention than they usually receive. The humor of Lewis Carroll or that of William Gilbert is readily apparent, but we too often forget that a tolerant but pervasive irony characterizes the narration in much of the best Victorian fiction.

The work of Oscar Wilde is characterized by brilliant paradoxical humor and flashes of insight; but in his case serious meanings have largely been ignored. The protagonist of Wilde's novel *The Picture of Dorian Gray* is a lovely youth who, under the influence of Lord Henry Wolton (and Huysmans), succumbs to what is a radical extension to life of Pater's theories of the relationship between art and life. Pater, like Henry James, advocates that we be one of those on whom nothing is lost. But Dorian emphasizes the word "nothing"; his quest for sensual experiences leads to criminal depravity which is not, platonically, recorded on his face but on his portrait: the confusion of art and life is complete. Though Wilde argues that "all art is quite useless" and that beauty is the aim of art, and though Lord Henry argues that "art has no influence upon action," the novel itself is an attack on those who confuse life with art and thereby pervert both. The novel attacks those who, like Dorian, try to live an amoral life by questing for sensation and ignoring all human values. Wilde himself publicly said his book was too moral to be good, and Pater said Dorian's career was an "unsuccessful experiment in Epicureanism, in life as a fine art." But the book is moral in much the same way that *Huckleberry Finn* is moral despite the prefatory warning, for Dorian's confusion of life and art works to the detriment of both. (Dorian's attraction to the church is not uncharacteristic; we should be remiss if we did not remark that many intellectuals and artists were similarly attracted "not for the doctrine but the music there.")

Wilde himself led the extravagant life of a dandy, much of which was an elaborate masquerade, but which titillated and outraged the public. Wilde satirized and shocked the bourgeois but was paid back by another of the great Victorian comic artists, William Schwenck Gilbert. "Bunthorne's Song," from Gilbert and Sullivan's *Patience*, mocks the decadents' love of the natural and the old as well as the gullibility of those who swallowed the elaborate put-on. (Wilde was notorious for wearing velvet clothes and sporting an exotic flower in his buttonhole.)

Wilde's homosexual activities are the subject of another poetic attack too amusing not to be reprinted here.

> When Oscar came to join his God,
> Not earth to earth, but sod to sod,
> It was for sinners such as this
> Hell was created bottomless.

Swinburne, to whom this quatrain is attributed, was a marvelous parodist, and dreadfully easy to parody. As others have shown, much of his work seems like or is self-parody. "The Higher Pantheism in a Nutshell" exemplifies Swinburne's talent for parody, though we ought to note that if read unsympathetically, Tennyson's "The Higher Pantheism" needs no parodying from without. The same may be true of Swinburne's "Dolores," delightfully savaged by A. C. Hilton's "Octopus"; but it is surely not true of FitzGerald's version of the *Rubáiyát* and Robert Browning's "Rabbi ben Ezra." Browning and FitzGerald had personal grievances, but those are not exhibited in these poems. Browning attacks the worldly, hedonistic philosophy he finds in FitzGerald's version of the poem and by changing in emphasis the basic metaphor successfully challenges the poem on its own grounds. Browning's manner was striking and individual enough to be frequently parodied, but never more in the spirit we discussed earlier than in the poem by J. K. Stephen we reprint.

We can conclude by emphasizing that Victorian controversies about art are typical of the period: while they are not always conducted with the utmost decorum there is always evident an earnestness which elevates issues above personalities. Even issues raised humorously have grave implications. We should also see that the problem of relating art to society without betraying art's very nature is a problem the twentieth century has not solved, although public attention has abated. We have much to learn from the Victorians, but more not to forget.

35. MORLEY:
Attack on Swinburne

The works of John, Viscount Morley (1838–1923), statesman, editor, liberal, agnostic, and critic, are complete in fifteen volumes (1921). F. W. Hirst's *Early Life and Letters* (2 vols., 1927) is standard. See also Warren Staebler's *The Liberal Mind of John Morley* (1943) and J. D. MacCallum's *Lord Morley's Criticism of English Poetry and Prose* (Princeton, 1921). The importance of Morley's review is set forth in the introduction to this section. Morley, who was an editor of two influential literary magazines, *Fortnightly Review* and *Pall Mall Gazette*, was also the editor of the important critical biographies, the "English Men of Letters" series.

This selection is given as it appeared in *Saturday Review*, August 4, 1866, titled "Mr. Swinburne's New Poems: *Poems and Ballads*."

It is mere waste of time, and shows a curiously mistaken conception of human character, to blame an artist of any kind for working at a certain set of subjects rather than at some other set which the critic may happen to prefer. An artist, at all events an artist of such power and individuality as Mr. Swinburne, works as his character compels him. If the character of his genius drives him pretty exclusively in the direction of libidinous song, we may be very sorry, but it is of no use to advise him and to preach to him. What comes of discoursing to a fiery tropical flower of the pleasant fragrance of the rose or the fruitfulness of the fig-tree? Mr. Swinburne is much too stoutly bent on taking his own course to pay any attention to critical monitions as to the duty of the poet, or any warnings of the worse than barrenness of the field in which he has chosen to labour. He is so firmly and avowedly fixed in an attitude of revolt against the current notions of decency and dignity and social duty that to beg of him to become a little more decent, to fly a little less persistently and gleefully to the animal side of human nature, is simply to beg him to be something different from Mr. Swinburne. It is a kind of protest which his whole position makes it impossible for him to receive with anything but laughter and contempt. A rebel of his calibre is not to be brought to a better mind by solemn little sermons on the loyalty which a man owes to virtue. His warmest prayer to the gods is that they should

> Come down and redeem us from virtue.

His warmest hope for men is that they should change

> The lilies and languors of virtue
> For the raptures and roses of vice.

It is of no use, therefore, to scold Mr. Swinburne for grovelling down among the nameless shameless abominations which inspire him with such frenzied delight. They excite his imagination to its most vigorous efforts, they seem to him the themes most proper for poetic treatment, and they suggest ideas which, in his opinion, it is highly to be wished that English men and women should brood upon and make their own. He finds that these fleshly things are his strong part, so he sticks to them. Is it wonderful that he should? And at all events he deserves credit for the audacious courage with which he has revealed to the world a mind all aflame with the feverish carnality of a schoolboy over the dirtiest passages in Lemprière. It is not every poet who would ask us all to go hear him tuning his lyre in a stye. It is not everybody who would care to let the world know that he found the most delicious food for poetic reflection in the practices of the great island of the Ægean, in the habits of Messalina, of Faustina, of Pasiphaë. Yet these make up Mr. Swinburne's version of the dreams of fair women, and he would scorn to throw any veil over pictures which kindle, as these do, all the fires of his imagination in their intensest heat and glow. It is not merely "the noble, the nude, the antique" which he strives to reproduce. If he were a rebel against the fat-headed Philistines and poor-blooded Puritans who insist that all poetry should be such as may be wisely placed in the hands of girls of eighteen, and is fit for the use of Sunday schools, he would have all wise and enlarged readers on his side. But there is an enormous difference between an attempt to revivify among us the grand old pagan conceptions of Joy, and attempt to glorify all the bestial delights that the subtleness of Greek depravity was able to contrive. It is a good thing to vindicate passion, and the strong and large and rightful pleasures of sense, against the narrow and inhuman tyranny of shrivelled anchorites. It is a very bad and silly thing to try to set up the pleasures of sense in the seat of the reason they have dethroned. And no language is too strong to condemn the mixed vileness and childishness of depicting the spurious passion of a putrescent imagination, the unnamed lusts of sated wantons, as if they were the crown of character and their enjoyment the great glory of human life. The only comfort about the present volume is that such a piece as "Anactoria" will be unintelligible to a great many people, and so will the fevered folly of "Hermaphroditus," as well as much else that is nameless and abominable. Perhaps if Mr. Swinburne can a second and third time find a respectable publisher willing to issue a volume of the same stamp, crammed with pieces which many a professional vendor of filthy prints might blush to sell if he only knew what they meant, English readers will gradually acquire a truly delightful familiarity with these unspeakable foulnesses; and a lover will be able to present to his mistress a copy of Mr. Swinburne's latest verses with a happy confidence that she will have no difficulty in seeing the point of every allusion to Sappho or the pleasing Hermaphroditus, or the embodiment of anything else that is loathsome and horrible. It will be very charming to hear a drawing-room discussion on such verses as these, for example:—

> Stray breaths of Sapphic song that blew
>   Through Mitylene
> Shook the fierce quivering blood in you
>   By night, Faustine.
> The shameless nameless love that makes
>   Hell's iron gin
> Shut on you like a trap that breaks
>   The soul, Faustine.
> And when your veins were void and dead,
>   What ghosts unclean
> Swarmed round the straitened barren bed
>   That hid Faustine?
> What sterile growths of sexless root
>   Or epicene?
> What flower of kisses without fruit
>   Of love, Faustine?

We should be sorry to be guilty of anything so offensive to Mr. Swinburne as we are quite sure an appeal to the morality of all the wisest and best men would be. The passionate votary of the goddess whom he hails as "Daughter of Death and Priapus" has got too high for this. But it may be presumed that common sense is not too insulting a standard by which to measure the worth and place of his new volume.

Starting from this sufficiently modest point, we may ask him whether there is really nothing in women worth singing about except "quivering flanks" and "splendid supple thighs," "hot sweet throats" and "hotter hands than fire," and their blood as "hot wan wine of love"? Is purity to be expunged from the catalogue of desirable qualities? Does a poet show respect to his own genius by gloating, as Mr. Swinburne does, page after page and poem after poem, upon a single subject, and that subject kept steadily in a single light? Are we to believe that having exhausted hot lustfulness, and wearied the reader with a luscious and nauseating iteration of the same fervid scenes and fervid ideas, he has got to the end of his tether? Has he nothing more to say, no further poetic task but to go on again and again about

> The white wealth of thy body made whiter
>   By the blushes of amorous blows,
> And seamed with sharp lips and fierce fingers,
>   And branded by kisses that bruise.

And to invite new Félises to

> Kiss me once hard, as though a flame
> Lay on my lips and made them fire.

Mr. Swinburne's most fanatical admirers must long for something newer than a thousand times repeated talk of

> Stinging lips wherein the hot sweet brine
> That Love was born of burns and foams like wine.

And

> Hands that sting like fire,

And of all those women,

> Swift and white,
> And subtly warm and half perverse,
> And sweet like sharp soft fruit to bite,
> And like a snake's love lithe and fierce.

This stinging and biting, all these "lithe lascivious regrets," all this talk of snakes and fire, of blood and wine and brine, of perfumes and poisons and ashes, grows sickly and oppressive on the senses. Every picture is hot and garish with this excess of flaming violent colour.

Consider the following two stanzas:—

> From boy's pierced throat and girl's pierced bosom
> Drips, reddening round the blood-red blossom,
>   The slow delicious bright soft blood,
> Bathing the spices and the pyre,
> Bathing the flowers and fallen fire,
>   Bathing the blossom by the bud.
>
> Roses whose lips the flame has deadened
> Drink till the lapping leaves are reddened
>   And warm wet inner petals weep;
> The flower whereof sick sleep gets leisure,
> Barren of balm and purple pleasure,
>   Fumes with no native steam of sleep.

. . . It was too rashly said, when *Atalanta in Calydon* appeared, that Mr. Swinburne had drunk deep at the springs of Greek poetry, and had profoundly conceived and assimilated the divine spirit of Greek art. *Chastelard* was enough to show that this had been very premature. But the new volume shows with still greater plainness how far removed Mr. Swinburne's tone of mind is from that of the Greek poets. Their most remarkable distinction is their scrupulous moderation and sobriety in colour. Mr. Swinburne riots in the profusion of colour of the most garish and heated kind. He is like a composer who should fill his orchestra with trumpets, or a painter who should exclude every colour but a blaring red, and a green as of sour fruit. There are not twenty stanzas in the whole book which have the faintest tincture of soberness. We are in the midst of fire and serpents, wine and ashes, blood and foam, and a hundred lurid horrors. Unsparing use of the most violent colours and the most intoxicated ideas and images is Mr. Swinburne's prime characteristic. Fascinated as everybody must be by the music of his verse, it is doubtful whether part of the effect may not be traced to something like a trick of words and letters, to which he resorts in season and out of season with a persistency that any sense of artistic moderation must have stayed. The Greek poets in their most impetuous moods never allowed themselves to be carried on by the swing of words, instead of by the steady, though buoyant, flow of thoughts. Mr. Swinburne's hunting of letters, his hunting of the same word, to death is ceaseless. We shall have occasion by and by to quote a long passage in which several lines will be found to illustrate this.

Then, again, there is something of a trick in such turns as these:—

> Came flushed from the full-flushed wave.
> Grows dim in thine ears and deep as the deep dim soul of a star.
> White rose of the rose-white water, a silver splendour and flame.

There are few pages in the volume where we do not find conceits of this stamp doing duty for thoughts. The Greeks did not wholly disdain them, but they never allowed them to count for more than they were worth. Let anybody who compares Mr. Swinburne to the Greeks read his ode to "Our Lady of Pain," and then read the well-known scene in the *Antigone* between Antigone and the Chorus, beginning *zowc avizars puxov*, or any of the famous choruses in the *Agamemnon*, or an ode of Pindar. In the height of all their passion there is an infinite soberness of which Mr. Swinburne has not a conception.

Yet, in spite of its atrocities, the present volume gives new examples of Mr. Swinburne's forcible and vigorous imagination. The "Hymn to Proserpine" on the proclamation of the Christian faith in Rome, full as it is of much that many persons may dislike, contains passages of rare vigour.

The variety and rapidity and sustention, the revelling in power, are not more remarkable here than in many other passages, though even here it is not variety and rapidity of thought. The anapæst to which Mr. Swinburne so habitually resorts is the only foot that suffices for his never-staying impetuosity. In the "Song in Time of Revolution" he employs it appropriately, and with a sweeping force as of the elements:—

> The heart of the rulers is sick, and the high priest covers his head!
> For this is the song of the quick that is heard in the ears of the dead.
> The poor and the halt and the blind are keen and mighty and fleet:
> Like the noise of the blowing of wind is the sound of the noise of their feet.

There are, too, sweet and picturesque lines scattered in the midst of this red fire which the poet tosses to and fro about his verses. Most of the poems, in his wearisomely iterated phrase, are meant "to sting the senses like wine," but to some stray pictures one may apply his own exquisite phrases on certain of Victor Hugo's songs, which, he says,

> Fell more soft than dew or snow by night,
> Or wailed as in some flooded cave
> Sobs the strong broken spirit of a wave.

For instance, there is a perfect delicacy and beauty in four lines of the hendecasyllabics—a metre that is familiar in the Latin line often found on clocks and sundials, *Horæ nam pereunt et imputantur:*—

> When low light was upon the windy reaches,
> Where the flower of foam was blown, a lily
> Dropt among the sonorous fruitless furrows
> And green fields of the sea that make no pasture.

Nothing can be more simple and exquisite than

> For the glass of the years is brittle wherein we gaze for a span.

Or than this:—

> In deep wet ways by grey old gardens
> Fed with sharp spring the sweet fruit hardens;
>   They know not what fruits wane or grow;
> Red summer burns to the utmost ember;
> They know not, neither can remember,
>   The old years and flowers they used to know.

Or again:—

> With stars and sea-winds for her raiment
>   Night sinks on the sea.

Up to a certain point, one of the deepest and most really poetical pieces is that called the "Sundew." A couple of verses may be quoted to illustrate the graver side of the poet's mind:—

> The deep scent of the heather burns
> About it; breathless though it be,
> Bow down and worship; more than we
> Is the least flower whose life returns,
> Least weed renascent in the sea.

> *   *   *   *

> You call it sundew: how it grows,
> If with its colour it have breath,
> If life taste sweet to it, if death
> Pain its soft petal, no man knows:
> Man has no right or sense that saith.

There is no finer effect of poetry than to recall to the minds of men the bounds that have been set to the scope of their sight and senses, to inspire their imaginations with a vivid consciousness of the size and the wonders and the strange remote companionships of the world of force and growth and form outside of man. "*Qui se considérera de la sorte*," said Pascal, "*s'effraiera, sans doute, de se voir comme suspendu dans la masse que la nature lui a donnée entre ces deux abîmes de l'infini et du néant.*" And there are two ways in which a man can treat this affright that seizes his fellows as they catch interrupted glimpses of their position. He can transfigure their baseness of fear into true poetic awe, which shall underlie their lives as a lasting record of solemn rapture. Or else he can jeer and mock at them, like an unclean fiery imp from the pit. Mr. Swinburne does not at all events treat the lot of mankind in the former spirit. In his best mood, he can only brood over "the exceeding weight of God's intolerable scorn, not to be borne;" he can only ask of us, "O fools and blind, what seek ye there high up in the air," or "Will ye beat always at the Gate, Ye fools of fate." If he is not in his best mood he is in his worst—a mood of schoolboy lustfulness. The bottomless pit encompasses us on one side, and stews and bagnios on the other. He is either the vindictive scornful apostle of a crushing iron-shod despair, or else he is the libidinous laureate of a pack of satyrs. Not all the fervour of his imagination, the beauty of his melody, the splendour of many phrases and pictures, can blind us to the absence of judgment and reason, the reckless contempt for anything like a balance, and the audacious counterfeiting of strong and noble passion by mad intoxicated sensuality. The lurid clouds of lust or of fiery despair and defiance never lift to let us see the pure and peaceful and bounteous kind aspects of the great landscape of human life. Of enlarged *meditation*, the note of the highest poetry, there is not a trace, and there are too many signs that Mr. Swinburne is without any faculty in that direction. Never have such bountifulness of imagination, such mastery of the music of verse, been yoked with such thinness of contemplation and such poverty of genuinely impassioned thought.

36.   ROSSETTI:
Defense of Swinburne

William Michael Rossetti (1829–1919), civil servant and critic, published prolifically on his brother, Dante Gabriel Rossetti, and the Pre-Raphaelites. For biographical information see R. D. Waller's *The Rossetti Family 1824–1854* (University of Manchester Press, 1932). For further information, see the article "The Third Rossetti" by Jerome Thale, *Western Humanities Review*, X (Summer, 1956), 277–84.

The acumen and modernity of Rossetti's critical stance as evidenced in this article from *Swinburne's Poems and Ballads: A Criticism*, are explored in the introduction to this section.

The advent of a new great poet is sure to cause a commotion of one kind or another; and it would be hard were this otherwise in times like ours, when the advent of even so poor and pretentious a poetaster as a Robert Buchanan stirs storms in teapots. It is therefore no wonder that Mr. Swinburne should have been enthusiastically admired and keenly discussed as soon as he hove well in sight of the poetry-reading public, for he is not only a true but even a great poet; still less wonder, under all the particular circumstances of the case, that, with his last volume, admiration and discussion should have ended in a grand crash of the critical orchestra, and that all voices save those of denunciation and repudiation should have been well-nigh drowned. As with many poets of whom our literature is or might be proud—a Shelley, a Byron, a Landor, a Whitman, a Mrs. Browning—the time had to come to Mr. Swinburne when the literary interest in his writings paled before some other feeling excited by them—when the literary gauge was thrown aside by his examiners, and some other one was applied, not to the present advantage of himself or his book. Be it added that Mr. Swinburne has done his very best, or worst, to hasten this time, and to aggravate the crisis. He has courted critics to be—and still more to profess themselves—indignant and horrified; they have responded to his invitation, have exorcised his book with

abundant holy water of morals and religion, the salt of literary dis-
quisition being sparingly used—and the result is, that the book is
withdrawn from publication in England. It is practically certain,
however, to have reappeared, with no alteration save that of the
London publishing-house, long before these remarks are in print.
We shall endeavour to look upon this book, along with Mr. Swinburne's other writings, calmly, to appraise them justly in literary
and all other respects, and to assign him his due place among poets.
We will at once and unreservedly say, we are satisfied that this place
will, in the judgment of posterity, be a lofty one, and that Algernon
Swinburne is one of that rare and electest class—the writers whom
contemporaries, even the well-affected among them, are likely to
praise too little rather than too much. . . .

On the "Heterodox or Religiously Mutinous" influence we have
already commented to some extent: it is closely connected with the
Classic influence, and is equally genuine, though hardly so deep-
seated. Mr. Swinburne, as we have said, is, in intellectual sympathy
and culture, a pagan. This gives a positive direction to his thought on
religious subjects, which otherwise seems to amount to little beyond
negation—materialism, and the absence of faith in a beneficent Providence. The negative and the positive currents, encountering and
joining, roll a considerable volume of turbidity, tumult, and spray.
In saying this we desire to guard ourselves carefully against any suspicion of levitical or pharisaic intolerance: we make no complaint of
Mr. Swinburne's speculative opinions, but, on the contrary, recognise
his right to entertain and express them, whatever they may be. They
have done us no harm; and we recommend other readers to persuade
themselves of the fact that to them also these opinions of a great
poetic genius will do no harm. We say "opinions," feeling that, although
Mr. Swinburne very seldom writes otherwise than dramatically, and
could not therefore be legally fixed with entertaining as his own the
opinions which he puts into the mouths of others, it would nevertheless
be affectation to profess serious uncertainty on this point: he, in fact,
dramatizes certain opinions, and not their contraries, so continually,
because he sympathises with them, and rejoices in giving them words.
We would make him welcome to do so. This world, which scandalized
readers believe to be regulated by a beneficent Providence, and which
Mr. Swinburne (we infer) believes to be regulated by some power of
some sort or other which is absolutely inscrutable, unfathomable,

and in its operations unamenable to the human reason or sense of right, is big and surprising enough for both opinions: and in the infinite there are possibly infinite disclosures to be made which may prove as astonishing to such readers as to Mr. Swinburne.

... This is one of the most curious specialties of Mr. Swinburne's writings, and may be best commented by a reference to individual poems in his volume. We take them pretty nearly in the order which they hold in the index of contents. The first brace of poems, "A Ballad of Life" and "A Ballad of Death," are Italian canzoni of the exactest type, such as Dante, Cavalcanti, Petrarca, and the other mediæval, with many modern, poets of Italy have written; and more especially taking the tinge which works of this class have assumed in Mr. Dante G. Rossetti's volume of translations, "The Early Italian Poets." The "Laus Veneris," itself sufficiently independent of models, is prefaced by a paragraph in old French purporting to be extracted from a "Livre des Grandes Merveilles d'Amour, escript en Latin et en Françoys par Maistre Antoine Gaget, 1530," but which we confidently father upon Mr. Swinburne himself, along with the extract from the "Grandes Chroniques de France, 1505," appended to "The Leper," and the Greek lines from "Anth. Sac." that serve as motto to "A Litany," which poem is a cross between the antiphonal hymnal form and the ideas and phraseology of the Old Testament. These latter are hardly less prominent in the "Song in time of Revolution." "Phædra" is in the form of a scene from a Greek tragedy, with the interpolated remarks of the Chorus. "A Ballad of Burdens" is moulded upon some of the old French poems, with an "envoy." "Hendecasyllabics" and "Sapphics" speak for themselves as regards literary relationship. "At Eleusis" is an exceptionally long speech spoken by Demeter, as from a Greek tragedy—recalling also such modern work as some of Landor's "Hellenics," or Browning's so-called "Artemis Prologizes." "A Christmas Carol" presents quaint, cunning analogies to mediæval writings of the same order. "The Masque of Queen Bersabe" is professedly "a miracle play," and treated accordingly. "St. Dorothy" is Chaucerian work, even to the extent of intentional anachronisms in the designations of the personages and otherwise. "The Two Dreams," from Boccaccio, is almost in equal measure Keatsian. "Aholibah" brings us back again to the Old Testament. Lastly, we have a quintette of ballads, carefully varied in shade, but mainly conforming to the type of the old ballads of North Britain—"The King's Daughter,"

"After Death," "May Janet," "The Bloody Son," and "The Sea-Swallows."

Now, there is nothing uncommon or surprising in imitative poetry. It is generally bad in itself, and inefficient in imitation; sometimes clever, without imitative success; sometimes imitative to the point of intentional, and very rarely of realized, illusion. The singular thing about Mr. Swinburne's reproductive poems is that they are exceedingly fine pieces of work, exceedingly like their adopted models, startlingly so from time to time, and yet that they belong strictly and personally to Mr. Swinburne, and stand distinctly on the level of original work, with the privileges, difficulties, and responsibilities thereto belonging. It seems quite clear that this poet could do, if he chose, an imitation, a "take-off," of almost any style, so close that only the most knowing critics could detect it: but he always stops short of that extreme point, preserving his own poetic individualism and liberty, exhibiting (as we have already said in speaking of the "Atalanta") "the independence and remoulding force of an original work." This state of the case can only, as far as we know, be referred to one cause—the fact that Mr. Swinburne, being truly a poet, a man of imagination, penetrates, by the force of imagination as well as of studentship, into the imaginative identity of poetic models of past time, and thence into their embodying forms. He can create for himself, as he has amply proved; but the determined set of his intellect towards art, and consequently towards literary art, possesses him with so sharp a sympathy for the literary or poetic models of highest style that, as the mood varies, he can pitch his mind into true harmonic concert with Chaucer now, and now with Dante, Sophocles, Keats, or Hugo, and sing, as it were, new vocal music to the accompaniment of these most definite, dominant, and unperishing melodies. In all the roll of poets, we certainly know none who has given such signal proof of his power to enter with re-creative, not imitative, sympathy into so many poetic models of style and form, so diverse and so high; to search their recesses, and extract their essential aroma. A true critic can discern with equal clearness that Mr. Swinburne is a very different sort of writer from a Greek tragedian or a Chaucer, writing things which have a very different ring, and also that his voluntary assimilation to these and other poets is both a genuine and a most singular effort of poetry. Such a critic would find it alike impossible to suppose that he was reading in the "St. Dorothy" a work really produced by Chaucer, or to miss wondering at the intimate and indwelling Chaucerism of the product.

The foregoing observations, singly and collectively, lead up to the central fact already curtly indicated, that the largest and most fundamental of all the influences acting upon Swinburne is the artistic, or (as one terms it in reference to this particular form of art) the literary, and that his poetry is literary poetry of the intensest kind. It is not only metric eloquence, still less versified rhetoric—something far higher than either: but one hesitates to say whether the primary conception in the poet's mind, the poetic nucleus, of the accretion of images and expressional form which grows and clings to this, the poetic investment, is the more important constituent in the general result. In several instances, however, we would say that the poetic investment is beyond a doubt the more important. Both the great beauties and the faults of Mr. Swinburne's writings are closely connected with this specially artistic or literary turn of his genius, as we shall have occasion to show in the sequel. Shelley has been termed "the poet for poets:" Swinburne might not unaptly be termed "the poet for poetic students." His writings exercise a great fascination over qualified readers, and excite a very real enthusiasm in them: but these readers are not of that wide, popular, indiscriminate class who come to a poet to be moved by the subject-matter, the affectingly told story, the sympathetic interpreting words which, in giving voice to the poet's own emotion or perception, find utterance also for those of the universal and inarticulate heart. Mr. Swinburne's readers are of another and a more restricted order. They are persons who, taking delight in the art of poetry, rejoicing when they find a poet master of his materials and the employment of them, kindle to watch so signal a manifestation of poetic gifts and poetic workmanship, and tender him an admiration which, if less than that of an adept, is more than that of a dilettante. It should be added that, while the beauty of execution is the more special attraction to the more special Swinburnian readers, it is by no means the only one: the poet's conceptions are in fact as vivid as his expressions, and he writes with a fire, and even vehemence, which keep his work, elaborate as it often is in verbal or rhythmical sublety, lifted clear above any such level as that of euphuism or "word-painting."

The indecencies in the "Poems and Ballads," about which more than enough has been said in other quarters, and something in the present review, may here once more be glanced at, to be noted as very much dependent upon this literary direction of mind in the author.

Of positive grossness or foulness of expression there is none—nor yet of light-hearted, jocular, jovial libertinism. The offences to decency are in the subjects selected—sometimes too faithfully classic, sometimes more or less modern or semi-abstract—and in the strength of phrase which the writer insists upon using on these as on other topics. He refuses to have his literary liberty abridged; and, as his own indifference or hostility to the common standards of right and wrong, and to the platitudes of their upholders, is necessarily active when he is writing on such subjects, he lashes out with a kind of exasperated and gladiatorial outspokenness which is, after all, as much in the line of literary as of anti-moral licence. We have already expressed our objection to such demonstrations; but we think that these considerations respecting them, being not wiredrawn but simply true, ought in justice to be stated and taken into account. . . .

A still larger question arises here—How far artistic excellence can and ought to be pursued to the neglect or disregard of moral truth? We cannot undertake to give this question the full discussion which it would merit *per se*, but will endeavour to state in a few sentences the conclusions which we believe a candid discussion would elicit, to the following effect:—1st. Minds of the highest order unite moral with artistic energy, and produce work—poetic work when that is in question—which is poetic in so far as it is artistic, but which is also moral because the writer belongs to this highest order of minds. Thus "Macbeth," "Othello," "Romeo and Juliet," and the body of Shakespear's Sonnets, are great poems because they are great works of art; but they are also moral because Shakespear was too great a mind to be otherwise than moral essentially. If even the worst charges which have been hinted against Shakespear on the evidence of some of the Sonnets were established as true, the Sonnets would equally continue to be great poems: the only difference would be that Shakespear's mind or personality, in its total range, would be shown to be of a less grand order than had previously been supposed. Thus again Dante, who professed himself the Poet of Rectitude, is subject to very various constructions on the ground of morals. Some persons believe his ideas on the subject (for instance) of hell to be truly moral; others, at the present date of thought, believe them to be decidedly anti-moral; others believe that the whole external scheme of his poem is a mere veil, or even an introversion, of his real meaning. Whichever of these opinions is adopted, the "Commedia" remains an equally great poem, because it is a great work of art: the only difference is as to the ultimate calibre of Dante's mind. And so again with Milton, who under-took to "justify the ways of God to men" on grounds which appear to many people to be fallacious, and the opposite of morally true. 2d. It follows that the poet, or artist, can, in so far as he is an artist, and with-out any express cognizance of morals, write poems whose rank as such will not be thereby lowered; and if he happens to be a man with-out a strong moral side to his nature, or one who has false or perverse moral tendencies, and even if he exhibits these in his writings, the loss will be to himself in his grade in the intellectual hierarchy, not to his poems, considered as concrete expressions of such intellect and art as were actually in him. His mind will rightly be classed as falling short of those other minds of the grandest order; but his poems will retain their own absolute value, whatever that may be, determinable by the quality and amount of the art which has gone to their production. (We need hardly explain that the term "Art," as here used, includes imagination, conception, and so on, as well as actual execution.) 3d. A poem which is *founded* upon morals rather than art is likely to be a poem of an inferior class; because the intrinsic constituent of poetry is art, and a thorough artist founds his work of art upon that which is not subsidiary but essential to it—namely, art. . . . 4th. A moralist, simply as such, has no title to attempt poetry, because art cannot be approached from the side of morals—the two things are extraneous one to the other, though in no wise conflicting. But an artist may, in a certain semi-paradoxical sense, approach morals from the side of art, because, the more and more he elevates his mind by the gifted practice of art, the nearer and nearer he will come to that highest order of minds which unites morals with art. 5th. Morals do not therefore directly produce, or conduce to the production of, poetry. Art does conduce to its production, and does indeed produce it. The very best poems give morals in, over and above the art. 6th. Consequently, in answer to our primary question, we find that artistic excellence can be pursued to the neglect or disregard of moral truth, and even *ought to be* so pursued with a view to the poetic result. But, if it is pursued to the *negation* of morals, that is a symptom that the mind of the author, or the particular poetic work, is not of the very highest class—still more so, if the artistic excellence is pursued with a purpose which can truly, on broad and positive grounds, be pronounced anti-moral. To this—passing from the essence of the work itself to its effect upon the student of it—we may add that it is not the direct function of a poem or other work of art to improve the morals of the reader, or other person addressed, according to the formulated, matter-of-fact sense in which that term "morals" is ordinarily used. This function is, as we said of morals embodied in the poem itself, "given in," over and above the direct function of the work, which is to enlarge the mental energy, add delicacy to the perceptions, stimulate and refine the emotions, satisfy the sense of beauty. When this has been done to some purpose, a right moral influence has also been exerted—and not the less substantially because indirectly exerted.

37. HOPKINS:

Poets and Poetry

The poetry of Gerard Manley Hopkins, though not published in his lifetime (1844–1889), has recently been reedited by W. H. Gardner (4th ed., New York, 1967), whose *Study* (2 vols., New Haven, 1948–49) is central to our understanding of the poet. The letters reprinted here are from C. C. Abbott's edition of Hopkins' letters to Robert Bridges* and correspondence with R. W. Dixon, published by Oxford University Press. John Pick's critical study, *Gerard Manley Hopkins, Priest and Poet*, and W. A. M. Peter's *A Critical Study*, both valuable, are also published by Oxford.

The Hopkins letters in this section not only reveal his estimates of aesthetic currents of the time but also provide an insight into his own intentions as an artist.

I think I have seen nothing of Lang's but in some magazine; also a sonnet prefixed to his translation of the Odyssey. I liked what I read, but not so that it left a deep impression. It is in the Swinburnian kind, is it not? (I do not think that kind goes far: it expresses passion but not feeling, much less character. This I say in general or of Swinburne in particular. Swinburne's genius is astonishing, but it will, I think, only do one thing.) Everybody cannot be expected to like my pieces. Moreover the oddness may make them repulsive at first and yet Lang

* From *The Letters of Gerard Manley Hopkins to Robert Bridges*, C. C. Abbott, ed. (Oxford University Press, 1960). Reprinted by permission.

might have liked them on a second reading. Indeed when, on some-body returning me the *Eurydice*, I opened and read some lines, reading, as one commonly reads whether prose or verse, with the eyes, so to say, only, it struck me aghast with a kind of raw nakedness and un-mitigated violence I was unprepared for: but take breath and read it with the ears, as I always wish to be read, and my verse becomes all right. I do warm to that good Mr. Gosse for liking and, you say, "taking" my pieces: I may then have contributed fuel to his Habitual Joy. . . .

By the by, inversions—As you say, I do avoid them, because they weaken and because they destroy the earnestness or in-earnestness of the utterance. Nevertheless in prose I use them more than other people, because there they have great advantages of another sort. Now these advantages they should have in verse too, but they must not seem to be due to the verse: that is what is so enfeebling (for instance the finest of your sonnets to my mind has a line enfeebled by inversion plainly due to the verse, as I said once before "'Tis joy the falling of her fold to view"—but how it should be mended I do not see). As it is, I feel my way to their use. However in a nearly finished piece I have a very bold one indeed. So also I cut myself off from the use of *ere, o'er, wellnigh, what time, say not* (for *do not say*), because, though dignified, they neither belong to nor ever cd. arise from, or be the elevation of, ordinary modern speech. For it seems to me that the poetical language of an age shd. be the current language heightened, to any degree heightened and unlike itself, but not (I mean normally: passing freaks and graces are another thing) an obso-lete one. This is Shakespeare's and Milton's practice and the want of it will be fatal to Tennyson's Idylls and plays, to Swinburne, and per-haps to Morris. . . .

By the bye the Paravicinis gave me Richard Crawley's *Venus and Psyche*, which I had long wanted to see. Did not like it. He is a true poet, but this poem is no success or at least it does not please. It is in the metre and manner markedly of *Don Juan*, mocking and discur-sive about modern life and so on. The verse very flowing and, where he took any pains, finely phrased. It is not serious; the scenes are scarcely realised; the story treated as a theme for trying style on. There is not the slightest symbolism.

This leads me to say that a kind of touchstone of the highest or most living art is seriousness; not gravity but the being in earnest with your subject—reality. It seems to me that some of the greatest and most famous works are not taken in earnest enough, are farce (where you ask the spectator to grant you something not only conventional but monstrous). I have this feeling about *Faust* and even about the Divine Comedy, whereas *Paradise Lost* is most seriously taken. It is the weakness of the whole Roman literature. . . .

By the bye, I say it deliberately and before God, I would have you and Canon Dixon and all true poets remember that fame, the being known, though in itself one of the most dangerous things to man, is nevertheless the true and appointed air, element, and setting of genius and its works. What are works of art for? to educate, to be standards. Education is meant for the many, standards are for public use. To produce then is of little use unless what we produce is known, if known widely known, the wider known the better, for it is by being known it works, it influences, it does its duty, it does good. We must then try to be known, aim at it, take means to it. And this without puffing in the process or pride in the success. But still. Besides, we are Englishmen. A great work by an Englishman is like a great battle won by England. It is an unfading bay tree. It will even be admired by and praised by and do good to those who hate England (as England is most perilously hated), who do not wish even to be benefited by her. It is then even a patriotic duty τῇ ποιήσει ἐνεργεῖν* and to secure the fame and permanence of the work. Art and its fame do not really matter, spiritually they are nothing, virtue is the only good; but it is only by bringing in the infinite that to a just judgment they can be made to look infinitesimal or small or less than vastly great; and in this ordinary view of them I apply to them, and it is the true rule for dealing with them, what Christ our Lord said of virtue, Let your light shine before men that they may see your good works (say, of art) and glorify yr. Father in heaven (that is, acknowledge that they have an absolute excellence in them and are steps in a scale of infinite and inexhaustible excellence). . . .

I want Harry Ploughman to be a vivid figure before the mind's eye; if he is not that the sonnet fails. The difficulties are of syntax no doubt. Dividing a compound word by a clause sandwiched into

* 'To be active in producing poetry.' Presumably a phrase coined by G.M.H. [Abbott's note.]

it was a desperate deed, I feel, and I do not feel that it was an unquestionable success. But which is the line you do not understand?
I do myself think, I may say, that it would be an immense advance in
notation (so to call it) in writing as the record of speech, to distinguish
the subject, verb, object, and in general to express the construction to
the eye; as is done already partly in punctuation by everybody, partly
in capitals by the Germans, more fully in accentuation by the Hebrews.
And I daresay it will come. But it would, I think, not do for me:
it seems a confession of unintelligibility. And yet I don't know. At
all events there is a difference. My meaning surely *ought* to appear
of itself; but in a language like English, and in an age of it like the
present, written words are really matter open and indifferent to the
receiving of different and alternative verse-forms, some of which the
reader cannot possibly be sure are meant unless they are marked for
him. Besides metrical marks are for the performer and such marks
are proper in every art. Though indeed one might say syntactical
marks are for the performer too. But however that reminds me that
one thing I am now resolved on, it is to prefix short prose *arguments*
to some of my pieces. These too will expose me to carping, but I do
not mind. Epic and drama and ballad and many, most, things should
be at once intelligible; but everything need not and cannot be. Plainly
if it is possible to express a sub[t]le and recondite thought on a subtle
and recondite subject in a subtle and recondite way and with great
felicity and perfection, in the end, something must be sacrificed, with
so trying a task, in the process, and this may be the being at once, nay
perhaps even the being without explanation at all, intelligible. Neither,
in the same light, does it seem to be to me a real objection (though this
one I hope not to lay myself open to) that the argument should be even
longer than the piece; for the merit of the work may lie for one thing
in its terseness. It is like a mate which may be given, one way only,
in three moves; otherwise, various ways, in many. . . .

No, I do not ask "enthusiastic praise". But is it not the case that the
day when you could give enthusiastic praise to anything is passing
or past? As for modern novels I will only say one thing now. It is in
modern novels that wordpainting most abounds and now the fashion
is to be so very subtle and advanced as to despise wordpainting and
to say that old masters were not wordpainters. Just so. Wordpainting
is, in the verbal arts, the great success of our day. Every age in art
has its secret and its success, where even second rate men are masters.

Second rate, third rate men are fine designers in Japan; second rate men were masters of painting in Raphael's time; seeond rate men were masters of sculpture in Phidias' time; second rate men of oratory in Cicero's; and so of many things. These successes are due to steady practice, to the continued action of a school: one man cannot compass them. And wordpainting is in our age a real mastery and the second rate men of this age often beat at it the first rate of past ages. And this I shall not be bullied out of.

For my case I shd. also remark that we turned up a difference of taste and judgment, if you remember, about Dryden. I can scarcely think of you not admiring Dryden without, I may say, exasperation. And my style tends always more towards Dryden. What is there in Dryden? Much, but above all this: he is the most masculine of our poets; his style and his rhythms lay the strongest stress of all our literature on the naked thew and sinew of the English language, the praise that with certain qualifications one would give in Greek to Demosthenes, to be the greatest master of bare Greek. . . .

Canon Dixon says your *Achilles* is very beautiful. He also says you "hate" his *Eudocia*. I have not seen it yet, but I have the *Saturday's* disagreeable review. If anything made me think the age Alexandrine (as they say), an age of decadence (a criticism that they sling about between the bursting Yes and blustering No, for want of more things to say, as also that the Academy is or is not "above the average"— for what does it matter?—but it reminds me of my aunt's question when she went shopping with her mother as a child, "Is goose a poultry?"—not an unreasonable question in itself and even philo-sophical, for strictly speaking everything either is or is not poultry, but for the purposes of criticism not enough) well, it would be to see how secondrate poetry (and what I mean is, not poetry at all) gets itself put about for great poetry, and that too when there are plenty of real, however faulty, poets living. I am thinking of people like Alfred Austin and Edwin Arnold and Austin Dobson and Lewis Morris, who have merits of course I know, but . . . you can finish up and I know you will think harder than anything I am likely to write. I must copy it for you, more by token: Mr. Skeat has written, out of pure gall (*facit indignatio versum*), a downright good villanelle in mockery of villanelle-writing*. If I were Russian censor of the press it would

---

* This villanelle accompanies the letter, and is here printed from G.M.H.'s copy, with his comment below:

be my joy to force rondeliers to print this piece on the titlepage of each new volume of roundels. There is one of that crew has written (did I tell you before?) the very worst line I ever remember to have read in English. It is from a villanelle in praise of the villanelle and says it, the kickshaw in question, cannot reach the roll and swell

> *Of organs grandiose and sublime*
> (A dainty thing's the Villanelle).

An effeminate thing: I wish we were rid of them.

Villanelle.

How to compose a *villanelle*, which is said to require 'an elaborate amount of care in production, which those who read only would hardly suspect existed.'

> It's all a trick, quite easy when you know it,
> As easy as reciting ABC;
> You need not be an atom of a poet.
>
> If you've a grain of wit, and want to show it,
> Writing a *villanelle*—take this from me—
> It's all a trick, quite easy when you know it.
>
> You start a pair of rimes, and then you 'go it'
> With rapid-running pen and fancy free;
> You need not be an atom of a poet.
>
> Take any thought, write round it or below it,
> Above or near it, as it liketh thee;
> It's all a trick, quite easy when you know it.
>
> Pursue your task, till, like a shrub, you grow it,
> Up to the standard size it ought to be;
> You need not be an atom of a poet.
>
> Clear it of weeds, and water it, and hoe it,
> Then watch it blossom with triumphant glee.
> It's all a trick, quite easy when you know it;
> You need not be an atom of a poet.

> *Walter W. Skeat*
> (*Academy* 19 May 1888)

This has the inspiration of annoyance, a very much more vital and spontaneous thing than the pieces it satirises have. [Abbott's note.]

Swinburne has a new volume out, which is reviewed in its own style: "The rush and the rampage, the pause and the pull-up of these lustrous and lumpophorous lines". It is all now a "self-drawing web"; a perpetual functioning of genius without truth, feeling, or any adequate

matter to be at function on. There is some heavydom, in long water-
logged lines (he has no real understanding of rhythm, and though he
sometimes hits brilliantly at other times he misses badly) about the
Armada, that pitfall of the patriotic muse; and *rot* about babies, a
blethery bathos into which Hugo and he from opposite coasts have
long driven Channel-tunnels. I am afraid I am going too far with the
poor fellow. Enough now, but his babies make a Herodian of me.

38. PATER:
The Bases of Impressionism

The best life of Walter Pater (1839–1894) is that by Thomas
Wright (2 vols., New York, 1907); the edition of *The Works* published in
London in 1920 is standard. René Wellek's "Walter Pater's Literary Theory
and Criticism," *Victorian Studies*, I (1956), 29–46, is a crucial article. Pater's
importance and modernity are discussed in the introduction to this section.

The Preface and Conclusion to *The Renaissance*, presented here, are
perhaps Pater's most famous statements, and present a clear perspective on
the movement toward decadence in the late years of the century.

Many attempts have been made by writers on art and poetry to
define beauty in the abstract, to express it in the most general terms,
to find some universal formula for it. The value of these attempts has
most often been in the suggestive and penetrating things said by the
way. Such discussions help us very little to enjoy what has been well
done in art or poetry, to discriminate between what is more and
what is less excellent in them, or to use words like beauty, excellence,
art, poetry, with a more precise meaning than they would otherwise
have. Beauty, like all other qualities presented to human experience,
is relative; and the definition of it becomes unmeaning and useless in
proportion to its abstractness. To define beauty, not in the most
abstract but in the most concrete terms possible, to find not its universal formula, but the formula which expresses most adequately this
or that special manifestation of it, is the aim of the true student of
æsthetics.

"To see the object as in itself it really is," has been justly said to be the aim of all true criticism whatever; and in æsthetic criticism the first step towards seeing one's object as it really is, is to know one's own impression as it really is, to discriminate it, to realise it distinctly. The objects with which æsthetic criticism deals—music, poetry, artistic and accomplished forms of human life—are indeed receptacles of so many powers or forces: they possess, like the products of nature, so many virtues or qualities. What is this song or picture, this engaging personality presented in life or in a book, to *me*? What effect does it really produce on me? Does it give me pleasure? and if so, what sort or degree of pleasure? How is my nature modified by its presence, and under its influence? The answers to these questions are the original facts with which the æsthetic critic has to do; and, as in the study of light, of morals, of number, one must realise such primary data for one's self, or not at all. And he who experiences these impressions strongly, and drives directly at the discrimination and analysis of them, has no need to trouble himself with the abstract question what beauty is in itself, or what its exact relation to truth or experience—metaphysical questions, as unprofitable as metaphysical questions elsewhere. He may pass them all by as being, answerable or not, of no interest to him.

The æsthetic critic, then, regards all the objects with which he has to do, all works of art, and the fairer forms of nature and human life, as powers or forces producing pleasurable sensations, each of a more or less peculiar or unique kind. This influence he feels, and wishes to explain, by analysing and reducing it to its elements. To him, the picture, the landscape, the engaging personality in life or in a book, *La Gioconda*, the hills of Carrara, Pico of Mirandola, are valuable for their virtues, as we say, in speaking of a herb, a wine, a gem; for the property each has of affecting one with a special, a unique, impression of pleasure. Our education becomes complete in proportion as our susceptibility to these impressions increases in depth and variety. And the function of the æsthetic critic is to distinguish, to analyse, and separate from its adjuncts, the virtue by which a picture, a landscape, a fair personality in life or in a book, produces this special impression of beauty or pleasure, to indicate what the source of that impression is, and under what conditions it is experienced. His end is reached when he has disengaged that virtue, and noted it, as a chemist notes some natural element, for himself and others; and the rule for those who would reach this end is stated with great exactness in the words of a recent critic of Sainte-Beauve:—*De se borner à connaître de près les belles choses, et à s'en nourrir en exquis amateurs, en humanistes accomplis.**

What is important, then, is not that the critic should possess a correct abstract definition of beauty for the intellect, but a certain kind of temperament, the power of being deeply moved by the presence of beautiful objects. He will remember always that beauty exists in many forms. To him all periods, types, schools of taste, are in themselves equal. In all ages there have been some excellent workmen, and some excellent work done. The question he asks is always:— In whom did the stir, the genius, the sentiment of the period find itself? where was the receptacle of its refinement, its elevation, its taste? "The ages are all equal," says William Blake, "but genius is always above its age."

CONCLUSION

Δέγει που Ἡράκλειτος ὅτι πάντα χωρεῖ καὶ οὐδὲν μένει†

To regard all things and principles of things as inconstant modes or fashions has more and more become the tendency of modern thought. Let us begin with that which is without—our physical life. Fix upon it in one of its more exquisite intervals, the moment, for instance, of delicious recoil from the flood of water in summer heat. What is the whole physical life in that moment but a combination of natural elements to which science gives their names? But those elements, phosphorus and lime and delicate fibres, are present not in the human body alone: we detect them in places most remote from it. Our physical life is a perpetual motion of them—the passage of the blood, the waste and repairing of the lenses of the eye, the modification of the tissues of the brain under every ray of light and sound—processes which science reduces to simpler and more elementary forces. Like the elements of which we are composed, the action of these forces extends beyond us: it rusts iron and ripens corn. Far out on every side of us those elements are broadcast, driven in many currents;

---

* "To confine themselves to know at first hand beautiful things, and to develop themselves by these, as sensitive amateurs do, and accomplished humanists."

† "Heraclitus says, 'All things give way; nothing remaineth.'" [Pater's translation.]

and birth and gesture and death and the springing of violets from the grave are but a few out of ten thousand resultant combinations. That clear, perpetual outline of face and limb is but an image of ours, under which we group them—a design in a web, the actual threads of which pass out beyond it. This at least of flame-like our life has, that it is but the concurrence, renewed from moment to moment, of forces parting sooner or later on their ways.

Or, if we begin with the inward world of thought and feeling, the whirlpool is still more rapid, the flame more eager and devouring. There it is no longer the gradual darkening of the eye, the gradual fading of colour from the wall—movements of the shore-side, where the water flows down indeed, though in apparent rest—but the race of the mid-stream, a drift of momentary acts of sight and passion and thought. At first sight experience seems to bury us under a flood of external objects, pressing upon us with a sharp and importunate reality, calling us out of ourselves in a thousand forms of action. But when reflexion begins to play upon those objects they are dissipated under its influence; the cohesive force seems suspended like some trick of magic; each object is loosed into a group of impressions—colour, odour, texture—in the mind of the observer. And if we continue to dwell in thought on this world, not of objects in the solidity with which language invests them, but of impressions, unstable, flickering, inconsistent, which burn and are extinguished with our consciousness of them, it contracts still further: the whole scope of observation is dwarfed into the narrow chamber of the individual mind. Experience, already reduced to a group of impressions, is ringed round for each one of us by that thick wall of personality through which no real voice has ever pierced on its way to us, or from us to that which we can only conjecture to be without. Every one of those impressions is the impression of the individual in his isolation, each mind keeping as a solitary prisoner its own dream of a world. Analysis goes a step farther still, and assures us that those impressions of the individual mind to which, for each one of us, experience dwindles down are in perpetual flight; that each of them is limited by time, and that as time is infinitely divisible, each of them is infinitely divisible also; all that is actual in it being a single moment, gone while we try to apprehend it, of which it may ever be more truly said that it has ceased to be than that it is. To such a tremulous wisp constantly reforming itself on the stream, to a single sharp impression, with a sense in it, a relic more or less fleeting, of such moments gone by, what is real in our life fines itself down. It is with this movement, with the passage and dissolution of impressions, images, sensations, that analysis leaves off—that continual vanishing away, that strange, perpetual weaving and unweaving of ourselves.

Philosophiren, says Novalis, *ist dephlegmatisiren, vivificiren.* The service of philosophy, of speculative culture, towards the human spirit, is to rouse, to startle it to a life of constant and eager observation. Every moment some form grows perfect in hand or face; some tone on the hills or the sea is choicer than the rest; some mood of passion or insight or intellectual excitement is irresistibly real and attractive to us,—for that moment only. Not the fruit of experience, but experience itself, is the end. A counted number of pulses only is given to us of a variegated, dramatic life. How may we see in them all that is to be seen in them by the finest senses? How shall we pass most swiftly from point to point, and be present always at the focus where the greatest number of vital forces unite in their purest energy?

To burn always with this hard, gemlike flame, to maintain this ecstasy, is success in life. In a sense it might even be said that our failure is to form habits: for, after all, habit is relative to a stereotyped world, and meantime it is only the roughness of the eye that makes any two persons, things, situations, seem alike. While all melts under our feet, we may well grasp at any exquisite passion, or any contribution to knowledge that seems by a lifted horizon to set the spirit free for a moment, or any stirring of the senses, strange dyes, strange colours, and curious odours, or work of the artist's hands, or the face of one's friend. Not to discriminate every moment some passionate attitude in those about us, and in the very brilliancy of their gifts some tragic dividing of forces on their ways, is, on this short day of frost and sun, to sleep before evening. With this sense of the splendour of our experience and of its awful brevity, gathering all we are into one desperate effort to see and touch, we shall hardly have time to make theories about things we see and touch. What we have to do is to be for ever curiously testing new opinions and courting new impressions, never acquiescing in a facile orthodoxy of Comte, or of Hegel, or of our own. Philosophical theories or ideas, as points of view, instruments of criticism, may help us to gather up what might otherwise pass unregarded by us. "Philosophy is the microscope of thought." The theory or idea or system which requires of us the sacrifice of any part of this experience, in consideration of some interest into which we cannot enter, or some abstract theory we have not identified with ourselves, or of what is only conventional, has no real claim upon us.

One of the most beautiful passages of Rousseau is that in the sixth book of the *Confessions*, where he describes the awakening in him of the literary sense. An undefinable taint of death had clung always about him, and now in early manhood he believed himself smitten by mortal disease. He asked himself how he might make as much as possible of the interval that remained; and he was not biased by anything in his previous life when he decided that it must be by intellectual excitement, which he found just then in the clear, fresh writings of Voltaire. Well! we are all *condamnés* as Victor Hugo says: we are all under sentence of death but with a sort of indefinite reprieve— *les hommes sont tous condamnés à mort avec des sursis indéfinis:* we have an interval, and then our place knows us no more. Some spend this interval in listlessness, some in high passions, the wisest, at least among "the children of this world," in art and song. For our one chance lies in expanding that interval, in getting as many pulsations as possible into the given time. Great passions may give us this quickened sense of life, ecstasy and sorrow of love, the various forms of enthusiastic activity, disinterested or otherwise, which come naturally to many of us. Only be sure it is passion—that it does yield you this fruit of quickened, multiplied consciousness. Of such wisdom, the poetic passion, the desire of beauty, the love of art for its own sake, has most. For art comes to you proposing frankly to give nothing but the highest quality to your moments as they pass, and simply for those moments' sake.

39.   WILDE:
Dorian Gray, Aesthete

The best life of Oscar Fingall O'Flahertie Wills Wilde (1854–1900) is St. John Ervine's study, but Rupert Hart-Davis' 1962 edition of the letters is more informative. Wilde's reputation is rising in the late sixties, though no thoroughgoing critical study has yet appeared. G. E. Woodcock's *The*

Paradox of Oscar Wilde (New York, 1950) should be consulted. The standard edition is that edited by G. F. Maine, published in 1948. As was pointed out in the introduction, we should beware of misreading Wilde: there is more to champagne than bubbles.

The selection is taken from Chapter 11 of *The Picture of Dorian Gray*, which indicates some of the abuses to which Pater's notion of the "hard, gemlike flame" was to lead.

"Nothing can cure the soul but the senses, just as nothing can cure the senses but the soul."

. . . He sought to elaborate some new scheme of life that would have its reasoned philosophy and its ordered principles, and find in the spiritualizing of the senses its highest realization.

The worship of the senses has often, and with much justice, been decried, men feeling a natural instinct of terror about passions and sensations that seem stronger than themselves, and that they are conscious of sharing with the less highly organized forms of existence. But it appeared to Dorian Gray that the true nature of the senses had never been understood, and that they had remained savage and animal merely because the world had sought to starve them into submission or to kill them by pain, instead of aiming at making them elements of a new spirituality, of which a fine instinct for beauty was to be the dominant characteristic. As he looked back upon man moving through History, he was haunted by a feeling of loss. So much had been surrendered! and to such little purpose! There had been mad wilful rejections, monstrous forms of self-torture and self-denial, whose origin was fear, and whose result was a degradation infinitely more terrible than that fancied degradation from which, in their ignorance, they had sought to escape; Nature, in her wonderful irony, driving out the anchorite to feed with the wild animals of the desert and giving to the hermit the beasts of the field as his companions.

Yes: there was to be, as Lord Henry had prophesied, a new Hedonism that was to re-create life, and to save it from that harsh, uncomely puritanism that is having, in our own day, its curious revival. It was to have its service of the intellect, certainly; yet, it was never to accept any theory or system that would involve the sacrifice of any mode of passionate experience. Its aim, indeed, was to be experience itself, and not the fruits of experience, sweet or bitter as they might be. Of the asceticism that deadens the senses, as of the vulgar profligacy that dulls them, it was to know nothing. But it was to teach man to concentrate himself upon the moments of a life that is itself but a moment.

There are few of us who have not sometimes wakened before dawn, either after one of those dreamless nights that make us almost enamoured of death, or one of those nights of horror and misshapen joy, when through the chambers of the brain sweep phantoms more terrible than reality itself, and instinct with that vivid life that lurks in all grotesques, and that lends to Gothic art its enduring vitality, this art being, one might fancy, especially the art of those whose minds have been troubled with the malady of reverie. Gradually white fingers creep through the curtains, and they appear to tremble. In black fantastic shapes, dumb shadows crawl into the corners of the room, and crouch there. Outside, there is the stirring of birds among the leaves, or the sound of men going forth to their work, or the sigh and sob of the wind coming down from the hills, and wandering round the silent house, as though it feared to wake the sleepers, and yet must needs call forth sleep from her purple cave. Veil after veil of thin dusky gauze is lifted, and by degrees the forms and colours of things are restored to them, and we watch the dawn remaking the world in its antique pattern. The wan mirrors get back their mimic life. The flameless tapers stand where we had left them, and beside them lies the half-cut book that we had been studying, or the wired flower that we had worn at the ball, or the letter that we had been afraid to read, or that we had read too often. Nothing seems to us changed. Out of the unreal shadows of the night comes back the real life that we had known. We have to resume it where we had left off, and there steals over us a terrible sense of the necessity for the continuance of energy in the same wearisome round of stereotyped habits, or a wild longing, it may be, that our eyelids might open some morning upon a world that had been refashioned anew in the darkness for our pleasure; a world in which things would have fresh shapes and colours, and be changed, or have other secrets; a world in which the past would have little or no place, or survive, at any rate, in no conscious form of obligation or regret, the remembrance even of joy having its bitterness, and the memories of pleasure their pain.

It was the creation of such worlds as these that seemed to Dorian Gray to be the true object, or amongst the true objects, of life; and in his search for sensations that would be at once new and delightful, and possess that element of strangeness that is so essential to romance, he would often adopt certain modes of thought that he knew to be really alien to his nature, abandon himself to their subtle influences, and then, having, as it were, caught their colour and satisfied his intellectual curiosity, leave them with that curious indifference that is not incompatible with a real ardour of temperament, and that indeed, according to certain modern psychologists, is often a condition of it.

It was rumoured of him once that he was about to join the Roman Catholic communion; and certainly the Roman ritual had always a great attraction for him. The daily sacrifice, more awful really than all the sacrifices of the antique world, stirred him as much by its superb rejection of the evidence of the senses as by the primitive simplicity of its elements and the eternal pathos of the human tragedy that it sought to symbolize. He loved to kneel down on the cold marble pavement, and watch the priest, in his stiff flowered vestment, slowly and with white hands moving aside the veil of the tabernacle, or raising aloft the jewelled, lantern-shaped monstrance with that pallid wafer that at times, one would fain think, is indeed the *panis cælestis*, the bread of angels, or, robed in the garments of the Passion of Christ, breaking the Host into the chalice, and smiting his breast for his sins. The fuming censers, that the grave boys, in their lace and scarlet, tossed into the air like great gilt flowers, had their subtle fascination for him. As he passed out, he used to look with wonder at the black confessionals, and long to sit in the dim shadow of one of them and listen to men and women whispering through the worn grating the true story of their lives.

But he never fell into the error of arresting his intellectual development by any formal acceptance of creed or system, or of mistaking, for a house in which to live, an inn that is but suitable for the sojourn of a night, or for a few hours of a night in which there are no stars and the moon is in travail. Mysticism, with its marvellous power of making common things strange to us, and the subtle antinomianism that always seems to accompany it, moved him for a season; and for a season he inclined to the materialistic doctrines of the *Darwinismus* movement in Germany, and found a curious pleasure in tracing the thoughts and passions of men to some pearly cell in the brain, or some white nerve in the body, delighting in the conception of the absolute dependence of the spirit on certain physical conditions, morbid or healthy, normal or diseased. Yet, as has been said of him before, no theory of life seemed to him to be of any importance compared with life itself. He felt keenly conscious of how barren all intellectual speculation is when separated from action and experiment. He knew that the senses, no less than the soul, have their spiritual mysteries to reveal.

40.   TENNYSON:

"The Higher Pantheism"

Tennyson's poem "The Higher Pantheism" is a serious attempt to convey the poet's belief in a God who is imminent in the universe but who transcends it, is not coextensive with it.

For bibliographical information on Tennyson, see headnote, Selection 17.

The sun, the moon, the stars, the seas, the hills and the plains—
Are not these, O Soul, the Vision of Him who reigns?

Is not the Vision He, tho' He be not that which He seems?
Dreams are true while they last, and do we not live in dreams?

Earth, these solid stars, this weight of body and limb,
Are they not sign and symbol of thy division from Him?

Dark is the world to thee; thyself art the reason why,
For is He not all but thou, that hast power to feel "I am I"?

Glory about thee, without thee; and thou fulfillest thy doom,
Making Him broken gleams and a stifled splendor and gloom.

Speak to Him, thou, for He hears, and Spirit with Spirit can meet—
Closer is He than breathing, and nearer than hands and feet.

God is law, say the wise; O Soul, and let us rejoice,
For if He thunder by law the thunder is yet His voice.

Law is God, say some; no God at all, says the fool,
For all we have power to see is a straight staff bent in a pool;

And the ear of man cannot hear, and the eye of man cannot see;
But if we could see and hear, this Vision—were it not He?

41. SWINBURNE:

"The Higher Pantheism in a Nutshell"

Algernon Charles Swinburne (1837–1909) is the subject of a
recent critical book by Robert Peters, *The Crowns of Apollo* (Detroit, 1965).
His letters are available in a six-volume modern edition edited by Cecil Lang
(New Haven, 1959–62); the standard edition of his works is that edited by
Edmund Gosse and T. J. Wise in twenty volumes (New York, 1925–27).
Lafourcado's *Swinburne: A Literary Biography* (London, 1932) should be
consulted, as should C. K. Hyder's *Swinburne's Literary Career and Fame*
(Durham, 1933).

Swinburne, the subject of several selections in this section, may well be
one of the most significant figures of the later nineteenth century, and is
surely one of the most fascinating, both as a poet and as a person. His talent
for parody is well exemplified in this *tour de force*.

One, who is not, we see: but one, whom we see not, is:
Surely this is not that: but that is assuredly this.

What, and wherefore, and whence? for under is over and under:
If thunder could be without lightning, lightning could be without
   thunder.

Doubt is faith in the main: but faith, on the whole, is doubt:
We cannot believe by proof: but could we believe without?

Why, and whither, and how? for barley and rye are not clover:
Neither are straight lines curves: yet over is under and over.

Two and two may be four: but four and four are not eight:
Fate and God may be twain: but God is the same thing as fate.

Ask a man what he thinks, and get from a man what he feels:
God, once caught in the fact, shews you a fair pair of heels.

Body and spirit are twins: God only knows which is which:
The soul squats down in the flesh, like a tinker drunk in a ditch.

One and two are not one: but one and nothing is two:
Truth can hardly be false, if falsehood cannot be true.

Once the mastodon was: pterodactyls were common as cocks:
Then the mammoth was God: now is He a prize ox.

Parallels all things are: yet many of these are askew:
You are certainly I: but certainly I am not you.

Springs the rock from the plain, shoots the stream from the rock:
Cocks exist for the hen: but hens exist for the cock.

God, whom we see not, is: and God, who is not, we see:
Fiddle, we know, is diddle: and diddle, we take it, is dee.

42. SWINBURN:
The Aesthetic Lady

William Michael Rossetti's comments on Swinburne's "Dolores"
provide an excellent approach to the poem, "Dolores: Notre-Dame des Sept
Douleurs." Additional information about Swinburne is provided in the headnote to Section 41.

"Dolores" seems, at first, hardly related to anything in one's experience of
facts, or scope of speculation: by thinking over it, however, one perceives that
it does contain an ample amount of meaning, and even that its loud-rustling
attire of immoralities is not so *very* immoral, after all—rather comparable to
the seamy, the extra-seamy, side of the moral texture.
                                                        —W. M. Rossetti

Cold eyelids that hide like a jewel
    Hard eyes that grow soft for an hour;
The heavy white limbs, and the cruel
    Red mouth like a venomous flower;
When these are gone by with their glories,
    What shall rest of thee then, what remain,
O mystic and somber Dolores,
    Our Lady of Pain?

Seven sorrows the priests give their Virgin;
   But thy sins, which are seventy times seven,
Seven ages would fail thee to purge in,
   And then they would haunt thee in heaven:
Fierce midnights and famishing morrows,
   And the loves that complete and control
All the joys of the flesh, all the sorrows
   That wear out the soul.

O garment not golden but gilded,
   O garden where all men may dwell,
O tower not of ivory, but builded
   By hands that reach heaven from hell;
O mystical rose of the mire,
   O house not of gold but of gain,
O house of unquenchable fire,
   Our Lady of Pain!

O lips full of lust and of laughter,
   Curled snakes that are fed from my breast,
Bite hard, lest remembrance come after
   And press with new lips where you pressed.
For my heart too springs up at the pressure,
   Mine eyelids too moisten and burn;
Ah, feed me and fill me with pleasure,
   Ere pain come in turn.

In yesterday's reach and tomorrow's,
   Out of sight though they lie of today,
There have been and there yet shall be sorrows
   That smite not and bite not in play.
The life and the love thou despisest,
   These hurt us indeed, and in vain,
O wise among women, and wisest,
   Our Lady of Pain.

Who gave thee thy wisdom? what stories
    That stung thee, what visions that smote?
Wert thou pure and a maiden, Dolores,
    When desire took thee first by the throat?
What bud was the shell of a blossom
    That all men may smell to and pluck?
What milk fed thee first at what bosom?
    What sins gave thee suck?

*   *   *

Could you hurt me, sweet lips, though I hurt you?
    Men touch them, and change in a trice
The lilies and languors of virtue
    For the raptures and roses of vice;
Those lie where thy foot on the floor is,
    These crown and caress thee and chain,
O splendid and sterile Dolores,
    Our Lady of Pain.

There are sins it may be to discover,
    There are deeds it may be to delight.
What new work wilt thou find for thy lover,
    What new passions for daytime or night?
What spells that they know not a word of
    Whose lives are as leaves overblown?
What tortures undreamt of, unheard of,
    Unwritten, unknown?

Ah, beautiful passionate body
    That never has ached with a heart!
On thy mouth though the kisses are bloody,
    Though they sting till it shudder and smart,
More kind than the love we adore is,
    They hurt not the heart or the brain,
O bitter and tender Dolores,
    Our Lady of Pain.

As our kisses relax and redouble,
  From the lips and the foam and the fangs
Shall no new sin be born for men's trouble,
  No dream of impossible pangs?
With the sweet of the sins of old ages
  Wilt thou satiate thy soul as of yore?
Too sweet is the rind, say the sages,
  Too bitter the core.

*   *   *

By the ravenous teeth that have smitten
  Through the kisses that blossom and bud,
By the lips intertwisted and bitten
  Till the foam has a savor of blood,
By the pulse as it rises and falters,
  By the hands as they slacken and strain,
I adjure thee, respond from thine altars,
  Our Lady of Pain.

*   *   *

Who has known all the evil before us,
  Or the tyrannous secrets of time?
Though we match not the dead men that bore us
  At a song, at a kiss, at a crime—
Though the heathen outface and outlive us,
  And our lives and our longings are twain—
Ah, forgive us our virtues, forgive us,
  Our Lady of Pain.

Who are we that embalm and embrace thee
  With spices and savors of song?
What is time, that his children should face thee?
  What am I, that my lips do thee wrong?
I could hurt thee—but pain would delight thee;
  Or caress thee—but love would repel;
And the lovers whose lips would excite thee
  Are serpents in hell.

Who now shall content thee as they did,
    Thy lovers, when temples were built
And the hair of the sacrifice braided
    And the blood of the sacrifice spilt,
In Lampsacus fervent with faces,
    In Aphaca red from thy reign,
Who embraced thee with awful embraces,
    Our Lady of Pain?

Where are they, Cotytto or Venus,
    Astarte or Ashtaroth, where?
Do their hands as we touch come between us?
    Is the breath of them hot in thy hair?
From their lips have thy lips taken fever,
    With the blood of their bodies grown red?
Hast thou left upon earth a believer
    If these men are dead?

They were purple of raiment and golden,
    Filled full of thee, fiery with wine,
Thy lovers, in haunts unbeholden,
    In marvelous chambers of thine.
They are fled, and their footprints escape us
    Who appraise thee, adore, and abstain,
O daughter of Death and Priapus,
    Our Lady of Pain.

What ails us to fear overmeasure,
    To praise thee with timorous breath,
O mistress and mother of pleasure,
    The one thing as certain as death?
We shall change as the things that we cherish,
    Shall fade as they faded before,
As foam upon water shall perish,
    As sand upon shore.

We shall know what the darkness discovers,
   If the gravepit be shallow or deep;
And our fathers of old, and our lovers,
   We shall know if they sleep not or sleep.
We shall see whether hell be not heaven,
   Find out whether tares be not grain,
And the joys of thee seventy times seven,
   Our Lady of Pain.

43. HILTON:

"Octopus"

Arthur Clement Hilton (1851–1877), one of the best parodists of the Victorian period, is almost forgotten today. His works, together with a life and his letters, were edited by Sir R. Pearce-Edgcumbe in 1904. This poem is entitled "Octopus: by Algernon Charles Sin-Burn."

Strange beauty, eight-limbed and eight-handed,
   Whence camest to dazzle our eyes?
With thy bosom bespangled and banded
   With the hues of the seas and the skies;
Is thy home European or Asian,
   O mystical monster marine?
Part molluscous and partly crustacean,
   Betwixt and between.

Wast thou born to the sound of sea trumpets?
   Hast thou eaten and drunk to excess
Of the sponges—thy muffins and crumpets,
   Of the seaweeds—thy mustard and cress?
Wast thou nurtured in caverns of coral,
   Remote from reproof or restraint?
Art thou innocent, art thou immoral,
   Sinburnian or Saint?

Lithe limbs, curling free, as a creeper
  That creeps in a desolate place,
To enrol and envelop the sleeper
  In a silent and stealthy embrace;
Cruel beak craning forward to bite us,
  Our juices to drain and to drink,
Or to whelm us in waves of Cocytus,
  Indelible ink!

Oh breast, that 'twere rapture to writhe on!
  Oh arms 'twere delicious to feel
Clinging close with the crush of the Python,
  When she maketh her murderous meal!
In thy eight-fold embraces enfolden,
  Let our empty existence escape;
Give us death that is glorious and golden,
  Crushed all out of shape!

Ah thy red lips, lascivious and luscious,
  With death in their amorous kiss!
Cling round us, and clasp us, and crush us,
  With bitings of agonized bliss;
We are sick with the poison of pleasure,
  Dispense us the potion of pain;
Ope thy mouth to its uttermost measure,
  And bite us again!

                    Written at the Crystal Palace Aquarium.

44.   FITZGERALD:

Turkish Bards and English Hedonists

Edward FitzGerald's version of *The Rubáiyát of Omar Khayyám* has been superseded by the recent translation of Robert Graves, but as it is edited by Carl J. Weber, (Maine, 1958) it will never be supplanted in the minds and anthologies of English-speaking people. FitzGerald's life

(1809–1883) has been written by A. M. Terhune (New Haven, 1947). George Bentham edited the *Variorum and Definitive Edition* of all FitzGerald's works (7 vols., New York, 1902–3).

Probably the debates about this work will never end: How faithful is it to the original? Is it a translation? A version? Is it properly considered as a Victorian poem? Is it a faithful reflection of its times or did it induce in others the points of view it posits?

Whatever answer we give, we must all thank Dante Gabriel Rossetti for rescuing it from obscurity.

LXXXII

As under cover of departing Day
Slunk hunger-stricken Ramazán away,
 Once more within the Potter's house alone
I stood, surrounded by the Shapes of Clay.

LXXXIII

Shapes of all Sorts and Sizes, great and small,
That stood along the floor and by the wall;
 And some loquacious Vessels were; and some
Listen'd perhaps, but never talk'd at all.

LXXXIV

Said one among them—"Surely not in vain
My substance of the common Earth was ta'en
 And to this Figure moulded, to be broke,
Or trampled back to shapeless Earth again."

LXXXV

Then said a Second—"Ne'er a peevish Boy
Would break the Bowl from which he drank in joy;
 And He that with his hand the Vessel made
Will surely not in after Wrath destroy."

LXXXVI

After a momentary silence spake
Some Vessel of a more ungainly Make;
 "They sneer at me for leaning all awry:
What! did the Hand then of the Potter shake?"

LXXXVII

Whereat some one of the loquacious Lot—
I think a Súfi pipkin—waxing hot—
   "All this of Pot and Potter—Tell me then,
Who is the Potter, pray, and who the Pot?"

LXXXVIII

"Why," said another, "Some there are who tell
Of one who threatens he will toss to Hell
   The luckless Pots he marr'd in making—Pish!
He's a Good Fellow, and 'twill all be well."

LXXXIX

"Well," murmur'd one, "Let whoso make or buy,
My Clay with long Oblivion is gone dry:
   But fill me with the old familiar Juice,
Methinks I might recover by and by."

XC

So while the Vessels one by one were speaking,
The little Moon look'd in that all were seeking:
   And then they jogg'd each other, "Brother! Brother!
Now for the Porter's shoulder-knot a-creaking."

45. BROWNING:

Optimism

    Robert Browning's "Rabbi ben Ezra" provides one of the clearest statements of the poet's brand of optimism. The savaging of FitzGerald's *Rubáiyát* is not attributable to the feud between the two resulting from FitzGerald's low opinion of Mrs. Browning's verse, for that occurred much later; it is rather attributable to the strength of Browning's religious convictions.

For bibliographical information on Browning, see headnote, Selection 32.

XXVI

Aye, note that Potter's wheel,
That metaphor! and feel
    Why time spins fast, why passive lies our clay,—
Thou, to whom fools propound,
When the wine makes its round,
    "Since life fleets, all is change; the Past gone, seize to-day!"

XXVII

Fool! All that is, at all,
Lasts ever, past recall;
    Earth changes, but thy soul and God stand sure:
What entered into thee,
That was, is, and shall be:
    Time's wheel runs back or stops: Potter and clay endure.

XXVIII

He fixed thee 'mid this dance
Of plastic circumstance,
    This Present, thou, forsooth, would fain arrest:
Machinery just meant
To give thy soul its bent,
    Try thee and turn thee forth, sufficiently impressed.

XXIX

What though the earlier grooves
Which ran the laughing loves
    Around thy base, no longer pause and press?
What thought, about thy rim,
Skull-things in order grim
    Grow out, in graver mood, obey the sterner stress?

XXX

Look not thou down but up!
To uses of a cup,
    The festal board, lamp's flash, and trumpet's peal,
The new wine's foaming flow,
The Master's lips a-glow!
    Thou, heaven's consummate cup, what need'st thou with
        earth's wheel?

XXXI

But I need, now as then,
Thee, God, who mouldest men;
    And since, not even while the whirl was worst,
Did I,—to the wheel of life
With shapes and colors rife,
    Bound dizzily,—mistake my end, to slake Thy thirst:

XXXII

So, take and use Thy work:
Amend what flaws may lurk,
    What strain o' the stuff, what warpings past the aim!
My times be in Thy hand!
Perfect the cup as planned!
    Let age approve of youth, and death complete the same!

46. STEPHEN:

"Sincere Flattery of R.B."

James Kenneth Stephen (1859–1892), journalist, lawyer, and editor, is the author of *Lapsus Calami and Other Verses*, which was edited together with a life by H. Stephen (Cambridge, 1909). Both Browning's stylistic habits and his occasional lapses into cliché are skillfully pilloried in the following selection.

Birthdays? yes, in a general way;
For the most if not for the best of men:
You were born (I suppose) on a certain day:
So was I: or perhaps in the night: what then?

Only this: or at least, if more,
You must know, not think it, and learn, not speak:
There is truth to be found on the unknown shore,
And many will find where few will seek.

For many are called and few are chosen,
And the few grow many as ages lapse:
But when will the many grow few: what dozen
Is fused into one by Time's hammer-taps?

A bare brown stone in a babbling brook:—
It was wanton to hurl it there, you say:
And the moss, which clung in the sheltered nook
(Yet the stream runs cooler), is washed away.

That begs the question: many a prater
Thinks such a suggestion a sound "stop thief!"
Which, may I ask, do you think the greater,
Sergeant-at-arms or a Robber Chief?

And if it were not so? still you doubt?
Ah! yours is a birthday indeed if so.
That were something to write a poem about,
If one thought a little. I only know.

P.S.

There's a Me Society down at Cambridge,
Where my works, *cum notis variorum*,
Are talked about; well, I require the same bridge
That Euclid took toll at as *Asinorum:*

And, as they have got through several ditties
I thought were as stiff as a brick-built wall,
I've composed the above, and a stiff one *it* is,
A bridge to stop asses at, once for all.

47. GILBERT:
Wilde with a Lily in His Hand

Sir William Schwenck Gilbert (1836–1911) is the subject of a biography by Hesketh Pearson (London, 1957). W. A. Darlington's *The World of Gilbert and Sullivan* (New York, 1950) is an important study. "Bunthorne's Song," from *Patience*, is exemplary of Gilbert's verse, which ranks high among the most delightful light verse of this or any other period, and is a good antidote to our stuffy notions of the stuffiness of Victorianism.

If you're anxious for to shine in the high aesthetic line as a man of
    culture rare,
You must get up all the germs of the transcendental terms, and plant
    them everywhere.
You must lie upon the daisies and discourse in novel phrases of your
    complicated state of mind,
The meaning doesn't matter if it's only idle chatter of a transcendental
    kind.
                    And every one will say,
                    As you walk your mystic way,
"If this young man expresses himself in terms too deep for *me*,
Why, what a very singularly deep young man this deep young man
    must be!"

Be eloquent in praise of the very dull old days which have long since
    passed away,
And convince 'em, if you can, that the reign of good Queen Anne was
    Culture's palmiest day.
Of course you will pooh-pooh whatever's fresh and new, and declare
    it's crude and mean,
For Art stopped short in the cultivated court of the Empress Josephine.
                    And every one will say,
                    As you walk your mystic way,
"If that's not good enough for him which is good enough for *me*,
Why, what a very cultivated kind of youth this kind of youth must be!"

Then a sentimental passion of a vegetable fashion must excite your
    languid spleen,
An attachment *à la* Plato for a bashful young potato, or a not-too-
    French French bean!
Though the Philistines may jostle, you will rank as an apostle in the
    high aesthetic band,
If you walk down Piccadilly with a poppy or a lily in your mediæval
    hand.
              And every one will say,
              As you walk your flowery way,
"If he's content with a vegetable love which would certainly not suit
    me,
Why, what a most particularly pure young man this pure young man
    must be!"

Suggestions for Further Reading

ALTICK, RICHARD D. *The English Common Reader: A Social History of the Mass Reading Public, 1800–1900.* Chicago: University of Chicago Press, 1957. An excellent, necessary social history, illuminating the tastes of nineteenth-century readers and the forces which shaped them.

BUCKLEY, JEROME H. *The Victorian Temper.* Cambridge, Mass.: Harvard University Press, 1952. Twelve essays on a "few centers of literary influence," which, though not detailed, suggest clearly the variety of meanings of "Victorianism."

BURN, W. L. *The Age of Equipoise: A Study of the Mid-Victorian Generation.* London: Allen and Unwin, 1964. Although including only the years 1852–1867, a "generation in which old and new . . . achieved a balance," the conclusions of this fine historical study are valid for much of the century.

CLARK, GEORGE KITSON. *The Making of Victorian England.* Cambridge, Mass.: Harvard University Press, 1962. An important history, emphasizing the necessity of continuing revision in our view of the Victorians.

FORD, GEORGE H. *Dickens and His Readers: Aspects of Novel-Criticism Since 1836.* Princeton: Princeton University Press, 1955. An introduction to the study of Dickens' fiction, but also a reputable guide to the literary history of Dickens' times.

HOLLOWAY, JOHN. *The Victorian Sage: Studies in Argument.* London: Macmillan and Co., 1953. An informative study of the philosophy and rhetoric of Carlyle, Disraeli, George Eliot, Newman, Arnold, and Hardy.

HOUGHTON, WALTER E. *The Victorian Frame of Mind, 1830–1870.* New Haven: Yale University Press, 1957. A standard work, tracing the "bundle of various and often paradoxical ideas and attitudes of Victorianism."

YOUNG, G. M. *Victorian England: Portrait of an Age* (2d ed.). London: Oxford University Press, 1953. A standard history by one of the most noted of English historians. Brief, graceful essays delineating the age.